The Path to Mechanized
Shoe Production in
the United States

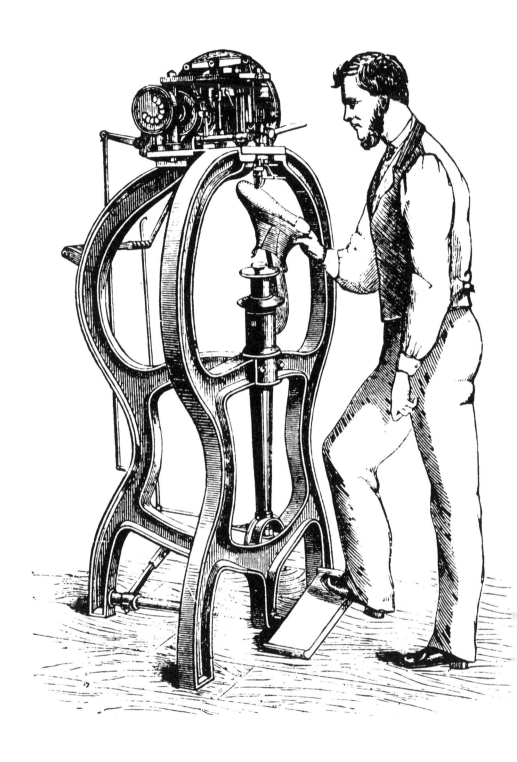

The Path to Mechanized Shoe Production in the United States

Ross Thomson

The University of North Carolina Press
Chapel Hill and London

© 1989 The University of North Carolina Press

Library of Congress Cataloging-in-Publication Data

Thomson, Ross.
    The path to mechanized shoe production in the United States /
Ross Thomson.
      p. cm.
      Bibliography: p.
      Includes index.
      ISBN 0-8078-1867-4 (alk. paper)
      1. Shoe industry—United States—History. I. Title.
HD9787.U45T48   1989
338.4′768531′0973—dc19   89-5444
                                           CIP

Printed in the United States of America

93 92 91 90 89   5 4 3 2 1
TP

To Floria and Justin

Contents

Tables

Figures

Acknowledgments

Like the mechanical creation the book documents, intellectual creation involves the inputs of many. William Parker has read and insightfully commented on my dissertation and two book drafts. Over two drafts, Robert Heilbroner's unerring eye for needless tangents and obscure arguments has kept the book on track and, indeed, helped identify what track it was on. Others have helped clarify the ideas of the book, including David Levine, David Weiman, Richard Garrett, Robert Urquhart, Carol Heim, Julie Matthaei, Nina Shapiro, Ron Blackwell, participants of the economic history seminars at Columbia and Yale and of the General Seminar and Historical Studies seminars at the New School, and a generation of New School students. The perceptive comments of the editors and two anonymous readers of the University of North Carolina Press have considerably strengthened the final draft. Carol Stock typeset the tables with skill and care. Without the capable research assistance of John Nader, Bryan Snyder, Togu Oppusunggu, Martin Kohli, and Luis Guevara, I would no doubt still be sitting in the Patent Library. Finally, I owe a great deal to Floria Thomson's incisive insights and steady support and to Justin Thomson's willingness to share his father with an effort older than he is and equally demanding.

**The Path to Mechanized
Shoe Production in
the United States**

1

The Problem

The mechanized production of modern capitalism, with its dynamic of continuous technological change, so contrasts with the craft production that preceded it that its origin forms a difficult problem. The difficulty lies not simply in the genesis of mechanized techniques out of craft techniques; more fundamentally, it is one of economic transformation: how could institutions that supported an ongoing revolution in mechanized production emerge from the quite different institutions that supported the relative stability of craft techniques?

The problem begins with the contrast between craft and mechanized techniques. In craft production, laborers hold a conception of the product and the method of its formation, which they then implement by the acquired, skillful use of tools. Determined by the brain and hand of the craftsman, such production is governed by what Marx called a subjective principle; labor is purposive and tools are means to achieve this purpose. Mechanized production is structured by an objective principle. Machines embody the idea of the product and its fabrication in the design of their working mechanisms; when activated, parts of the machine so constrain one another that the desired transformations are effected. This internally controlled motion differentiates a machine from a tool. Labor simply allows the machine to function, and is therefore separated from the activity of conceiving and fabricating the product.[1]

From these differences in technique came barriers to the origin of mechanized production. Craft techniques limited conceptions of the product and the method of production to those that workers could implement. Simply to conceive the transformation of the material outside of the tool-manipulating skills of workers is a great innovation. Even if this innovation is made, craft techniques do not in general provide knowledge of the principles of machine design and construction. The principles embodied in machines form a system of general engineering concepts and particular applications that Marx called "the modern science of technology"; machines can be most readily developed when others form a context of technological knowledge.[2]

Technical differences are historically tied to contrasts in social organization, and these social contrasts determine the relevance of technical barriers for the possibility of transition. In modern capitalism, ongoing technological change exists as an integral aspect of an economy-wide accumulation of capital. Firms produce commodities through the organized consumption of purchased means of production and labor power. Profitability is not essentially fixed by such factors given to capital as the abilities of workers or the productivity of nonproduced means of production, and may change with technological advances. Investment for the whole economy generates the market growth that justifies the investment of particular industries. For any firm, accumulation provides both a rationale for introducing new machinery and a necessary condition when the cost and scale of operations are large. More rapid accumulation increases the profits and sales of capital goods firms and hence their ability and incentive to engage in developing and marketing new machines. To develop novel machines, firms tap markets both for laborers with related technological knowledge and inventive experience, and for equipment serving as the means for technical development.

When compared to those of industrial capitalism, the institutions within which craft production was exercised formed a number of barriers to the introduction, generation, and diffusion of machinery. Craft techniques may have been valued in themselves so that mechanization was resisted. This was so in the guild system, in which the aim of production was in part the quality of the product and the virtuosity of the craftsman. Not simply an economic expedient, the hierarchy of masters, journeymen, and apprentices was valued for its moral, familial, aesthetic, and even political and religious qualities, and the education it imparted was inseparably moral and technical. Although this classical form had broken down prior to mechanization, craft systems retaining many classical elements persisted long after the Industrial Revolution.

Even when techniques were not valued in themselves, the scale of craft production, bound to restricted local markets and limited per capita consumption of craft products, may have been too small to introduce machinery. Practices of custom design would find little use for the mass-production capabilities of machinery. Laborers retaining possession of the means of production may have resisted factory employment. Moreover, mechanization may have required the reorganization of production, particularly in putting-out systems.

Craft institutions also limited the generation of machinery. Barriers to the introduction of machines reduced incentives to develop machinery. This is true whether or not the machine was intended for direct use by the inventors. Craft tools were often sold as commodities, but largely in local markets, which restricted the extent of sales that machine makers could expect. Further, the system of craft training limited the spread of knowledge outside the craft and therefore impeded the discovery of similarities of technical solutions among crafts.

Diffusion of machinery was also constrained within craft systems. Machinery long antedated capitalism, but this fact by itself did not lead to ongoing technological development. The insignificance for industrialization of the basic technological innovations brought to use in the French luxury trades and documented in Diderot's encyclopedia powerfully illustrates this point. Typically, new techniques were carried by the movement of workers, and diffusion was thus constrained by the pace, direction, and accidentality of mobility. Some capitalists who developed and used machines within their own plants tried to suppress movement. Even where diffusion occurred through sale, the local and custom structure of tool and machine markets posed barriers to the geographic extent of diffusion.

Thus industrial capitalism had both technology and institutions to support ongoing mechanization, but craft economies had neither. The difficulty of accounting for the transition lies in the magnitude of the qualitative break between these systems. They differed in technique, in industry organization, and in the structure of the larger economy. The extent of discontinuity makes explanation difficult; there were no fixed points in terms of which changes at other points can be grasped. Rather, the system changed together in one intertwined dynamic.

Insights of Marx and Mantoux

The classical formulations of Marx and Mantoux form a useful starting point for understanding industrialization. For Marx the problem is stark. Industrialization is understood as an aspect of the transition from feudalism to capitalism. It thereby poses a dilemma: on the one hand, history is a lawful process in which for prolonged periods the evolution of productive forces and therefore productivity is supported by the social relations surrounding production. The support for technological change provided by capitalist social relations is only the clearest example of a more general phenomenon. On the other hand, social relations pertinent to production may limit the progress of productivity, as is clear in the limits posed by feudal guilds and serfdom to mechanization or even to the transformation of craft techniques. If technical change emerges as a result of supportive institutions, how can technical change occur when constrained by the institutional structure?

Marx attempts to solve this problem through a transitional process in which social relations changed in a way that supported changes in technique. In the transition to capitalism, feudalism gave way to a stage of manufacturing in which nascent capitalist social relations came to foster industrialization. While not posing the question so broadly, Mantoux likewise begins his study of the Industrial Revolution by identifying the "preparatory changes" occurring in a stage of manufacture.[3]

For both Marx and Mantoux, focusing principally on England, manufacturing involved changes in agriculture, trade, and the crafts. The social organization of agriculture was transformed by enclosure, land sale, engrossment, the decline of the yeomanry, and the growth of the capitalist farm. Concomitantly, large-scale, intensive agricultural techniques arose. In these changes lay a principal source of the growth and increased mobility of the proletariat, as well as a source of agricultural surpluses, industrial entrepreneurs (especially for Mantoux), and the home market (as emphasized by Marx).[4]

A revolution in trade expanded and integrated markets abroad and at home. The ascendancy of English international merchants, fostered by commercial policy, led to the growth of commercial centers, and these centers, along with improvement of communications, brought the integration of the home market.

Market growth and integration, in turn, fostered the birth of capitalist craft production in the forms of a putting-out system and larger workshops employing divisions of labor. Marx argues that "today, industrial supremacy brings with it commercial supremacy. In the period of manufacture it is the reverse: commercial supremacy produced industrial predominance."[5] Mantoux concurs; the rapid technical progress of factory production itself created conditions for commercial expansion, but the comparative slowness of productivity growth in craft production implied that "industry had to be regulated by the condition of trade connections." Regulation took the form of a Smithian connection of exchange and the division of labor: "Every extension or multiplication of exchanges, by throwing open more channels to production, gives rise to an ever more elaborate and effective division of labour, a more and more narrow distribution of functions between producing areas, between trades and between different parts of the same trade."[6]

At least in some industries, the changes of the manufacturing period created conditions supporting machine introduction: large, integrated, well-organized markets; firms of ample size; and a proletariat. The craft system supported diffusion. Machines spread readily when, like the jenny, they could be used in the putting-out system. Merchant manufacturers provided finance and organization to form factories.

The craft system also supplied the principal agents of machine invention and diffusion. For Mantoux, "Every technical question is first and foremost a practical question. Before ever it becomes a problem to be solved by men with theoretic knowledge, it forces itself upon the men in the trade as a difficulty to be overcome, or a material advantage to be gained."[7] Craftsmen posed and answered most of these practical questions. Invention was a collective effort; inventors made use of the knowledge of the trades and communication with other tradesmen. Textile inventors were frequently weavers, mechanics, or both. Deficiencies in mechanical knowledge were overcome by "emergency engineers": carpenters, locksmiths, clockmakers, and especially millwrights.[8]

The Industrial Revolution was an outcome of the manufacturing period in the sense that the earlier period generated an economic interest in inventing which the activity of tradesmen could satisfy. Once begun, industrialization took on a dynamic of its own. The introduction of some machines helped develop others by providing technical knowledge (as the jenny did for the mule) or bottlenecks (as spinning did for weaving). From one operation to another, from one industry to another, mechanization spread until industrial capitalism was complete.

Issues and Directions

Here is a solution to the problem of the transition from craft to mechanized production from which our study begins: a manufacturing stage generated new kinds of craft institutions and techniques which fostered a phase of initial mechanization which in turn became ongoing. But Mantoux's account (or Marx's less complete reflections) leaves two critical unresolved issues which this book must address.

First, little is said about the institutions that generated and spread machines. In capitalism, altered techniques are means to economic ends. For Mantoux, the end—profitability—requires a sufficient scale of the firm and the market, and the means—machinery—rests on the evolution of craft skill. He misses a third factor: the social organization of the generation and diffusion of techniques. In market societies, individuals are typically separated from knowledge of techniques, potential markets, and sources of finance outside their specialization. Sufficient incentive and capacity to invent may be present for society taken as a whole but for no individual within it. Yet structured relations may exist which allow individuals to overcome barriers to invention and which therefore are determinants of technical change in their own right.

Mantoux's neglect of the social relations of technical change leads to several weaknesses in his analysis. He writes that the principal inventions of the Industrial Revolution occurred in a phase that "is sufficiently accounted for by economic needs and the spontaneous efforts they call forth," but he does not adequately consider how these needs induced the required efforts.[9] The social form taken by invention is critical here; market growth provided quite different incentives for inventions used in the inventor's shop and for those widely sold as commodities. The extent of the incentive to invent thus varied with the forms of diffusion and introduction of the new machine, but these receive scant attention.

Furthermore, whose spontaneous efforts were called forth? Mantoux emphasizes craftsmen, but, beyond providing skills and focusing attention, their trade backgrounds are accorded little role. There is little discussion of the relation of mechanization to the ways in which techniques were developed and diffused in the craft period. The social form of the new technique is again pertinent. The role of craftsmen making spinning wheels, hand looms, and other instruments of production is not considered; Marx, for one, emphasizes their role when he writes: "One of its [manufacture's] most finished products was the workshop for the production of the instruments of labour themselves. . . . This workshop, the product of the division of labour in manufacture, produced in its turn—machines."[10]

Mantoux barely touches on how inventions were developed to adequacy. His accounts of major inventions each focus on one or two major figures, yet other craftsmen may have been decisive in developing (or suppressing) these inventions. The form of diffusion is again relevant, because it influenced the spread of technical information and hence further invention. Here Mantoux does not sufficiently develop his own notion of invention as "collective experience." Instead, he focuses on the personality of inventors, and therefore gives more than he would like to the genius theory of invention which he criticizes as "romantic."[11]

If institutions generating new techniques are neglected, then so are changes in these institutions. As a result, the problem of the transition from craft to mechanized production is defined in a one-sided way. The evolution of craft and the birth of mechanized techniques occurred through different institutions, and the transition altered the institutions generating techniques as much as it changed the techniques themselves. Mechanization therefore could not be the straightforward outcome of the institutions of the manufacturing period.

Moreover, the institutional changes brought about by industrialization are also underdetermined. Mantoux rightly emphasizes the novelty of the factory system and the industrial firm, and grasps their role in further technical change. But he neglects the formation of the industry making and selling machinery, and this industry proved critical for making technical change ongoing.

The English focus of the Marx-Mantoux account of the process of mechanization gives rise to the second issue. As the first successful industrialization, the English Industrial Revolution was unique. How then can its explanation shed light on later processes of industrialization?

Answers to this question are bounded by two extremes. Mechanization after the Industrial Revolution could be a simple widening of the successes of British industrialization. No industry would then have to duplicate the stages of British mechanization; machinery would emerge, full grown, from the mills of Manchester. A stage of manufacturing might create adequate incentives to mechanize, but would play no part in generating machines in response to these incentives. At the other extreme, subsequent mechanization might be independent of Britain's Industrial Revolution. Each instance would recapitulate the stages of Britain's mechanization, and hence the arguments of Marx and Mantoux would apply without modification.

An adequate answer will no doubt lie between these extremes. In industries closely related in technique and markets to those of the Industrial Revolution, later mechanization will be more dependent on earlier, as was the case for the spread of textile machinery across fabrics and space. Elsewhere, mechanization will be more independent and perhaps for this reason slower. Whether industries are integrated will also depend on how the institutions generating and diffusing technology have developed over the course of industrialization.

This book takes up the problem of transition from craft to mechanized production for the case of the shoe industry in the United States.[12] This case is important historically owing to its size and impact on other industries and countries. It also takes on methodological significance because, to explain mechanization, both issues of the Marx-Mantoux account—the neglect of social relations generating technical change and the focus on the first industrialization process—must be addressed.

The shoe industry exhibited the intertwined technical and institutional transformations that make the problem of transition so difficult. During the nineteenth century, it developed from a craft system of mostly small shops selling in regional markets to a factory system of much larger firms selling in national markets. This transition occurred in relation to—and by means of—another, the evolution of the social form generating new techniques from innovations for use within the shop spread by the movement of craftsmen, to new capital goods produced by new firms, and then to organized product development by well-established firms.

In each phase of its evolution, mechanization elsewhere in the economy influenced shoemaking; the transition therefore must differ from that of the case of the English textile industry where the problem has classically been posed. Yet shoe mechanization had enough autonomy from the development of other machinery that it can be studied by itself. Shoe mechanization had its own history, indeed its own social history, which must begin with the American shoemaking craft.

Part I

The Manufacturing Dynamic

2

The Evolution of Markets

Craft shoemaking was fundamentally restructured in the first half of the nineteenth century. Small shops retailing locally gave way to a capitalist putting-out system selling in national wholesale markets. Labor too was affected; a division of labor, altered products, and novel means of production all emerged. These changes in markets, social relations of production, and labor together formed the manufacturing dynamic of the industry.

An account of mechanization must examine this dynamic for two kinds of reasons. One Marx and Mantoux emphasize: that the changes of the manufacturing period brought about conditions favorable to mechanization. The other they largely neglect: that the social processes generating these changes informed the processes of mechanization. What changes occurred and how they occurred must both be understood.

Insights into the origin and character of the manufacturing dynamic are provided by the classic interpretations of the evolution of the American shoe industry advanced by John R. Commons and Blanche Hazard. Both adopt periodizations that emphasize transformations prior to mechanization; both identify a period of wholesale production between a handicraft stage of retail sale and a factory stage. For Commons, focusing largely on urban Philadelphia, the growth of wholesale production first pitted merchant employers against journeymen. The merchant then transformed masters into dependent suppliers who opened sweatshops and divided labor. For Hazard, concentrating on small-town and rural Massachusetts, wholesale production led to the formation of full-time merchant capitalists, the growth of putting-out, and the specialization of labor.[1]

Commons and Hazard agree that the driving force transforming the industry was the evolution of the market, not changes of instruments of production. The merchant was the central agent; in Commons's words, "Throughout the course of industrial evolution the part played by the merchant stands out as the determining factor. The key to the situation is at all times the price-bargain. It is the merchant who controls both capital and labor."[2] Market development was the independent force; it provided opportunities and competitive pressures to which production adjusted.

Marx and Mantoux would concur that growth was market-led in this phase. But particularly between Marx and Commons there remain differences that raise important issues for understanding the manufacturing dynamic. For Commons, Marx's standpoint—"that of the mode of production and not the extension of the market"—leads him away from the critical factor of market growth and toward determinants of surplus value (the length of the working day and the cost of living), which "are secondary factors, results not causes."[3] This criticism is misdirected because Marx accepts the dominance of merchant capital in the manufacturing stage. But it contains an important insight: Marx would argue that market growth was neither sufficient to change the mode of production nor independent of such changes.

For Marx, the consequences of market development depend on the organization of production. "To what extent it [commerce] brings about a dissolution of the old mode of production depends on its solidity and internal structure. And whither this process of dissolution will lead, in other words, what new mode of production will replace the old, does not depend on commerce, but on the character of the old mode of production itself."[4]

Production also generates agents of market transformation. Marx describes two paths to capitalism, one in which the producer becomes an employer and merchant, and a second in which merchants integrate into production. Commons focuses principally on the second, a path that in Marx's view ultimately conserves the old mode of production. It is the first that is "the really revolutionizing path." The difference between the two is not just the identity of the agent but the content of the innovation. In the revolutionary path, alterations in the organization and techniques of production help secure market growth.[5]

At issue is the sense in which the market led the evolution of production. If production adapted to an independently given rate of market growth, then the history of production must focus on the sources of product demand. Mechanization too might have responded to market growth through incentives for machine invention. But if production was more autonomous, attention must be paid more to dynamic processes within the social organization of production. To examine this issue, we will consider the evolution of the market in this chapter and the alteration of the organization and means of shoe production in the next two.

Shoe Production in 1800

The American shoe industry of 1800 was, according to Commons and Hazard, in transition from a stage of retail shops to wholesale production. In terms of market structure, this is quite right. Shoemakers working in their own shops for retail consumers were spread throughout northern cities and towns. Wholesale markets originated in the 1790s in Philadelphia and earlier in Massachusetts. Lynn was the leader; from 1750 it undertook production for distant markets and by 1795 was reported to export 300,000 pairs of shoes, chiefly to the South. In the 1790s, other Massachusetts towns followed, including Haverhill, Abington, Milford, Danvers, Reading, and Braintree.[6]

The rise of wholesale production challenged the craft system by supplanting direct relations between producers and consumers. Capital requirements rose; the journeyman status became more permanent; competition between cities put pressure on wages, and "the conflict of capital and labor begins."[7] Employment grew; one manufacturer in seven months of 1795 is reported to have made 20,000 pairs of shoes, an output that must have required the labor of 50 to 100 workers. Means to sell this output were put in place. By the late 1790s, several shoe jobbers in Boston made regular large shipments to such southern ports as Savannah and Charleston, and, in smaller quantities, to the Caribbean.[8]

These glimmerings of a capitalist future were still faint. Techniques had not altered. Simply, a shoe was formed by sewing together parts of the top of the shoe (the upper), attaching the upper to the last (a wooden form in the shape of the foot), and sewing the soles of the shoe onto the lasted upper. Tools like those employed in England for centuries were used: a knife, a lapstone, an awl, a needle, pincers, a hammer, and a stirrup or strap. The quality of the product was determined by the conception of the shoe held by the craftsman and his virtuosity in implementing that conception.

In ways, craft social relations were also the rule. Shoemakers continued to make the whole shoe. Even in wholesale production, the proportion of masters to journeymen and apprentices was not high. The 600 journeymen and apprentices employed by 200 Lynn masters in 1795 were within accepted craft limits for the town as a whole, though not for each master. In this regard, the American craft system had purer form than the British, where as early as 1738 some large London and Northampton masters employed over 160 workers and divided labor between cutters, bottomers, and unapprenticed upper binders.[9]

In other ways, traditional craft social relations no longer existed. The classical craft system was not just an economic form; it was a community with its own ethical standards. The product was not just a source of income; it was a medium through which the prowess and creativity of the craftsman were recognized by consumers and other shoemakers. Craft hierarchies were a means through which masters trained apprentices in the ethics of the craft along with the skills, and, by following these norms, apprentices could expect to rise in position and esteem.

In England, this ethos had long degenerated, undercut by the permanence of journeyman status and the decline of formal craft training, especially outside the custom trade. Still, an ethos of craft education and independence persisted throughout the nineteenth century, manifested in journeymen's defense of craft training and ownership of the tools of the trade. Likewise a muted craft tradition existed in northern U.S. cities, one weak enough that masters could act for craft solidarity yet still sell in wholesale markets, increase employment, and live away from their journeymen and even their apprentices.[10]

Outside cities, the craft ethic had less reality, including in those Massachusetts small towns and rural areas where wholesale shoemaking was already arising. The village was organized around landed property, so that consciousness of a society of crafts could not easily develop. Even those who left the village to seek apprenticeship elsewhere often intended to acquire land later. Moreover, in many towns crafts had not been established long enough to take on a traditional status as a part of the town division of labor. For example, Brookfield, by 1830 a major shoemaking center, had probably had a settled shoemaker only since 1770.[11] America's history as a settler colony helps explain the distinctiveness of its craft system.

The easy mobility between occupations also undercut the craft conception that one's person was defined through a single kind of labor. Of the account books of 15 shoemakers before 1800, 10 contained entries for income received from one or more other occupations, including not only farming and stock raising, but also tanning, butchery, fishing, shipbuilding, blacksmithing, weaving, milling, brick making, and storekeeping.[12]

Embedded in rural society, the education of apprentices lost much of its craft ethos. Masters often possessed little craft consciousness and could not easily instill a craft ethic in apprentices coming from and perhaps intending to return to rural villages. Such apprentices were numerous enough to affect the entire craft in Massachusetts; their availability is one reason why Massachusetts newspapers, unlike those of Philadelphia, carried few advertisements for apprentices or journeymen. Rules of craft training were less formalized than in England or even Philadelphia. Shoemakers often trained their own sons without formal apprenticeship, and to secure employment journeymen did not have to prove that they had completed an apprenticeship.[13]

The weakness of the craft tradition helps account for the widespread willingness to produce for wholesale markets in the 1790s. Shoemakers were used to innovation; within the lifetimes of many, production had evolved from itinerancy to custom production to noncustom production for retail markets. From here the step to wholesale production was not a difficult one.

But the step to mechanization would have been formidable. The financial requirements, scale, and centralized organization required to introduce shoe machines were beyond the reach of shoemakers in 1800. Nor were the skills needed to design and make shoe machines available in the United States. The industry was poised to develop, but to develop within craft production.

Market Formation and Growth

During the first half of the century, a substantially integrated national market for ready-made shoes formed and grew. As Commons noted, it was a wholesale market; shoes typically flowed from producer to wholesaler to retailer to consumer. Only early and again late in the century did a few shoe firms set up their own retail outlets. Integrated markets originated before firms

Table 2.1
The Value of Shoe Output by Region, 1810, 1840, and 1850
(millions of 1860 dollars)

	1810[a]	1840[b]	1850
New England	5.51	17.44	45.52
(Massachusetts)	(3.00)	(13.31)	(36.64)
Middle Atlantic	6.44	13.04	25.52
(New York)	(2.50)	(6.60)	(11.82)
(Pennsylvania)	(2.59)	(3.62)	(8.57)
West	0.21	2.89	7.20
South	2.16	1.99	3.79
United States	14.32	35.82	82.03

Sources: U.S. Treasury Department, Third Census, *Arts and Manufactures of the United States*; U.S. Census Office, Sixth Census, *Statistics of the United States,* and Seventh Census, *Abstract of the Statistics of Manufactures*; U.S. Bureau of the Census, *Historical Statistics of the United States,* ser. E 52–63. Shoe values have been deflated by the Warren-Pearson wholesale index for hides and leather products.

Note: New England = Massachusetts, Connecticut, Rhode Island, Maine, New Hampshire, and Vermont; Middle Atlantic = New York, New Jersey, Pennsylvania, Delaware, Maryland, and the District of Columbia; West = Ohio, Indiana, Michigan, Illinois, Wisconsin, Iowa, Missouri, and Minnesota; and South = the remaining states.

[a]States reporting totaled about two-thirds of population. Pennsylvania reported only pairs of shoes and the value of all leather goods; an output estimate was made by assuming that shoe prices equaled the average for reporting Middle Atlantic states and the District of Columbia. Nonreporting states were assumed to have shoe output equal to regional per-capita averages.

[b]The 1840 manufacturing census did not separate shoes from other manufactured leather products. Estimates of shoe output have been formed by assuming that the share of shoes in all leather manufactures was the same in 1840 and 1850.

divided labor between wageworkers or had come to employ many workers. At least in the beginning, market transformation led the alteration of production.

As sales expanded, so did output. The real value of shoe output in the United States increased from an estimated $14 million in 1810 to $36 million in 1840 and $82 million in 1850 (see Table 2.1). Because these figures are deflated by an index of the prices of hides and leather products, the number of pairs of shoes rose in something like the same proportion. Net exports were insignificant relative to output, so that the domestic market approximated domestic output.[14]

Market growth need not entail transformation; increasing demand in principle could have been met by expanded localized custom or retail sale. But sale to the national market did grow and in some producing areas came to domi-

Table 2.2
Lynn Producers by Employment and Markets, 1832

Number of Employees	Number of Producers	Producers Listing Markets	Location of Markets		
			Mass. Only	Mass. and Outside	Only Outside
0–9	14	12	8	0	4
10–19	9	8	5	1	2
20–39	8	7	3	2	2
40–59	7	7	3	2	2
60–79	6	6	0	3	3
80–99	7	7	0	0	7
100–149	3	2	0	1	1
150–199	6	6	0	2	4
Over 199	2	1	0	0	1
Total	62	56	19	11	26

Sources: U.S. Treasury Department, Documents Relative to the Manufactures in the United States, 1:224–35.

nate. Massachusetts was the chief center. The *McLane Report* supplies useful evidence about the structure of the market in 1832. Among 62 Lynn shoe producers surveyed, 56 gave meaningful answers to the question of the location of their markets. As Table 2.2 shows, 19 sold solely in Massachusetts, 11 in Massachusetts and elsewhere, and 26 only outside Massachusetts. Moreover, those selling outside Massachusetts were noticeably larger. None of the producers selling only in Massachusetts employed over 59 workers and 8 employed fewer than 10. By contrast, 16 of the 26 selling wholly outside Massachusetts employed 60 or more workers.[15]

Other Massachusetts shoe towns were similarly oriented to wholesale production for markets outside the state. As Table 2.3 indicates, only 9 of the 23 towns providing useful market information took Massachusetts as a principal market (in which, say, a quarter or more of output was sold). None of the 4 largest centers other than Lynn sold extensively in Massachusetts. Southern and western markets were particularly significant for men's shoe and boot centers such as Randolph.

Markets varied widely in location. Massachusetts was largely supplied by its own shoe towns, as manifested by the paucity of shoemakers in Boston. Other eastern states were large and growing markets for cheap and medium-quality Massachusetts shoes, as the regular complaints of Philadelphia and New York artisans evidence. Southern markets were important throughout the century; the shoe industry was one of the few for which this was true. As early as 1800 Boston jobbers specialized in this market, and with time the numbers grew. Finally, demand in the West grew rapidly; many western frontier areas in the second half of the century never knew a stage of custom production.[16]

Table 2.3
Shoe Output, Employment, and Markets
in Selected Massachusetts Towns, 1832
(output in thousands of dollars or pairs)

Town	Output	Employment	Markets
Abington	300 pr.	650	¾ in Middle, S, W; ¼ in West Indies
Bedford	71 pr.	n.a.	¾ in Mass., 1/8 in Rhode Island, 1/8 in S
Bradford	203 pr.	475	S and W
Braintree	$75	n.a.	Mass.
Brookfield	114 pr.	180	S, W, West Indies, South America
Danvers	$351	990	Middle, S, W
Grafton	170 pr.	251	Mass., Middle
Haverhill	575 pr.	939	United States
Holliston	180 pr.	160	Mostly S and W
Hopkinton	47 pr.	n.a.	Mass., S
Malden	350 pr.	500	New Eng.
Milford	60 pr.	140	Middle, S, W
North Bridgewater	126 pr.	170	S and W
North Brookfield	130 pr.	149	Outside Mass.
Quincy	41 pr.	205	Mass. and S
Randolph	$508	970	1/8 in Mass., 3/8 in W, 1/8 in S, 3/8 in Middle
Reading	180 pr.	460	¾ in Mass.; Middle; S
Southborough	$57	156	¼ in New Eng.; ¾ in S, W
South Reading	300 pr.	500	7/8 in Mass.; New Eng.
Stoneham	300 pr.	370	¾ in Mass.; S
Stoughton	$190	325	New Eng., Middle, S
Upton	87 pr.	110	Middle, S
Weymouth	$163	450	Mostly S
Woburn	252 pr.	n.a.	7/8 in Mass.; New Eng.; Middle
Wrentham	$60	210	n.a.

Source: U.S. Treasury Department, *Documents Relative to the Manufactures in the United States,* 1:232-719.

Note: Under *Markets,* the following abbreviations are used: Mass. = Massachusetts; Middle = Middle Atlantic region; New Eng. = New England; S = the South; and W = the West. These regions largely correspond to those defined in Table 2.1, but in cases where markets are reported in general terms—for example, "southern states" or "western states"—the correspondence may not be exact.

Table 2.4

Unevenness of Shoe Production by Region, 1810, 1840, and 1850

(1860 dollars; excess production in millions)

	Per Capita Shoe Output			Excess Production[a]		
	1810	1840	1850	1810	1840	1850
New England	3.7	7.8	16.7	2.6	12.7	35.9
(Massachusetts)	(6.3)	(18.0)	(36.8)	(2.1)	(11.8)	(33.1)
Middle Atlantic	2.6	2.6	3.9	1.5	2.3	2.1
(New York)	(2.6)	(2.7)	(3.8)	(0.6)	(1.5)	(0.9)
(Pennsylvania)	(3.2)	(2.1)	(3.7)	(1.0)	(0.0)	(0.4)
West	0.7	0.9	1.3	−0.4	−4.1	−12.6
South	0.7	0.3	0.5	−3.8	−11.4	−25.4
United States	2.0	2.1	3.5			

Sources: See Table 2.1; U.S. Bureau of the Census, Historical Statistics of the United States, ser. A 195–209.

Note: For definition of regions, see Table 2.1.

[a]Excess production E is production above the national average. Definitionally, for region i, it is:

$$E_i = (V_i/P_i - V_{US}/P_{US})P_i$$

where V = the value of shoe output and P = population.

The location of shoe output provides some indication of the concentration of production for the national market. As Table 2.4 shows, shoe output was unevenly distributed among regions, and the unevenness increased over time. New England regularly had per capita shoe output well above the national average, the South and West well below average, and the Middle Atlantic region somewhat above average. The disparity between New England and other regions increased over time; its per capita shoe output, not quite double the national average in 1810, stood at close to five times the national average in 1850.

The absolute importance of divergences in per capita output is measured by a region's excess production, the difference between actual regional output and output if the region had average per capita output. New England regularly led in excess production, and its lead increased greatly over time. Its excess production increased from 47 percent of its total production in 1810 to 79 percent in 1850. The South and the West were regularly deficit regions, and the Middle Atlantic region went from substantial to modest excess production; its ratio of excess to total production fell from 24 percent in 1810 to 8 percent in 1850. A measure of the unevenness of production for the country as a whole can be formed by comparing the total of regional excess production in surplus regions with national output. This measure stood at 29 percent in 1810, and increased to 42 percent in 1840 and to 46 percent in 1850.

Growing divergences of shoe output per capita would indicate increasing interstate markets if the distribution of per capita shoe consumption among states were constant over time. If, to take the simplest case, per capita shoe consumption were equal among states, then excess production would directly measure net interstate shipments, and the measure of the unevenness of production for the country would also measure the share of interstate markets. New England's domination of wholesale production is indicated by its increase in the share of positive excess production from 63 percent in 1810 to 95 percent in 1850.

Of course, one would not expect per capita shoe consumption to be the same in Massachusetts and Mississippi; consumption would be expected to rise when per capita income was higher and more evenly distributed. Interstate markets would then differ from excess production. Assume that shoes were consumed in proportion to per capita income and that regional differences in per capita income were constant over time. Compared to equal per capita consumption, shoe consumption would rise in New England and the Middle Atlantic region, and regional shoe exports—output minus regional consumption—would decline for New England and become negative for Middle Atlantic states.[17] Net interregional wholesale markets for the whole country would decline; the ratio of net shoe exports to total shoe production would decline from 29 to 12 percent in 1810, from 42 to 31 percent in 1840, and from 46 to 40 percent in 1850. On the other hand, the growth over time of the share of interregional markets would be much higher than in the case where shoe consumption was proportional to per capita income.[18]

The centrality of Massachusetts to wholesale production is clear from the tables. Its per capita shoe output was by far the highest of the states, and rose from three to ten times the national average from 1810 to 1850. Its excess production was half of the nation's total in 1810, and increased to three-quarters in 1840 and seven-eighths in 1850. If shoe consumption varied with per capita income, Massachusetts' share of interstate markets was about 80 percent in 1810 and rose to over 95 percent in 1840 and 1850.

By mid-century, a new kind of market, called by Polanyi an "internal market," had come into being. An integrated, national market, supplied by competing producers from many areas, had replaced the earlier combination of local retail exchanges and still irregular exports to agricultural regions in the South and the Caribbean. This market would not basically change over the rest of the century. Regional excess production for surplus regions increased only modestly from 46 percent of national shoe output in 1850 to 51 percent in 1880, or, if regional consumption was proportional to income, surplus production expanded from 40 to 46 percent of the national output from 1850 to 1880. One facet of the great transformation had been completed.[19]

Accounting for Market Growth

For Commons, the extension of the market was "solely external" to the shoe industry; he says little about why it grew.[20] Hazard emphasizes marketing innovations. Both agree that the growth of the potential market as tapped by merchants, rather than the transformation of the mode of production, was the principal source for the expansion of the wholesale market.

No doubt both the potential market and marketing innovations played important roles in market growth. The near doubling of per capita shoe consumption from 1810 to 1850, at a time when the population tripled, multiplied output sixfold. This growth rested on the growth of per capita income and wages, themselves dependent on transportation improvements, the integration of markets, and productivity growth in craft and agricultural production. The manufacturing dynamic in the economy as a whole thus supported the development of a home market in the first half of the nineteenth century, as it had in Britain in the eighteenth.[21]

The rapidity of shoe market growth had to do with the distinctiveness of the nineteenth-century United States. The same dynamics of settler colonies that inhibited the formation of craft tradition supported rapid population growth and immigration. Mechanization also supported market growth. The expansion of the textile industry contributed to American productivity growth and augmented the demand for cotton and hence the expansion of southern markets.

Mechanization also fostered market growth in another way. If, as Marx and Mantoux maintain, the action of merchant capital governed industrial development in the manufacturing stage, then the predominant effect of mechanization may have come in transforming the market. For its locomotives, steamboats, and even canals, the transportation revolution of the first half of the nineteenth century depended on the development of steam engines and civil engineering. These innovations cheapened shoe transportation costs, but had greater consequences by reducing the costs of moving agricultural products, increasing income levels, and fostering regional divisions of labor.[22]

Without altered forms of marketing, growing potential markets might have been supplied by a proliferation of retail shops. Marketing innovations for Commons fell within the merchant function, but were not necessarily the actions of specialized merchants. Commons and especially Hazard rightly emphasize the activity of shoe producers in forming new marketing systems. Small-town Massachusetts shoemakers were particularly important in this regard. They sold in auctions, consigned shoes to country stores, and set up their own retail shops. One dogged Worcester County shoemaker brought shoes by the horse load to Boston in 1811 for auction, marketed in Albany in 1812, sold 700 pairs to army contractors in 1814, and from 1815 consigned shoes to country stores around Spencer. Producers also became shoe dealers; large shoe manufacturers from North Brookfield, East Bridgewater, Hopkinton, and Spencer all became dealers in the 1820s. Marketing innovation was widespread; shoemakers from half of the 25 towns listed in Table 2.3 are known to have sought out new marketing forms.[23]

By about 1830 a wholesale shoe marketing system had been established in which purchasers bought shoes from the salesrooms of jobbers in New York and Boston and from the outlets and factories of manufacturers, typically on 6 to 10 months' credit. This system was part of a more general merchandising development in the United States in which southern factors and western store-keepers purchased many kinds of goods in semiannual trips to eastern cities. Types of purchasers were numerous; one shoe dealer wrote: "We had a large trade South and West with the grocery men, the dry goods men, the hardware men."[24]

In this context jobbers and wholesalers specialized and grew quickly. The Boston jobbing trade in 1828 amounted to $1 million, and in 1856 that city had about 200 wholesale and jobbing houses with sales on the order of $50 million. New York also grew; its 3 houses with about $130,000 sales in 1828 had expanded to 56 with business of $15 million in 1858. Shoe merchants continued to innovate; they sold by sample and financed the formation of shoe dealers in the West.[25] The wholesaling system drew shoe producers from many regions into indirect contact, some planning for growing sales, others fearing the effects.

Yet there was more to the growth of wholesale markets than marketing innovations and the expansion of the potential market. Marketing innovations alone could not overcome the transportation and marketing costs of long-distance trade and, therefore, in the absence of cost or quality advantages, could not account for the concentration of wholesale production in Massachusetts. Changes in production provided such advantages. Shoe firms contributed to wholesale market expansion not simply as merchants, but also as producers. To the evolution of shoemaking we must turn.

3

Reorganizing Production

The American shoe industry in the mid-nineteenth century was like the British cotton textile industry a century earlier. Both were about to mechanize, and both had experienced the development of capitalist firms putting out work to large numbers of producers. But the transformation of craft shoemaking was more radical; the several centuries over which putting-out had expanded in Britain were compressed to a half century, and in this time wage laborers also specialized by task.

The restructuring of craft shoemaking, like that of textiles, may have prepared the way for mechanization. It might have contributed to market growth and hence the incentive to invent. The larger, reorganized firms might have more readily introduced machinery. Moreover, the process of craft innovation may have spilled over into machine development. To account for mechanization, we must first understand the process transforming craft production.

Capitalist Production and the Central Shop System

Begun in the eighteenth century, capitalist production was well established by 1830. Lynn provides a clear illustration. By 1810 a Lynn manufacturer employed 70 workers, many times the level allowed masters by the craft ethic. In 1832 such employment levels were common. As Table 2.2 indicates, almost 40 percent of establishments employed 60 or more workers. Close to 80 percent employed 10 or more, and eight firms employed 150 and up. The mean establishment employed 57, the median 40. The largest firms continued to grow; in 1850, employment of 300 or 400 workers was not uncommon.[1]

Other centers of capitalist production developed. Mean 1832 employment levels in other Essex County towns approached that of Lynn, including 45 for Haverhill and 30 for Bradford. Towns south and west of Boston also developed wage labor. Grafton had an average employment of 13. Weymouth became a center after Harvey and Quincy Reed discovered in 1809 that they could sell large quantities of shoes in Boston. Quincy noted that "most of the shoes were made by people in South Weymouth. We had nearly every man there working for us before long." East Bridgewater expanded through the efforts of Seth

Bryant, who sold 3,000 pairs of shoes in an order of unprecedented size in 1822 and in 10 years employed 200 to make 150,000 pairs of shoes.[2]

By mid-century Massachusetts was the unrivaled center of capitalist shoemaking. In 1850 it averaged 37 employees per establishment, compared to 5 in the rest of the country. It stood alone; no other state averaged 10, and Pennsylvania, its traditional rival, had only 5 employees per establishment.[3]

The division of labor also centered in Massachusetts. According to Hazard, it began around 1810. The division of labor was a specifically capitalist relation; it refers not simply to a specialization of individuals among the shoemaking operations—wives and daughters of shoemakers had long stitched uppers—but rather to a specialization among wage laborers.

Labor was divided in traditional parts. Following preexisting roles, upper stitching, called binding or fitting, typically was performed by women. Binding involved sewing relatively thin upper leather, along with subsidiary operations such as attaching eyelets and buckles. Men continued to bottom or "make" the shoes. Bottoming began with lasting, in which the insole was tacked to the foot-shaped wooden last, and the upper was stretched around the last and was tacked to the insole. The lasted upper was next permanently fastened to inner and outer soles, at first by sewing and later by pegging. Afterward heels were added. The division between binding and making necessitated mediating activity to prepare, distribute, and collect shoes.[4]

The three kinds of activities were performed in three types of units. Binding was done in the home. Finished uppers could be transported without damage, so that binding could be spatially separated from bottoming. Some bottoming was conducted in the home, but most was performed where the whole shoe had previously been made, in the "ten-footer," a 10- to 14-foot square building with benches for several shoemakers. All bottoming operations were carried out in the same place, because lasted shoes that had not been bottomed could not be transported readily. Finally, the central shop distributed materials, inspected work, and undertook some cutting and finishing operations. Here the upper leather was cut, the pieces put out, the stitched upper returned, the upper put out along with sole pieces or leather to be bottomed, and the bottomed shoe finished. One central shop worker supplied about 40 outworkers. The central shop was the distinguishing institution of the division of labor.

The division of labor expanded quickly, as shifts in word usage document. In accounts and records before 1815 the term "making" referred to shoe production as a whole but after 1815 its meaning was restricted to bottoming operations.[5] By the 1830s, the bulk of Massachusetts shoe output was the product of the central shop system. As Table 3.1 indicates, in 1832 and 1837 virtually every major shoe town in Massachusetts employed large numbers of women, a sure sign of the generality of the division of labor. In towns like Lynn, as many women and girls were employed as men and boys. Moreover,

Table 3.1
Employment by Sex in Selected Shoe Towns, 1832 and 1837

Town	Men and Boys		Women and Girls		Share (%) of Women and Girls	
	1832	1837	1832	1837	1832	1837
Abington	500	847	150	470	23	36
Brookfield	140	262	40	215	22	45
Danvers	698	666	292	411	29	38
Grafton	188	906	63	486	25	35
Haverhill	690	1,715	249	1,170	27	41
Holliston	155	312	5	149	3	32
Lynn	1,757	2,631	1,770	2,554	50	49
N. Bridgewater	120	750	50	375	29	33
N. Brookfield	120	550	29	300	19	35
Randolph	670	804	300	671	31	45
Reading	310	338	150	494	33	59
Stoughton	225	495	100	386	31	44
Weymouth	350	828	100	519	22	39

Sources: For 1832, see Table 2.2; for 1837, see Barber, *Historical Collections of Every Town in Massachusetts,* as summarized in Hazard, *The Organization of the Boot and Shoe Industry,* pp. 207–10.

the dramatic growth in the proportion of women and girls between 1832 and 1837 expressed the rapid spread of the division of labor in the 1830s. By 1850 Massachusetts had a far more developed division of labor than elsewhere; women comprised 43 percent of all Massachusetts shoe workers, but only 20 percent for the rest of the country.[6]

Over time the division of labor was refined. When the shoemaker made the whole shoe, the capitalist put out whole sides and skins of leather to be cut and made. The shoemaker was allowed to retain the "cabbage," leftover leather pieces. Upper leather was cut from paper patterns, the dimensions and shape of which were derived from the size of the last on which the shoe was to be made. When labor was divided, the central shop cut the upper leather and put out upper pieces. Beginning about 1820, central shops also cut sole leather. Specialized cutters reduced waste of materials, and central shops appropriated scrap leather made valuable by the birth of a scrap leather market; one of the last vestiges of the craft right of the shoemaker to the product was thus eliminated. Later patternmaking became a specialization in large shops. Finally, the central shop took on finishing operations to improve the appearance of the shoe, and then divided these operations into upper and bottom finishing. In some shops bottom finishing was divided into sandpapering and polishing, done by a two-person team.[7]

Near the end of the period, the division of labor entered the ten-footer. Teams or gangs were formed, composed of specialized bottoming workers. One common pattern grouped one laster, two or three sewers or more commonly one pegger, one edge trimmer, one polisher, and perhaps one heeler. These workers were trained not to make the whole shoe, or even to bottom it, but to trim, last, peg, or heel.[8]

Innovation and the Craft System

In the conclusion of *The Industrial Revolution in the Eighteenth Century*, Mantoux wrote: "One of the objects we have always kept in mind was precisely to show the continuity of the historical process underlying even the most rapid changes."[9] We too must keep this object in mind in order to understand how capitalist production and the division of labor so quickly and widely transformed Massachusetts shoemaking.

Marx's notion of paths to capitalism presupposes the same objective by grounding the emergence of capitalist production in the activity of previously existing merchants and producers. In the distinction between paths, Marx furthermore argues that the kind of innovation depends on who innovates, but he never makes clear why the innovations of producers have more revolutionary consequences than those of merchants.[10]

We can clarify the issue by tying agents to social structures that can influence the generation and diffusion of innovations. Producers are more than individuals who fabricate useful objects; they also occupy a social position, defined by a set of institutions that structure the relation of producers among themselves and to others in society. These institutions contain media of communication that can help undertake and spread innovations. Producers may then be more revolutionary than merchants because their institutions foster innovations not just in the distribution of the product but in the very organization and techniques of fabrication.

The institutions of the shoe craft were decisive for the reorganization of American shoe production. Shoemakers did not act alone; not only the merchant function emphasized by Commons but also merchants themselves were involved. Alan Dawley contends that in Lynn shopkeepers successfully became shoe manufacturers and reduced independent masters to the status of contractors or even wage laborers.[11]

But there is far more evidence for the involvement of shoemakers. Craft institutions could, of course, inhibit innovation, but they did not do so in the American shoe trade, particularly in the Massachusetts areas where capitalist shoemaking prospered. Craft restraints on the scale of employment had little force. Never strong, formal apprenticeship ceased to be practiced in Massachusetts in the 1830s. It had lost all meaning when Henry Wilson, who later became vice-president of the United States under Ulysses S. Grant, secured training from a shoemaker in exchange for five months' labor and only a few weeks later bought back the time he owed and started producing for himself. Training was merely the imparting of technique.[12]

Shoemakers initiated large-scale employment in many towns and were probably even more important in the origin of the division of labor. The central shop system appears to have originated independently in several Massachusetts towns. Harvey and Quincy Reed of Weymouth began selling shoes in Boston in 1809 and opened a store in which, in Quincy's words, "I used to cut out what would promise to be $100 worth a day. We couldn't have them made equal to that, but I could cut them. One day I cut 350 pairs of boot fronts and tended store besides." Upper cutting was separated from fitting and making. The store was not fully a central shop, since upper pieces were taken to Weymouth to be stitched but were not brought back to Boston to be redistributed to bottomers. About the same time, however, a true central shop was built in Weymouth; "the work done here was the cutting, treeing and dressing, the rest of the process being performed outside in homes and ten-footer shops."[13]

Lynn was another early developer of the central shop. Samuel Brimblecom, a shoemaker trained in Danvers who had been selling wholesale shoes since 1800, built a central shop around 1810. His operations expanded until his shop employed up to 3 or 4 cutters; in 1832 he employed 35 men and 45 women. The central shop was also initiated in Randolph around 1810, when a wholesale shoemaker and the main general store each opened up a central shop. In 1819 Ariel Bragg of Milford built a shop 30 feet wide, 20 feet in depth, and 2 stories high at a cost of $260.[14]

Moreover, the craft system supplied the principal mode of diffusion of capitalist development and the division of labor. The organizational knowledge and contacts provided by employment were put to use by the formation of new firms. The families of shoemakers were important beneficiaries, with the result that many family members set up their own large-scale central shops. This is apparent in Lynn, where, in 1832, four different Breeds employed 19, 22, 174, and 200 workers respectively; four Mudges hired 4, 16, 40, and 190; two Pratts, 190 and 250; six Newhalls, between 2 and 68; and five Chases, between 40 and 160 workers each. Together these five families ran 21 shops employing 1,668—about a third of Lynn's shoe establishments and close to half of its employment. Half of the employees of these families were women and girls.[15]

Other shoemakers used learning from their employment to set up their own shops. Two major Lynn manufacturers and initiators of the shoe factory, Samuel Bubier and Lyman Frazier, had both worked for Samuel Brimblecom. In North Brookfield, Tyler and Ezra Batcheller were trained in a shop producing for the southern market and in the 1820s established their own firm which produced 65,000 pairs of shoes in 1832 and over a million in 1860. Of course, upward mobility was not general; in Lynn only a few percent of shoemakers became manufacturers. But for these few, craft training was a means for capital accumulation.[16]

Similarly, the expansion of the central shop system was supported by the structures of the shoemaking craft. Christopher Robinson was apprenticed to

Micajah Newhall of Lynn and then worked for him as a cutter. In 1819 Robinson opened his own business, utilizing the division of labor. By 1822 he employed 12 shoemakers and 12 binders; by 1824 the number had doubled, and by 1848 Robinson employed 250. Others in Lynn adopted the central shop in the 1810s and 1820s.[17]

The shoe trade also structured the geographic spread of capitalist production and the division of labor. Craft shoemakers had long been mobile. European journeymen well earned their name, and in America land settlement and village formation provided additional reasons for movement. Lewis Prentiss was unique only in the extent of his travels. Apprenticed in Grafton in 1826, over the next half century he worked mostly as a custom producer in the Massachusetts towns of Hardwick, Mansfield, Northbridge, Millbury, Worcester, and Billerica, and went north to Springfield and Barre, Vermont, south to six shops in Providence, Rhode Island, and west to Louisville, Kentucky; Cincinnati, Ohio; and Rock Island, Illinois.[18]

Journeymen who had been trained in capitalist, wholesale shoemaking centers brought these new practices with them when they moved to other towns. The novelty of capitalist production gave them an incentive to move: to become manufacturers in areas where they would face less competition for laborers. Shoe towns thus became centers for the diffusion of capitalist shoemaking.

Instances of the journeyman-carried diffusion of the central shop system spanned the state (see Figure 3.1). A Randolph shoemaker initiated large-scale production in North Bridgewater (later Brockton) in 1811. About the same time two Grafton shoemakers began capitalist production in North Brookfield. One, joined by his brother, built a shop about which it was written: "Their shops were immense, as much as 25 by 50 feet." In the 1830s, a Beverly sailor and fisherman, trained in shoemaking in Danvers, returned home to organize his own central shop. The Worcester wholesale trade began around 1835 when two large-scale Hopkinton producers arrived and set up shop.[19]

Natick is an interesting example. It only began wholesale shoemaking on any scale in the mid-1830s, but by 1840 was both a center of attraction and diffusion of large-scale production. Henry Wilson was a farm boy from Farmington, New Hampshire, when he arrived in Natick around 1833. He became a major Natick producer, employing 18 workers to make 18,000 pairs of shoes in 1838 and 109 workers to form 122,000 pairs in 1847. Another country boy, Martin Hayes, had been bound to a country shoemaker in 1827 who still made his own leather. Hayes went to Natick in 1832, then returned to his hometown of Framingham to initiate wholesale production in 1837 or 1838. Another established Natick manufacturer, George Herring, left Natick and began wholesale production in the village Wilson had left.[20] As a new shoe town, Natick began with the central shop system and became another center of diffusion when its shoemakers moved elsewhere.

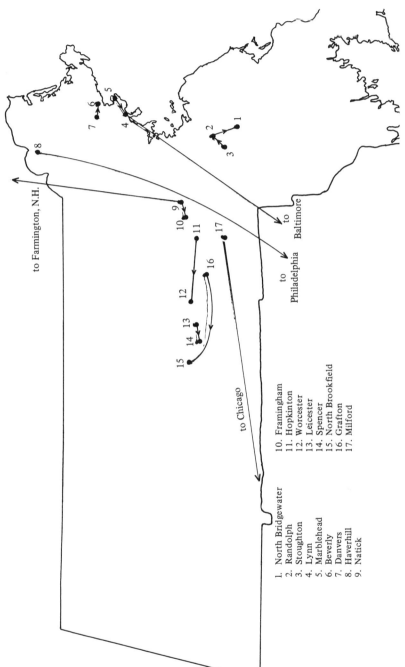

1. North Bridgewater
2. Randolph
3. Stoughton
4. Lynn
5. Marblehead
6. Beverly
7. Danvers
8. Haverhill
9. Natick

10. Framingham
11. Hopkinton
12. Worcester
13. Leicester
14. Spencer
15. North Brookfield
16. Grafton
17. Milford

to Farmington, N.H.

to Baltimore

to Philadelphia

to Chicago

Figure 3.1 The Movement of Massachusetts Shoemakers and the Spread of Capitalist Production and the Central Shop.

The trained craftsman organized the bottoming gang and often was the only trained shoemaker on the team. He contracted with the central shop to make shoes by the case; hired, directed, and perhaps trained workers who were proficient at one task; and performed one operation in the division of labor. Specializing labor benefited the contractor by some combination of lower wages for less skilled tasks, increased productivity, and, by removing less skilled laborers from skilled operations such as lasting and trimming, improved quality.[21]

The extension of the division of labor and the growth of capitalist production were connected. As firms grew, labor was divided, as indicated by the higher share of women and girls in larger firms. The division of labor affected new firm formation; bottomers could no longer make the whole shoe and as a result were less likely than cutters to become shoe manufacturers.[22]

That the division of labor and capitalist production both evolved in Massachusetts in the first half of the nineteenth century was more than a coincidence of time and place. Both were parts of a single process of capitalist development, undertaken by the same agents and supported by the structures of the craft system. The process was self-sustaining; once begun, inherited forms of training and mobility were transformed into carriers of the new system.

The process, moreover, was bounded by the spatial structure of the craft system; craftsmen moved readily in and around eastern Massachusetts, but much less frequently elsewhere. As a result, Massachusetts employed relatively more women in shoemaking; in 1850, women formed 43 percent of Massachusetts shoe workers, 28 percent for other New England states, 21 percent for the Middle Atlantic region, and only 7 percent for the rest of the country.[23]

The concentration of the division of labor in Massachusetts helps account for its domination of wholesale production. The division of labor may have reduced unit labor time and training costs. Lower wages for women and less skilled men also reduced unit shoe costs. In Massachusetts shoe towns the daily wage of women was a quarter to a half of that of men in 1832.[24] As a result, annual wage income per worker (and presumably also daily wages) was lower in Massachusetts; in 1850, the $178 per worker in Massachusetts was far lower than the $227 of the Middle Atlantic region or even the $217 of the rest of New England. Competition of Massachusetts shoes, expressed in the ongoing complaints of shoemakers in other states, was based on lower prices. To the extent that prices for shoes of each quality were driven toward equality, the lower average wages of Massachusetts workers, other things equal, gave shoe producers in that state higher profits and growth.[25] Through this mechanism, competition expanded wholesale markets at the expense of custom and retail, and concentrated wholesale production in Massachusetts. Contrary to Commons's argument, changes in production may thus have helped form and expand the wholesale market.

If the reorganization of shoemaking, like the Industrial Revolution for Mantoux, can be understood by reference to "economic needs and the spontancous efforts they call forth," spontaneity must be interpreted in relation to the institutions and activities of shoemakers. The question is whether and in what sense spontaneous efforts responded to economic need.

Markets and the Evolution of Production

The reorganization of shoemaking in the first half of the nineteenth century was not the result of production innovations alone; it also rested on conditions quite outside the industry. Among these were not only the product markets so central to Commons's account, but also markets for labor and inputs.

As Commons claimed, market evolution was both largely independent from and an important determinant of the reorganization of production. The evolution of the wholesale market surely rested on factors outside the industry to determine transportation costs and the potential demand for shoes. Nor can it be doubted that transition to wholesale markets facilitated the reorganization of production by overcoming the need for direct contact with the consumer. Production could become abstract, aimed not at this or that consumer but at the market per se. It could therefore achieve a scale not easily gained through custom or even retail sales.

But a closer link between market growth and production innovation is difficult to find. The division of labor altered production "to secure rapid work" according to Hazard, and as a cost-reducing change it would have been adopted as easily in the context of stagnant markets.[26] Firms needed only modest scale and investment to introduce the division of labor. Circulating capital predominated over fixed, and small central shops were often simply modified stores and ten-footers. Capital costs could constrain the entry of new firms, but these were more circulating capital costs than fixed capital associated with the central shop system. Because growth beyond a minimal scale multiplied the same operations, small firms could enter without facing competitive disadvantages.[27]

Nor were there any discernible costs of generating the new organization of production. In this the division of labor differed from mechanization. To justify the substantial costs of inventing, developing, and producing new machines required sufficient size of potential markets for machinery, and, by extension, the products made by machinery. Costs of development thus linked new machines to market size. This link did not exist for organizational changes, which did not entail costs of developing and disseminating any new means of production.

Capitalist shoe production, of course, required a supply of labor power; here is Marx's problem of primitive accumulation. For Marx the English manufacturing period formed a stage in which workers lost ownership or effective control of the means of production, principally land. This separation was required for widespread proletarianization. The provision of a labor force was far more difficult in the United States, so much so that Marx conceived the

United States to be a settler colony in which land was freely available. As such it was the antithesis of Britain, and the recruitment of a proletariat was correspondingly harder. The society in which feudal tradition was the weakest was also one in which free labor power was the most difficult to acquire.[28]

The structure of the manufacturing period gave form to labor power. Workers retained ties to the land through ownership, usage, residual rights, or bonds to rural communities, and these ties gave much proletarianization the form of rural putting-out. As Marx points out, Mantoux and Bucher emphasize, and the protoindustrialization literature thematizes, capitalist production can most readily arise when and where agricultural labor requirements are declining. Particularly when there are no advantages of large-scale operations stemming from heating or power requirements or the scale of the product, capitalist production can be spread out to homes or small independent workshops. Wage labor in a putting-out system thus has the paradoxical result that it maintains ties to the land and rural communities and thus forms a barrier to proletarianization.[29]

The Massachusetts shoe industry was overwhelmingly organized in a putting-out system, with perhaps 5 percent of total employment in the central shop. Some outwork occurred in the town where the central shop was located, but most was outside. In Lynn, for example, laborers outside town generated at least 60 percent of the output of Lynn manufacturers.[30]

The protoindustrialization thesis helps account for the location of shoe production in Massachusetts. The decline of Massachusetts agriculture in the first half of the century, in the context of limited geographic mobility, created a pool of potential workers which the shoe industry could and did tap. As Alexander Field argues, growing competition from agricultural products from the Middle Atlantic states, upper New York, and later the West resulted in part from the use of the steamboat on rivers and the Long Island Sound and the locomotive on lines connecting Boston with New York City and Albany. Therefore by facilitating the integration of markets, machinery supported primitive accumulation and the growth of capitalist production in declining agricultural areas.[31]

The putting-out system can supply an indirect link between market growth and the reorganization of production. When market growth was rapid, the supply of labor power provided by the putting-out system was often insufficient. Even if adequate for the industry as a whole, the labor supply was limited for individual manufacturers. Several kinds of evidence suggest that this was so. Manufacturers put out over greater distances, and the growing costs of transporting materials and semifinished products would not have been incurred had labor been available at comparable wages. Lynn came to put out as far as 150 miles.[32]

Wages were higher in older centers, consistent with the contention that these centers faced tighter labor markets. In 1832 Lynn employers hired male shoemakers in Lynn at wages from 67 to 87 cents per day, but hired Marblehead workers at daily wages varying from 40 to 67 cents. Moreover, some capitalists moved their operations to new centers where a ready supply of labor was available. Though Natick had only taken up wholesale shoe production a decade earlier, in 1843 it could not secure an adequate supply of labor locally, which led one manufacturer to move to a southern New Hampshire town. The limits to labor supply in established areas gave advantages to producers setting up operations in areas new to shoemaking.[33]

In the context of rapidly growing markets and constraints on supplies of labor, reorganizing production allowed firms to increase output. The division of labor could both increase shoe output per laborer and extend employment to workers untrained to produce the whole shoe, thereby allowing other workers to concentrate on more skilled operations. The limits to American proletarianization could therefore have tied market growth to the reorganization of production. The unavailability of labor may have been a bottleneck that directed attention to innovation, just as for Mantoux weaving advances directed inventive attention to spinning prior to the Industrial Revolution.

Still, protoindustrialization in the context of rapid market growth does not adequately account for the localization of shoe production in Massachusetts. First, there was substantial mobility of labor into shoemaking towns, including a significant in-migration from outside Massachusetts. Labor was not tied to localities, though its mobility may have centered on nearby areas. Second, wage data do not suggest that New England was unique. Indeed, as Sokoloff has argued, from 1820 through 1850 money wage rates were as high in New England as they were in the Middle Atlantic states, rural wages were generally higher, and the rural-urban difference was less in New England than in the Middle Atlantic states. This is not to deny the logic of protoindustrialization, but at a minimum it suggests that wage differentials do not account for the unique success of Massachusetts shoemaking. Rather, it is to the cumulative logic of the innovation within the industry that we must look to account for localization.[34]

Input markets also contributed to the reorganization of production. In much of the eighteenth century, leather had been supplied locally, which constrained the growth of shoe output. By about 1825, this limit was overcome by the birth of international trade in hides and national markets for sole and upper leather. Sole leather was concentrated in New York and to a lesser extent in Pennsylvania, and upper leather was tanned in these states and in such North Shore, Massachusetts, towns as Lynn, Peabody, and Salem. The presence of upper-leather production supported the concentration of shoemaking in Massachusetts, but, if anything, New York would gain more from its proximity to tanning of all sorts. Large-scale leather production benefited wholesale shoe-making wherever it was, but did not single out Massachusetts.[35]

Finally, making shoe tools and forms also concentrated in Massachusetts, and, because these had mostly local markets, the Massachusetts shoe industry was the main beneficiary. The evolution of the instruments of labor, which

Commons held to be insignificant in determining production, may have had some role after all.

In the history of the shoe industry in the first half of the nineteenth century, market evolution and productive innovation were mutually reinforcing. The evolution of markets for shoes, labor power, and inputs fostered but did not compel the expansion of capitalist production and the division of labor. The reorganization of production, in turn, contributed to the formation of national markets for mass-produced shoes and leather and a regional market for labor power.

In this mutuality, the shoe industry exemplified a more general phenomenon. New retailing, wholesaling, and transport systems fostered the integration of markets for many industries. Some developed national markets, like tanning, textiles, and firearms, but others produced for regional markets, including furniture, wagons, and carriages. In industries of both types, small producers with little commitment to craft traditions reorganized production, increased shop size, and, in hats, clothing, and—until industrialization— textiles, developed putting-out.[36] Particularly where capital requirements were large or production was an adjunct to trade, merchants invested. Moreover, changes in the size and structure of product markets augmented specialization by region and industry, and helped provide a labor force for all industries.

That changes of production in turn contributed to market growth reflects the progressiveness of the American manufacturing dynamic. Two kinds of alterations of production contributed to this progressiveness. One, paramount in England's manufacturing period, was, in Mantoux's words, "of a purely economic and not of a technical nature. It was a change in organization and not in the apparatus of production."[37] The second did alter instruments of production. Mechanization in industry and especially in trade accelerated market growth and changes in production. Alongside the power loom, locomotive, and steamboat, more modest changes in craft instruments had the same effect.

4

New Means of Production

The division of labor among workers making a commodity was the principal transformation of the labor process within the manufacturing period; on this Marx, Mantoux, Commons, and Hazard all agree. Here manufacturing differed from mechanized production. In Marx's words, "In manufacture the transformation of the mode of production takes labour-power as its starting-point. In large-scale industry, on the other hand, the instruments of labour are the starting-point."[1] Means of production may of course change within manufacturing, but these changes must accommodate to the handicraft skills of workers and are therefore limited in importance.

Means of shoe production did change; new means of uniting soles and uppers, kinds of lasts, and tools all developed in the first half of the nineteenth century. An account of mechanization must investigate these changes because, like the division of labor and marketing innovations, they may have influenced the manufacturing dynamic of shoemaking in ways that met conditions for mechanization. But there are further reasons that single out craft means of production. They may have been technically related to machinery, diffused in similar ways, and developed through similar institutions. Understood in relation to the institutions generating them, craft instruments of labor may have been the historical starting point of mechanized production.

The Pegged Shoe

The *Scientific American* wrote in 1869 that the shoe peg "worked perhaps as great a revolution in a most important branch of industry as was ever effected by a single device,"[2] for the nail-like, pointed wooden peg came with a new kind of shoe that dominated the industry by mid-century. The pegged shoe united the upper and soles by one or two rows of driven pegs, each as long as the combined width of the soles and upper. It thus dispensed with the stitched seams that had bottomed sewed shoes.

Pegged shoes originated around 1810. They were introduced almost simultaneously in the Massachusetts towns of Milford, Byfield, Hopkinton, and Spencer, as well as in Homer, New York, and Norwalk, Connecticut. According to one well-placed shoe manufacturer, who filled orders for pegged shoes as large as 3,000 pairs in 1822, "Pegged shoes were introduced in 1815; previous to that all boots and shoes were sewed, or nailed with copper nails, for the Spanish market."[3]

From these beginnings, the pegged shoe grew to predominance. Workers in the boot-making town of South Randolph first saw pegged boots in 1827 and produced them extensively only a decade later. Pegging diffused rapidly in the 1840s and 1850s, so that in 1860 their manufacture "constituted at least three-fourths of the general business" according to the census of that year.[4]

Compared to the sewed shoe, the pegged shoe reduced costs; here lay the principal rationale for its introduction. Shoes varied in style and construction. Style distinguished boots, shoes, and slippers, men's from women's shoes, Balmorals from Bluchers and both from moccasins, laced from buttoned shoes. The mode of construction was defined by the method used to unite soles and uppers. Style influenced the design and size of pieces and the materials and subsidiary operations used, yet shoes of many styles could be sewed, pegged, or nailed. Differences in style affected marketability but not the form of manufacturing.[5]

The advantages of the pegged shoe over sewed shoes can be seen by comparing their construction. Sewed shoes were of two types, welt and turn. Welt shoes were bottomed by means of two seams. Uppers were first sewed to the insole and to a welt, a strip of leather about one-half inch wide extending around the sole except at the heel. The welt was then stitched to the outsole inside a cut in the outsole, called a channel. When the channel was glued shut, the stitching was protected. In turn shoes, the uppers were sewed inside out to a single sole, and the inside was then turned outside. The pliability required for their construction restricted the turning process to light shoes and slippers. The pegged shoe was simpler. It trapped the edges of the upper between the insole and the outsole and united them all by short wooden pegs, six to eight per inch.

The simplicity of pegged shoe construction substantially reduced labor time. The pegged shoe substituted mechanically elementary hole-punching and hammering operations for the sole-placing, hole-making, stitching, channeling, and gluing operations needed to sew welt shoes. As a result, one pegger could do the work of two or three stitchers on bottoming teams. For a number of enterprises in the 1850s and 1860s, more precise differences of labor times are presented in the U.S. Commissioner of Labor's 1898 report. Whereas 123 labor hours were required to sew and turn 100 pairs of cheap women's turn shoes by hand, only 42 hours were needed to hand peg that many shoes of the same quality. In similar fashion, hand pegging 100 pairs of men's cheap brogans took about 22 hours and the same number of boots 50 hours, but 298 hours were needed to channel and sew the bottoms of medium-grade men's welt shoes.[6]

The pegged shoe was not without its faults. It was more rigid and therefore less comfortable than sewed shoes because the insole was directly united with the outsole, whereas the two seams of the welt shoe allowed the insole to lift off the outsole. But the lower price of pegged shoes increased their market share. For example, Howard and French, wholesale Randolph boot makers, sold a dozen pairs of pegged boots for $25.50 in 1845, compared with $39.00 per dozen for sewed boots of the same quality. Pegged shoes came to dominate markets for cheap and medium-quality shoes, largely leaving the highest-quality markets to sewed shoes, often still the domain of custom producers. The simple shoe peg was indeed a revolutionary device.[7]

Lasts and Standardization

In the second quarter of the nineteenth century, standardized lasts came into use. Their significance lies in fulfilling a condition for creating a standard shoe, a shoe built to standardized measures of length and, later in the century, width. Standardization transformed the conception of the product and its production. The standard shoe was built to satisfy an abstract need; it was designed to fit no particular foot but a conception of the foot, a "standard" foot. From this conception were derived measurements of each part of the shoe which then constituted standards, norms to be met in making the shoe.

Standardization had two objectives. Standard shoes could be marketed more easily and widely. They could be sold by sample; the buyer had no need to go to the warehouse of the producer or jobber. Designed for the average foot, standard shoes would fit a larger share of the population.

Standard shoes were also of higher quality, and here the standard last was critical. The last played two roles in shoemaking. It functioned first as a model. The shoe design determined the shape of the last, and the last was then used to form patterns for upper pieces by wetting tissue paper, folding it around the last, and marking on the paper the location of joints between upper pieces. When dry, the paper was cut into patterns from which individual pieces were cut.

The last also functioned as a form around which the shoe was made. The inner sole was cut roughly against the bottom of the last, tacked or pegged to the last, and trimmed to its finished shape. The stitched upper was mounted on the last, secured to the inner sole, and permanently fastened to the soles by sewing or pegging. The last was both a standard and a means to conform to the standard.[8]

This dual function led to poorer-quality shoes when the last was not standardized. If the last used to cut upper pieces differed in shape and size from that used to make the shoe, the upper would not correctly fit the last on which it was to be bottomed. The upper would be too wide, leading to baggy shoes, or too tight, so the product tended to rip, or too short to be lasted, or too tight in some parts and too loose in others.

The problem of nonstandard lasts worsened when a division of labor was instituted. For then different lasts were used to form upper patterns in the central shop and to make shoes in ten-footers. If lasts were not homogeneous, a nonstandard, badly fitting shoe was the likely outcome. Workers with sufficient skill and interest could only at times compensate. Before the division of labor, the shoemaker cut the uppers on the last on which the shoe was made. The resulting product was not standardized, but could be well made and comfortable. With the division of labor, standard lasts became a condition for consistently making well-fitting, comfortable shoes.

A concerted dynamic toward standardization among wholesale producers emerged in the second quarter of the century. Earlier shoes had little uniformity. Wholesale shoes had been sold by size since the second half of the eighteenth century, but rarely conformed to standards defining each size. Connected to this was the heterogeneity of lasts for shoes of the same size and style. At least from the mid-1830s, standard lasts were made in Lynn and Brockton, and spread quickly elsewhere.[9]

A standard shoe depended not only on a standard last but also on accurate patternmaking, cutting, fitting, and bottoming. To improve precision, capitalists brought cutting operations into the central shop and inspected outwork. In cutting, new means of production aided the quest. In 1832, the first complete set of diagram patterns for cutting uppers was produced in Boston; made of strawboard, tin, or some other enduring material, the diagram patterns replaced earlier tissue-paper patterns.[10] Tin sole patterns came into use in the 1840s. Their significance was described by a Lynn shoemaker: "The use of tin patterns for shaping the soles, in place of the old method of 'rounding on' by the last . . . gave uniformity to the shape of the shoes—a thing impossible, as experience has shown, under the ancient plan, which left every man to the free exercise of his choice in determining the width and shape of the shoes, and especially of the shanks." Soles cut from a sole pattern would be the same size and would conform to the last in the same way. Previously, "when it came to the 'shank,' there was a chance for the display of original genius."[11] As elsewhere, genius was sacrificed for uniformity.

New Tools

The manufacturing dynamic to tools is aptly described by Marx: "In Birmingham alone 500 varieties of hammer are produced, and not only is each one adapted to a particular process, but several varieties often serve exclusively for the different operations in the same process. The manufacturing period simplifies, improves and multiplies the implements of labour by adapting them to the exclusive and special functions of each kind of worker."[12]

Along with lasts and patterns, shoe tools and work support devices were refined and specialized. In 1800 quality shoe tools had to be imported from England. By about 1830 Massachusetts shoe tools had closed the gap. Lynn became an important shoe toolmaking town. So did the old South Shore iron-making center of North Bridgewater (later Brockton). By 1835 it was an acknowledged center of shoe tools purchased throughout Massachusetts, and in 1865 it had 11 shoe toolmakers, not to mention makers of lasts, awls, shoe boxes, and shoe blacking.[13]

The growth of toolmaking was accompanied by innovation in tool design. As new shoe types emerged, so did new shoe tools. Made at first with tools adopted from other operations, the pegged shoe acquired its own specialized instruments. One of the most important was the pegging haft invented by Herrick Aiken of Dracut, Massachusetts, in 1833. It was a socket for holding the awl in pegging and was "deemed one of the most useful among the minor inventions connected with shoe manufacturing." A series of pegging jacks supported and in cases rotated the lasted shoe during pegging. After pegging, pegs protruded inside the shoe; tools to cut and rasp these pegs were introduced and improved. At least five peg cutters were patented from 1852 through 1860.[14]

Bottoming tools evolved in every operation. Pincers were patented to simplify lasting and to perform specialized lasting. A tool was invented to cut sole channels a desired distance from the edge; if standard lasts and soles were used, it cut the channel in a way that standardized sewing could take place. Over a dozen sole and heel edge trimmers were patented through 1860, as well as about two dozen treeing devices used to reshape the shoe after bottoming and a number of polishing tools.[15]

Upper tools were also developed. Knives, needles, and awls all evolved. Far and away the most patents for upper manufacturing were issued for crimping devices, which exerted pressure to shape wet leather, most importantly for the fronts of boots. Three patents for crimping and other upper-shaping devices were issued in each of the 1810s and 1820s, and close to 20 in the 1830s, in the 1840s, and again in the 1850s. Crimping devices became increasingly complex, involving holding, grasping, and pressure-applying mechanisms. They, like pegging jacks and some sole-cutting devices, were passing over into machines.

The Innovative Process

As innovations, altered means of production had an objectivity that the division of labor did not possess. They were embodied; new pegs, standard lasts, and new tools outlived the labor that formed them. Their objectivity was manifested in their patentability: unlike the division of labor, these innovations could themselves be recognized as property.

Objectivity implied that the inventor could be remunerated by everyone using the innovation in the form of patent royalties or payment for new means of production. Self-interest and use by others could both be realized; indeed, when diffusion occurred through sale, the latter was a condition of the former. Particularly in an industry with many firms, the returns to invention extended beyond the reduced costs secured by use of the new technique in the inventor's own shop.

The division of labor, by contrast, was disembodied. It was not directly observable in the product and entailed no changes in means of production. It diffused personally, through emulation and spatial mobility among craftsmen. In this regard it was similar to the spread of craft skills. Just as the immigration in 1750 of the Welsh shoemaker John Dagyr brought skills held to be important to the improvement of the quality of Lynn shoes, so also the movement of other shoemakers carried the division of labor among towns.[16] Dividing labor fostered the interest of innovators by reducing costs in their own production processes, but not more widely. Indeed, through the spread of the division of labor, the innovator lost competitive advantages.

But the objectivity of new means of production by itself accounts for neither the form nor the agents of development and diffusion. The contrast of new commodities and the division of labor suggests two paths of technical development and associated types of social organization. In the path of new commodity development, firms develop new techniques for sale. Use is preceded by a social relation of capital goods producers and users. The firm is an institution of generation and diffusion, and the capital goods market is an institution not only of sale but also of learning and secondary invention. In the path of self-usage, firms undertake invention to change their own production processes. Diffusion occurs mainly through the movement of workers to firms that use the technique in their own production, often new firms the workers themselves establish; it is unintended and perhaps suppressed by the inventor.

In the manufacturing stage, new techniques, especially major new techniques, often develop and spread for self-usage. Means of production most readily develop as new commodities when a well-developed capital goods sector supplies trained inventors and adequate marketing institutions. New shoe means of production found no such contexts. They were embedded within a craft milieu in which innovations took a disembodied form. The movement of workers had been a principal means through which British shoe tools had been acquired. This mode of diffusion extended beyond craft techniques; textile machinery had come in the same way, and the great American firearms machine tool innovations spread principally through the mobility of workers.[17]

Similarly, new means of shoe production were often invented by shoemakers (or shoe merchants) and spread by craft movement. The pegged shoe in part originated and diffused in this way. Two pegging innovators, Rufus Chapin of Milford and Josiah Green of Spencer, were both shoemakers who made pegged shoes for wholesale markets. Neither tried to appropriate larger returns through patenting. Chapin even made his own pegs. Especially when pegs were not purchased, diffusion occurred by personal contact among shoemakers, perhaps spurred by merchants marketing pegged shoes.[18] No doubt many shoe tools evolved along the same path.

Innovations also emerged as commodities sold by producers of lasts, tools, and pegs. Just as "men wore clothes before there were any tailors," so were there shoe means of production in the United States before people specialized in making them.[19] In 1800 America had few, if any, craftsmen specializing in making lasts, shoe tools, or shoe pegs, but all three specializations developed over the following half century. By 1850 shoemaking towns like Lynn, Brockton, Haverhill, and Braintree had their own toolmakers and last makers.[20]

The origin of independent shoe input producers followed the Smithian logic of deepening the division of labor as the market expanded. The growth and spatial concentration of the market for shoes surely increased the potential markets for inputs, and the transportation improvements that Smith emphasized played a part in extending the market. So did the reorganization of production; what Marx termed the technical division of labor—the specialization of laborers in the production of a single commodity—may thus have fostered the extension of the social division of labor—the division between those producing separate commodities. Still, market growth only removed a limit to specialization; advantages from superior input design and knowledge of the iron and wood manufacturing methods combined to realize this potential.[21]

Once in existence, input producers readily innovated. Indeed, specialized shoe input producers and new inputs grew together, each supported by the other. As last makers originated, so did the standard last, variable widths, and such improved last designs as the replacement of "straights" by right and left lasts. Toolmakers refined and differentiated shoe tools. Vertical disintegration was at times the result of invention.

Sale by input producers diffused new techniques. Some were sold on custom bases; here a personal, largely localized interaction persisted. But others were sold throughout Massachusetts and beyond. Pegs made in Massachusetts and New Hampshire came to be marketed throughout New England and were even exported. Unlike the shoe peg, the standard last was never made by shoe producers; it spread by the marketing efforts of last makers. Many tools were widely sold; by 1860, both Lynn and Boston directories advertised shops selling a number of tools and forms.[22]

Inventions for both self-usage and commodity usage were tied to institutions of the shoe industry. The size of the potential market for new means of production posed no barriers; they typically could be introduced on a small scale, and particularly in Massachusetts there was more than enough shoe output to fully utilize the capacity of even mechanized peg and last shops. But invention was also tied to the knowledge provided by proximity to shoe and shoe input producers. This tie is suggested by the location of patenting. Table 4.1 presents shares of nonmachine shoe manufacturing patents, including tools, lasts, work support devices, crimping devices, and manufacturing processes.[23] There were 29 such patents from 1806 through 1825, 77 from 1826 to 1845, and 53 in the next decade. The increase in patenting over time mirrored shoe output growth. The regional shares of nonmachine patents varied closely with regional shoe output shares. New England's output share

Table 4.1
Regional Shares of Shoe Output and Nonmachine Shoe Patents,
1806–1855

	1806 - 1825		1826 - 1845		1846 - 1855	
	Output	Patents	Output	Patents	Output	Patents
New England	38%	34%	49%	60%	55%	38%
(Massachusetts)	(21)	(21)	(37)	(35)	(45)	(18)
Middle Atlantic	45	62	36	34	31	53
(New York)	(17)	(28)	(18)	(18)	(14)	(28)
(Pennsylvania)	(18)	(21)	(10)	(10)	(10)	(25)
West	1	3	8	3	9	2
South	15	0	6	4	5	8

Sources: See Table 2.1; for the identification of American shoe patents, see U.S. Department of Commerce, *U.S. Patent Classification–Subclass Listing,* class 12, "boot and shoe making"; U.S. Patent Office, *Subject-Matter Index;* Research Publications, Inc., *Early Unnumbered Patents, 1790–1836.*

Notes: For 1806–25, 1810 output is used; for 1826–45, 1840 output is used; for 1846–55, 1850 output is used. For definition of regions, see Table 2.1.

varied from 38 to 55 percent and its patent share from 34 to 60 percent. The Middle Atlantic states were significant but generally declining in both output and patenting. The South and West were minor producing and inventing states in all periods.[24]

Within shoemaking (and shoe input) regions, the development of shoe inputs was also supported by institutions outside the shoe industry and associated means of production trades. Regions with concentrations of shoe patenting and output typically also were centers of machinery production, and, as the origin of the pegged shoe and the standard last demonstrate, knowledge of machinery influenced the development of shoe inputs.

One of the principal inventors of the pegged shoe was Paul Pillsbury. He was born near Newburyport, Massachusetts, into one of those New England families that spanned the division of labor; his six brothers included one blacksmith, one mechanic, two farmers, and two ministers. Pillsbury became a mechanic, making wind and water mills in his leisure and later building a lathe and manufacturing shuttles for woolen mills in Amesbury. He moved a few miles to Byfield, where he farmed, worked as a machinist in a cotton factory, and invented a corn sheller and bark mill. The latter, patented in 1808, ground bark for leather production but also embodied a principle later used to grind corn, coffee, and spices. The patent proved so valuable for leather tanning that Pillsbury sold it for $2,000.[25]

In Byfield an enterprising shoemaker approached Pillsbury to make a heel peg machine around 1810. Through this contact Pillsbury acquired knowledge of shoemaking. He generalized the problem of heel attaching to include the more important problem of uniting soles and upper. To make pegs, he "plowed and cross-plowed" a piece of maple to form the points, split it into combs and then into pegs. This innovation was probably similar to those of Rufus Chapin, Josiah Green, and other shoemakers, but Pillsbury took it in a different direction. Rather than making shoes with his pegs, he concentrated on making the pegs themselves. He spent three years to design peg-making machinery and build his own forge, lathe, and foundry, and opened a peg mill in 1815. His inventive and marketing efforts were successful enough that, according to the *Shoe and Leather Reporter*, "he became known throughout the State as 'Peg Pillsbury.'" By selling pegs, he also spread knowledge of the pegged shoe.[26]

The genesis of the standard last was even more independent of the shoe industry. It came as the product of a machine, the last-turning lathe. Being neither flat nor cylindrical, a last could not be cut by either a circular saw or the usual wood lathe. The pattern lathe solved the problem. It fastened a model last and a block to be cut to a rotating shaft. Tracing and cutting wheels were attached to the machine frame so that the tracing wheel followed the contours of the revolving model while the cutting wheel duplicated the contours in the block. Either the rotating shaft or the cutting and tracing wheels moved laterally so that the tracing wheel spiraled over the entire model, thereby cutting the block into the shape of the model.[27]

The lasting lathe was not invented by last makers or even for the purpose of making lasts; it was, rather, a minor adaptation of the Blanchard pattern lathe. Thomas Blanchard perfected the pattern lathe to produce gunstocks. The invention was part of a process entirely separate from the shoe industry, a process of initial mechanization that generated a whole system of woodworking and metalworking machines. The process had different agents, a remarkable set of craftsmen in western Massachusetts and the Connecticut River valley including Blanchard, the successful inventor of a tack-making machine, several versions of the pattern lathe, and later a wood-bending machine. This process also had different results; it led to the factory and a dynamic of ongoing technological change. Such techniques applied most directly to firearms, but were also applied more generally. The pattern lathe could copy any irregular wooden model, and its technological principles also applied to copying irregular objects of other materials. Other firearms machines, like the milling machine, had similar breadth of applicability.[28]

The lasting lathe was simply the pattern lathe applied to last making. Lasts were not the only beneficiaries; the pattern lathe also came to make axe handles, wheel spokes, oars, hat blocks, and wooden sculptures. About 10 years after the pattern lathe had come into general use in the Springfield Armory, it was introduced to make lasts and shoe trees in Lynn, Brockton, and elsewhere. The machine took a mere minute and a half per last, so that even though finishing and model building remained hand operations, labor productivity in last making increased fourfold. The resulting fall in last prices led to the spread of the lathe to virtually all last making by 1840.[29]

The dependence of the manufacturing dynamic of shoemaking on mechanization was already seen for the evolution of the market and the formation of a proletariat, in which the steamboat and railroad played a role. Pillsbury's peg making and the origin of the standard last makes it clear that the evolution of craft production was also influenced by mechanization. This is not to deny that shoemakers helped to generate and spread the pegged shoe, and to set and enforce standards. Rather, it emphasizes the complementarity of developments internal to the craft with others coming from the mechanized sector of the economy. This complementarity is one reason why the manufacturing dynamic in the United States was more thoroughgoing than that which preceded the Industrial Revolution in Britain.

The regional confines of the interaction of mechanization and shoemaking deserve emphasis. It was within Massachusetts and adjoining sections of surrounding states that the pegged shoe, standard last, and many shoe tools were developed. Within this area, communication among producers in different industries was easiest, due to the predominance of regional labor mobility and machinery markets and to the ongoing interactions within families and communities. Innovations of course spread beyond Massachusetts, but more irregularly as distance increased; so eminent an English engineer as Joseph Whitworth first saw the Blanchard lathe a quarter century after its introduction, and then only because he systematically toured American workplaces.[30]

Once in existence, inputs developed their own inventive processes. Fostered by growing demand and the widespread development of woodworking machinery in New England, peg production came to employ a series of machines to saw, plane, groove, and split, with the result that peg prices fell from $2.00 per bushel in 1841 to 70 cents in 1855.[31]

The lasting lathe formed the basis for a variety of further developments. The lathe itself developed when the application of the pantograph principle allowed lasts of many sizes to be cut from the same model last. The standard last made standard patterns possible, and in 1848 George Parrot used the pantograph to make patterns of many sizes from one model. By cutting right and left lasts from one model, the lasting lathe also made it practical to form right and left shoes of the same size and shape.[32]

The development of new means of shoe production thus took a distinctive path. Compared to the division of labor, originated and spread by shoemakers and shoe merchants, new pegs and lasts followed a more universal path, integrated with machinery sharing similar technical principles and diffused via commodity sales. Once begun, this path took on its own dynamic. Lasts and pegs were refined as products, their production became increasingly mechanized, and complementary products evolved, such as the pegging haft, rasper, and other pegging tools, channeling tools, sole patterns, and patternmaking machines. Shoemaking had come to develop through the new products of capital goods firms.

New Means of Production and the Manufacturing Dynamic

The evolution of means of production had important consequences for shoe production and markets. The pegged shoe altered the division of labor. It reduced bottoming time and thus the share of makers among shoe workers. It also modified the proportions of the bottoming gang; whereas "in the case of hand-sewed shoes 2 or 3 sewers were needed to keep the rest of the gang busy," one pegger was sufficient. The makeup of the team altered; pegging was increasingly the domain of children and less skilled men. Indeed, pegging contributed to forming the bottoming gang, because the lower wages of peggers cut costs and enabled skilled makers to specialize in other operations.[33]

New means of production also contributed to the formation and growth of the wholesale market. Compared to the sewing operations it replaced, pegging reduced labor time by one-half to two-thirds, and, because sewers formed about a quarter of bottoming time and about an eighth of total labor time, pegging reduced expended labor time by about 6 to 8 percent.[34] The lower wages of peggers in bottoming teams further reduced costs. Lower costs were passed on in lower prices, which was a factor in the increase of per capita shoe consumption and in the concentration of shoemaking in Massachusetts, near the invention and production of new inputs.

The standard last also contributed to the formation of the national market by improving the quality of the central shop's product. Standardization moreover influenced the organization of the market. In Lynn in the 1830s, "The buyers always came to the factory and no salesmen went on the road to solicit trade, nor was such a thing known as selling by sample. In fact, the sizes were so ill-made and assorted that no sample could have been duplicated in large quantities." This soon changed, and sales by sample had come into being by the Civil War.[35]

The evolution of means of shoe production, it can therefore be argued, was an independent force contributing to the formation of the wholesale market and the reorganization of production. Commons's claim that the market determined the mode of production, not the converse, can thus be faulted on two grounds. First, the counterposition of the market to production as a cause of change is inaccurate because the evolution of production depended on the birth and evolution of markets for labor and means of production. Second, the claim is one-sided; the evolution of production also contributed to market growth. New means of production already had a dynamic of their own, tied to the evolution of means of production in other sectors, and these new means contributed to both the division of labor and the extent of the market.

But the development of instruments of production was still stamped by the manufacturing period. The two principal changes, the shoe peg and the standard last, both gained significance by altering the shoe as a product. Commons grasps the importance of product changes and sees the limits of much of Marx's analysis that takes the product and its usefulness as given.[36] Productivity increases were limited by the givenness of craft techniques; the most important increase came as the result of a product innovation, the pegged shoe. This would change when the evolving instruments of labor no longer accommodated themselves to craft techniques of production.

Part II
Initial Mechanization

5

The Introduction of Shoe Machines

The transformation of shoemaking which began in the first half of the nineteenth century continued in the second half, but became a process of mechanization. The 1850s was the transitional decade; by 1860 mechanization had left an imprint on the labor of the sole cutter, the binder, and the bottomer. If Marx and Mantoux are correct—and this chapter will argue that they are—mechanization was revolutionary: it marked a break in economic evolution, was a principal cause of this break, and resulted from a different process than that which had reorganized craft production. Initial mechanization, in short, brings us to the problem of understanding an industrial revolution.

The First Shoe Machines

Machines transformed the labor of each of the units of the central shop system. Cutting and preparing machines altered the labor of the central shop. One leather-preparing machine had been introduced much earlier to split upper leathers. Invented around 1809, the upper-splitting machine spread slowly. Seth Bryant wrote that in 1822 he had "procured a machine, the first that was ever brought to that section of the country, with which to prepare leather, and the tanners on the south shore and vicinity brought to my place their leather to be split."[1] A generic leather machine, the splitter was constructed simply: it held leather down under pressure and fed it into a knife.

Sole leather machines were also introduced. Soles were prepared for cutting from 1845 by leather-rolling machines, which compressed leather under great pressure, and shortly after by sole-splitting machines, which cut leather to the desired thickness. Sole cutting was first mechanized in the 1840s when a stripping machine cut leather into straight strips the length of the sole. A machine to cut strips into sole blanks was perfected by David Knox in the mid-1850s.[2]

The sewing machine transformed the home work of the binder. In 1852, the foreman of the shop of a Lynn manufacturer, John Wooldredge, introduced the first known upper-stitching machine, a Singer. It sewed light uppers with a dry thread. A second sewing machine, to sew heavier leathers with a waxed thread, was not long coming. From these beginnings, the sewing machine spread quickly among Lynn producers; already 1,000 were used in 1856. It rapidly diffused to other major shoemaking centers and was in widespread use by 1860.[3]

Machines also invaded the domain of the ten-footer, though they had not penetrated far by 1860. Pegging was one point of entry. In the 1850s, several machines were introduced that used an awl to punch holes in the soles and upper, then inserted and hammered a peg while the machine made the next peg hole. The machine that was to become the most popular even fed and cut its own pegs. Another machine trimmed soles after bottoming, and others formed heels and shaped the uppers of boots.[4]

The breadth of shoe machines is manifested by the 1860 offerings of Boston companies. The Canton Boot and Shoe Machine Company sold the widest range, including machines to split, roll, strip, and cut sole leather, machines to crimp boot uppers, three different heeling machines, and a variety of tools and forms. Other firms were more specialized. Two Boston firms made and sold pegging machines and a third peg wood. Far and away the largest sales were obtained by sewing machine companies, of which there were 29 in Boston alone (though only a few had extensive shoe markets) and a number in major shoemaking towns.[5]

A further machine adopted in shoe production, as in many other industries, was the steam engine. Sewing machines could be and at first were run by hand, as were leather-rolling, sole-cutting, and pegging machines. But all were run by steam in some of the larger factories in 1860, and by waterpower in a few others. The steam engine was also applied to other machines, including heel-making machinery, in Wooldredge's plant in 1858.[6]

However diverse their operations, shoe machines transformed labor in a similar manner. As machines, they were composed of parts mutually constraining each other to move in a way that effected the desired alteration of the material. The machine now performed the operation; *it* cut leather, sewed, and pegged. The subjective principle was overthrown; no longer did the purposive activity of workers direct the knife, needle, and hammer. Labor became industrial; its activity was determined by the machine it operated. Rather than manipulate awl, hammer, and pegs by hand movements, the pegger now merely placed the shoe on the machine, activated the machine, and guided the shoe as it was pegged. That there remained acumen in guiding the shoe should not obscure the fact that the worker's activity was now determined by the requirements of the machine. It was this transformation of the character of labor that Marx and Mantoux held to be epoch making.

The Importance of Mechanization

Mechanization is not the only criterion for dividing epochs of eighteenth- and nineteenth-century production, and may not even be the most important. Two others have also been advanced. For Hazard, the 1850s initiated a factory stage. The factory was a workplace producing the whole shoe through direct supervision of the quality and duration of labor. The need for supervision accounted for the factory's origin: "The Factory Stage did not come into existence in the boot and shoe industry because . . . of the installation in it of heavy expensive machinery, nor the use of power to run it, but because industrial organization, in order to secure uniformity of output, economy of time, labor, and stock, demanded foremen to superintend, and regular hours of steady work on the part of men and women employed in all of the processes of shoemaking."[7]

The factory is conceived in contrast to the decentralization of the putting-out system, and can encompass the labor of both craftsmen and machine operatives. This notion contrasts with that of Marx, who stresses the importance of machinery. For him, manufacturing as a form of capitalist production (to be distinguished from manufacturing as a historical stage) concentrated under one roof specialized but tool-using workers, whereas industrial production was the form concentrating machine-using workers. He termed the analogous places of work the manufactory and the factory respectively.[8] Because Hazard's factory refers to both, the key transition for her was from putting-out to either the manufactory or the factory.[9]

Epochs of production can also be characterized by standardization. The 1900 census of manufacturing adopts this strategy:

> The true criterion for manufactures, as opposed to the hand trades, is found in the standardization of the process. This latter word, however, requires some definition. It describes all operations which produce "standard" products; that is, similar products which conform to a general demand. Tailoring and custom shoemaking, for example, are not standardized, for dissimilar articles are produced, each being suited to the taste and need of the individual consumer. But the manufacture of ready-made clothing and shoes is standardized, for here the products all conform to a single standard, even the variations for sizes being standard variations.[10]

Such a definition does not require that production take an industrial or even a manufacturing form.

Each of these criteria can be applied to shoemaking in the 1850s; it did become more mechanized, directly supervised, and standardized. Each highlights an aspect of the evolution of production that was significant to the structure and growth of shoe firms. But if Marx and Mantoux are right, it was mechanization that had the greatest impact on productivity, the formation of the proletariat, the spatial organization of labor, and the technical division of labor.

Most directly, mechanized labor substantially reduced unit labor time and cost. Declining labor costs fostered firm growth, the perception of which furthered machine diffusion. Labor costs fell in each unit of the central shop system. The rolling machine mechanized a simple hammering operation; with it, "a man could do in a minute what would require half an hour's hard work with a lapstone and hammer."[11] The stripping machine could cut 250 sides into strips in one day, compared to 10 by hand.[12]

Binding costs also fell. It was estimated around 1860 that the piece rate for machine sewing was one-fourth the rate for hand sewing, but daily wages could still rise.[13] Reduced cost and improved durability of the seam combined to bring about rapid introduction. As a Lynn shoemaker put it, "The introduction of the sewing machine soon made the old-fashioned method of binding shoes by hand well nigh a lost art. . . . The saving of labor was so great, and the nicety of the work, which could be done with almost mathematical exactness, was so far beyond the old-time product of the hand needle that in a few years the shoe-binder and her mission, became historical reminiscences."[14]

Bottoming machines similarly cut costs. The pegging machine could peg a whole shoe in 10 seconds. Bishop estimated that a single operative could each day machine peg 1,000 pairs of shoes with a single row of pegs or 400 to 500 pairs of double-rowed shoes. Machine pegging cost about five-sixths of a cent per pair, whereas hand pegging cost from four to six cents.[15] Other bottoming machines had similar effects.[16]

By greatly reducing unit labor requirements, mechanization overcame limits to the size of the proletariat. Requiring relatively fewer workers, capitalists relied more on the full-time, skilled labor force in shoemaking towns. Mechanization thus facilitated the regular, supervised employment that defined the factory for Hazard.

This result is seen most clearly in fitting. The rapid introduction of the sewing machine implied that from 1850 to 1860 Lynn output increased while employment of women fell from 6,500 to 3,900. By contrast, male employment grew from 3,900 to 5,900 over the decade. The *Lynn Reporter* identified the scarcity of labor to be one cause of the adoption of machinery: "The introduction of sewing machines for the stitching and binding of shoes was the result of absolute necessity. There was a time when women's busy fingers were able to do all that was required of them; but the time came when they could not, and machinery was called to their aid."[17] Likewise, the pegging machine reduced labor requirements among bottomers, though not to the same extent, due to its slower introduction and the smaller proportion of bottoming labor needed to peg. Largely as a result of the disproportion between productivity growth in fitting and bottoming, the share of women in Massachusetts shoe employment fell from 43 percent in 1850 to 31 percent in 1860.[18]

Mechanization also helped provide a future proletariat. Falling unit labor requirements and the growth of factory towns reduced rural outwork. Left without work, rural shoe producers often migrated to shoe towns seeking employment. In the case of Lynn, Alan Dawley demonstrates the plausibility of this intraindustry migration. About four-fifths of the factory proletariat of 1870 had not lived in Lynn a decade earlier, and about half of the shoemakers had not been born in Massachusetts; the vast majority of those born outside Massachusetts but inside the United States came from New Hampshire and Maine, states in which Lynn shoe manufacturers had employed substantial numbers of outworkers.[19] The factory thus became a means of primitive accumulation; by undercutting putting-out, it removed a transitional form of wage labor that had allowed workers to remain tied to land or rural communities.

Mechanization played a central part in eliminating the central shop system and concentrating shoemaking within single workshops. Here we must address Hazard's thesis that the centralized shoemaking workshop arose through organizational changes to secure regularity and uniformity of supply and reduced costs, not through mechanization. That supervision in a manufactory could have had these effects was surely possible, and efforts were made to bring about these results. The central shop imposed minimum-quality standards and inspected outwork. To mitigate the irregularity of supply, the central shop took on more processes and subcontracted to bottoming gangs that worked regularly, often in or near the central shop.[20]

But capitalists did not widely introduce the manufactory. Supervision alone did not greatly increase the speed of hand fitting and making operations, and therefore could not counteract the decentralization required to get sufficient supplies of labor. The difficulty of expanding employment for Lynn shoe manufacturers led to a growing recourse to part-time and irregular employees and to the decline of the average annual output of fitters from 1,018 pairs in 1837 to 754 in 1845 and 689 in 1850. The difficulty of recruiting workers extended to bottomers as well. With this constraint, one would expect the manufactory to displace putting-out gradually, if at all.[21]

Moreover, rather than concentrating authority in the hands of the capitalist and his foremen, the centralized workshop of 1860 united a number of distinct authorities inside and outside the shop. Subcontracting flourished; machine-stitching shops either sewed precut upper parts at a piece rate or bought their own material to make uppers as a distinct commodity. Some mechanized bottoming and heeling teams subcontracted and produced in their own shops. Many other teams subcontracted inside the factory itself.[22]

Mechanization provided a control of a different kind, a determination of *labor* that did not necessarily entail authority by the capitalist over the *laborer*. The early factory system, in shoemaking and more generally, retained large elements of the control craftsmen had had over their labor. Without the skill and management brought by contractors, machinery would have been introduced more slowly and fitfully.[23]

Sole-preparing and sole-cutting machines were from their inception brought into the central shop, but their introduction did not influence the putting-out of shoes to be fitted and made. To revolutionize the organization of production, the relations of central shop work to outwork had to be transformed. This the sewing machine accomplished. The employment of the sewing machine, according to the census of 1860, "along with the sole-cutting machine, and other appliances, is gradually bringing about a silent revolution in boot and shoe manufacture, which is daily assuming the characteristics of a factory system."[24]

Sheer technological advantage necessitated use of the sewing machine, but did not require that it be used in the factory.[25] As in clothing, some machines were purchased by operatives for use in their own homes. Hazard and others argue that owner-operatives were atypical even in the 1850s.[26] By 1860 most fitting was done in subcontractors' shops or in shoe factories. Both commonly employed 25 to 50 fitters whose labor was divided and supervised. Contracting shops were often started by new producers adept at sewing machine use, such as John Nichols, who had adapted the sewing machine to work leather. Initial factories were frequently the old central shop with a story or a back room added to house fitters. But soon factories were designed specifically for industrial production; they organized machines into a system, often driven by steam, so that materials could flow smoothly and quickly through the series of operations needed to make a shoe. With this development, "An era in the history" of the shoe trade had been marked, and, "as in every other department of the clothing trade, the principal agency had been the Sewing Machine, operated by steam power."[27]

The pegging machine began to bring bottoming into the factory. With the pegger, the rest of the bottoming gang entered the factory. Even in factories mechanization was incomplete; for example, in 1862 one steam-powered factory in Beverly, Massachusetts, employed 160 men, of whom 60 still worked outside the factory.[28] But the direction of movement was clear. By eliminating the difference between putting-out operations and those of the central shop, the factory destroyed the distinctiveness of the central shop system. The factory system had been born, as this contemporary account recognized:

> That [the steam-powered sewing machine] and other labor-saving machines for cutting out the soles, heels, and uppers, for pegging, burnishing, and other operations, are now driven by the exhaustless energy of steam, whereby the entire system of manufacture has been imperceptibly but effectually revolutionized. Their use has silently brought about a transfer of the work from small shops to large factories, several stories high, in which all parts of the manufacture are carried on under the same roof, each floor being devoted to a separate portion of the work, which is conducted in a manner similar to the factory system of other countries, and of our large cotton centres. In pegged work, which forms the bulk of the manufacture, every operation, except fitting shoes to the last, even to the polishing and cutting the pegs from the inside, is done by machinery.[29]

Mechanization altered the division of labor. Machines each had their own specialist operatives, and, as new machines were introduced, the division of labor was extended. The division of labor had a new dynamic; where workers' "capacity for labor was only limited by the capabilities of the machines over which they presided," both the positions in the division of labor and their relative proportions evolved with machine development.[30]

The form of learning was in part modified in the factory. Frequently training followed the system of the bottoming team: workers were trained in one specialization by fellow workers in the same shop. The craftlike training gave a personal character to the early spread of mechanization not unlike the way the division of labor had diffused. But this craft form of learning was already threatened by another; when John Wooldredge installed his first sewing machine in 1852, he brought in an expert from Philadelphia to instruct the operatives. Sewing machine firms deepened this practice by establishing training schools to complement the informal training conducted by their agents.[31]

By distinguishing mass production from custom orders, standardization was clearly important; the question is how it was achieved. Careful supervision played a part, but mechanization had done its share through the standard last and continued to do so with the introduction of shoe machines. Industrial labor could more readily work up to standard because a well-designed machine could undertake and repeat an operation with precision. Ideally, in the factory "everything is reduced to system. The exactness of scientific measurement is substituted for random guesses."[32] The machine overcame the variability of craft skill. Labor was no longer the expression of the individual artistry of the craftsman; displays of individuality were now defects, violations of the standards of production.

The realization of this ideal was limited not only by the persistence of craft operations, but also by the construction of machines and by the maintenance of hand skills among machine operatives. That the fitter fed leather to the sewing machine could be a source of inaccuracy yet could also compensate for errors in other operations. The trend was toward standardization; in 1864, it could be said about pegged shoe construction that "the work being almost entirely accomplished by machinery, gives it a uniformity as to style, shape, and general appearance, which it is impossible to obtain by hand."[33]

An industrial revolution had occurred. It swept away the manufacturing system, together with its characteristic limits—productivity constrained by the subjective principle of production, diffusion restricted by craft mobility, and a localized proletariat. The division of labor, standardization, and tools continued to evolve, but now they were mediated by the evolution of machinery. An account of the generation of shoe machinery is thus an indispensable part of the explanation of the evolution of shoemaking.

Understanding Initial Mechanization

Industrial production began with a change in instruments of production; the problem is to understand how new instruments were generated and diffused.

If, as Hazard suggests, the factory were simply a change in supervision, then it could be understood as an outcome of the same process that brought the central shop. But machinery introduced an element foreign to craft production whatever its form. Commons acknowledges the problem by arguing that the cause of changes in production shifts from "external" to "internal," from new markets to machinery, but he provides no account of the transition.[34]

Some light on the problem can be shed by the contention of Marx and Mantoux that the manufacturing period created conditions and agents of initial mechanization. The manufacturing dynamic realized conditions for the introduction of shoe machines. Most fundamentally, American shoemaking had introduced capitalist production for large, integrated markets. Wage labor was and would remain the form in which labor was secured; ethical restraints on the legitimate size of employment had been long overcome. The factory abridged the independence of outworkers, but subcontracting persisted and, more strongly, was a means through which factories acquired needed expertise.[35]

The wholesale market was well organized to sell factory output. Single capitalists already sold hundreds of thousands of pairs of shoes annually, a scale large enough to fully utilize the gamut of machines of the 1850s. The scale necessary to fully utilize the sewing machine was not large, but it was considerably larger for the pegging machine, which could bottom from 400 to 1,000 pairs of shoes per day.

The prior accumulation of capital facilitated machine introduction. Many firms had grown to the point where they could afford to mechanize. The mean output of shoe establishments rose from $2,700 in 1840 to $7,300 in 1850. Capital costs were modest; in 1854, for example, Christopher Robinson of Lynn owned one sole-cutting machine, one splitting machine, one stripping machine, three sewing machines, and one punching machine, which had a combined value of $469, not quite 10 percent of the value of leather held at the time.[36] Machines could be introduced piecemeal to spread out the cost. Wholly new factories were more expensive, but still required less capital than that invested in leather and credit.

Not all firms were large enough to afford or fully utilize machines. Small producers were always numerous and became more so over time. The median size of establishments (and of firms, because almost all firms had only one plant) actually decreased from an output, in 1860 dollars, of $3,075 in 1820 to $2,375 in 1860. For median firms, machine purchase might not be possible or desirable. In 1850 and in 1860, 84 percent of establishments had output values less than $10,000, a level that might utilize upper-sewing machines but not specialized bottoming machines.[37]

The concentration of wholesale production in Massachusetts also concentrated large firms in that state. The value of shoe production per establishment was far higher in New England than in other regions (see Table 5.1). The

Table 5.1

Mean Shoe Establishment Size by Region, 1840, 1850, and 1860

(output valued in 1860 dollars)

	1840[a]	1850	1860
New England	3,900	13,900	22,500
(Massachusetts)	(9,600)	(26,300)	(34,100)
Middle Atlantic	2,700	4,800	4,500
(New York)	(3,100)	(5,600)	(4,800)
(Pennsylvania)	(2,000)	(4,000)	(3,900)
West	1,600	4,300	3,200
(Ohio)	(2,400)	(4,400)	(3,400)
South	1,100	3,800	2,800
United States	2,700	7,300	7,400

Sources: See Table 2.1.

Notes: For definition of regions, see Table 2.1. Kansas, Nebraska, and the Pacific states are classified with the West.

[a]Shoes were not distinguished from other leather products in the 1840 census; shoe output and establishments have been estimated by assuming that the share of shoes in all leather manufactures was the same in 1840 and 1850.

contrast was starker between states; the mean 1850 Massachusetts output of $26,300 per establishment was about five times that of the next highest major shoemaking state. Moreover, whereas mean establishment size for the industry as a whole was constant in the 1850s, in Massachusetts it rose by 30 percent. It was thus precisely in the center of wholesale production that firms were commonly large enough to introduce the range of machinery developed by 1860.

The earlier transformation of production also facilitated machine introduction. Without the division of labor, each shoemaker would have had to possess all machines and would have utilized each (in the absence of sharing) only a fraction of the time. Mechanization could have occasioned the division of labor, but would surely have been slowed as a result. The earlier development of the pegged shoe and peg making obviously facilitated the introduction of the pegging machine, and the standard last provided a basis for the accurate measurements required by many bottoming machines.

As the scale of the wholesale market grew, so did the potential market for shoe machinery. Real shoe output in 1850 was about six times as large as it was in 1810, and wholesale production had become a far larger share of the total. Significant incentives to develop and sell machines had come into being.

The introduction of shoe machines, like other instruments of production, was eased by the commodity form of diffusion. But by the simple fact that machines were the products of capital goods firms, their generation cannot be accounted for within the shoe industry. Nor were they principally the products of shoemakers or shoe tool, last, or peg producers. The standard last and pegged shoe had depended on technological developments outside the shoe sector, and so did shoe machinery.

The manufacturing dynamic within the shoe sector can therefore account for the introduction of shoe machines, but not readily for their generation. Just as Mantoux turned outside the textile industry to grasp the generation of textile machinery, so we must look to the American economy more broadly. The dynamics of the economy as a whole might be able to account for initial mechanization, but only by moving outside the evolution of craft production within each sector.

6

Prospects

Initial mechanization transformed not simply techniques but also the process through which techniques evolved. Along with new machines came a new machine-making industry composed of new firms organized in novel ways. In the intertwined qualitative changes of techniques and institutions lies the problem of understanding the origins of mechanization.

To focus, as economic theory predominantly does, on the introduction of new techniques is to radically underestimate the difficulty of technical change. The institutional break was only secondarily one of the institutions using the new techniques; new units of mechanized production had to be introduced, but shoe firms were large enough to finance the transition and numerous enough to provide incentives to invent. The primary institutional break lay in the process generating and diffusing machines. It is this process, not the potential demand for machinery, that the manufacturing dynamic cannot account for. But it is precisely here, in understanding the social organization of the generation and spread of machines, that explanations of Marx and Mantoux are weakest.

To clarify the problem, we will begin by examining the technological and institutional barriers to shoe mechanization. Technical change is a complex problem-solving activity; its prospects can be assessed in terms of the barriers to posing and solving a series of technical and economic problems. The analysis of the sources and extent of these barriers in turn helps to identify the path, agents, time, and place of the development and spread of machinery.

Barriers to Mechanization

Barriers vary with the social form of the mechanization process. Machines can diffuse as commodities, new capital goods. To come into use, they have to be adequately designed, produced, marketed, priced, and serviced. Machines can also develop for self-usage. They will then face no problem of marketing and pricing. For innovating firms that are unwilling to license rights to usage, the problem is quite the opposite: how to prevent diffusion and the loss of competitive advantages. Here the firm is itself a barrier to diffusion.

Three kinds of barriers may block mechanization along either path.[1] First, there may be little incentive. Constricted machine usage coming from market narrowness for machine-made goods or the size of the using firm may make net monetary benefits too low to warrant innovative activity. Expansion of market potential or of the firm may be needed to stimulate innovation.

Second, individuals may not have the capacity to develop or disseminate a practical machine. Capacity has technical, production, financial, and marketing aspects. Technological discontinuity will inhibit mechanization when the machine requires new technological principles or complex adaptations of established principles. When new techniques are required to produce the machine, production discontinuity will make a well-functioning invention difficult to achieve. Mechanization may also be prevented by discontinuities of finance if the economy cannot provide the necessary funds, and of marketing when inadequate sales procedures lead to the underestimation of market potential.

Third, social organization may prevent the use of the capabilities that individuals and firms possess. Technological advance may be limited by technological or production isolation when those trying to design or produce a new machine cannot readily find and use existing knowledge and skills. Financial and marketing isolation prevent the movement of funds and, when expectations and marketing procedures are not communicated to prospective inventors, reduce perceived incentives.

In short, mechanization may not occur because the potential for machine usage is too restricted, the capability to realize this potential is limited, or the communication that supplies skills, market awareness, and finance is lacking. We will begin with the barrier that the manufacturing dynamic most directly affected.

Potential Usage

Mechanization could be inhibited by too little expected usage. The appropriate measure of usage varies with the social form of mechanization. For capital goods, the measure is industry-wide; a threshold potential market size is required to justify expenditures to develop, produce, and sell a machine. For self-usage the threshold is specific to the user, whose output must be large enough to warrant the costs of development.[2]

The processes of the manufacturing period helped meet both thresholds. In the case of commodity usage, as has been seen, the evolution of wholesale, capitalist shoe production had gone far to achieve a potential market of threshold size by 1850. In output, the shoe industry was among the largest, well above such successful industrializers as firearms and clocks.

Other sectors added to the potential demand for those shoe machines that performed operations used outside shoemaking; shoe machines may thus have arisen in response to the needs of quite different sectors. Far and away the most important instance was the sewing machine. The clothing industry was surely large enough to provide substantial sales. The output of the men's clothing industry, in 1860 prices, stood at $47 million in 1850 and rose to $73 million in 1860. To this should be added the smaller ladies' and children's clothing and men's furnishing industries. In output value, the shoe and clothing industries together exceeded even cotton textiles.[3]

The shoe and clothing industries were favorably organized to introduce machines. For both paths, mechanization could be stifled when machine costs were high relative to the investment funds of firms, when machines were expected to be little utilized, when major changes of industrial organization were a condition of introduction, and when employers or workers opposed machine use. Expected machine usage was highest and most certain, in short, when the break with the organization and scale of craft production was least.

Due to the growth of wholesale production, scale was no barrier to machine introduction for many shoe firms, especially those in Massachusetts. Scale was even less of a problem in clothing. Large capitalistic producers had appeared by 1850 in both custom and ready-made branches. Mean establishment output in men's clothing exceeded that of shoemaking in 1850 and was over twice as large in 1860. Even many smaller producers could afford the relatively inexpensive sewing machine.[4]

The putting-out system posed organizational difficulties. Little organizational change was needed to introduce machines to be used in the central shop for such operations as cutting and finishing. But most work was done outside the central shop. The same was true of clothing, as is illustrated by the case of the nation's largest clothing producer in 1850, Lewis and Hanford, which is reported to have employed 72 workers inside its shop and 3,600 outside around 1850.[5] A capitalist introducing machines for operations formerly put out had to overcome problems of factory organization and labor recruitment. Outworkers could mechanize for themselves, but capital requirements and organizational barriers made this unlikely.

The extent of this barrier varied by operation. Barriers were more pressing for shoe-bottoming machines, which, when compared to dry-thread sewing, were more expensive, often required mechanical power, and could be used most fully with a more extensive division of labor than that typical among bottomers. The extent of organizational changes needed to mechanize ascended from operations performed in capitalists' shops to urban garment sewing, to urban and then rural upper binding, and finally to urban and then rural bottoming.

As the cotton textiles demonstrated, putting-out posed formidable, but hardly insuperable, barriers to mechanization. These barriers made the extent of potential machinery usage uncertain, but the history of innovations in craft techniques and organization left little doubt that, given the opportunity, some shoe and clothing firms would attempt to mechanize.[6]

Potential demand varied by kind of machine. Standard dry-thread sewing machines had the widest potential usage. Sewing comprised about 25 percent of the total labor time of craft shoemaking, and, compared to other machines, sewing machines could be effectively used by smaller firms and with fewer organizational changes. By contrast, bottoming machines faced less certain and smaller usage. Not only were capital costs and organizational barriers greater, but each bottoming operation involved less total labor time than upper sewing. Lasting formed about 5 percent of the labor time of shoemaking; sole trimming, 2 percent; and pegging, 3 percent.[7]

Dry-thread machines diffusing as commodities had one other advantage: they could also be sold to families for their own use. Indeed, after the Civil War, this would become their primary market, absorbing hundreds of thousands of machines annually. Because U.S. population and per capita income levels were lower in 1850 than two decades later, mid-century family sewing machine sales would have been less but, it seems clear with the benefit of hindsight, still substantial.[8]

Differences of incentives provide some insights into why shoe machinery followed a commodity path. The commodity path becomes more advantageous when the number of firms that can mechanize grows, because then the cost of product development can be spread over more units. In an industry with many small, similarly sized firms, all might be able and willing to purchase machinery but none to develop it. The shoe and clothing industries approached this limit far more than did cotton textiles or firearms. Of course, self-usage may be combined with licensing to others, thus combining elements of both paths, but this would lose the competitive advantages entailed by sole use.

However much potential machinery usage fostered industrialization, it cannot by itself account for how machinery was supplied. Nor did the growth of potential usage account for the timing of machinery development. In the 1850s, real output slowed in its growth, and mean and median firm size stagnated. Moreover, after having grown substantially over the previous three decades, the real wage was roughly constant and therefore cannot account for the introduction of machinery.[9]

Nor did potential usage translate directly into economic incentives. A first mediation was the social form of mechanization, which determined whether industry or firm measures of usage were appropriate. A second came with expectations. Prospective inventors were motivated not by potential usage itself but by their expectations concerning it. Particularly for commodity usage, the two were likely to differ because inventors were unaware of the potential usage or of how to reach it.

To understand the process generating machines and the expectations about machine usage takes us beyond the determination of market potential. We must move to barriers of capacity and communication, and to economic processes outside the shoe industry.

Capacity

Mechanization may be beyond the capabilities of individuals. Developing any new machine involves overcoming difficulties, but the extent of these difficulties varies with the character of the challenge and the capacity to respond.

The operations and the materials of shoemaking precluded straightforward application of existing mechanical technology. The simple hand operation of sewing posed a series of technical problems. On simpler materials such as cloth and light uppers, the sewer penetrated the material with a needle that had a thread-carrying eye at the end opposite the point, then altered the angle of the needle with one hand and of the cloth with the other so that the needle repenetrated the material from the underside. Next, the sewer pushed the needle part way back through the cloth, grasped the point of the needle, let go of the eye, pulled the needle the rest of the way through the material, and finally extended his or her arm to take up the slack thread.[10] A sewing machine hence had to solve an interlinked set of stitch-forming, material- or needle-feeding, and tension-regulating problems.

Pegging was a simpler operation, involving the formation of holes on the uppers and soles into which wooden pegs were driven; the problems here came in finding a way for the machine to feed the shoe to the pegging mechanism and to form and feed pegs quickly enough. Lasting entailed the simultaneous operation of all the fingers to pull, twist, fold, and tack the material; its complexity rendered invention difficult.

The material added complications to the inventive process. The greater resistance of heavier leather necessitated use of an awl. Dies could not readily cut the leather, since they tended to veer to one side when force was applied. The waxed thread used to sew heavier leathers clogged the eyes of needles; a suitable thread-carrying implement had to be discovered.

Although fully aware of craft methods, shoe and shoe input producers were limited in their ability to solve the technological problems of mechanization. The very conception of mechanized shoe production was foreign to the shoemakers, last makers, and toolmakers who had been the principal agents developing craft production. The training of these craftsmen gave them few skills to pose and solve the complex problems involved in inventing and producing shoe machinery.

Technological similarities with other sectors eased the problem of designing adequate machines. The technological convergence that, as Nathan Rosenberg has noted, tied together the production of firearms, sewing machines, bicycles, and automobiles was one instance of a much wider phenomenon.[11] The mechanical technologies developed in the United States over the first half of the nineteenth century—the Industrial Revolution combination of textile machinery, machine tools, and steam engines, later locomotive and railroad technology, and indigenous agricultural, woodworking, and mass-production metalworking machinery—all embodied principles applicable to shoe machinery. Whereas the growth of the potential demand for machinery depended on the evolution of craft shoemaking, the ability to supply that demand depended on wider forces of mechanization.

Engineering principles formed a conceptual system that provided categories to meaningfully identify and evaluate solutions to problems of machine design. Some principles, especially those of the application and transmission of power, could be directly applied. Awareness of widely shared principles and of particular convergences facilitated discovery of mechanical means to copy hand operations and, perhaps more importantly, ways of transforming these operations to gain mechanical advantage.

Technological convergence carries implications for the machinery-generating process. William Parker contended that "things which are simple to invent get invented first."[12] Shoe operations varied in their uniqueness and complexity; operations that were simple, such as leather rolling and cutting, or that shared elements with other machinery, such as dry-thread upper sewing and peg forming, might be mechanized more readily and quickly than sole-sewing and lasting operations.

To extend the proposition, invention would be easiest for producers in technologically convergent sectors. Knowledge of thread manipulation in textile machinery and of wood-forming techniques relevant for peg construction and pegging would give advantages to producers in these sectors.

Many trades had technological knowledge, including the clockmakers and millwrights central to the Industrial Revolution. Machinists were particularly important bearers of mechanical principles. By the mid-nineteenth century, machinists were widespread in sections of England, Scotland, France, Belgium, and the United States. Negligible in 1800, employment in the American machinery industry stood at 13,000 in 1840, almost 28,000 in 1850, and over 41,000 in 1860.[13] There were also many who made and repaired machinery not sold as commodities.

Machinists occupied a critical position in the transition from craft to mechanized production. In many ways, machinists were distinctive of the new age of mechanized production. Their product eliminated craft techniques. The rapid growth of their numbers attests to the pace of this displacement. Their own production was mechanized; lathes, planers, and other machine tools fabricated their products. Although much machinery was made for self-use, machine shops increasingly produced for well-defined markets. Even shops founded as adjuncts to factories, such as Locks and Canals in Lowell, had come to produce for the market. Moreover, machinists were often employed in large shops, led in 1860 by the locomotive works which averaged 220 workers, not to mention the railroad lines themselves.

Yet machinists were organized very much like a craft. Their product was typically still custom designed and made. Many worked in relatively small, general-purpose shops. They were trained by other machinists and were highly skilled; along with proficiency on the lathe came mastery of the file. Journeymen still had real possibilities to open their own shops.

Machinists represented a unique craft, a craft whose product eliminated craft techniques, an anticraft craft. Their innovations were also revolutionary. Formed out of a process of technical change, machinists were ready agents of ongoing mechanization. The origin and growth of machinery firms had rested on machinists' involvement in spreading and developing new techniques. From at least the time of Samuel Slater, whose immigration brought to Rhode Island spinning mills knowledge gained as an apprentice with Arkwright and Strutt, machinists had successfully transferred the techniques of the British Industrial Revolution. American steam engine and locomotive production had similarly benefited. Machinists were central to the birth of an indigenous technological dynamic. They had their hand in the evolution of textile production, engine making, and locomotive construction and in that remarkable series of machine tool innovations around the firearms sector.[14]

The social organization of the mid-century machinery sector remained conducive to technical change. Existing firms refined and developed machinery, largely for already mechanized production processes. Inventions by machinists were often marketed in new firms; in a revolutionary path to capitalism, innovations were the means through which producers became capitalists. Some inventions were self-used, especially machine tool inventions used to make not only machines, but also tools, hardware, and such mechanisms as clocks and firearms. But when machinery was used in production processes radically different from the machine shop, new machines were diffused principally through sale in local and regional markets. Machinists were agents who tied initial mechanization in some sectors to ongoing mechanization in the economy as a whole.

By 1850 the production of shoe machines posed few barriers. Machinists in the best shops employed high-quality engine lathes, boring machines, drilling machines, planers, milling machines, and measuring devices. Use of iron and to a much smaller extent steel secured sufficient durability. The machine tools and shop practice utilized for other light machinery could be applied directly to make shoe machines.

The investment required to develop shoe machines was comparatively modest. Light in weight, they could be made in general machine shops. They varied in complexity from leather rolling and sewing to lasting; development costs accordingly differed. But all were simple relative to such machines as the locomotive. Marketing costs could have been met out of profits from the sales of established outlets. Unlike the cases of the railroad, canals, and even textiles, many individuals possessed sufficient funds to finance shoe machine development and sale.

Marketing discontinuity presented a greater barrier to widespread diffusion through machine sale. The problem was not in selling per se; methods used to market other machinery could be adopted readily. The problem was more that these methods could not realize the market potential of shoe and sewing machines and thus lowered incentives to invent.

The mid-nineteenth-century economy had not yet solved the problem of nationally (and internationally) marketing technically complex products to small, mechanically unsophisticated consumers. Most machinery was sold in local or regional markets, typically to customers close enough that agents operating out of the machine shop could install and service machinery. Extra-regional markets existed—for example, among northern engine makers exporting to southern rice and sugar mills—but were clearly secondary. Because each firm typically operated out of a single plant, the location of sales near production limited the firm's sales revenue. Innovators following this pattern would be limited to only parts of the potential market, supplemented perhaps by some licensing revenue from the rest of the market.

The localization of machinery markets no doubt weakened incentives, but to degrees varying greatly by area. The inhibiting effect was least in Massachusetts, as Table 6.1 indicates. Already in 1810 Massachusetts produced an estimated 21 percent of the value of shoe output (and more of total pairs). Concentration grew over the next half century.[15] Massachusetts' share of output in value terms rose to 45 percent in 1850 and to 50 percent in 1860. By contrast, Pennsylvania's output share was significant but falling, and the shares for western and southern states were never great. Given that Massachusetts had far and away the greatest establishment scale, its potential shoe machinery markets were far larger than those of any other area.

Similarly, for men's clothing in 1850, New York produced 33 percent of the nation's product, and Massachusetts, Ohio, and Pennsylvania added another 38 percent. The industry was more urban-centered than shoemaking; in 1860, New York City, Boston, Cincinnati, and Philadelphia together fabricated 73 percent of the clothing of their states. Establishments in these states were larger, but the contrast was neither as sharp as in shoemaking nor, given that small firms could fully utilize sewing machinery, so important a determinant of potential machine demand.

When the United States in 1850 is compared to the country in 1800, the improved capacity to develop shoe machinery is striking. A growing core of machinists supplemented the "emergency engineers" of the Industrial Revolution. The geographic concentration of shoe production greatly eased the problem of market adequacy in at least one region. Market potential and inventive capabilities existed; the question was whether they would come together.

Communication

A society may have ample capability and incentive to invent yet fail to coordinate the knowledge and finance needed to do so. For society does not act as a unit, and individuals possessing the technological, production, financial, and marketing capacities to successfully mechanize may never perceive the

Table 6.1
Geographic Concentration of Output, 1810, 1840, 1850, and 1860

	Shoes				Clothing	
	1810	1840	1850	1860	1850	1860
New England	38.5%	49.3%	55.4%	59.7%	25.5%	15.6%
(Massachusetts)	(20.9)	(37.2)	(44.7)	(50.3)	(18.1)	(8.3)
Middle Atlantic	45.0	36.8	31.1	25.0	59.1	61.8
(New York)	(17.5)	(18.4)	(14.4)	(11.9)	(33.1)	(34.3)
(Pennsylvania)	(18.1)	(10.1)	(10.4)	(9.2)	(14.5)	(16.8)
West	1.5	8.1	8.8	10.3	9.9	17.6
(Ohio)	n.a.	(5.1)	(4.3)	(4.0)	(5.7)	(12.0)
South	15.1	5.6	4.6	5.0	5.4	5.0

Sources: See Table 2.1.
Note: New England = Massachusetts, Connecticut, Rhode Island, Maine, New Hampshire, and Vermont; Middle Atlantic = New York, New Jersey, Pennsylvania, Delaware, Maryland, and the District of Columbia; West = Ohio, Indiana, Michigan, Illinois, Wisconsin, Iowa, Missouri, Minnesota, Kansas, Nebraska, and the Pacific states; and South = the remaining states.

potential demand or make contact with one another. Isolation may prevent mechanization.

This isolation was built into the organization of shoe production. Knowledge of shoemaking was largely confined to shoemakers, and no regular mechanisms disseminated this knowledge outside the craft. Hence a breaking-in problem existed.

Breaking-in problems were, of course, quite general. Technological change occurred within already mechanized sectors much more readily than it expanded into new sectors. This is evident in Britain where mechanization remained located largely within the key sectors of the Industrial Revolution. Machinists helped generalize factory methods to most fabrics, develop the locomotive and marine engine, and improve the variety and precision of machine tools, but did not extend mechanization much beyond that range.[16] To a lesser extent the problem existed in the United States where by 1850 well-institutionalized processes developed machine tools, engine making, and textile and firearm manufacturing much more readily than they spread mechanization elsewhere. Beginnings are always hardest.

The significance of isolation barriers varied with several circumstances. First, individuals might have worked as both shoemakers and machinists. Intercraft mobility was common in the United States. To take one notable example, Matthias Baldwin was apprenticed as a jeweler, then made bookbinders' tools, engraved rolls for printing cotton goods and bank notes, built machinery including hydraulic presses, calender rolls, and steam engines, and, after having built a model locomotive for a museum, began producing locomotives in earnest in 1834.[17]

Second, isolation would be less significant for machinists with economic contacts with shoemaking. As Part I showed, some connections already had been made in the invention and production of shoe pegs and lasts. Peg and last producers surely had significant knowledge of shoemaking techniques, but were probably more concerned with the requirements shoemaking placed on their own products. In any case, peg and last makers were few; in the 1860 census, only 6 establishments making shoe pegs and peg wood were listed, employing 29 workers, and 48 last-making units employed 511. Shoe tool manufacturers might also invent; they had some mechanical knowledge, had a history of developing new tools, and in 1860 employed 249 toolmakers in 27 establishments.

Third, isolation from craft shoemaking would be less limiting for operations shared by other production processes. Knowledge of dry-thread sewing was widely spread and easily gained. But isolation barriers were greater for more specialized pegging and waxed-thread sewing operations, and greater yet for operations specific to shoemaking, such as lasting.

Fourth, developing and producing shoe machinery met less significant isolation barriers than initial invention. Invention typically required the greatest knowledge of craft techniques, whereas development began with knowledge of an invention and the problem it intended to solve, and often utilized general mechanical knowledge to make improvements. Production of the new machine required even less knowledge of the particular craft.

Inventors often initiated contact with machinists to develop and produce the invention, and machinists then spread knowledge of the new technique through their own channels. Here the possibility arises of a collaboration— whether intended or not—of machinists and other craftsmen in the birth of new machines. The barriers faced by each craft could then be overcome by the complementary craft.

Finally, machinists in close proximity to centers of craft production could more readily gain knowledge of craft techniques. Learning was most possible within everyday life, and for the machinist this life was local and regional. Business and family connections could take machinists to nearby towns, but these ties much less often took them long distances.[18] Hence, the significance of isolation barriers was less in areas with concentrations of both machine making and shoemaking or a technically related craft.

Each of the major shoe- and clothing-producing states also had major concentrations of machinists in 1850, as Table 6.2 indicates.[19] For the shoe and clothing industries, employment was more concentrated than was the value of output. In shoemaking Massachusetts employed about half the industry total in 1850, and in men's clothing New York's share stood at 43 percent. Employment was also concentrated in relation to population; Massachusetts, New York, and Pennsylvania had about two and one-half times as many shoemakers and garment makers per capita as the nation as a whole. Employment was concentrated further within these states. In 1860, 87 percent of

Table 6.2
Geographic Distribution of Employment by Industry, 1850

	Shoes	Clothing	Machinery
New England	59.1%	23.1%	32.0%
(Massachusetts)	(49.0)	(14.9)	(18.6)
Middle Atlantic	30.0	65.4	53.6
(New York)	(13.1)	(42.5)	(27.8)
(Pennsylvania)	(10.2)	(11.7)	(17.5)
West	6.9	7.7	9.9
(Ohio)	(3.6)	(4.7)	(6.1)
South	3.9	3.8	4.4

Source: U.S. Census Office, Seventh Census, Abstract of the Statistics of Manufactures.

Note: For definition of regions, see Table 6.1.

Massachusetts shoe workers were located in Essex, Plymouth, Middlesex, and Worcester counties.

Machinery production was concentrated in the same three states. They together employed 64 percent of the nation's machinists and millwrights in 1850. All machinists had design and production knowledge relevant to shoemaking, but those who made cotton textile and woodworking machinery had more directly relevant skills than did engine and locomotive makers. The major textile machinery center was located in an arc from the Merrimack Valley to Worcester and down to Rhode Island; Paterson, New Jersey, and Philadelphia were secondary centers. Woodworking machinery was more dispersed, but included a belt from Worcester into southern New Hampshire. The heavy engineering that made steam engines and locomotives was centered more in the Middle Atlantic region.

The locational overlaps of the craft skills of shoemakers and tailors with the technological knowledge of machinists surely lessened isolation barriers. All major clothing cities were also machinery centers, and at least Essex and Worcester counties in Massachusetts combined substantial shoe and machinery production.

This overlap largely overcame problems of production isolation, but not technological isolation. New England machinery towns were seldom centers of shoemaking. As Allan Pred has shown, invention was disproportionately urban; 16 major cities in 1860 had 30 percent of all U.S. patents but only 10 percent of population.[20] This may have supported invention in New York and Philadelphia, which were also shoemaking centers, but hardly in Massachusetts, where virtually all shoe production was outside Boston. Moreover, even where both machinery and shoes or clothing were made, there existed no organized media of technical communication connecting machinists, shoemakers, and tailors.

Marketing isolation also could have inhibited invention and diffusion. The problem here is the separation of innovators from the marketing knowledge that others possess. To sell machines, inventors trained as shoe or shoe input makers would have to learn machine marketing techniques. New lasts, tools, and materials had been sold, but their producers did not address problems of installation, training, and servicing which would confront machine manufacturers.

Even machinists near expected markets faced a breaking-in problem involved in learning who producers were and how to market to them. Machinists who sold to a few large firms might find it difficult to sell to numerous small shoe and clothing firms. This problem might be mitigated by forming partnerships or other close relationships with shoe or clothing producers. Among innovators outside producing areas, marketing isolation would be more severe, further inhibiting invention in these areas.

For the dry-thread sewing machine, marketing isolation could also limit expectations about markets in the home. Growing numbers and kinds of consumer durables were sold to families, but knowledge of this potential and how to gain it was separated from machinists and craftsmen, who sold to other firms and to dealers.

Isolation barriers were much more severe for machines developed for self-use. By setting up their own firms, inventors might avert problems marketing machinery, but they had to acquire substantial knowledge of both machine design and production and shoemaking techniques, products, and markets. Moreover, they learned less from use of the technique. They had only their own feedback, whereas capital goods firms had the feedback of many users and of their own marketing agents.

These inventors also isolated their technique from others who might develop and use it. This isolation was in part intentional, as inventor-users tried to maintain their competitive advantage by suppressing diffusion. The mobility of skilled producers could spread knowledge of the technique, but successful emulation could be blocked by patent control or by the necessity of emulators to develop and produce the machine. And if inventors were willing to license patent rights, they would face barriers like those of capital goods producers, with the added difficulty that licensees would have to build and frequently perfect the machine.

Finally, inventors were often isolated from those who possessed sufficient funds to finance the development of shoe machines. This isolation was based on the institutional structure in which much nineteenth-century invention was embedded: inventors typically acted on their own account without access to either substantial profits from an ongoing firm or long-term credit from organized capital markets. Established firms would find this barrier easier to overcome, but they rarely attempted to develop new products outside their own lines of business. By reducing expected sales, marketing isolation may have made funds harder to acquire. The limit imposed by financial isolation would be greater for the more complex bottoming machines than for simpler leather-preparing and dry-thread sewing machines.

Prospects and Processes

Barriers to mechanization have a complex relation to the processes over-coming them. Immediately, barriers simply identify the prospects for success, not the character of the process realizing these prospects. This is not an insignificant conclusion; if barriers are significant, the process of mechanization may not be undertaken at all, or if begun may falter and fail. One cannot conclude that invention must or will occur where barriers are the least, but differences in the level of barriers help determine when mechanization could more readily occur—1850 as opposed to 1800; where it could occur—Massachusetts more easily than New York, and New York more easily than the West or South; who could succeed—machinists and others mechanically skilled; and for which operations—dry-thread sewing machines more than waxed-thread, and these more than sole-sewing and lasting machines.

Less directly, barriers were connected to the process overcoming them through the operation of economic institutions, particularly the institutions of the machinery sector. The rise of this sector increased the capacity to invent and reduced isolation by locating near centers of shoe and clothing production. The sector formed agents for whom invention was a normal mode of advancement. It also formed a commodity path diffusing new machines, especially when the machine was used in production processes unlike those of the machine shop. It even helped develop incentives by creating a commodity form of diffusion and—through transportation machinery, lasting lathes, and peg-making machines—by increasing the size of integrated shoe markets and the concentration of production.

That the machinery, shoe, and clothing industries did not overcome all barriers has a bearing on the process of mechanization: shoe machinery may not have developed out of any established sector or relation of sectors without the formation of new institutions and perhaps even new types of institutions. Knowledge of shoemaking and engineering techniques was isolated within each field, knowledge of the economic organization of shoemaking and machinery marketing was similarly fragmented, and no institutions existed that could readily bridge these gaps. There was no equivalent of the modern corporation, which can develop, finance, and market new techniques within its own organization.

Significant barriers therefore could be overcome only in the course of the process that developed shoe machinery. Economic circumstances may have allowed the mechanization process to start and supported its continuation, but the process then acquired its own momentum. Mechanization was cumulative and path-dependent; each step in the development process supplied a critical context forwarding that process. As some barriers were overcome, others came into focus. Successful mechanization in some times, places, and operations reduced obstacles to mechanization elsewhere.

Two expected features of the path of initial mechanization can be identified. Technological change is expected to be social, involving both contractual and noncontractual relations between interested individuals. Because of isolation problems, individuals faced different barriers and may have played complementary roles in bringing machinery into use. Machinists may have been more involved in production, technological development, and machine marketing than in invention. Shoemakers might have played more of a role in the first stages of invention. The path of mechanization may depend on who first invented; machinists were more likely to take the commodity form, whereas shoemakers might opt for self-usage. But even when shoemakers invented for self-use, contact with machinists to develop and produce the invention might lead to a commodity path. Actions to develop and especially to diffuse the technique might encourage others to take up the same end. In this way, innovation would result from the effective cooperation, both intended and not, of individuals tied together by the process of technical change.

Furthermore, for technical changes that diffused as commodities, the innovation process was structured into stages by the requisites of new product development. In a first stage, the commodity must achieve a useful form, its potential market must be conceived, and media to realize this market must be discovered. Success in this stage created the conditions for a stage of market penetration. Sales here would function not only as a goal but as a communication medium that could overcome isolation barriers and therefore sustain the mechanization process.

Barriers to mechanization influenced but did not foreordain the process overcoming them. Mechanization need not have occurred when and only when barriers were least, nor need it have followed the path of least resistance. Accounting for the initial mechanization of shoemaking requires more than an examination of the factors conditioning innovation; it requires an understanding of the particular path followed. Having clarified the obstacles to any path, we must identify the path taken.

7

The Birth of the Sewing Machine

Among the machines introduced into shoe production in the 1850s, the most important was not designed to produce shoes at all. Rather, the sewing machine was developed principally to make clothing. The history of this most important shoe machine therefore may begin without any reference to shoemaking.

Invention

An account of the birth of the sewing machine must start with Elias Howe, whose sewing machine, patented in 1846, was the basis of the practical machine of a decade later. Howe grew up in a milieu where the reorganization and mechanization of production were common. His was one of those Massachusetts farm families that raised crops; operated a gristmill, a saw mill, and a shingle machine; made cards for mechanized cotton mills; and with its combined income barely supported a family of 10. In his youth, the central shop system of shoemaking had expanded in his hometown of Spencer until in 1837 it employed almost one-tenth of the town's 2,000 inhabitants. Howe left home in 1835, at age 16, to learn the machinists' trade in a Lowell machine shop that produced and repaired cotton textile machines. Laid off in the depression of 1837, he found employment in a Cambridge machine shop that made newly invented hemp-carding machinery, and later moved to the Boston shop of Ari Davis, who produced nautical and scientific instruments and had invented commercially successful woodworking machinery.[1]

Howe's career illustrates the importance of machinists for ongoing mechanization. His background as a machinist shaped his interest in inventing and gave it a particular object. The Lowell shops had long been a training ground for machinists turning their hand to invention, and the hemp-carding and dovetailing machines made by Davis manifested a more general pattern: self-seeking through invention on one's own behalf.

A discussion in the Davis shop helped focus Howe's attention on the sewing machine. The financier of a knitting machine sought Davis's advice about its mechanical problems. During the conversation, Davis suggested that a sewing machine was a more lucrative project and one he thought he could himself

Figure 7.1 Greenough's Hand-Stitch Machine. (Smithsonian Photo 45525-G)

accomplish. The capitalist responded that such a machine would be worth a fortune, a remark Howe noted with interest.[2]

To see how training as a machinist aided Howe, consider his process of invention. Taking current practice as his starting point, Howe tried to mechanically reproduce the hand stitch he observed his wife making. He thus took the through-and-through stitch, in which the needle went entirely through the cloth and back out through a different hole, as a condition of the problem. To gain mechanical advantage, he designed a two-pointed needle with an eye in the middle which, after it left one hole, would not have to be turned around to enter another. Howe's solution closely resembled that of the first U.S. sewing machine patent, issued to John Greenough in 1842. (See Figure 7.1.)

After months of effort, Howe rejected both this design and the hand conception of sewing on which it was based. He recognized that any such design was made complex and slow by the sequence of operations it had to perform. Fingerlike pincers pushed the needle through the fabric, then another pair of pincers grasped the needle, allowing the first pair to let go. In an armlike motion, the pincers pulled the needle to the full length of the thread, reversed direction, and advanced back through the cloth. These operations were complicated by the varying distances that the thread had to be pulled as it was used up. In addition, the needle had to be rethreaded when the short length of thread it carried had been consumed.

Howe then tried to discover a stitch in which the needle moved in and out the same hole. He understood that some mechanism would have to retain the thread when the needle returned through the hole and to form a stitch with this thread. The solution to this problem comprised the most important claim in his 1846 patent: "The forming of the seam by carrying a thread through the cloth by means of a curved needle on the end of a vibrating arm, and the passing of a shuttle furnished with its bobbin, in the manner set forth, between the needle and the thread which it carries." (See Figure 7.2.) An eye-point needle, which carried the thread near its point, penetrated the fabric far enough to leave a loop of thread and then returned through the material. The shuttle, carrying a second thread, advanced through this loop, leaving a length of this thread which was locked to the needle thread when the latter was tightened. The shuttle was then free to move through the loops of all the following stitches in the same way until the bobbin of thread had been consumed. Howe's patent also claimed a mechanism to open the thread loop and tension devices to tighten the stitch and prevent the shuttle thread from unraveling. Through these mechanisms, the lockstitch was born, or, as shall be seen, reborn.[3]

A sewing machine had to do more than stitch; Howe also developed instruments to hold and feed the cloth. The material was hung from a baster plate, a long, narrow, horizontal piece of metal with a series of pins pointing away from the machine. The fabric was fed to the stitching mechanism by a toothed wheel which moved the baster plate forward automatically the length of a stitch after the needle had been withdrawn from the fabric.

Though inferior for hand use, Howe's stitch was superior for mechanization. It was faster, simpler, and could be used more continuously. The needle reciprocated over a fixed short distance and had no need to be transferred between separate needle holders. The shuttle reciprocated in its shuttle race, again over a fixed short distance. Both threads drew continuously from bobbins, and so had to be rethreaded much less frequently than hand-stitch machines.

Howe's invention not only mechanized sewing operations; it also transformed them, together with the tools employed and the kind of seam produced. The invention evidenced the ability to abstract from craft techniques in order to inquire how a machine might best form a seam. This investigation can be conducted most readily within a suitable conceptual system, the system of mechanical technology Howe learned as a machinist.

A particular technological context was useful for his invention. The producers of a later sewing machine wrote that Howe's machine could not sew a seam; it could only weave one. Howe likely adapted the shuttle mechanism from the loom, with which his Lowell experience made him familiar. Both loom and sewing machine shuttles carried a bobbin of thread which was interwoven with other threads. In addition, both reciprocated in shuttle races of similar design.[4]

Howe's machine shop practice also aided in production. Even his first

Figure 7.2 Howe's Patent Model. Note the horizontal needle motion and the baster plate and pin feed mechanism. (Smithsonian Photo 45525-B)

machines were made almost completely of metal and were well enough constructed that they worked effectively from the start. Soon after his first machine was completed, Howe used it to stitch whatever clothes tailors brought. He also raced and beat five Boston seamstresses, his 250 stitches per minute surpassing their combined total and his work judged better in quality.[5]

In these ways, Howe's invention followed a path of least resistance. As a machinist, and particularly one connected with textile and precision construction, Howe minimized technological barriers to invention, development, and production. Breaking-in problems were insignificant because he intended to mechanize not specialized craft operations, but activities that were performed in every home. Working in metropolitan Boston, Howe faced ample potential markets which could be tapped through traditional machine marketing methods.

Still, institutions of the machinery sector in America (or the whole world) were neither necessary nor sufficient to generate the sewing machine. These institutions facilitated invention, but, even abstracting from the adequacy of potential markets, they were not sufficient by themselves. Howe's invention depended on contingencies of experience. Mobility of journeymen machinists from shop to shop and discussions about machine improvement were both common practice, but that Howe heard one such discussion at a time when he previously had mastered relevant loom technology was accidental and perhaps decisive for his invention.

Moreover, the institutions of the machinery sector were insufficient to overcome at least one barrier to invention, the need for finance. Howe's weekly wage of $9 could hardly support his family and also meet the estimated $500 needed for materials and tools to construct the machine. The problem was the circularity facing all artisan inventors: how could one with little wealth finance the considerable capital costs required to develop a practical machine when that machine could itself yield no revenue until it had already taken practical form? The craftsmen initiating the division of labor did not face this problem, because this innovation had no costs of development and only modest costs of introduction. The modern corporation solves the problem by financing technical change out of revenue from other products or from institutional borrowing.

Howe found the solution outside the machinery sector; like many others in the nineteenth century, he got minor financing from his family and then resorted to personal contacts to get more. In the fall of 1844, his machine already conceived, he formed a partnership with a wealthy friend, George Fisher, in which they agreed to split any income from Howe's invention if Fisher would board Howe and his family and pay $500 for machine construction costs. Howe then quit his job and in half of a year had constructed his first machine.[6]

Neither was the American machinery sector necessary for inventing a sewing machine. Well-developed machinery sectors existed elsewhere, including London, northwestern England, and places on the Continent; in any case, technological barriers did not preclude invention by nonmachinists. Moreover, at least 17 stitching mechanisms had been invented before Howe's, only 1 of which came out of the American machinery sector. Designed to mechanize commodity production, most were invented in areas with concentrations of both potential users and mechanical skills. (See Table 7.1.) Some reflection on this experience will help gain a more general understanding of the invention of the sewing machine.[7]

Most of these inventions were not the product of machinists, much less

Table 7.1
Stitching Mechanism Inventions, 1790–1846

Inventor	Year	Location	Stitch	Purpose
Thomas Saint	1790	Middlesex, Eng.	Chain	Leather sewing
Thomas Stone and James Henderson	1804	France	Hand	Sewing
John Duncan	1804	Glasgow, Scot.	Chain	Tambour embroidery
Edward Chapman	1807	Newcastle-on-Tyne, Eng.	Hand	Rope stitching
Balthasar Krems	ca. 1810	Mayen, Rhineland	Chain	Cap sewing
Josef Madersperger	1814	Vienna, Aus.	Hand	Sewing, embroidery
M. Heilmann	1829	Mulhouse, Fr.	Hand	Embroidery
Barthelemy Thimonnier	1830	St. Etienne, Fr.	Chain	Sewing
Walter Hunt	ca. 1833	New York City	Lock	Sewing
Josef Madersperger	1839	Vienna, Aus.	Lock	Sewing
Edward Newton and Thomas Archbold	1841	Leicester, Eng.	Chain	Embroidery
John Greenough	1842	Washington, D.C.	Hand	Leather sewing
Benjamin Bean	1843	New York City	Hand	Sewing
George Corliss	1843	Greenwich, N.Y.	Hand	Leather sewing
James Rodgers	1844	New York City	Hand	Sewing
John Fisher and James Gibbons	1844	Nottingham, Eng.	Lock	Lace embroidery
John Fisher and James Gibbons	1844	Nottingham, Eng.	Chain	Lace embroidery
Elias Howe	1846	Cambridge, Mass.	Lock	Sewing

Sources: Alexander, "On the Sewing Machine"; Grace Cooper, *The Sewing Machine;* Ure, *A Dictionary of Arts, Manufactures and Mines.*

American machinists. Of the ten inventors prior to Howe whose occupations are known, only one, the prolific inventor Walter Hunt, was well connected with the American machinery sector. Only one other, John Fisher, was a machinist outside the United States. The clockmaker James Rodgers had professional technological knowledge. But as many were employed in the clothing trades; Josef Madersperger and Barthelemy Thimonnier were tailors, and Balthasar Krems made hosiery. Finally, Thomas Saint was a cabinetmaker and George Corliss kept a store.

This diversity of backgrounds does not deny the importance of technological continuity for invention. Knowledge of mechanical technology did help overcome the limitations of the hand stitch. Two of the three lockstitch machines before Howe's were invented by machinists; John Fisher and probably also Hunt were familiar with the loom shuttle mechanism and adapted it to their machines. The difficulty of coming to this invention without mechanical background is illustrated by the case of the third lockstitch machine, which Madersperger did not arrive at for 25 years after his hand-stitch machine. The inventions of machinists were also superior in design and construction.

The continuity of principles of the sewing machine with established practice also helped other inventors conceive another stitch adequate for machine sewing, the chain stitch. Although this stitch had not been used for hand sewing, it was employed for embroidering on a tambour in much of nineteenth-century Europe. Familiar with such embroidery, Thimonnier and perhaps also John Duncan incorporated this stitch and the barbed needle that formed it in their inventions. An adequate sewing machine could copy hand techniques, though not techniques of sewing.

Many paths led to the stitching inventions; the principles of a practical stitching mechanism were hardly a unique product of Howe's genius or particular experience. Training as a machinist facilitated but was not necessary to form adequate stitching principles. But all stitching mechanisms were similar in one way; none succeeded commercially as sewing machines by the efforts of their inventors. This was not for lack of trying; Howe demonstrated his machine in a Boston clothing manufactory, but to no avail. Discouraged by his reception in the United States, Howe sold the English patent rights for a mere 250 pounds and, in February 1847, left for England to try to adapt his machine to corset making. With this departure, his direct contribution to the development of a practical machine ended.

The commercial failure of these machines rested on their impracticality for sewing. A practical machine had to stitch durable seams of a variety of shapes with greater speed or higher quality than hand work. None of the stitching mechanisms could do this. Howe's machine was probably the most adequate, but like the rest its material-holding and feeding mechanisms were inadequate. The baster plate effectively limited the machine to straight seams, because a tight, curved seam of evenly spaced stitches could not be formed when the fabric was pinned to the straight baster plate. Moreover, since the machine could only stitch the length of the baster plate before the cloth had to be repositioned, it could not realize the possibility for continuous sewing offered by the lockstitch. Even the stitching mechanism needed refinement, as was recognized in the first improvement patent on Howe's machine, which called the lifting rod that opened the loop of the needle thread "a very bungling device."[8]

Marketing barriers further reinforced the machine's impracticality. The practice of marketing machines locally limited Howe to the area around Boston, which was declining as a center of ready-made clothing relative to New York. The machine was not generally known even in this market. Finally, not only tailors resisted adoption, but so did manufacturers, who faced an estimated unit price of $300 in 1845 and the organizational difficulties of introducing the factory in what had been a putting-out system.[9]

The Commodity Path of Mechanization

What Howe could not do by intention developed as an unintended consequence. Practicality came quickly; within a decade of Howe's invention, others in the United States created practical machines of several varieties and a dynamic of continuing technological change. The pace of this development is notable because, unlike Hunt or Thimonnier, Howe neither contributed to this development nor sold his patent to others who did so.

The problem in accounting for the development of Howe's machine is not the lack of technological skills or of incentives, or the inadequacy of the machine to provide a basis from which development could ensue, but rather the isolation of the invention from those with appropriate knowledge and interests. The principal medium overcoming this barrier was Howe's marketing activity in 1845 and 1846. A failure in itself, this activity initiated a commodity path of mechanization.

Let us examine the logic of the commodity path. Sales efforts fostered further technical change through a process called learning by selling. Sales were attended by interactions around marketing, use, servicing, and production, and each helped overcome technological isolation. Marketing involved demonstration of the machine's functioning, discussion of its durability and adaptability to the particular needs of the user, and training in machine usage. The user learned through experience with the machine; machinery producers by testing, complaints, maintenance, and repairs; and inventors from contact with machine users and producers. Communication extended to other firms in the machine-using and machine-producing industries, to other machinists, and to family and community members.[10]

Learning by selling fostered technical improvements in two different ways. It widened the sphere of inventors by extending the numbers and widening the location of those familiar with sewing machine design. It also led to repeat invention among existing inventors when efforts to bring inventions into use occasioned responses about the adequacy of the machine or the need for other machines.

Other learning theories likewise identify a process of technical change in which experience leads to the recognition and transcendence of deficiencies of technique. These notions typically refer to the content of learning. Some learning identifies appropriate product designs and principles before commercial usage (research and development); other learning improves manufacturing skills with a fixed or changing plant (called by Paul David short-run and long-run learning by doing respectively). Finally, experience using an input can lead to improved design of that input or to its improved usage—better or cheaper maintenance, reduced downtime, or increased life (termed by Rosenberg embodied and disembodied learning by using).[11]

By contrast, learning by selling refers to the social form of learning: learning through the medium of commodity sale. It thus links diffusion to technical change; as diffusion broadens, so does learning about the use and the limitations of the commodity. Part of this learning alters production skills or the usage of the inputs, but part redesigns the inputs and as such comprises embodied learning by using. Improvements then diffuse as altered capital goods. Thus, the wider the diffusion, the greater the technical change. Moreover, because such technical change takes as its object the alteration of a commodity, learning need not take the uses of the good as given. Invention may aim at reducing labor costs or downtime in a given process, but it may also attempt to apply the product to new uses.

Compared to commodity usage, self-usage constrains the scope of learning and hence limits further invention. Knowledge spreads to managers and workers in the factory of the inventor (or the purchaser of the invention), perhaps to outside shops that make and maintain the machine, and then fans out to others through personal contact. Worker mobility can spread machine knowledge, but is constrained to the shops where the workers go, is threatened by patent action, and requires significant knowledge to duplicate the invention. By contrast, in the commodity form interaction can extend to large numbers of users, to other inventors, to the production and marketing personnel of the machinery firm, and to the broader community in which they live.

Fostered by sales, new inventions in turn stimulate the growth of sales. They are particularly likely to augment sales early in the machine's product cycle. The first stage of this cycle, called commodity definition, forms a practical machine, identifies the need it will fulfill, and creates an appropriate marketing apparatus. During this stage, technical changes can solve problems basic to the commodity's practicality, and can therefore have a major effect on sales. Refinement can extend sales to new uses or compete for the sales of other firms. The sales of new firms formed around inventions can further increase industry output. The commodity definition stage prepares the way for rapid sales growth in the stage of market penetration. As sales and learning expand, inventions multiply, but, because basic improvements were made in the previous stage, these inventions have less effect on sales.[12]

In this way, sales, learning, and invention form a cumulative process. Changes in each occasion changes in the others, and, once started, mechanization develops through its own momentum. Complementary innovations to define the market and marketing procedures and, particularly when the scale of output rises, to reduce costs and improve the quality of production contribute to the momentum of mechanization. Conditions in the broader economy matter, but as they influence the internal processes of the commodity path. Because the new commodity is expanding to fill a potential defined by the existing economy, changes in that economy have only secondary importance. The machine, as a produced commodity, has its own dynamic.

Prospects for Technological Development

At its beginning, the commodity path was difficult to follow and easily abandoned. With little capital and facing no organized markets for the labor of those trained in developing new techniques, even the most active entrepreneur could be stifled by isolation.

The marketing medium could only inadvertently overcome isolation barriers. The object of marketing was to sell, not to develop; to this end, design deficiencies may have been covered up. Tailors and other prospective buyers had relatively little technological knowledge. To avoid potential competition, contact with machinists may have been actively discouraged. In this way, the self-interest of those selling a machine could have impeded the effective cooperation conducive to technical improvement. The local character of machine marketing also limited the spread of knowledge about the invention.

Nor did other media overcome isolation barriers. Knowledge could have spread through use in the inventor's own shop, through demonstrations at fairs and exhibitions, or through public documents like patents, reports of exhibitions, and journals. As far as is known, none of these media was important in Howe's case. He did not exhibit his machine at fairs, journals like the *Scientific American* did not report it in detail, and, unlike William Thomas, to whom he sold the English patent rights, Howe did not sew in his own workshop.

But unlike most stitching mechanisms, marketing as a sewing machine had at least the possibility of developing Howe's invention. Some, such as the Fisher and Gibbons machines, were intended for use inside the inventors' shop and were never marketed more widely. Six embroidery and rope-stitching inventions were not conceived or marketed as sewing machines, so that the narrowness of focus of those aware of these machines hindered recognition of their applicability to sewing.

Other machines faced barriers that marketing could not overcome. Dependable machines could not be produced by means of the wood-using construction methods current at the beginning of the nineteenth century. Inadequate incentives were relevant barriers for inventions in isolated locations, such as that of Krems, or machines made for specialized purposes for which demand was falling, including John Fisher's lace-embroidering machine. By their design, running-stitch machines could form temporary but not permanent stitches. Through-and-through stitch machines were complex, slow, and inherently inferior to lockstitch and chain-stitch machines. Inadequate mechanical skills limited the development of machines in some locations, including those of Krems in a small Rhinish town, Madersperger in Vienna, and perhaps John Greenough in Washington, D.C.[13]

Nodality

Howe's machine was not developed to practicality by those few who observed it. Rather, this observation began a process of development in which, from 1845 through 1850, a series of new, small firms formed nodes in a communication network which, through the production, sale, use, and servicing of their machines, spread knowledge of mechanical sewing to innovators who overcame weaknesses of established machines. The process was cumulative; each nodal machine developed out of earlier nodes. It was also progressive; each of these machines expanded its sales, use, and technological influence relative to earlier ones.

While not sold or regularly used at all, Howe's was the first nodal machine because it was noticed and improved by John Bradshaw, who was granted a patent in 1848. As far as is known, the Bradshaw machine was used in only one establishment, to make ready-made sailors' clothing in New Bedford, but it qualifies as nodal because it stimulated the invention of the third such machine, that of Charles Morey and Joseph Johnson. At least 50 Morey and Johnson machines were produced and used, according to the *Scientific American*, "in most of the Print Works and Bleach Works in New England."[14] They spread knowledge of mechanical sewing both to a wider range of users and to the machinists who contracted to make them. This impact was great enough that an 1849 improvement patent could refer to "the machine well known as the 'Morey machine.' "[15]

The Morey and Johnson had one last importance: it influenced the development of the fourth nodal machine, the Blodgett and Lerow. This was the first sewing machine to have any significant acceptance in the clothing industry; in 1849 and 1850, several hundred of these machines were used to sew coats, pantaloons, caps, and bags in Boston, New York City, and other places. Moreover, it was known by the machinists in Boston, New York, and Worcester who licensed rights to produce and sell it.

As these machines developed, new media of diffusion came into use. The *Scientific American* reported on sewing machine inventions from 1848, when it included one short article on a machine it speculated to be Howe's and another on Thimonnier's machine. From its January 1849 article on the Morey and Johnson machine, it began a series of illustrated, often front-page articles providing detailed technical descriptions of inventions along with purchasing information. In the case of the Blodgett and Lerow, it even made its offices available for ordering the machine. Exhibitions provided a means of diffusion tapped by the Blodgett and Lerow, which received an award at the Massachusetts Charitable Mechanics Association Exhibition in 1850 and a better-known medal at the Crystal Palace Exhibition a year later.[16]

The process developing the practical machine was structured by the influence of these nodal machines, as Figure 7.3 depicts. The Howe machine affected not only Bradshaw, but also John Bachelder, a Boston machinery maker who attended a demonstration. The major impact of the Bradshaw machine was on the Morey and Johnson, perhaps on the Blodgett and Lerow, and on Allen Wilson, who responded to a falsely claimed infringement of the Bradshaw patent by altering the shuttle mechanism on his 1850 machine. The Morey and Johnson had a much wider impact, affecting not only the Blodgett and Lerow, but several other inventions as well.[17]

The Blodgett and Lerow also had broad importance; it influenced two and perhaps all of the three machines that were to dominate the industry. Isaac Singer turned his attention to the sewing machine when, attempting to sell a print type-carving invention in Boston, a center of the book manufacturing trade, he displayed his invention in the shop of the Blodgett and Lerow licensee, Orson Phelps. There Singer noted the deficiencies of the Blodgett and Lerow, and Phelps interested him in developing the machine. Singer had become involved in type carving when employed in a type-carving factory after a traveling theatrical troupe that he had financed through another invention ran out of funds. Moreover, the Blodgett and Lerow was the dominant machine around Boston when the tailors William Grover and William Baker began their inventive efforts. It may also have affected the evolution of the Wilson machine through the display of both at the same industrial expositions.[18]

Nodal inventions other than Howe's had no major technological importance in themselves. Bradshaw advanced only minor improvements in the loop-forming, tension, and cloth-support mechanisms. Morey and Johnson introduced a useful device to restrain the cloth as the needle left. Blodgett and Lerow developed a flawed rotary shuttle machine.

But inventions stimulated by nodal machines were of greater consequence. John Bachelder's 1849 patent overcame important deficiencies of Howe's baster plate cloth-supporting and feeding mechanism. Bachelder's machine introduced the horizontal worktable and the vertically reciprocating straight needle. (See Figure 7.4.) It effected a continuous or perpetual feed by means of a revolving endless belt (e.g., a belt in the form of a circle) which formed the surface supporting the cloth and advanced the length of a stitch each time the needle rose above the fabric. Vertical pins at the edge of the belt entered the cloth and advanced it toward the needle as the belt moved forward. After being stitched, the cloth rose over a metallic receiver plate on the belt, which lifted it off the pins. This machine allowed a seam of unlimited length to be sewed without resetting the material, but remained restricted to straight seams.[19]

Singer also contributed to the development of the Howe machine. His 1850 machine, patented in 1851, held the needle on a stationary arm overhanging the worktable, replacing the reciprocating needle arms of other machines. (See Figure 7.5.) This gave the machine more stability and allowed it to be used for heavier industrial purposes. To hold the cloth down as the needle rose or as the cloth was fed, Singer designed a vertical presser foot which incorporated a

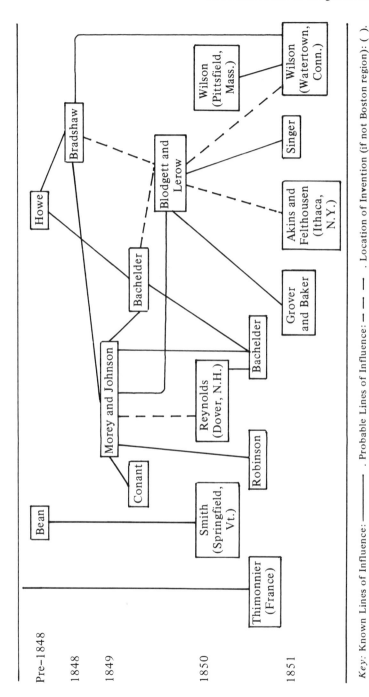

Figure 7.3 Lines of Influence of American Sewing Patents, 1848–1851.

Key: Known Lines of Influence: ———— . Probable Lines of Influence: — — — . Location of Invention (if not Boston region): ( ).

Figure 7.4 The Bachelder Feed Mechanism. The endless belt was horizontal and the needle now reciprocated vertically. (Smithsonian Photo 45572)

spring to allow it to pass readily over seams and different thicknesses of material.[20]

The machines of this developmental path also reintroduced three other types of stitches. The Morey and Johnson machine, followed by several others, employed a single-thread chain stitch, which was formed when a hook grasped the thread loop left by the retreat of the needle and secured it around the loop left by the needle's next penetration. (See Figure 7.6.) Grover and Baker reinvented the double-thread chain stitch, formed when a second thread-carrying eye-point needle penetrated the loop of the first and left its own loop which encircled the next loop left by the first needle. This machine overcame the need of lockstitch machines to rewind thread onto the shuttle bobbin. Finally, in 1850 Frederick Robinson made use of the evolution of lockstitch and especially chain-stitch machines to invent a more mechanically adequate hand-stitch machine. Dispensing with pincers, this machine passed the thread between two hooked needles with movable pins to form closed eyes. The loop of thread left by the first needle was caught in the barb of the second, which then closed, held the thread by a spring, and moved away from the cloth.[21]

Sewing technology also developed outside the dynamic Howe initiated, including 3 of the 15 sewing machine patents issued from 1848 through 1851. Two of these had neither technological nor commercial importance. In 1850, D. M. Smith patented an acknowledged improvement of the Bean running-

Figure 7.5 Singer's Patent Model. Of early machines, this most anticipated the form of the practical machine. (Smithsonian Photo 45572-D)

stitch machine, but this type of machine could only be used to make temporary seams. Into the American scene came the French invention of Thimonnier, patented in 1850 but described in an 1848 *Scientific American* article which prophesied about the inventor that "his fame will go down to posterity with that of Jacquard." Yet the machine was quickly forgotten, and, in reviewing the rise of the sewing machine 30 years later, the *Scientific American* wrote of Thimonnier's invention: "This had no feed motion, and our object in publishing it, if we recollect aright, was to exhibit its inferiority to the American machine." By 1849, the time when Thimonnier's machine could have been revolutionary had passed; by accident of time and place, the success that might have been his was realized instead by Howe.[22]

The third of these independent inventions was central to the development of Howe's machine. In a machine designed in 1848, constructed in 1849, and

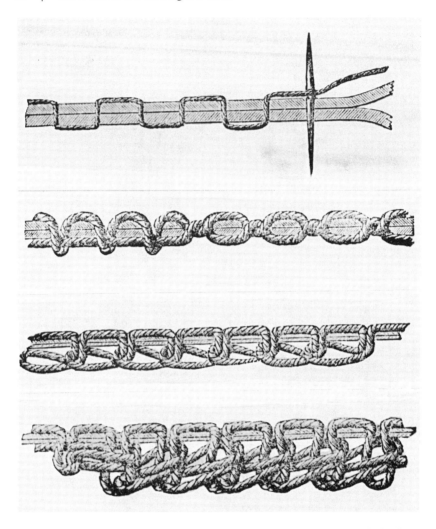

Figure 7.6 Types of Stitches. From top to bottom: shoemaker's hand stitch (Greenough); lockstitch (Howe); single-thread chain stitch (Morey and Johnson); double-thread chain stitch (Grover and Baker). (*Journal of the Society of Arts*, April 10, 1863)

patented in 1850, Allen Wilson incorporated a new, far more adequate feeding mechanism, called the two-motion feed. Operating in conjunction with a smooth, stationary, horizontal worktable, this feed consisted of a serrated bar embedded in a slot in the table such that the bar's teeth protruded above the table. When the needle had risen above the table, the cloth, caught between a metal plate and the serrations of the bar, was advanced the length of a stitch. When the needle descended into the cloth, the bar returned to its starting point, ready to feed the cloth again, and the cloth could be pivoted around the needle.

Figure 7.7 Wilson's Patent Model. The two-motion feed allowed the table to be stationary. (Smithsonian Photo 45504-H)

This feed was far superior to Bachelder's, since only a small bar moved, rather than the whole table, so that the hands of the operative could rest on the table and hence more accurately guide the cloth. (See Figure 7.7.) Moreover, by eliminating the pins, this feed began to extend the sewing machine to seams of all shapes.[23]

The product of an inventor with little prior technological training, Wilson's invention illustrates the abstractness of mechanical technology. Wilson had worked as a farmer and a carpenter, and had forged tools in a local blacksmith's shop. At age 16, he was apprenticed as a cabinetmaker. He followed his trade to Adrian, Michigan, where in 1847 he initially conceived his invention, and then to Pittsfield, Massachusetts, where he built his first machine. His technological knowledge came at first more through play than work. Like many other youths in the period when the steamboat had come into use and the railroad was just beginning, Wilson made machinery as a hobby; he went so far as to construct his own workshop, including a turning lathe and tools, in which he built miniature waterwheels and sawmills.

That he could arrive at the most adequate principles of mechanical sewing without professional technological training makes Wilson the most creative of the stitching machine inventors. An inventor can be said to be more creative when the gap is greater between the technical adequacy of the invention and his or her prior technological knowledge. Wilson was one of only five to independently discover the lockstitch, and three of the others had considerable technological knowledge probably including an awareness of loom shuttle mechanisms. He was one of the few with a horizontal worktable, and his feed was superior to those of all prior stitching inventions.[24] Moreover, Wilson's talents went beyond sewing. In 1858, the *Scientific American*, already reminiscing about sewing machine inventors, wrote of a day in 1849 when Wilson entered its office: "Feeling a degree of security that he could trust to our integrity and honor, he carefully untied a handkerchief, and brought out two models—one a sewing machine, and the other a rotary steam engine." Wilson could afford to patent only one, and, at the journal's suggestion, patented the sewing machine through the Scientific American Patent Agency.[25] From that point, the Wilson machine became intertwined with the development Howe had begun.

The Virtuous Circle of Failure

The birth of the sewing machine formed a virtuous circle in which attempted sale engendered technological learning, learning led to the invention of new machines, and invention overcame barriers to sale. The circle involved both inadvertent and intended outcomes of the actions of inventors. Marketing efforts intended to bring sewing machines into contact with prospective users, not potential developers. Yet machinists observed demonstrations, and tailors and clothing manufacturers did not remain only users. Challenged by the stark deficiencies of the machines they knew and directed by the evident requirements of an adequate machine, such tailors as Joseph Johnson, inventor of the Morey and Johnson machine, Sherburne Blodgett, William Grover, and William Baker all became inventors.[26]

Tailor-inventors faced barriers to success that they alone could not readily overcome. They had inadequate financing and little knowledge of machine design, production, and marketing. Realizing these limits, tailors and other inventors formed partnerships and contracting relationships. Capital costs, though not high compared to those of many inventions (George Fisher's total expenditure in supporting Howe and developing his machine was around $2,000), were a barrier that the partnership helped overcome. In part for this reason, Johnson was joined by Morey and Blodgett by John Lerow. Likewise, Singer financed the building of a model by ceding a share of his patent to George Zieber, who had financed his type-carving machine. Allen Wilson's partnership with Nathaniel Wheeler in 1851 secured financing in a more modern form: Wheeler was a metalwares manufacturer who could finance development with revenue from existing products. Partnerships also supplied marketing knowledge. Lerow had been the agent for the Morey and Johnson machine, and Wheeler's marketing experience had some relevance to sewing machine sales.[27]

Technological and production skills were acquired in the same way. The concentration of machinists in areas where sewing machines were made and sold eased the difficulties of skill acquisition. The Morey and Johnson was made by contractors, and the Blodgett and Lerow came to be built by contracting shops in Boston, New York, and Worcester. Singer and Grover and Baker both took mechanics as partners, as did Wilson by allying with Wheeler. Machine shops also developed their products, as is evidenced by the dramatically different construction of Blodgett and Lerow machines made in different shops. These shops also marketed and serviced machines, especially the Blodgett and Lerow, which was distributed by machine shops that had purchased geographic rights to produce and sell.

Sales widened as firms integrated the efforts of tailors and of machinists, especially for the Morey and Johnson and the Blodgett and Lerow. Invention followed; these 2 machines probably influenced all but 3 of the 12 other sewing machine patents issued from 1849 through 1851. Inventors of new machines in turn sought out machinists to develop, produce, and sell their machines. Quite unintentionally, the sale of machines to users outside the machinery sector led to a closer integration of the sewing machine with other machinery.

Events would have taken a different course—indeed, perhaps no course at all—had inventors attempted to set up clothing factories of their own. Without learning by selling, knowledge might not have spread beyond Howe, and it surely would have spread more slowly. British sewing technology had begun on the path of self-use when Howe sold his British patent to a large corset maker, and thereafter lagged behind American developments. American inventors pursued commodity usage from the start. Howe, Bradshaw, and other machinists probably would not have undertaken sewing invention in the absence of the possibility of machine sale. Tailors followed the same path, often through licensing out patent rights to machinists who sold the machines. Singer and Wilson never had any intention of making clothing.

The process that developed the sewing machine was tied to its starting point. Invention remained concentrated in the region where the machine had originated, because media of learning—sale and the mobility of machinists and other craftsmen—operated most readily within regions. Regional institutions fostered development not only through the skills and marketing mechanisms they provided, but also through the accidents they occasioned, including those that interested both Howe and Singer in mechanized sewing.

This is not to say that the sewing machine was simply accidental. Conditions favored sewing invention in many parts of the United States and Western Europe, and many took up the challenge. Had Howe's machine not been developed in the United States, it might have been in England, where he went to develop his machine in 1847. If his machine had failed, Thimonnier's might have succeeded in any of three countries where it had been patented: France, Britain, and the United States. Or Wilson's machine might have concentrated development around New York. If simultaneous development by those facing few significant barriers can be taken as evidence that an invention is "immanent" to an age, then the sewing machine was an invention whose time had come.

But at the time things looked differently. At the end of 1850, sales were small and localized, and deficiencies of design and production remained. Agents who could overcome these limits had not yet taken a stable form; none of the firms making nodal machines achieved commercial success or long continued in business. Nor was future success apparent to the actors; as Singer testified in a patent suit, in 1851 Sherburne Blodgett "said he was a tailor by trade, and knew more about sewing than I could; that his had been the leading machine in the market, and he could assure me sewing-machines would never come into use. Three factories which he had established to operate with sewing-machines had failed."[28] The rapid diffusion of the sewing machine would await an evolution of its usefulness, its marketing, and the firms making it.

8

Self-Sustaining Success

A process quite different from that which gave birth to the sewing machine completed its development to practicality. Growing out of the earlier process, it continued to take its momentum from an interrelation of sewing machine inventors, producers, and users structured by the sales of nodal machines. But now nodal firms succeeded, most major technical changes occurred on their machines, and their success occasioned a far wider, deeper innovational process. These attributes of the new phase reinforced one another; sales created conditions for technical change inside and outside nodal companies, and technical change engendered more sales. The virtuous circle of failure had become a spiral of success.

Redefining Product and Market

The three nodal machines of this new phase, the Singer, the Grover and Baker, and the Wheeler and Wilson, gained superiority over their predecessors through a remarkably similar set of innovations. Technologically, even the first models of these machines achieved greater adequacy by introducing stationary, horizontal tables, workable stitching mechanisms, and two-motion or similar feeding devices. Organizationally, the requisites of development and diffusion were increasingly met within the firm. Inventors formed partnerships with others who supplied metalworking abilities, knowledge of marketing, and some finance. Production was undertaken within the firm. Each concentrated on nearby markets and licensed out rights to sell in more distant areas but did not license out the right to produce machines; in this they broke with the method employed by Blodgett and Lerow.

By means of this combination of continuity and innovation, these companies—and virtually only these companies—secured substantial sales. Singer sold about 800 machines in each of its first two full years, 1851 and 1852, and Grover and Baker sold 500 in each. Wheeler and Wilson sold 200 machines in 1851, the first year of their partnership, and increased to 450 machines the next year. By contrast, the sales of earlier machines plummeted; the only producer known to have remained in business, Blodgett and Lerow's New York licensee A. Bartholf, produced 30 machines in 1851 and 50 in 1852. Sales of nodal machines were unprecedented not so much in their scale—Blodgett and Lerow had made almost as many—but in their persistence. Average sales expanded from 590 per company in 1852 to 1,070 in 1855 and skyrocketed thereafter.[1]

Learning by Selling and Ongoing Invention

As sales grew, so did learning and invention. The number of patents indicates the expansion of inventive effort. Of course, patents did not capture all inventions, especially minor modifications. But they did include almost all major improvements, as would be expected in a period of active patent litigation and struggle over patent control.[2] From an average of 4 per year from 1849 through 1851, sewing machine patents rose to 23 annually over the next four years.

Sales affected learning in distinct ways for new and established inventors. For all inventors, learning expanded with experience with the machine. For those who had not invented, experience gained through demonstration, training, use, and repair provided knowledge about the machine's mechanisms, deficiencies, and potential. Such experience could overcome isolation barriers and direct attention to invention.[3] Sales growth also increased expected markets and hence incentives to invent. Thus the growing extent and widening location of sales should have increased the number and locational breadth of inventors.

Established inventors had an added kind of experience on which further technical change depended: that of inventing. Inventing is itself a process of learning. The inventor must pose a problem; consider alternative solutions, reject some, and settle on others; identify and solve complementary problems; design, build, and test mechanisms embodying these solutions; and, for many, present models, drawings, and specifications for patenting. These inventive skills having been employed, later reflection on the invention may pose new challenges and lead to new responses.

Use increased the extent and quality of reflection about an invention. Through use, the inventor entered into contact with others who produced, tested, demonstrated, sold, used, and serviced the machine. The varying perspectives of others offered distinct insights into the requirements and possibilities of further invention. By extending the range and kinds of use, commodity usage broadened the feedback the inventor received, as well as increasing incentives. Hence for inventors, usage of an invention, especially as a capital good, could lead to further inventive activity, particularly for those who were owners or employees of the firms making their machines or who maintained contact with the firms assigned their patents.

New inventors took out most of the 91 sewing machine patents issued to American residents from 1852 through 1855 (see Table 8.1). First patents, defined to be those issued to individuals without previous sewing machine

Table 8.1
Sewing Machine Patents, 1846-1861
(number issued to U.S. residents)

	First Patents	Repeat Patents	Total Patents
1846	1	0	1
1847	0	0	0
1848	1	0	1
1849	4	0	4
1850	4	1	5
1851	3	1	4
1852	4	3	7
1853	6	2	8
1854	24	13	37
1855	16	23	39
1856	13	15	28
1857	33	23	56
1858	48	54	102
1859	53	33	86
1860	49	30	79
1861	43	24	67
Total	302	222	524

Sources: Patents were identified from U.S. Department of Commerce, *U.S. Patent Classification–Subclass Listing,* class 112. Patents were then individually consulted.

patents, grew from 4 in 1852 to 6 in 1853 and then jumped to 24 in 1854; 16 were issued in 1855.[4]

This surge of patenting paralleled, but lagged behind, the accelerated diffusion of nodal machines in late 1851 and early 1852. The lag would be expected since the discovery of technical problems and solutions, the building and testing of models, and the preparation of patent applications would take a year or two and the issuance of the patent another six months. The correlation of patenting and sales is also consistent with a demand-determined technical change hypothesis, which might maintain that present sales are a determinant of future expected sales so that growing sales can induce more inventive effort.[5]

The location of new inventors, as indicated by the places of residence listed on patents, was also tied to machine sales. Invention continued to congregate around places where nodal machines were used and made. Nodal machines were made in Massachusetts, Connecticut, and New York, and inventors residing in these states took out 37 of the 50 first patents issued to new American inventors from 1852 through 1855, led by the 21 in Massachusetts.

Concentration near the location of machine use and production was also true within states. Only 1 of Massachusetts' new inventors lived west of Worcester, and 10 of New York's 14 patents were issued to new inventors living in metropolitan New York, with another 3 in Ithaca, where W. H. Akins had invented. Moreover, of the 13 first patents outside of these states, 7 were issued to inventors in Philadelphia and Newark, which had agencies of the nodal companies. Altogether then, 90 percent of the patents to new American inventors were located in or around centers of machine use and manufacture.

As use was extended, many inventors took out other patents. The patents they took out after their first, called repeat patents, comprised 45 percent of sewing machine patents issued to American residents from 1852 through 1855. With the growth of sales and the return flow of information to inventors, the number of repeat patents rose from 3 in 1852 to 13 in 1854 and 23 in 1855.

Repeats occurred most readily when first patents had come into use. In virtually all known cases, sewing machines came into use as the products of capital goods firms. New firms adopted the practices of nodal companies, which as such led not only in usage but also in disseminating a mode of usage. The only exception was Frederick Robinson, the inventor of a hand-stitch machine, who used his machine in his Worcester shoe factory. Yet even his machine was also sold. Usage began through the commodity path and would continue along this path.

Nodal companies led the way in repeat patenting. Issued all 4 repeat patents in 1851 and 1852, nodal firm members took out 40 percent of the repeats through 1855. Singer took out 13 repeat patents, Wilson had 3, and Grover and Baker had 1. Other early inventors continued in the field, but less actively. Other than Singer, Wilson, and Grover and Baker, 10 Americans had been issued first patents from 1846 through 1851. Four of these were granted 5 repeat patents from 1852 through 1855, and 2 others, along with 2 Blodgett and Lerow licensees, were issued patents later in the decade. All of the 4 who were issued repeat patents by 1855 either established their own firms (Robinson and Akins) or assigned the patent to a company already owning other patents (Blodgett to Nehemiah Hunt) or to an individual who presumably expected to use it (J. S. Conant).[6] New inventors quickly followed suit. About half of all repeats from 1852 to 1855 were issued to 12 inventors who took out first patents within these years, 8 of whom brought their patents into use in this period.

Technical Change and Sales

Just as sales fostered secondary invention, so technical change stimulated sales, closing the circle of mutual support. Improvements made machines more salable in several ways. Led by the innovations of nodal companies, new techniques completed the development of practical, general-purpose sewing machines. By far the most important improvement was the four-motion feed that Allen Wilson invented in 1852 and patented in 1854. This device introduced an up-and-down motion on the serrated feed bar which allowed the material to be turned easily when not in contact with the bar and therefore overcame the deficiency of the earlier two-motion feed. With this device, the cloth was fed forward by the bar as on the earlier feed, but, when the needle entered the cloth, the bar moved down, broke contact with the cloth, and permitted the cloth to freely pivot around the needle in any direction. While under the cloth, the bar moved backward and then ascended to its initial position, in contact with the cloth, as the needle rose from the cloth. In this way, a continuous seam of any shape could finally be constructed.[7]

Isaac Singer added another contribution to the practical machine. While demonstrating his machine, Singer introduced a foot treadle to allow him to use both hands to guide the cloth to be stitched. This mechanism became the standard means used in the United States to activate machines not driven by power, replacing the hand cranks of earlier machines.[8]

Second, less basic improvements added to the usefulness of machines, besides also giving competitive advantages to companies utilizing them and perhaps also avoiding patent infringements. The most important of these were Wilson's rotary hook and stationary bobbin, which replaced his earlier reciprocating shuttle. To form the stitch, the hook entered the loop of the needle thread, expanded the loop, and rotated the loop around the bobbin, enclosing the thread of the bobbin in the loop of the upper thread. When the hook entered and expanded the next loop, it also tightened the previous stitch. The loomlike shuttle was dispensed with, and the resulting stitching mechanism was faster, quieter, and, since the power loss in changing the direction of the shuttle was eliminated, more efficient mechanically.[9]

Other nodal companies also improved their machines. Singer led the way. Nine of his 13 repeat patents through 1855 improved the standard machine. Six of these altered the feeding mechanism. Others protected the needle, applied tension to the needle thread, modified the lockstitch, improved the shuttle, and developed a chain-stitching mechanism. Many other improvements were not patentable.[10]

New inventors also contrived many refinements and alternative mechanisms. To compete through machines that were better, cheaper, or noninfringing, they patented 11 new shuttle machines, 17 chain-stitch machines, 13 improvements in feeding mechanisms, and a variety of improvements in needles, thread take-ups, tensioning devices, and presser foots.

Finally, inventors extended the range of operations of the sewing machine. Most importantly, Singer, Grover and Baker, and others developed dry-thread leather-sewing machines. Several new inventors designed machines to stitch leather with waxed thread. Patents were also issued for specialized buttonhole, zigzag, and embroidery machines and for attachments to bind, hem, and gather.

Singer was particularly active in expanding sewing machine applications.

He added a linseed oil lubricant to reduce needle friction on his leather-sewing machine. He developed a multiple-needle machine and a vibrating-needle machine with a continuous feed motion that was useful in overcoming friction in stitching sails, harnesses, and other heavy work. He also patented an embroidery machine that used a double-thread chain stitch (which had been invented by John Fisher and James Gibbons as an ornamental stitch) with a third thread thrown back and forth under the needle for further embellishment.[11]

Technical changes also augmented industry sales through the formation of new firms by inventors or those to whom they assigned patents. By 1855, companies had been formed to make and market machines embodying about half of the patents taken out by inventors who first patented after 1851. These inventors were located near nodal companies. Inventors from Massachusetts, New York, and Connecticut were issued 28 of the 33 patents taken out by new inventors, led by the 17 of the Bay State. Companies were even more concentrated: all of the 20 companies formed between 1852 and 1855, whether or not they produced a newly patented machine, were located in these three states. As secondary nodes of communication, new firms themselves fostered ongoing invention.[12]

Complementary Innovations

Other innovations supported the cumulative process binding technical change and sales. Most fundamental were the marketing innovations of nodal firms. To realize the potential market, a machine had to be affordable, accessible, and usable. The initial marketing system, which combined local sales by sewing machine companies and the sale of patent rights in more distant areas, failed to realize this potential. Unlike most other commodities, usability entailed not only practicality but also training and servicing. Territorial rightholders provided neither the elaborate showrooms preferred by companies nor a sufficiently trained sales and maintenance staff. Moreover, the right-holder system was not financially advantageous. The sale of rights supplied little capital. Nor were profit margins high; Singer right-holders paid only $60 and, from 1853, $70 for a machine selling for $125.[13]

Led by Singer, from 1852 nodal companies began replacing this system by networks of commission agents and then company agencies. Commission agents set up their own showrooms and hired a staff to sell and repair machines, but sewing machine companies could replace them if facilities or sales were inadequate. The new system increased sales and the profit margins of nodal firms; Singer sold its machines at prices varying from $87.50 for its most important agents to $100 for others, an increase of some $20 to $30 per machine over the older system. Together with Cyrus McCormick's similar organization for selling reapers, this system brought about mass machinery production for the national market.

The system that ultimately was to prevail eliminated any reliance on independent agents by establishing branch sales and servicing offices. At about the same costs of selling, averaging 28 percent of the retail price for Singer, this system overcame a barrier to sales by ensuring that demonstrator models and a stock of finished machines would be available at every office. It transcended another barrier by transferring technically competent personnel within the company to manage some branches. For Singer, branch managers included machinists from its factory and those connected to Singer's invention, including Orson Phelps, John Lerow, and George Zieber. Here technological skills contributed to marketing development. This system had one other important benefit: agents gathered information about machine performance that was used to improve later models. Technological development had come to depend on the structure of marketing directly, as well as through its effect on sales and learning.[14]

Company agencies had already been placed in many major centers by the mid-1850s. Singer opened its first branch office in 1852 and by 1855 had offices in Philadelphia, Boston, Baltimore, Newark, and Gloversville, New York, besides its main office in New York City. Others followed suit. In 1855, Grover and Baker had offices not only in the eastern cities of New York, Albany, Gloversville, Philadelphia, Baltimore, and Boston, but also in the southern and western centers of Augusta and Columbus, Georgia; St. Louis; Nashville; and New Orleans.

One other innovation affected the scale and distribution of sales: the formation of a patent pool. Sales depended on enforceability of the right to sell. A barrier here lay in the social character of invention: because the practical sewing machine was the product of many, no one could produce without infringing on the rights of others. Through the struggle to control rights to the idea of the sewing machine, the unintended character of the effective cooperation of the inventive process was made explicit and took on competitive importance.

Two struggles were paramount: the opposition of Elias Howe to those who developed and produced his machine, and of these major developers to one another. Returning in 1849 from England, Howe discovered that others were producing machines infringing on his patent. In 1850 he began a series of infringement suits against Blodgett and Lerow, John Bradshaw, and Singer which were not to end until 1854. To finance the costs of litigation, Howe enlisted the support of a Massachusetts shoe manufacturer, George Bliss, who bought a share of the patent and loaned Howe money, though only with Howe's father's farm as collateral.[15]

It was apparent that these, like all machines making other than a through-and-through stitch, did infringe on Howe's patent. In the most important case, which pitted Howe against Singer, the defense argued that the sewing machine had been invented by Walter Hunt a decade before Howe, and that the principles of this machine, unpatented by Hunt, were public knowledge. In this way, the question of what constituted invention became of critical practical concern to sewing machine producers.[16]

The court ruled in favor of Howe, offering the following rationale: "A machine, in order to anticipate any subsequent discovery, must be perfected— that is, made so as to be of practical utility, and not merely experimental and ending in experiment. Until of practical utility, the public attention is not called to the invention; it does not give to the public that which the public lays hold of as beneficial."[17] To confer property rights upon its holder, an invention was not merely a novel principle embodied in a mechanism, but was also capable of fulfilling needs and, in appropriate circumstances, of becoming a commodity. Because Howe, unlike Hunt, had tried to develop his machine, he gained rights to his conception. Singer was forced to pay Howe $15,000 for past infringement and to pay a royalty for any future usage. In return, Singer agents, like those of other nodal companies already paying royalties, could sell machines without fear of suits by Howe.[18]

Still, this decision did not establish who had the right to sell practical machines. Howe's machine was not fully adequate and basic improvement patents were owned by competing companies. In 1855 a second round of litigation began, pitting Singer against the other two nodal companies. Wheeler and Wilson claimed that Singer's wheel feed infringed on their two-motion feed. Singer, on the other hand, sued for infringement of the Bachelder feed and vertical needle patent and the Morey and Johnson spring arm patent, both of which it had purchased. When a U.S. circuit court judge suggested in 1856 that the matter be settled out of court, Orlando Potter, president of Grover and Baker, secured the agreement of his company, Singer, Wheeler and Wilson, and Howe to organize a patent pool, called the Sewing Machine Trust or Sewing Machine Combination. A means whereby firms could right-fully sell their machines had been found.[19]

The formation of novel marketing systems and the patent pool not only fostered sales and hence technical change, but also maintained the domination of nodal firms. Marketing innovations transcended the traditional tie of ma-chinery sales and firms to a locality. The patent pool, at Howe's insistence, agreed to license at least 24 manufacturers, but conferred competitive advan-tages on nodal firms. All companies, including pool members, were licensed to use the pooled patents for $15 per machine. Of the proceeds, Howe received $5 on every machine sold in the United States and $1 on each export; the remainder, after litigation and other expenses, was divided evenly between Howe and the 3 nodal companies.[20] Through their innovations in marketing, patent control, and technology, nodal companies set the stage for the penetra-tion of the potential market, the widening of technical change, and their continued centrality to both.

Market Penetration and Ongoing Technical Change

Adequate in its basic technological principles, the sewing machine of 1855 lacked technical refinement and had only begun to diffuse among shoe and other commodity producers. Both diffusion and refinement were accomplished in the market penetration stage of the sewing machine and its producers. Beginning in 1855, this stage continued through 1872. To portray initial shoe mechanization, this chapter will concentrate on the pre–Civil War years.

Expansion in this stage was substantially determined by agents and conditions within the industry, led by established nodal firms. This is not to say that factors outside the industry were irrelevant. The state of commercialization of sewing, national income and its distribution, and mechanical knowledge had provided and would continue to provide conditions for industry expansion. No doubt changes in such factors mattered; that Civil War sales stagnated obviously had causes external to the industry. But though changes in these outside factors affected the timing of expansion, they were neither large nor continuous enough to account for the trend of sales growth. It is on the internal dynamic that attention must focus.

Sales and Market Construction

Market penetration was not so much a period in which all barriers to market realization had been overcome as it was one in which rapid growth could bring with it a process overcoming remaining barriers. In the mid-1850s firms making practical machines still faced three barriers that their efforts could challenge. The first was financial: because investment was largely financed from retained profits, future sales were limited by present sales. The second was organizational: staffing a company agency system increased in difficulty with the pace of company growth. The third was conceptual: firms had limited understanding of their potential markets.

Each of these barriers was addressed in the second half of the 1850s. Increased sales resulting from earlier innovations provided funds that nodal firms used to expand plants, repurchase territorial patent rights, and increase company agencies. These investments lowered unit costs of production, reduced selling expenses, and thus increased profit margins and the capacity of the firm to finance growth.

Agencies were formed sequentially, so that established agencies supplied the personnel and profits to create new ones. In the second half of the 1850s, Singer bought back territorial rights and opened new offices in Albany, Chicago, and New Haven in 1856, in Brooklyn, Charleston, and Nashville in 1857, and in Rochester, Troy, and Syracuse in 1859. These agencies soon helped form others; already in 1859 the Chicago, Nashville, and Charleston offices totaled about $50,000 in sales. A survey of directories of cities with population exceeding 10,000 revealed that Singer had at least 27 outlets in 1860. Other nodal firms lagged behind only slightly; Grover and Baker had 23 outlets, and Wheeler and Wilson 22. Among the cities represented were the Massachusetts shoemaking towns of Lynn, Taunton, and Worcester.[21]

The growth of agencies was connected to marketing innovations. Capitalists often misperceived both the extent and composition of potential demand. In the late 1850s, Nathaniel Wheeler had to convince his stockholders that an increase in plant capacity from 12 to 25 machines per day would not be reckless; when he succeeded, he "proudly declared his belief that the company would then be able to supply the demands of the whole world." Within a few years Wheeler and Wilson alone annually manufactured several times that output.[22] In part, this misperception was based on another: that the principal demand for sewing machines would come from commodity producers. The leading members of firms had been tailors and machinists; for them the prospect of families buying machines as consumption goods was a great unknown.

A number of innovations began to define and institutionalize the family market, until by 1862 it absorbed one-quarter of the sewing machines in use and the large majority a decade later.[23] The agency system made this dispersed market more accessible; manufacturing sales thus provided the profits and agencies used to penetrate the family market. Advertising attempted to define the need for sewing machines by appealing to both the compassion of men and the independence of women. Recognizing the emulative and conspicuous character of consumption, companies attempted to place machines with re spected community leaders. Singer reasoned that no group was more re spected, more public, and more widespread than the clergy, and therefore offered to sell one machine at half price to a minister, a church sewing society, or a person designated by the minister. Agencies were luxuriously equipped and operatives elegantly attired to convey the propriety of sewing machines in respectable, well-to-do homes.[24]

Machines were designed expressly for the family market. Fostered by Wheeler's previous experience with consumer metalwares and the quiet efficiency of the rotary-hook machine, Wheeler and Wilson led the way. They added ornate designs, brilliant finishes, and elaborate cabinetwork, and they designed models that when not in use functioned as a desk or even as a melodeon. Singer strove to catch up; it supplemented its noisy, heavy machine with the lightweight Turtle Back family machine in 1856 and the more mechanically adequate Letter A machine in 1859.[25]

Finally, the sewing machine was made more generally affordable. Besides its competitive function, reduced prices made the machine available to a wider segment of the population. The prices of Grover and Baker and of Wheeler and Wilson machines fell from $125 in the first half of the decade to $50 and up by 1859. Likely more important for the family market was the role of installment credit in reducing monthly payments to manageable levels. The "hire-purchase" system, as Singer called it, would come to involve a down

Table 8.2
Sewing Machine Sales and Agencies, 1852–1860
(number of machines and agencies)

	Sales of Nodal Companies	Agencies of Nodal Companies	Agencies of Other Companies	Total Agencies
1852	1,800	2	1	3
1853	2,300	7	11	18
1854	3,700	8	15	23
1855	3,200	22	25	47
1856	6,700	27	30	57
1857	11,900	37	61	98
1858	16,600	53	69	122
1859	42,500	79	163	242
1860	61,900	91	254	345

Sources: Grace Cooper, *The Sewing Machine;* city and business directories for 69 U.S. cities.

Note: Only agencies listed in city directories are included; thus, the actual number is understated.

payment of as little as $5 and monthly payments as low as $3.[26] The sewing machine was well on its way to being available, needed, and affordable.

With a practical machine and improving marketing institutions, sales surged. As Table 8.2 indicates, sales of nodal machines soared from 3,200 in 1855 to 61,900 in 1860. Growth was not only rapid but also accelerating; the annual growth rate of the number of nodal machines sold increased from about 20 percent in the period from 1851 through 1855 to about 80 percent from 1855 through 1860. The remarkable growth of the latter half of the decade resulted from both the widening and the deepening of the market. The quadrupling of the number of known agencies of nodal companies spread the sewing machine to new areas. At the same time, the market potential within each area was more fully realized by an increase in the average annual sales of known agencies from about 150 machines in 1855 to 680 in 1860, an increase made more notable by the fact that newer centers were generally less populous, had less commercial sewing, and hence comprised smaller potential markets.[27]

Sales also expanded dramatically for other companies. The perceived success of nodal companies encouraged entry. As in the commodity definition period, technical change continued to influence sales through entry. Successful entry was typically tied to the competitive advantages gained from innovation; at least 19 of the 23 nonnodal companies selling in more than one agency in 1860 incorporated their own patented improvements in their machines. The census of 1860 reported 71 nonnodal sewing machine firms, which made about 60,000 machines.[28] The machine outlets of these companies were far more numerous and even more widespread than those of nodal companies.

The number of outlets of these companies listed in surveyed city directories increased from 25 in 1855 to 254 in 1860, suggesting that these companies grew faster than nodal firms and that the annual industry growth rate in the second half of the 1850s exceeded the 80 percent achieved by nodal companies.

By 1860 the market for sewing machines was national in scope. In the absence of company records on the location of sales, business directories can help identify the geographic structure of the market. Directories for 69 cities were surveyed, including all cities with over 40,000 population in 1860 and all but two over 20,000. The survey covered 25 states and the District of Columbia with 88 percent of the nation's population in 1860. Already in 1855, 12 states had agencies. In 1858 the number had risen to 19 states and the District of Columbia. In 1860, as Table 8.3 indicates, agencies were located in 51 cities, spread over 24 states and the District of Columbia.[29]

Agencies were regionally dispersed throughout the period. In 1855, agencies were listed in four Middle Atlantic states, four southern states, three western states, and only Massachusetts from New England. Expansion occurred in every region; in 1860, agencies were located in five Middle Atlantic states and the District of Columbia, six states in the South, eight in the West, and five in New England. Nodal firms led the way in spreading agencies, but by 1860 over 20 nonnodal companies had agencies in more than one state. Agencies were denser in the East—in 1860 New England had 19 percent and the Middle Atlantic region 43 percent, whereas the West had 22 percent and the South 16 percent—but this reflected market potential, still centered on commodity production, as much as it did the uneven realization of that potential. The growth and the nationalization of the market were mutually reinforcing.

First Inventions

As sales soared, inventions proliferated, evidenced by the dramatic expansion of patenting in the latter half of the 1850s. After decreasing from 39 in 1855 to 28 in 1856, total sewing machine patents issued to American residents increased to a high of 102 in 1858 and then fell to 67 in 1861, after which the Civil War disrupted the pattern (see Table 8.1). Repeat patents formed 43 percent of the 418 patents issued from 1856 through 1861, almost exactly the proportion of the previous five years.

If learning through sale fostered invention, then the take-off of patenting was an intrinsic part of the market penetration stage of the industry, and innovations in technique were an outcome of innovations in marketing. Sales growth spread knowledge not only to more people, but to more kinds of people. Individuals in various regions and occupations came into contact with sewing machines, and invention would not only grow in scale but also spread

Table 8.3
U.S. Cities with Directories Listing Sewing Machine Agencies,
1860 and 1880

	Number of Agencies			Number of Agencies	
	1860	1880		1860	1880
New England			West		
Hartford, Conn.	8	6	Los Angeles, Calif.	n.a.	5
New Haven, Conn.	4	5	San Francisco, Calif.	7	28
Portland, Maine	4	6	Denver, Colo.	n.a.	8
Boston, Mass.	26	42	Chicago, Ill.	13	73
Cambridge, Mass.	1	n.a.	Indianapolis, Ind.	3	7
Fall River, Mass.	0	5	Dubuque, Iowa	1	n.a.
Lowell, Mass.	1	4	Topeka, Kans.	n.a.	6
Lynn, Mass.	5	n.a.	Detroit, Mich.	6	12
Roxbury, Mass.	1	n.a.	St. Paul, Minn.	n.a.	8
Salem, Mass.	3	n.a.	St. Louis, Mo.	6	38
Taunton, Mass.	1	n.a.	Cincinnati, Ohio	22	39
Worcester, Mass.	6	8	Cleveland, Ohio	9	15
Manchester, N.H.	1	10	Columbus, Ohio	0	8
Providence, R.I.	4	15	Dayton, Ohio	1	7
			Zanesville, Ohio	4	n.a.
Middle Atlantic			Milwaukee, Wis.	4	13
Wilmington, Del.	0	6			
Washington, D.C.	2	17	South		
Baltimore, Md.	5	28	Mobile, Ala.	0	5
Jersey City, N.J.	1	6	Atlanta, Ga.	3	8
Newark, N.J.	6	13	Augusta, Ga.	1	n.a.
Paterson, N.J.	4	7	Savannah, Ga.	3	3
Albany, N.Y.	9	11	Louisville, Ky.	5	14
Brooklyn, N.Y.	2	47	New Orleans, La.	7	23
Buffalo, N.Y.	4	14	Charleston, S.C.	6	4
Newburgh, N.Y.	3	n.a.	Memphis, Tenn.	8	9
New York, N.Y.	56	93	Nashville, Tenn.	5	11
Poughkeepsie, N.Y.	5	n.a.	Norfolk, Va.	4	3
Rochester, N.Y.	2	9	Richmond, Va.	9	7
Syracuse, N.Y.	4	8			
Troy, N.Y.	2	11			
Utica, N.Y.	1	7			
Harrisburg, Pa.	n.a.	5			
Philadelphia, Pa.	36	32			
Pittsburgh, Pa.	0	16			
Reading, Pa.	4	5			

Sources: Business and city directories for 1860 and 1880. In cases where cities did not have annual directories, directories in surrounding years were used.

geographically and take forms specialized to the needs of various kinds of production.

Again, this is not to deny any role to such extraindustry factors as expanded potential markets in the clothing, hat, and shoe industries and improved mechanical capability following from the growth of employment in the machinery sector. But changes of these factors were surely too little to account for the great acceleration of sewing machine invention in the late 1850s. The 12 percent growth of real shoe output in the 1850s, or the 55 percent expansion of the men's clothing output, or the 48 percent increase in the number of machinists did not approach the explosion of sewing machine output. Moreover, internal factors governed the effect of outside changes. Machines known through sales and other communication media formed the starting point for the application of altered incentives and skills, so that the relevance of external changes depended on the rapidity of machine diffusion. Finally, internal processes changed the importance of outside factors; for example, the growing sophistication of sewing machine technology put a premium on the possession of technological knowledge.

We shall begin by considering first patents, those issued to inventors with no previous sewing machine patents. These formed 57 percent of all patents from 1856 through 1861, and their inventors also were issued over two-thirds of the repeat patents of this period. Sales growth could foster first patents either through the technological learning or through improving expected profitability and access to financing.

Other media could have had similar effects, including specialized publications like the *Scientific American* and magazines and newspapers intended for a more general audience. For at least one important improvement, these media were decisive. The rural Virginian James Gibbs began the process that led to his rotary-hook chain-stitch mechanism when he saw a woodcut of a Grover and Baker machine. His account is revealing:

> Not being likely to have my curiosity satisfied otherwise, I set to work to see what I could learn from the woodcut, which was not accompanied by any description. I first discovered that the needle was attached to a needle arm, and consequently could not pass entirely through the material, but must retreat through the same hole by which it entered. From this I saw that I could not make a stitch similar to handwork, but must have some other mode of fastening the thread on the underside, and among other possible methods of doing this, the chain stitch occurred to me as a likely means of accomplishing the end. . . . After studying the position and relations of the needle and [driving] shaft with each other, I conceived the idea of the revolving hook on the end of the shaft, which might take hold of the thread and manipulate it into a chain stitch.

A later visit to a tailor's shop using Singer machines convinced Gibbs that his machine was superior. He took a model to Philadelphia, met the model builder

Table 8.4
Sales and First Patents, 1853–1861
(annual averages)

Patenting Period	Sales by Nodal Companies	Total Agencies	First Patents
1853–1855	1,860	11	15.3
1856–1858	4,530	42	31.3
1859–1861	23,670	154	48.3

Sources: See Tables 8.1, 8.2.
Notes: Sales and agency periods are defined to lead patenting periods by two years; thus for the 1859–61 patenting period, sales and agencies from 1857 through 1859 are considered. Because business directories did not include sewing machine agencies in 1851, total agencies in the first period are the average of agencies in 1852 and 1853.

James Willcox, and soon formed the Willcox and Gibbs Sewing Machine Company.[30]

The extent of first patenting supports both learning and incentive theses. Just as the substantial sales growth associated with the formation of nodal companies in 1852 led to growth in invention in 1854 and 1855, the growth in sales after 1855 was followed with a similar lag by the increased patenting of 1858 through 1861. Division into periods conveys a clearer sense of the trend. Table 8.4 presents annual averages of nodal company sales, total surveyed agencies, and first patents for three periods: 1851–53, 1854–56, and 1857–59 for sales and agencies; and, assuming a two-year lag, 1853–55, 1856–58, and 1859–61 for first patents. As sales and agencies increased from period to period, first patents did as well.[31]

Whether sales induced invention through their effect on learning or on incentives can be ascertained by examining the location of patenting. If technological learning spurred invention, then patents would be located near sales, and the share of patents in a region would vary with the share of sales. If incentives stimulated invention, patenting should vary with the extent of the potential market. Because the market was becoming national during the 1850s, incentives by the end of the decade should be the same everywhere in the country (assuming that people invent for markets in which they are located), and patenting should vary directly with population.

For convenience, location will be considered by state, and states will be divided into three types according to their concentration of both sewing machine sales and production. Nodal states are those where nodal companies were located—Massachusetts, New York, and Connecticut. Secondary states had substantial concentrations of agencies and of sewing machine production—Ohio, Pennsylvania, Rhode Island, and New Hampshire. The remaining states and territories are called tertiary states.

Table 8.5
First Patenting per Capita, 1853–1861
(annual averages per million population)

Patenting Period	Nodal States	Secondary States	Tertiary States
1853–1855	2.38	0.39	0.10
1856–1858	4.52	0.55	0.26
1859–1861	4.67	1.62	0.65

Sources: See Table 8.1; U.S. Bureau of the Census, *Historical Statistics of the United States,* ser. A 195–209.
Notes: Nodal States = Massachusetts, New York, and Connecticut; Secondary States = Pennsylvania, Ohio, Rhode Island, and New Hampshire; Tertiary States = all other states, territories, and the District of Columbia. Population is estimated by interpolation between census years.

Invention varied significantly among these groups. In each period, as Table 8.5 suggests, nodal states had well over twice as many first patents per capita as secondary states and eight times as many as tertiary states. Secondary states also doubled the first patents per capita of tertiary states in each period. The effect of sales on incentives cannot readily grasp this locational pattern.[32]

To examine whether learning induced invention, the geographic distribution of sewing machine agencies can be used to approximate the distribution of sales. Agencies, of course, do not precisely measure sales; the sales of Singer's New York office in 1859 did not equal that of its Gloversville agency or of Atwater's New York office or of Singer's New York agency in 1853. Still, the number of surveyed agencies moved in the same direction as the quantity of sales.

As the learning-by-selling thesis would suggest, shares of first patents varied closely with shares of agencies. For each period, as Table 8.6 indicates, the extent of patenting in each group of states was much more closely tied to agency shares than to population shares. Moreover, changes over time in patenting shares correspond to changes in agency shares. The contrast of nodal and tertiary states illustrates this point. From 1853–55 to 1859–61, the share of first patents in nodal states decreased from 76 to 54 percent, and their agency share in the corresponding periods fell from 82 to 46 percent. By contrast, tertiary states increased their patenting share from 11 to 27 percent and their agency share from 0 to 34 percent.

Invention occasioned by learning through sale would not be expected to be perfectly correlated with sales for two reasons. First, where firms operated between states, learning at the point of use could be transmitted to main offices and lead to invention near those offices. This interstate learning would imply that the share of patents in home states of sewing machine companies should be greater than the share of agencies in those states. Second, learning may have occurred at the point of sewing machine production, so that as sales

Table 8.6
Geographic Distribution of Agencies and First Patents, 1853–1861
(annual averages; population in millions)

| | Patenting Periods | | | | | |
| | 1853 - 1855 | | 1856 - 1858 | | 1859 - 1861 | |
	N	(%)	N	(%)	N	(%)
Nodal States						
Patents	11.7	(76)	23.7	(76)	26.0	(54)
Agencies	9	(82)	28	(67)	71	(46)
Population	4.9	(19)	5.2	(18)	5.6	(18)
Secondary States						
Patents	2.0	(13)	3.0	(10)	9.3	(19)
Agencies	2	(18)	4	(9)	31	(20)
Population	5.2	(19)	5.5	(19)	5.7	(18)
Tertiary States						
Patents	1.7	(11)	4.7	(15)	13.0	(27)
Agencies	0	(0)	10	(24)	52	(34)
Population	16.4	(62)	18.3	(63)	20.1	(64)

Sources: See Tables 8.1, 8.2, 8.5.

Note: See Table 8.5 for nodal, secondary, and tertiary state classifications and for method of population estimation.

increased, production employees, learning, and invention would also expand. Both reasons suggest that patenting should be disproportionately concentrated toward nodal states and away from tertiary states.

As expected, the ratio of first patents to agencies was highest in nodal states and lowest in tertiary states. This is expressed in Table 8.7's First Patent-Agency Index (F/A Index), which measures the ratio of first patents to agencies in relation to the U.S. average. Nodal states had 23 percent more first patents per agency than the national average over the 1856–61 period and tertiary states had 30 percent fewer.

These differences correspond to differences in both interstate learning and sewing machine employment. Through 1859, 16 different companies had a total of 82 agencies outside the type of states in which their main office and factories were located. Nodal states were the home bases for all interstate agencies through 1856 and 89 percent of these agencies over the whole period. The knowledge transferred to nodal states may thus account for their greater patenting relative to sales. The greater concentration of production employment may have had the same effect. Nodal states had about four times as much per capita employment making sewing machines as the national average, whereas tertiary states had only 5 percent of the national average.

But another explanation is possible: that the nodal states invented more because they had more mechanical skills. Nodal states had 83 percent more machinists per capita than the national average, while tertiary states had 41

Table 8.7
Interstate Learning, Machinists, and Invention

	Nodal States	Secondary States	Tertiary States
F/A Index (U.S. = 1)[a]	1.23	0.87	0.70
Interstate Firms	89%	11%	0%
S/P Index (U.S. = 1)[b]	3.94	1.48	0.05
M/P Index (U.S. = 1)[b]	1.83	1.65	0.59

Sources: See Tables 8.1, 8.2, 8.5; U.S. Census Office, Eighth Census, *Manufactures of the United States in 1860.*

Notes: Interstate firms had main offices in one type of state and agencies in other types of states. They are classified by the location of the main office (typically also the plant). F/A Index is the First Patent-Agency Index; S/P Index is the Per Capita Sewing Machine Employment Index, and M/P Index is the Per Capita Machinists Index. For type of state i, these indices are defined as follows:

$F/A_i = (\text{First Patents}/\text{Agencies})_i / (\text{First Patents}/\text{Agencies})_{US}$

$S/P_i = $ Sewing Machine Production Employees per Capita$_i$/ Sewing Machine Production Employees per Capita$_{US}$

$M/P_i = $ Machinists per Capita$_i$/Machinists per Capita$_{US}$

For nodal, secondary, and tertiary state classifications, see Table 8.5.

[a]Patents from 1856 through 1861 and agencies from 1854 through 1859 are considered.

[b]Numbers of sewing machine employees and machinists are from 1860 manufacturing censuses. Population figures are also for 1860.

percent fewer (see Table 8.7's Per Capita Machinists—M/P—Index). We return to the supportive role of technologically convergent knowledge for ongoing invention.

The same result emerges when all states are classified by technological skills, measured by per capita employment of machinists (see Table 8.8). In each period first patenting varied with machinists; states doubling the national average in machinists per capita had over ten times as many first patents per capita as states with less than half the national average.

Machinists no doubt influenced the pace of invention. They were represented among sewing machine inventors out of all proportion to their share in the population, as can be concluded from a study of the occupations of inventors listed in city directories in years prior to their first patents. Of 26 Boston and New York City inventors who could be identified, 15 were machinists, 3 of whom made sewing machines.

The impact of machinists cannot be grasped independently of learning by selling, however. Sales growth is needed to account for the upsurge of patenting over time. That annual first patenting increased from about 0.15 per million population from 1850 to 1852 to 0.58, 1.08, and 1.54 over the subsequent three-year periods cannot be explained by the modest 9 percent

Table 8.8
First Patenting per Capita by Nodality and Concentration
of Machinists, 1853–1861
(annual averages)

	Per Capita Machinists Index			
	Over 2.0	1.0 - 2.0	0.5 - 1.0	Under 0.5
1853–1855				
All States	4.70	0.94	0.16	0.03
Nodal States	5.82	1.40	–	–
Other States	0.00	0.57	0.16	0.03
1856–1858				
All States	5.18	1.69	0.22	0.20
Nodal States	6.07	3.84	–	–
Other States	0.00	0.60	0.22	0.20
1859–1861				
All States	5.39	2.37	0.78	0.50
Nodal States	5.72	4.21	–	–
Other States	3.48	1.44	0.78	0.50

Sources: See Tables 8.1, 8.5, 8.7.
Notes: For state classifications, see Table 8.5; for definition of the Per Capita Machinists Index, see Table 8.7. Population and machinists are interpolated between census years.

growth in machinists per capita over the 1850s. Within periods, as Table 8.8 shows, the importance of the learning associated with sales is manifested by the much higher per capita patenting of nodal states compared to nonnodal states with the same concentrations of machinists.[33]

Repeat Invention

Inventing made it easier to invent again. Inventive skills improved and knowledge of sewing technology deepened. From communication around use of the invention, inventors came to know the weaknesses of their machines, the characteristics of other machines, and pressing technical problems. Revenue from the sale of machines or patents or from contact with potential investors could finance further invention.

Established inventors took advantage of their better prospects. Of the 342 American residents who received sewing machine patents from 1842 through 1861, 28 percent took out repeat patents by 1861. They are called multiple inventors, in contrast to single inventors who were issued only one patent (see Table 8.9). Another 11 percent would take out repeats over the next 20 years. Clearly, invention fostered invention. The proportion of sewing machine inventors who took out additional patents was far above the share of sewing machine inventors in the population at large, or even those favorably located

Table 8.9
Patent Use and Repeat Invention, 1842-1861

	Used	Not Used	Total
Single (S)	59	187	246
Multiple (M)	56	40	96
Total Patentees (S+M)	115	227	342
Repeat Patents (R)	169	58	227
Frequency [M/(S+M)]	0.49	0.18	0.28
Extent (R/M)	3.02	1.45	2.36
Rate [R/(S+M)]	1.47	0.26	0.66

Sources: Table 8.1; city and business directories for 69 U.S. cities; Grace Cooper, *The Sewing Machine.*

Note: This table focuses on inventors, not patents. Patents issued to more than one individual are counted separately for each patentee. For this reason, and because this table includes three patents from 1842 and 1843, the 569 patents of this table (S+M+R) exceed the 524 of Table 8.1.

in it. Connecticut, for example, had less than one first patent per 10,000 residents. Advantages existed even for inventors whose machines were not known to have been used, some 18 percent of whom took out additional sewing machine patents.

Repeat patenting also depended on the use of earlier inventions. A word about the meaning of use is needed. We utilize a minimal definition of use: a patent is said to have been used when the inventor either (1) owned a firm making and selling sewing machines or attachments, or (2) sold, licensed, or assigned the patent to other such firms. Use here is restricted in form; it refers to machines that were sold, either as capital goods or as consumption goods. Self-usage is excluded.[34] To ascertain usage, business and to a lesser extent city directories provide information on companies, supplemented by Grace Cooper's data on sewing machine firms, and patent grants list assignments at the time of patenting to firms or members of firms.[35]

A third of American sewing machine inventors had at least one patent used by 1861; another 5 percent gained usage after 1861 (see Table 8.9). About three-quarters of those who secured use were members of firms. The large majority of these firms were formed within two years of the first patent. Firm members could be involved in all aspects of the business, and therefore had great scope for learning. Twenty-six of these firms had two or more agencies by 1860. The other quarter with used patents assigned or licensed their patent rights, half to firms with more than one agency by 1860. The connection of these inventors to the firms using their patents varied from those who simply gained a payment for their patent to those who worked or regularly invented for a company.

The role of use in fostering further invention is indicated by the contrast in repeat inventing between those with used patents and those without. The 96 multiple inventors took out 227 repeat patents by 1861 and another 129 from 1862 through 1882. Considering only patenting and usage by 1861, the share of inventors who repeated (the frequency of repeat inventing) was 49 percent when patents were used and 18 percent when unused. Moreover, the number of repeat patents per multiple inventor (the extent of repeat invention) was twice as high when first patents had been used. The product of these measures (the rate of repeat patenting) indicates that those with used patents were issued close to six times as many repeat patents as those without. If usage and patenting after 1861 were also considered, extents and rates of repeat patenting would both rise, but the marked superiority of inventors with used machines would persist.[36]

One refinement of these measures is needed. Usage that followed repeat patents obviously did not induce these inventions. If use resulted in later invention, then inventions used within a period would generate more repeat patents after that period (called sequenced repeats) than would inventions not so used. To examine this hypothesis, we have selected a one-year period, because, of used first inventions, about four-fifths gained usage within one year of patenting. We thus want to compare repeat patenting two or more years after the first patent between inventors who did and did not gain use within one year of their first patents. This is done in Table 8.10. Much the same results recur; 58 percent of inventors of machines used within one year were issued sequenced repeat patents, whereas the proportion was only 26 percent among inventors with machines not so used. Moreover, those whose machines were used took out three times as many sequenced repeats and had rates of sequenced repeat patenting over six times as high as those whose machines were unused within one year.

Inventors, of course, varied in the kind and extent of learning they derived from usage of their patents. A member of a nodal firm who regularly interacted with agents and machine users would surely learn more than the inventor of a short-lived, failing machine, and this learning (together with the financing gained from sales) may have fostered repeat invention.

The survey of business directories can illuminate one facet of differences in firm success. Firms can be divided into three categories: nodal companies, firms with more than one agency by 1860, and those with only one agency. Table 8.11 classifies inventors by the kind of user of their patents. Clearly repeat patenting among inventors increased with the success of firms using their patents; inventors for nodal companies had twice as many repeat patents as inventors for multiple-agency firms and four times as many as single-agency inventors. This result would be replicated if sequenced repeat patenting were examined. For both the industry as a whole and successful firms within it, a virtuous circle existed in which invention led to use which led to more invention.

The determinants of repeat patenting were quite different from those of first patenting. The use of earlier inventions was paramount; factors that influenced

Table 8.10
Patent Use and Sequenced Repeat Patenting, 1842–1861

	Use of First Patent	
	Within One Year	Not within One Year
No Sequenced Repeats (N)	33	120
With Sequenced Repeats (Y)	45	43
Total Patentees (N+Y)	78	163
Sequenced Repeat Patents (R)	85	28
Frequency [Y/(N+Y)]	0.58	0.26
Extent (R/Y)	1.89	0.65
Rate [R/(N+Y)]	1.09	0.17

Sources: See Tables 8.1, 8.9.
Notes: Sequenced repeat patents are those repeat patents issued two or more years after the first patent. Inventors without sequenced repeats are single patentees plus multiple patentees whose repeats occurred less than two years after the first patent. To examine sequenced repeat patenting for all inventors, only first patents issued through 1859 are considered.

first patenting, such as proximity to sewing machine sales and production, played little independent role. When inventors are categorized by the region of their first patents, as they are in Table 8.12, it can be seen that rates of repeat patenting differed markedly among types of states, but that this difference largely reflects the greater portion of patents used in nodal states. When patents are divided by use, the influence of location lessens dramatically. Nodal states had no advantage over tertiary states for nonused patents. Nodal states did have the highest rates of repeat patenting for used patents, but their margin over tertiary states is much less and is explained by the greater rates of repeat patenting of inventors for nodal companies. Location, then, continued to be important for repeat inventing, but more because of the variation of use with location than because of differences of the quality of further technological learning.

The Direction of Technical Change

The combined efforts of single and multiple inventors deepened and widened sewing machine technology. The vast majority of patents modified the standard dry-thread machine. Stitch-forming patents and improvements of needles, presser foots, take-ups, tension devices, and other parts formed from 70 to 90 percent of patents throughout the decade. Stitch-forming and feeding patents were the most numerous; lockstitch, chain-stitch, and material-feeding patents each formed from 11 to 17 percent of all patents throughout the period, except for the 38 percent of patents comprised by chain-stitch machines from

Table 8.11
Repeat Patenting by Type of Patent User

	Type of Patent-using Firm		
Patent Type	Nodal	Other Multi-Agency	Single Agency
Single (S)	3	8	32
Multiple (M)	6	21	29
Total Patentees (S+M)	9	29	61
Repeat (R)	38	59	70
Rate [R/(S+M)]	4.22	2.03	1.15

Sources: See Tables 8.1, 8.9.

1856 through 1858. Attachments and other work-manipulating devices made up 10 percent of patents, and special-purpose machines somewhat less.[37]

These inventions increased the speed, quality, dependability, and automaticity of mechanical sewing. Speed increased on all machines but especially those with rotary shuttles and hooks. The Wheeler and Wilson and the Willcox and Gibbs single-thread chain-stitch machine attained maximum speeds of from 2,000 to 3,000 stitches per minute. Specialized machines, such as those to sew parallel seams, reduced the time needed to perform standard sets of operations. Many stitch, take-up, and tensioning inventions increased product quality by tightening stitches and reducing missed stitches. The downtime of machines was diminished by eliminating or speeding up shuttle bobbin rewinding, by reducing resetting when the machine sewed various thicknesses of material, and by altering the design of parts to reduce breakage. Many of these changes more fully automated sewing and therefore reduced the number of operations that workers performed. Automatic bobbin rewinders and tensioning devices, parallel seam machines, and various guides all had this effect.[38]

Refinements also extended the operations performed by sewing machines. The substantial expansion of patents for attachments to bind, braid, cord, trim, crease, ruffle, gather, hem, tuck, and fold all extended the usefulness of the sewing machine. Singer, Wheeler and Wilson, and two other large firms took out binder patents. Changes in work surfaces—needed, for example, to sew pant legs—likewise extended the utility of the machine. Finally, a few special-purpose machines were introduced to sew buttonholes, embroidery, hats, and leather.

As in the commodity definition stage, invention in the second half of the 1850s contributed to sales growth. Often refinements formed the basis for the entry of new firms, which in this stage could expand industry sales without necessarily changing product quality or price. Invention may have broadened the market by reducing machine prices. The search for inexpensive sewing machines led to the proliferation of chain-stitching patents after 1855. Single-thread chain-stitch machines were simpler and cheaper than two-thread ma-

Table 8.12
Variation in the Rate of Repeat Patenting
by Type of State

	Nodal States	Secondary States	Tertiary States
All	0.80	0.28	0.49
Used	1.61	0.60	1.38
Not Used	0.27	0.14	0.29

Sources: See Tables 8.1, 8.9.
Notes: Inventors are classified by the location of their first patent.
For nodal, secondary, and tertiary state classifications, see Table 8.5.

chines, and thus could challenge the domination of the nodal machines. The most important single-thread chain-stitch machine was the Willcox and Gibbs, but at least eight other multiple-agency firms also took out and used chain-stitching patents. New uses also extended sales, including adaptation to new materials, new attachments, and special-purpose machines. Seen from the perspective of sewing machine invention as a whole, shoe-sewing invention was but a small trail leading off the main path of advancement.

The Path of Sewing Machine Development

The sewing machine developed as a commodity, and as such was not only a means to satisfy a social need, but also, through its sale, a means of accumulation and a medium of learning. The latter two aspects structured the path of sewing machine development. The sewing machine was, for the firm producing it, a means to its profit and growth. Sale was thus a source of finance used to renew and expand the capacity to produce and market commodities. This was the aspect emphasized by Marx.

The second aspect Marx largely neglected. As a medium of learning, sales formed a circle of mutual support with invention. By spreading technical knowledge to potential users and from these users back to producers and inventors, sales created conditions for invention by both new and existing inventors. Invention in turn improved and simplified the machine and adapted it to new uses, augmenting the sales of established firms and supporting the entry of new firms. Growing sales communicated the success of firms, which improved expectations and fostered entry. From sales also came learning about how to sell, and marketing innovations then contributed to sales. Increased sales began the spiral again.

Both attributes of sales must be incorporated into an understanding of technical change. The logic of accumulation takes the qualities of the product, the need it satisfies, and the mode of marketing as given, but these elements are precisely what changes in the process of new product development. The logic of learning alters the product, identifies needs, and conceives ways of organizing the marketing process. Yet learning takes accumulation as its aim and is made real by the action of firms investing out of sales revenue.

The history of the sewing machine displays this fusion of accumulation and learning processes. Nodal firms led and structured the history. Efforts to market their products formed a network of interactions that gave form to the learning process. The principal significance of the earliest nodal firms lay in this communication; accumulation could not be sustained until innovation had better defined the commodity, its need, and its marketing. Accumulation failed, but learning continued.

Learning led to the innovations that could sustain accumulation. New nodal firms established the principles of the practical dry-thread sewing machine, defined needs the machine was to satisfy, and conceived solutions to the problems of selling to a mass market. Innovations were institutionalized. The new firms were Chandlerian; they secured rapid growth by organizing within the firm marketing systems, large-scale production facilities, and regularized procedures for invention by firm members, employees, and outside assignors.[39]

From their accumulation came more learning. Their leadership gave rise to invention by others in growing numbers and widening locations; the share of patents by nodal companies fell from half in 1851 and 1852 to a few percent in 1860 and 1861. When new firms formed to utilize new inventions, learning was once again a means to accumulate.

The growth and innovation of nodal firms gave the generation and usage of inventions a geographic structure. As sales and invention spread into new geographic areas, the sewing machine overcame its dependence on the markets and skills of a few localities. But the diffusion of sales did not spread invention or sewing machine production commensurately. Not only was patenting, in relation to sales, disproportionately centered in nodal states, but also patent use was even more concentrated. Especially among multiple inventors, patents were often used in states other than those of their first inventions; to gain usage, inventors either moved to other states or assigned patents to firms in other states. Nodal states were the principal beneficiaries; whereas through 1861, 80 percent of used sewing machine patents were issued to inventors with first patents in nodal states, 88 percent found usage in these states.

This cycle described a self-sustaining path of development. In every stage the path was conditioned by wider economic forces determining market potential, skills, and availability of labor power and finance. It drew on these forces for inventors, funds especially to finance new firms, and the usual inputs into growth. But the rapid growth and ongoing innovations of the firms themselves altered conditions that the firms faced, and these rapidly changing conditions were much more decisive determinants of sewing machine development than were the relatively slowly changing conditions in the economy at large. This dynamic of commodity development would continue to structure development in the decades that followed.

9

The Genesis of Shoe Machinery

Shoe machines developed as commodities, but through processes quite different from the path of sewing machine development. In many ways the sewing machine path formed an extreme type. Among machines, its scale of usage was unprecedented, as was its mode of marketing. Because the activity it mechanized was common to many industries and every household, it was unusually autonomous from the skills of particular trades. In scale, marketing, and breadth of application, it contrasted with cotton textile machines, locomotives, machine tools, and steam engines.

Shoe machines fell in between. Like the sewing machine, shoe machines were relatively small, light, and inexpensive. Small new firms could produce and market them. Moreover, their potential market consisted of many, modestly sized firms. Yet unlike the sewing machine, shoe machines were specific to an industry. Breaking-in problems influenced their development in a way they had not in sewing. As capital goods selling in a single industry, potential markets were far more restricted. Shoe machines were technologically more diverse than sewing machines; shoe-sewing machines were more similar to dry-thread machines than to pegging or sole-cutting machines, and operations to cut, peg, last, and finish differed significantly from one another. Hence shoe machines might have evolved in processes more varied and less interrelated than those of sewing machines.

The process developing shoe machines was different for one other reason: the existence of sewing machines. New machines typically developed in relation to old, but the kind of connections varied greatly. English cotton-spinning machinery influenced the mechanization both of weaving, and, by affecting American textile mechanization, of sewing, but to quite different degrees. The sewing machine had even more importance for the development of at least some shoe machinery than spinning machines had for weaving. Through its technology, its social form, and the firms that made it, the sewing machine led shoe mechanization. To understand how, we will begin with its closest follower.

Shoe-Sewing Machines

Shoe-sewing machines developed quickly out of early dry-thread machines. Barriers to applying the sewing machine to shoemaking were few. Dry-thread upper fitting was technically similar to cloth stitching. Communication barriers were minimized by the eastern Massachusetts location of the early nodal sewing machine companies and the shoe industry.

Still, a breaking-in problem existed. Looked at from the perspective of the economy as a whole, the sewing machine developed in a process that had a momentum internal to the emerging sewing machine industry. But looked at within that industry, the sewing machine was formed through a number of relatively distinct processes. To develop machines for glove making, hat making, and shoemaking, inventors faced technical problems learned through communication with producers in these industries and among the inventors and manufacturers of special-purpose sewing machinery. The more novel the machines and their uses, the more distinct were their paths of development.

Two aspects of the commodity path taken by sewing machines were decisive for shoe machine invention. The first was learning by selling. John Nichols designed the first successful leather-stitching machine. Nichols went to Lynn to learn shoe cutting from his cousin, a shoe manufacturer. There he bought a Singer machine, reportedly one of the first 25 made. Finding that seams formed by this machine were too loose and the stitches too coarse, he attempted to develop a practical machine. He failed at first, succeeded in adapting the machine to sew pantaloons, and turned his attention back to shoe stitching. By designing a smaller needle and a new thread, he successfully stitched light upper leathers.[1]

The second aspect was the diversification of firms. Noticing Nichols's efforts, Singer employed him to develop its leather-sewing capabilities and then to teach operatives to use the machine. But it failed to keep him. Having sold exclusive territorial rights to sell its machine in Essex County, Singer refused to equip a subcontracting shop in which Nichols could fit uppers; Nichols was a casualty of the right-holder marketing system. Nichols then took employment with Grover and Baker, whose dry-thread machine he designed.

Although located outside the shoe-producing areas, Wheeler and Wilson was not about to cede the leather-sewing machine market to its competitors. As early as 1852, the year after its machine was first sold, the *Scientific American* could report: "Mr. Wilson informs us that he is about to make one [a sewing machine] that will sew boots and shoes with a rapidity that will astonish all the sons of St. Crispin."[2]

New firms also entered. Not the least important was the company Nichols formed, at first in partnership with the one-time partner of Elias Howe, George Bliss. Frederick Robinson also applied his short-thread machine to shoemaking. But smaller firms had little success. The domination of nodal machines in dry-thread markets was to continue throughout the century; when shoe machinery had spread to many operations late in the century, Singer, still concentrating on dry-thread machines, sold more machines to shoe producers than any other company.[3]

Three attributes of the sewing machine account for the speed of its adaptation to light upper stitching. As a machine, it was easily adapted to shoemaking. As a commodity, its sale was a medium of learning that occasioned needed modifications. And as a means of accumulation, it provided revenues used by nodal firms to diversify into leather stitching. Because of this diversification, light upper-stitching machines never went through a period when nodal firms failed.

The commodity form was far superior to self-usage as a means to spread machinery between industries. Sewing machines self-used to make clothing could not readily be applied to make shoes; clothing producers knew or cared little about shoemaking, and shoemakers would have scant access to the sewing machine. Self-usage existed; Frederick Robinson opened a shoe factory in Worcester to use his machine. But his machine did not diffuse, nor was it successful in shoemaking. Firms selling sewing machines pursued all potential uses and organized to overcome breaking-in problems. It was as the product of nodal firms that the sewing machine swept through binding rooms in the 1850s.

By contrast, nodal dry-thread firms had little importance in waxed-thread sewing. Heavier upper leathers had to be sewed with waxed thread, but this thread clogged the eye-point needle of dry-thread machines. The problem and the opportunity it presented were most clearly perceived in shoemaking regions, and in 1853 a Boston machinist, William Wickersham, solved the problem by introducing a chain stitch with a barbed or hooked needle similar to that of Thimonnier over two decades earlier. Following a leather-piercing awl, the needle penetrated the leather, a looper placed a loop of thread in the needle's barb, and the needle ascended back through the leather. A hook then grasped the thread, the leather was fed forward, and the needle penetrated the material through the loop it had previously brought up. When the needle returned with a second loop, the stitch was completed. This machine not only allowed waxed thread to be sewed, it also was one of the first successful single-thread chain-stitching machines of any kind. The chain-stitch principle of the first known sewing machine, that of Thomas Saint, had finally been reapplied to the object of its invention, shoemaking.[4]

Relying on the experience of machinists, the Wickersham machine came into use quickly. The Boston machinists, Butterfield and Stevens, began selling it in 1853. In 1854 it was well enough known that one patent claimed to improve the "Wickersham waxed thread sewing machine" and two others used it as a model in patent drawings. Experience from the shoe industry also contributed. After threatened patent litigation, the rights to the machine were sold to Elmer Townsend, who brought the machine into widespread use.

Townsend was a wholesale shoe dealer, and knew well both the possibilities for a waxed-thread sewing machine and the shoe producers who might adopt it.[5]

The sale of leather-stitching machines became a learning medium that encouraged secondary invention. By 1861 at least 24 patents had been issued for machines to sew leather. Three or 4 were intended for dry-thread use, including Singer's linseed oil lubricating patent for sewing patent leather and an 1857 work support patent that marked the reemergence of Elias Howe as a sewing machine inventor.

Others improved waxed-thread machines. Several improved stitching, feed, tension, take-up, and waxing mechanisms. Two modified work support devices, including David Haskell's important patent which substituted a post arm for part of the table to allow counters to be sewed after the uppers had been closed. Three others added attachments to bind, trim welt seams, and guide parallel seam stitching. The most fundamental advance was Lyman Blake's bottom-stitching patent, but this machine had not come into use by 1861. From minor variants of dry-thread machines at the beginning of the decade, shoe-sewing machines became more complex and specialized to shoemaking as the decade progressed.

The location of patenting manifests the autonomy of shoe- from cloth-sewing machines. Shoe-sewing machines emerged around Boston and remained concentrated in the same area. Twenty-one of the 24 leather-sewing machine patents issued by 1861 were taken out by eastern Massachusetts inventors, a far higher share than the state's 23 percent of all sewing machine patents.[6]

Within Massachusetts, invention was associated with shoe production. Several inventors had been shoe manufacturers, contractors, and dealers or shoe-sewing machine producers. Invention often took place in shoe towns; Lynn had one patent, Haverhill had another, and Abington had five. The integration of the region implied that shoe machines need not be invented in shoe towns. Of the nine patents assigned to Elmer Townsend or Butterfield and Stevens, six were taken out by inventors in Boston and Lowell, which had virtually no shoe production.[7]

That early waxed-thread inventions were not controlled by nodal dry-thread firms may account for the exclusion of these firms from waxed-thread production. When waxed-thread technology was developing, nodal firms were perfecting dry-thread machines, organizing marketing networks, and fighting patent battles. The far larger potential markets for dry-thread machines combined with the many demands on modest funds to limit investment in waxed-thread machines. After about 1856, most basic waxed-thread patents had been issued and were held by Townsend, and patent control created barriers to entry. That Singer took out one of the three leather-sewing patents outside Massachusetts supports the point: it was used for dry-thread sewing.

In the other direction, waxed-thread firms saw little possibility of competing in dry-thread markets. Their attention was focused on the shoe industry, first on sewing and then on other shoe machines. A partition was formed—standard sewing machine firms in dry-thread markets and shoe machinery firms in waxed-thread markets—which would persist throughout the century.

Other Shoe Machines

Other shoe machines cannot be so easily accounted for. In contrast to the shoe-sewing machine, machines to peg, trim heels, and shape uppers, and to cut, trim, and lay soles were not adaptations of machines outside shoemaking. Their operations were specific to shoemaking (with some extension to other leather trades) and sufficiently unique that prospective inventors found few solutions elsewhere in the economy.

The technological autonomy of shoemaking operations other than sewing might suggest that shoe mechanization would be more internal to the shoe industry. Breaking-in problems would limit invention by those outside the industry. Shoemaking knowledge was needed to apply the sewing machine to shoe production, and played a bigger role for other shoe machinery. Machines might emerge from the well-established dynamic of craft production which had already introduced new shoe types, tools, and lasts. But the technological and organizational differences of craft and mechanized production posed barriers to this internal path. In particular, the technological discontinuities involved in machine design and production would have been daunting for those who made shoes or even shoe tools and lasts.

Thus, factors inside and outside the industry facilitated mechanization, yet each was intrinsically limited. The possibility arises that each could contribute to form a distinct path, one that neither simply extended the dynamic of craft shoemaking nor merely applied established mechanical technology. Shoe mechanization would then be similar to the birth of the sewing machine, which developed in relation to both the garment and machinery trades but formed its own path. One difference might influence the pace and organization of shoe mechanization: whereas the garment trades were entirely unmechanized when the sewing machine was introduced, after 1851 shoemaking was altered by leather-sewing machines and the firms that made them.

The Role of the Craft Dynamic

Mechanization was part of the broader shoe invention process, and the ties of shoe invention to the shoe industry are indicated by the occupations and locations of patentees. Like early steam engine technology and unlike sewing machines, many new shoe techniques in the first half of the century were not patented, but there is no reason to suspect that the occupations and locations of patentees differed greatly from those of other inventors. A study of city directories revealed occupations for 55 shoe inventors immediately prior to their first shoe patents. All but 1 first invented from 1852 through 1861, 22

Table 9.1
Geographic Distribution of Shoe Employment
and Patenting, 1837-1861

	Shoe Patents	Shoe Patents per Capita[a]	Shoe Employment per Capita[b]	Machinery Employment per Capita[b]
Massachusetts	164	164.8	51.8	5.2
Other New England States	40	23.1	6.1	2.2
Middle Atlantic	101	15.3	4.8	2.3
West	25	4.6	1.3	0.5
South	6	0.7	0.5	0.1
United States	336	14.5	4.5	1.2

Sources: U.S. Census Office, Seventh Census, *Abstract of the Statistics of Manufactures;* U.S. Bureau of the Census, *Historical Statistics of the United States,* ser. A 195–209; U.S. Department of Commerce, *U.S. Patent Classification–Subclass Listing;* U.S. Patent Office, *Subject-Matter Index* and *Annual Report.*

Note: For definition of regions, see Table 2.1.

[a]Total patents, 1837 through 1861, per million of 1850 population.

[b]Based on 1850 employment per thousand of 1850 population.

percent of those issued first patents in these years.[8] Twenty-three were tied to the shoe industry, including 17 shoemakers, 3 input producers, and 3 retailers. Three manufactured leather. Another 13 were machinists, 4 of whom made sewing machines. Three were professional inventors. Finally, 13 had other occupations, ranging from merchants, brass founders, iron manufacturers, and cutlers, to attorneys, architects, physicians, and members of the clergy.

In location, shoe invention paralleled shoe production. Even those not trained as shoemakers gained knowledge from proximity with shoe production. This learning was expressed in the correlation between per capita shoe patents and shoemakers per capita. Over the quarter century from 1837 through 1861, this correlation was very close. (See Table 9.1.) Massachusetts had over ten times the national average of both shoemakers and shoe patents per capita, far above any other state. Other New England states were somewhat above average in both, and Middle Atlantic states were at the average in both. By contrast, western states stood at 30 percent of the nation's average in both but were still ahead of southern states.[9]

Machinists and sewing machine patenting were concentrated in the same eastern states, but do not correlate as closely with shoe patenting. This is particularly true for Middle Atlantic states, which were average in shoe patenting but doubled the national average in both machinists and sewing machines per capita.

Patenting expanded in all types of operations, but grew especially rapidly among machines. Like most new techniques, shoe manufacturing inventions can be divided into machines, tools, forms (lasts primarily), work support

Table 9.2
Types of Shoe Patents, 1837–1861

	1837-1841		1842-1846		1847-1851		1852-1856		1857-1861	
	N	(%)	N	(%)	N	(%)	N	(%)	N	(%)
Crimping Devices	10	(43)	10	(42)	9	(25)	7	(8)	11	(7)
Tools	3	(13)	3	(12)	4	(11)	17	(18)	27	(17)
Forms	0	(0)	0	(0)	2	(6)	3	(3)	9	(6)
Designs	6	(26)	6	(25)	1	(3)	14	(15)	29	(18)
Work Support	0	(0)	0	(0)	3	(8)	7	(8)	15	(9)
Sole Machines	1	(4)	2	(8)	8	(22)	14	(15)	34	(21)
Pegging Machines	0	(0)	0	(0)	3	(8)	16	(17)	14	(9)
Stripping Machines	3	(13)	1	(4)	6	(17)	8	(9)	6	(4)
Other Machines	0	(0)	2	(8)	0	(0)	6	(7)	16	(10)
Total	23		24		36		92		161	

Sources: See Table 9.1.

devices, and new processes. Recall the definition of a machine: a mechanism in which parts are so related that in operation they transform the material in a desired way. Categorization is ambiguous in some cases, including pegging jacks, which often rotated the mounted last, and crimping devices, which used metallic jaws to grasp and shape wet upper parts. Still, the growth of machinery patents is unmistakable, as Table 9.2 indicates. Pegging machine and sole-cutting and sole-laying machine patents comprised only 7 percent of patents through 1851 but about 30 percent after. By contrast, tools maintained a constant share of patents, and crimping devices fell from about 40 to 7 percent. All in all, machines, including those to peg, strip leather, and cut and lay soles, increased from under 20 percent of patents from 1837 through 1846 to between 40 and 50 percent in each of the next three periods. In addition, the requirements of mechanized shoe production occasioned the invention of new lasts and manufacturing processes.

Craft shoemaking contributed to its own demise by providing contexts and agents supportive of mechanization. The role of the craft system is clear in the origin of sole-cutting machines. The growing scale of production and the incorporation of sole cutting in the central shop reduced barriers to introducing machines. The craft system also supplied inventive personnel. City directories reveal that six patentees of sole and related heel machines were employed in the shoe industry, three as shoemakers, one as a patternmaker, and two in sales. Moreover, seven American sole machine patentees had earlier taken out shoe patents of other types, mostly for edge-trimming and other tools.

A sole-cutting machine was invented in 1844 by Richard Richards, a Lynn last maker who had been one of the first to specialize in making lasts and to use the lasting lathe. The mechanical experience he gained facilitated sole-cutting and later peg-cutting inventions, though neither invention achieved much success.[10]

The most important sole-cutting machine, which cut strips of leather into sole blanks, was brought to practicality by David Knox. His location in Lynn enabled Knox to become familiar with advances by nearby inventors. He was likely acquainted with not only Richards's machine but also with at least some of the six shoe-cutting and shoe-trimming patents issued to residents of Lynn, Haverhill, Boston, and Stoneham before Knox's invention in 1855. From earlier machines Knox retained the arrangement of shoe blanks on a strip of sole leather and the curvature of cutting knives, but he overcame deficiencies in the design of the cutting apparatus.[11]

Pegging also developed in relation to the techniques and organization of craft shoemaking, though shoemakers were less active. Like the sewing machine, the pegging machine had a long history of failures and abandonments prior to achieving success. Two machines were designed in 1829 and another in 1835. Another machine was invented in 1833 by Amos Whittemore, a West Cambridge mechanic who had made textile machinery and optical implements; as a witness to its initial demonstration wrote, the machine performed "the work of pegging a shoe merely by turning a crank; that is, the said machine made the peg, punched the hole, put in the peg and drove the same, all apparently with one motion, with great rapidity and accuracy." In the next few years, Whittemore tried to introduce his machine in Danvers and Woburn, pegged a few hundred pairs of shoes commercially, but failed to gain much use and abandoned his efforts.[12]

Pegging inventions picked up in the late 1840s and particularly after 1852. From 1848 through 1861, 24 inventors were issued 33 pegging machine patents, all but 3 of which were taken out in 1853 or after. In addition, 18 patents were issued for pegging jacks, which held and often rotated shoes for hand pegging. Some simpler machines, called "hand pegging machines," retained craft operations. These inventions were not widely used but may have fostered the invention of more automated machines.

By 1860 a practical automatic pegging machine had been designed. It was the product of many, but the most important inventor was Benjamin Sturtevant. A shoe pegger by trade, Sturtevant received seven shoe patents from 1856 through 1861. His initial patent and one follow-up patent were taken out for lasting pincers. His first pegging machine patent in 1857 was followed by improvements in the feed mechanism in the same year.

By then he had identified the fundamental problem that his efforts would come to solve: to gain any real mechanical advantage, pegging machines had to cut and feed pegs, but existing machines were slow and often broke the pegs. Sturtevant first devised a cumbersome procedure to cut out knots and other imperfections from the peg wood, glue the wood together, and secure the wood in packages usable on machines. To avoid problems of splitting, another patent included a saw to cut pegs. But sawing wasted stock, and both sawing and splitting were limited by the length of the strip.[13]

Sturtevant's most important contributions were the continuous peg strip and a method for compressing the strip so that when driven the pegs expanded to

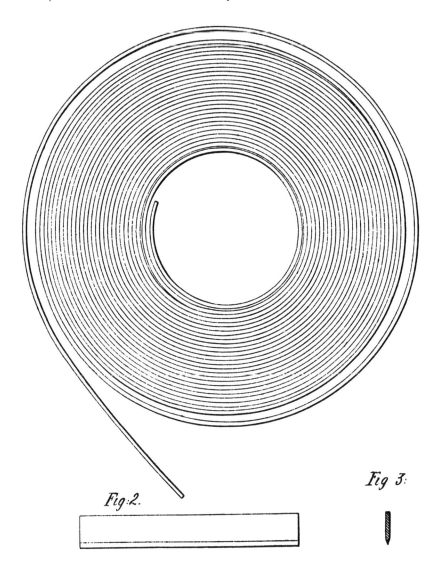

Fig 3:

Fig:2.

Figure 9.1 Sturtevant's Blank for Shoe-Pegging Machines. U.S. patent 24,149, August 16, 1859.

secure the fastening. The peg strip came in the form of a spiral the width of a peg and limited in length only by the diameter of the trees from which the pegs were made. (See Figure 9.1.) To produce the strip, Sturtevant invented a wood-veneer lathe. This machine cut a strip of wood across the grain of the log as wide as the length of the peg by rotating the log while holding a cutting edge to its outside. The machine fed the log forward the width of a strip with each rotation of the log, and cut a spiral of wood, according to the patent, 50 or 60 feet long. His invention, Sturtevant correctly claimed, "could make a blank of shoe pegs, of uniform width and thickness, with smooth surfaces, and at a less cost, both of labor and stock than by any other process."[14] The machine not only revolutionized pegging, it also became the standard machine for cutting wood veneers in making furniture.

Contributions from the Machinery Sector

Factors outside the shoe industry also helped mechanize sole cutting and pegging. Sole cutting depended less on the skills of outsiders than did pegging, but among the 11 sole machine patentees whose occupations are known, 5 were not employed in the shoe industry, including a leather producer, a machinist, a cutler, a wool factory superintendent, and a merchant.

Of all types of shoe invention, pegging depended the most on outside skills. Of the eight pegging machine inventors with known occupations, only Sturtevant was neither a machinist nor a professional inventor at the time of his first shoe machine patent, and Sturtevant was soon classified as a machinist. Three of the eight made sewing machines. The contrast with other shoe inventions is remarkable. Twenty-nine percent of pegging machine inventors are known to have been machinists or professional inventors when they began inventing shoe machines, whereas the share for other shoe inventions was less than 3 percent. Pegging machinery embodied a crossover technology, one that was the medium through which technological knowledge in some industries came to be applied to others.

Pegging was particularly tied to sewing machinery. Three pegging machine inventors were employed in manufacturing sewing machines, and each had taken out sewing machine patents prior to their pegging inventions. The only other sewing machine producer involved in shoe invention, William Butterfield, took out an upper-cutting patent which he assigned to Elmer Townsend. Two other pegging inventors had venerable places in the emergence of the sewing machine: John J. Greenough, the first American sewing machine patentee, and John Bradshaw, who received the first improvement patent on Howe's sewing machine and whose machine was one node communicating sewing machine technology.

Equally important, sewing machine firms diversified into pegging machinery. Nehemiah Hunt, of the Boston-based Hunt and Webster sewing machine company, was assigned one pegging patent, but never brought it into use. Waxed-thread sewing machine firms were more significant. Edgar Stevens, of the firm that first produced the Wickersham sewing machine, was assigned part of the hand-pegging machine patent of William Wells in 1857, himself took out an improvement patent the following year, and produced and sold machines by 1860.

The largest waxed-thread producer, Elmer Townsend, also became the biggest pegging machine manufacturer. Townsend had financed the waxed-thread patents of Alfred Swingle from 1854 through 1856 and acquired the Wickersham patent from Butterfield and Stevens when he claimed that this patent infringed on the Swingle patents. At the same time, Townsend became inter ested in other shoe machinery He was assigned a hand pegging machine patent in 1854 and three Swingle pegging machine and jack patents in 1855 and 1856. In 1856, he was assigned the first of six patents of Sturtevant, which included four pegging machines. Altogether, assignments to Townsend were included in the specifications of eight pegging machine patents and two related jack and last-holder patents. He also bought a number of other patents, including Greenough's, and employed Sturtevant, Greenough, and J. F. Sargent to perfect his pegging machine.[15] Townsend thus fostered shoe machine invention by facilitating the transfer of skills, by applying his organizational and marketing knowledge, and by shifting profits from sewing machine production.

Birth of an Internal Dynamic

Once in existence, sole-cutting, pegging, and other shoe machines evolved through cumulative processes of their own. Like the sewing machine, shoe machines took the social form of commodities, and this form not only structured their individual processes of development but also connected these processes with those of the shoe-sewing machine.

Shoe machines developed through a learning-by-selling process. This is particularly clear for pegging machines. These machines came into use in the mid-1850s. In 1856, a pegging machine patent could describe itself as an improvement on "others well known and in common use."[16] In 1860, several pegging machines were utilized. According to the manuscripts of the manufacturing census, Edgar Stevens and William Wells each sold pegging machines valued at $12,000. Townsend's sales are not known, but Sturtevant sold peg wood valued at $12,000.[17]

The sale of pegging machinery fostered the flurry of pegging inventions after 1853. Patenting centered in areas of machine use and production. The three known pegging machine firms in 1860 were located in Boston and sold most readily in eastern Massachusetts. Patenting came to concentrate in the same area. Massachusetts inventors took out only 7 of the 19 pegging machine patents through 1856, but received 11 of the 14 issued in the 1857–61 period.

Finally, inventors whose pegging inventions were used had far more repeat patents than those without use. The 7 with used pegging patents took out 8 more pegging machine and pegging jack patents and 14 more patents overall, while the 17 without used patents took out only 5 repeats. The difference in rates of repeat patenting—2.0 for those with used patents in contrast to 0.3 for others—amply attests to the importance of the learning and finance coming with use.[18]

Sole machinery also formed its own dynamic of development. Knox's sole-cutting machines came into use in the mid-1850s; Knox sold machines valued at $3,360 in 1860. Marketing by producers was supplemented by such firms as the Canton Boot and Shoe Machine Company of Boston, which sold 3 sole-cutting machines, including Knox's, and 2 heeling machines, each embodying the patent of a Massachusetts inventor. Patenting expanded with sales; from 8 sole machines patented from 1847 to 1851, the number rose to 34 from 1857 through 1861. Invention remained concentrated locationally; three-quarters of sole machine patents were issued to Massachusetts inventors in each of the periods.[19] Moreover, sole machine inventors patented sole designs, pegging jacks, and machines to peg, crimp, last, and burnish.

The commodity form also gave unity to shoe mechanization. Initial mechanization was not a single process. Prior to 1853, machines to sew, peg, cut soles, and crimp uppers had evolved in largely separate processes. The evolution of sole-cutting and pegging machines continued to differ in dependence on technical knowledge outside the shoe industry. But from about 1853, ties of marketing, the mobility of machinists and shoemakers, and the growth of firms established patterns of communication that connected processes developing different machines.

The most important connection linked shoe-sewing machines and pegging machines. The tie was less one of convergent technologies and more one of accumulation strategies of capital goods firms. Elmer Townsend played the principal role. Coming out of the shoe industry, he directed his invention not to mechanize sewing operations outside shoemaking, but rather to mechanize other shoe operations. Through his efforts, the path developing pegging machines, unlike that of dry-thread sewing machines, never went through a period of failure of nodal firms. Revenues from the rapid penetration of the waxed-thread market, used to induce sewing machine inventors to transfer their skills to pegging, brought the pegging machine to the point where it could begin to generate revenue that would in turn develop other shoe machines.

Waxed-thread sewing and pegging mechanization also influenced sole-cutting and crimping invention. Inventors moved between operations. Marketing practices and, in some cases, marketing outlets were shared. The introduction of some machines reduced barriers and directed attention to the development of other machines. These linkages, concentrated as they were in eastern Massachusetts, shed light on the simultaneity of shoe machine invention seen in Table 9.2. In this region in particular, a shoe machinery industry was emerging.

The success of mechanization influenced the dynamic of shoe invention as a whole. Not only did the share of machinery patents increase, but also the pace of growth of all shoe patents accelerated. Shoe patenting went through three phases over the half century prior to the Civil War. An average of 11 shoe patents were issued in each of the five-year periods from 1807–11 to 1822–26, with a high of 15 in the first of these periods. In the next 20 years, patenting doubled to 25 per period, peaking at 32 from 1832 through 1836.

With the beginnings of mechanization in the late 1840s, shoe patents doubled in each period. From 36 in 1847–51, patents jumped to 92 from 1852 through 1856 and to 161 over the next five years. Only after 1845 did patenting grow noticeably more rapidly than employment or output in the shoe industry.

Annual shoe patents per thousand employees quadrupled from 0.068 from 1847 through 1851 to 0.262 from 1857 through 1861. Patenting did not increase in relation to the real value of output until the 1850s.

The acceleration of inventing was in part the result of mechanization. Machines themselves formed a major portion of this expansion, having expanded from 17 percent of shoe patents in 1837–41 to from 43 to 48 percent in the three periods beginning in 1847. Mechanization also fostered tool, design, and form invention. Some last, work support, and manufacturing process patents were intended for use with machinery. Tools were sold at machine marketing outlets, which provided incentives and communication nodes for tool technology. One such outlet was the Canton Boot and Shoe Machine Company, which sold boot trees, shoe knives and shavers, edge planes, and a host of other shoe tools. Shoe machine inventors also took out other kinds of patents; besides 37 repeat patents for machinery, they were issued another 18 for tools, forms, designs, and work support. Their ongoing invention is reflected in the higher rates of repeat patenting for those who invented shoe machinery: 0.41 repeats per inventor, compared to 0.12 for those with only nonmachine patents.

The concentration of the emerging shoe machinery industry in Massachusetts accounts for the localization of machine invention in that state. As Table 9.3 indicates, the share of shoe machines patented in Massachusetts rose from 47 percent from 1847 through 1851 to 61 and 76 percent in the subsequent two five-year periods. As has been seen, leather-sewing machine production and patenting also concentrated in Massachusetts. Tool and form patenting likewise increased most rapidly in Massachusetts, suggesting their complementarity with machine patents. Other forces pulled invention elsewhere; 16 of the 19 rubber shoe patentees, for example, were located in New Jersey, New York, Pennsylvania, and Connecticut, states that produced about 80 percent of the nation's rubber goods in 1860. But this was another industry; leather shoe machine patenting was concentrating in location at just the time when sewing machine inventing was spreading out.

Ongoing Mechanization and New Sectors

The barriers to and the process of the mechanization of shoe production can be simply related: mechanization occurred when, where, in operations, and through processes for which barriers were least significant. Prior mechanization in the economy at large affected both barriers and the processes overcoming them. It formed technological knowledge that reduced the difficulty of shoe invention. It generated a sector of machinery firms, and the practices of the sector—production by some firms of a wide range of machinery, considerable mobility of machinists between firms, and ongoing invention frequently tied to new firm formation—reduced isolation barriers and formed agents who invented, improved, produced, sold, and repaired sewing and shoe machines.

Table 9.3
Number of Shoe Patents Issued to Massachusetts Inventors,
1837–1861

	1837 - 1841		1842 - 1846		1847 - 1851		1852 - 1856		1857 - 1861	
	N	(%)	N	(%)	N	(%)	N	(%)	N	(%)
Pegging Machines	0		0		1	(33)	6	(38)	11	(79)
Sole Machines	1	(100)	2	(100)	6	(75)	10	(75)	25	(74)
Other Machines	2	(67)	1	(33)	1	(17)	11	(79)	17	(77)
All Machines	3	(75)	3	(60)	8	(47)	27	(61)	53	(76)
Nonmachines[a]	7	(37)	4	(21)	4	(21)	15	(31)	43	(45)

Sources: See Table 9.1.

Note: Percentages are the ratios of Massachusetts patents for each type and period to the corresponding national total.

[a]Nonmachines include crimping devices, tools, forms, shoe manufacturing processes, and work support devices.

The initial mechanization of shoemaking was, from another vantage point, the ongoing mechanization of the economy.

But because of the isolation of machinists from shoemaking, initial shoe mechanization differed from ongoing mechanization in established sectors. It was instead a fusion of innovations from within the craft sector with the skills, inventiveness, and firms of the machinery sector. The fusion followed two paths. Breaking-in was much easier when established firms could apply their commodities with little modification, as was true of the sewing machine. When this could not occur, shoemakers and especially shoe input producers were more important innovators. The two paths came together when specialized shoe-sewing machine producers formed and spread to other shoe machinery.

The result was a distinctive technology, a group of new machinery firms, and a self-sustaining dynamic of technical change. Initial mechanization not only supplanted craft production; it also altered the process, changing production in content by increasing the share of machinery inventions, in pace by accelerating the rate of patenting, in location by geographically concentrating machinery invention, in context by integrating more with other machinery production, and in form through the birth of shoe machinery firms. Shoe machinery was acquiring a history of its own.

Shoe invention also contributed to mechanization at large. The sewing machine had developed in relation to shoemaking, though not decisively. Inventors of two of the first three sewing machines had aimed at mechanizing shoemaking, one—a Greenwich, New York, storekeeper—in order to remedy badly stitched shoes he retailed. These machines failed, but Sherburne Blodgett's role in developing Elias Howe's machine may have been influenced by his prior invention of a boot-tucking machine in 1835.

Even if the sewing machine evolved independently of shoemaking, the steam engine did not. The New York storekeeper who invented a sewing machine in 1843, George Corliss, tried to sell it to a Providence, Rhode Island, engine maker, who declined but hired Corliss to design steam engines. In another virtuous circle of failure, a central figure in American engine making found his calling.[20]

The shoe industry continued to contribute to mechanization elsewhere. Benjamin Sturtevant's peg-strip lathe became an important woodworking machine, and Sturtevant later invented highly successful air blowers and exhaust fans used in metalworking. Moreover, many shoe inventors developed sewing machines.[21]

Mechanization had come to shoemaking. It diffused most rapidly in upper sewing, where factories and mechanized binding shops were common by 1860. It also spread in the sole leather rooms of the old central shops and the new factories. Its inroads were least in bottoming. Judging from Sturtevant's peg-strip revenue, no more than 2 or 3 percent of American shoes were machine-pegged in 1860. Even less of other bottoming and heeling operations were mechanized. For shoes in 1860, like textiles at the end of the Industrial Revolution, mechanization had only begun.

10

The Evolution of Dry-Thread Sewing Machines

If the shoe industry's industrial revolution occurred in the 1850s, the revolution's consolidation took place in the remainder of the century. What was unprecedented became ordinary. Machines used in 1860 evolved, and other operations were mechanized. The novelty of new techniques became routine. The initiation of mechanization had given way to its continuation.

After the Industrial Revolution

Insights into the character of continuing shoe mechanization can be derived by considering a better-known mechanization process. The literature on the Industrial Revolution focuses principally on the contrast with what came before, but here the question is different: what followed the Industrial Revolution? A common answer, shared by Marx and Mantoux as well as Landes, Rostow, and others, is that the Industrial Revolution created a dynamic of self-sustaining technological change. Although the Industrial Revolution affected only a small part of the economy, it began a process that would transform existing machines and spread mechanization to other textile operations, to other regions, and to other industries.[1] The Industrial Revolution gave birth not only to machines but also to their ongoing development.

What makes technological change self-sustaining? Marx and Mantoux identify elements of an answer. Mantoux concludes the Industrial Revolution around 1800, when the factory had spread through whole districts, and an industrial firm, a bourgeoisie, and a proletariat had originated. From then on, technical change would be a means to further the accumulation of industrial capitalists. That firms had the financial means, the incentive, and the organizational abilities to introduce new vintages of machinery formed a powerful inducement to invent. Clearly this inducement was strongest in mechanized sectors and to a lesser extent in technically related sectors; ongoing textile mechanization faced rather different prospects than the beginnings of mechanization elsewhere.

Incentives were further improved by the growth of sales that followed mechanization. The stage of manufacturing was distinguished by the determination of market size and growth by merchant activities. By contrast, "Modern industry, driven forward by the internal force of technical progress, urges on trade and credit." Falling costs and prices were means to increase sales internationally and at home. The incentive to invent grew, and, if invention followed, the cycle began again.[2]

The Industrial Revolution also gave direction to later technical change. For Mantoux, labor and material bottlenecks occasioned such new machines as the power loom. In the case of the self-acting mule, Marx added the role of class organization as a factor directing technical change toward automation. Marx identified three ways that technological limits also directed invention. First, individual machines evolved to overcome the limits of mechanisms to work on the material and to supply and transmit power. Second, individual machines were integrated into a system, providing an impetus to mechanize operations inadequate in quality or quantity. Finally, attention was directed to other industries such as when—to make machines of needed size, durability, and precision—new machine tools were developed. More broadly, changing conditions of industry called forth new means of communication and transportation, including the railroad, steamship, and telegraph.[3]

Moreover, the Industrial Revolution developed knowledge required to overcome bottlenecks. Marx argues: "It is only after a considerable development of the science of mechanics, and an accumulation of practical experience, that the form of a machine becomes settled entirely in accordance with mechanical principles, and emancipated from the traditional form of the tool from which it has emerged."[4] The regular, incremental learning on the job supplied needed knowledge, as did the formulation and spread of the technological principles of applied science. After the inception of industrialization, science came to give "partial developments in different industries a common direction and a common speed." Experience and science were brought together in trained engineers.[5]

Marx and Mantoux say little about the institutional structure of machine generation, and this gap undercuts their ability to account for initial or continuing mechanization. Our own analysis can help to overcome this weakness. As Part II argued, the social organization of the machinists' trade—and not simply the skill of machinists—played a significant part in initiating shoe mechanization. There were, of course, few machinists before the Industrial Revolution, but the social organization of "emergency engineers" helped form not just machines but also machinists. Here was a new institution, a trade of machinists, tied to another, a machinery industry, making and selling steam engines by the end of the eighteenth century and cotton textile machinery by 1830.[6]

After the Industrial Revolution, the new institutions of the machinists' craft and the machinery industry increasingly structured the mechanization process. Through institutions of the machinery sector, individuals learned about technology, bottlenecks, markets, and finance. This knowledge was readily available in sectors already mechanized but not so elsewhere, which provides insights into why further mechanization occurred more easily within cotton textiles than woolens, and within woolens than the bulk of consumption goods.

Technological change therefore became self-sustaining in two senses. Within already mechanized sectors, ongoing mechanization comprised a cumulative process structured by the established social form of the generation and diffusion of new machines. When machines diffused as commodities, learning by selling led to further invention, and the sale of the altered products began the process anew. Macroeconomic factors increased the size of the potential market, but, because the market was still being penetrated, the virtuous circle of sales growth and invention would have occurred anyway. An internal dynamic was formed which developed new machines for related operations, as spinning did for weaving, spread machinery regionally, but did not readily develop machines outside the sector.[7]

Between sectors, technological change was self-sustaining in a weaker sense. The initial mechanization of some sectors was fostered by technological and production capabilities, structured by institutions, and conducted in part by agents that were formed by earlier industrialization processes. It was in this way that the American machinery sector had contributed to the birth of a sewing machine dynamic. Technical change was cumulative over the whole economy because mechanization in some sectors supported initial mechanization in others but did not determine when, where, how, or even whether mechanization would begin. Once started, mechanization took on its own dynamic.

Technological change in the economy as a whole consisted of a number of relatively distinct cumulative processes in different sectors. Taken together, these processes influenced the aggregate pace of accumulation, the growth of income, and the growth of actual and potential markets. Taken separately, these processes affected one another without merging, and supported the origin of new kinds of techniques which then developed within processes of their own.

The commodity path followed by initial shoe mechanization had culminated in two sets of institutions and an innovative process governing the evolution of both. Nascent shoe factories had already overcome organizational barriers that slowed or blocked the introduction of machinery a decade before. Shoe manufacturers were prepared to introduce—but not commonly to generate—new shoe machines. Shoe machines had originated as commodities, and the innovative process was itself institutionalized in established firms and among inventors associated with these firms or trying to form their own. It is to the institutions and individuals of the sewing machine and shoe machine industries that we must look to understand continuing mechanization.

The One and the Many

To argue that the forces propelling mechanization were internal to an industry is to argue that machine development was not a simple response to changes in potential demand or outside technology. But this does not identify the character of the internal process. For shoemaking, the problem was in part the social form of that process. Initial shoe machines had taken the form of commodities, and later machines would do so as well. Yet shoe manufacturers learned how to better use machinery and in cases also developed machinery that could then be sold. Self-usage and commodity usage were only in part alternatives.

The problem is also one of boundaries. There were many different machines, and the integration of their development remains a question. On the one hand, shoe machines can be considered as a group, their evolution connected through linkages of technology, of markets and marketing mechanisms, and of the diversification of firms. On the other hand, machines were autonomous, divided by technique and firm.

In initial mechanization, the leadership of upper-sewing machines and firms bridged the gap between the evolution of shoe machines individually and as a group, and the well-developed shoe machinery firms of 1860 had the capacity to make such leadership more pronounced in continuing mechanization. Later machines would not retrace the path taken by earlier machines; new machines would depend less on innovations from craft shoemaking and the broader machinery sector and more on established shoe machinery, and might develop within established firms.

Yet with the great expansion of the types and sales of shoe machines after 1860, specialization of firms might grow. From Adam Smith's notion that the division of labor is limited by the extent of the market, George Stigler infers that vertical disintegration is characteristic of growing industries. For the same reason, as output grew, the shoe machinery industry might disintegrate into subindustries with separate firms and processes of technical change.[8] Firms would then lead not by diversifying but rather by creating conditions for new firms to arise.

Initial shoe mechanization was led by dry-thread sewing machine firms, both directly and through their effect on waxed-thread firms. The dry-thread sewing machine was the most widely used shoe machine in 1860 and remained so afterward. Because it may have continued to lead, we will begin our account of continuing mechanization with the evolution of this machine. We must once again turn our attention away from shoemaking.

Market Penetration

Sewing machine sales had supported invention prior to 1860 and would continue to do so afterward. In 1860, dry-thread sewing machine firms were in the midst of a market penetration boom. The Civil War slowed expansion, but the upsurge of the late 1850s resumed after the war. From 61,900 in 1860, sales of the three nodal sewing machine companies grew to 83,400 machines in 1865, then surged to 144,000 machines in 1868, doubled to 288,400 machines in 1870, and, in spite of a decline in Grover and Baker sales, peaked at 445,900 in 1872. Other companies grew apace; from about 60,000 machines at the census of 1860, they sold about 330,000 a decade later.[9]

By 1872 the domestic market had been largely penetrated, and sales stagnated for the next quarter century. The output of sewing machine companies that was recorded by the sewing machine patent pool fell from 855,000 in 1872 to 588,000 in 1876, the last full year of the pool. Sales averaged around 500,000 annually through the mid-1890s and improved to 803,000 in 1900.[10]

The pace of the upsurge after the war cannot be understood by the pace of general economic expansion. Growth of population and per capita income expanded the potential market somewhat from 1865 through 1872, but at nothing like the pace of sales growth. Moreover, population and per capita income continued to increase when sewing machine sales stagnated.[11] Output growth in the clothing and shoe industries slowed, but by the 1870s markets for the sewing machine as a capital good were already secondary.

The factors internal to the industry that had accounted for growth in the late 1850s maintained their influence through 1872. Marketing innovations spread within and between companies. Nodal firms led the growth of installment credit. They also led the expansion of agencies. In 48 American cities with commercial directories available from the time of their first sewing machine agencies through 1880, there were 51 nodal agencies in 1862, 88 in 1866, and 127 in 1872, and agencies in nonsurveyed cities grew more rapidly.

Faced with stagnant industry sales after 1872, nodal companies intensified their marketing efforts to secure and increase their market shares. Singer was the most aggressive. It expanded its U.S. agencies to 200 in 1876, when it set a policy of forming branches in areas as small as 5,000 population. Its agencies increased to 1,500 in 1886, and, to bring its machines into closer touch with consumers, it added door-to-door canvassers. Now the norm, installment credit was extended for 85 percent of Singer sales in 1885.[12]

Others followed the lead of the nodal companies. In 1862, as Table 10.1 indicates, 11 nonnodal companies (and 3 nodal companies) had more than 1 agency listed in surveyed business directories. Nonnodal multiple-agency firms expanded quickly; they numbered 18 by 1866, stood at 38 by the boom year 1872, and increased to 51 by 1882. Whereas the largest nonnodal firms had 5 agencies in 1862, 4 had over 30 in 1872 and 3 had over 40 in 1882. For all companies, total agencies grew from an average of 238 in the Civil War years to 330 from 1866 to 1869, 621 from 1870 to 1872, and 709 from 1877 to 1880.[13]

New kinds of sewing machines contributed to sales growth. For standard manufacturing machines, already practical in 1860, refinements and the entry of new firms each added to the sales of individual firms but had little effect on

Table 10.1
Distribution of Multiple-Agency Sewing Machine Firms by
Number of Agencies, 1862, 1866, 1872, and 1882

Number of Agencies	Number of Firms			
	1862	1866	1872	1882
2–4	8	8	14	20
5–9	3	7	9	10
10–19	2	2	8	9
20–29	1	3	3	4
30–39	0	1	4	5
Over 39	0	0	3	6
Total	14	21	41	54

Sources: City and business directories for 48 U.S. cities.
Note: The number of agencies is cumulative and, because some firms went out of business, does not exactly reflect the distribution in any year. This procedure was adopted because it is difficult to determine when firms went out of business. Agencies were often listed by the name of the agent rather than the company or were not listed in one directory but were listed in earlier and later ones.

total industry sales. Lighter family machines did more to increase industry sales. In some cases, product-simplifying design changes reduced costs and prices. Compared to the period of initial mechanization, technical change was more the effect than the cause of sales growth.

Technical change also aided sales through its effect on sewing machine production. As firms grew, they expanded factory capacity to tens and even hundreds of thousands of machines. Just as Smith expected, when scale grew, labor was divided and specialized machinery introduced. And as he further anticipated, labor productivity rose. Sewing machines annually produced per worker rose from 45 in 1860 to 69 in 1870. One authority estimated that over the next decade productivity grew at least 20 percent for up-to-date establishments. Cost reductions fostered sales growth by allowing prices to fall and by providing funds for installment credit and the extension of the agency system.[14]

The growth of firm size influenced the choice of specialized machinery but did not explain why that choice was available. Like shoemaking, sewing machine production was transformed rapidly and from the outside, and, like the standard last, the transformation came as the unintended consequence of the generation of the technologically convergent machinery needed to make firearms. Beginning in the late 1850s with Wheeler and Wilson and with Willcox and Gibbs, the factory introduced updated versions of Blanchard lathes, milling machines, and standardized production devices such as jigs and fixtures. The factory also utilized major fruits of the later evolution of mass-production machinery including the turret lathe, the profiling machine, and drop forging techniques. Born through skills of the general-purpose machine shop of eastern Massachusetts and New York, the sewing machine industry now came to rely on the mass-production machinery sector of the Connecticut River valley.[15]

In contrast to shoemakers, who acquired their machinery ready-made from capital goods firms, sewing machine firms took an older, craftlike route. The major mass-production machine tools had emerged for self-usage, and they diffused by the movement of machinists who frequently became superintendents, foremen, and contractors in their new shops. In social form, such technical change resembled the birth and spread of the division of labor and craft skills. Because machinists' skills were applied to a variety of mechanisms, machinery techniques diffused between industries like craft skill improvements moved between men's and women's shoes.[16]

Once again like crafts, diffusion was fitful, particularly between regions. Companies in easy regional contact with New England firearms production were the first to adopt armory practice. Wheeler and Wilson utilized the skills of William Perry, J. D. Alvord, James Wilson, and Albert Eames, who between them had worked in such notable plants as Robbins and Lawrence, Sharps Rifle, Ames Manufacturing, Remington, and the Springfield Armory. Willcox and Gibbs acquired the same skills in a different way by contracting to have Brown and Sharpe build their machines. Practiced in precision work but not in interchangeable parts, Brown and Sharpe introduced mass-production techniques only with difficulty and the help of such Robbins and Lawrence mechanics as Frederick Howe. When Elias Howe entered sewing machine production, he could call on Alfred Hobbs, who had picked the famous Bramah lock at the 1851 Great Exhibition in London and then set up a lockmaking factory, and later Frederick Howe. The difficulty of introducing the system is seen clearly in the case of Singer, which—perhaps because of its New York and then Elizabethport, New Jersey, location—showed little interest in interchangeable parts production until around 1870 and did not successfully introduce this system for another 15 years.[17]

The sewing machine industry added new mass-production machine tools. The convergent problems of firearms and sewing machines, communicated through discussions between Frederick Howe of Providence Tool and Joseph Brown of the neighboring Brown and Sharpe, led Brown to develop the universal milling machine, a central tool room machine, and the turret lathe with a self-revolving head. The automatic turret lathe was developed to produce the bobbins of the Weed sewing machine, was quickly applied to make screws and other parts, and was later improved in the Cleveland works of the White Sewing Machine Company. Albert Eames introduced the molding press to cast Wheeler and Wilson sewing machine parts. Joseph Brown introduced grinding machines to make parts of the Willcox and Gibbs, and Joseph Billings, the superintendent of Weed and a veteran of the Remington and Colt armories, developed the board drop to improve drop forging.[18]

The sewing machine industry also helped alter the social form taken by the diffusion and development of mass-production machinery and devices. This equipment first secured large-scale sales in the mid-1850s, when George Lincoln of Hartford sold a milling machine and Brown sold his recently invented vernier caliper. Brown sold his turret lathe and universal milling machine soon after he introduced them in his own plant and followed the same pattern with the universal grinding machine and the micrometer caliper. Others, including Pratt and Whitney, joined in widely selling their machine tool inventions. Commodity purchase was not the typical way sewing machine firms acquired machinery—four-fifths of the 12,390 machines installed in Singer's Scotland plants from 1870 to 1914 were made in these plants—but particularly for Connecticut and Rhode Island firms near centers of mass-production machinery, it was increasingly common. Vertical disintegration was both a result of the growing use of mass-production machinery and a source of further usage.[19]

The processes transforming sewing machine production and the sewing machine itself were quite distinct. There was some overlap of personnel; Brown collaborated with Charles Willcox to develop an automatic tension control for the Willcox and Gibbs machine, J. D. Alvord designed a binder for the Wheeler and Wilson, and Phillip Diehl designed shuttles for the Singer and headed Singer's gauge department.[20] But the more important link came through sales: sewing machine sales provided a scale on which mass-production technology could fruitfully be applied, and the cost reductions and quality improvements coming from production innovations added to sales, and hence to learning and invention.

New Inventors

The mutual reinforcement between invention and sales changed only in scope after 1860. The knowledge communicated by sales led growing numbers to improve sewing machines. As sales expanded, so did first patents. The slow growth of the Civil War period was associated with a decline of first patents, the postwar boom with a doubling of patenting, and the stagnancy after 1872 with falling patenting (see Table 10.2). The trend of first patents was matched by that of patents per capita, and therefore was not the simple result of population growth.[21]

To examine regional differences in inventing, states are recategorized to reflect their changing importance as sewing machine centers. Because of the rise of the Willcox and Gibbs as the primary chain-stitching machine, Rhode Island is put among the nodal states. New Jersey and Illinois joined Ohio, Pennsylvania, and New Hampshire as secondary centers; all had companies with substantial sales and agencies outside their states. Given our interest in shoemaking, Massachusetts is separated from other nodal states.[22]

First patents continued to locate near agencies. The first patent share of

Table 10.2
Sewing Machine Patenting, Sales, and Agencies, 1862–1882
(annual averages)

	Patenting Period				
	1862-1867	1868-1871	1872-1874	1875-1878	1879-1882
First Patents	36.3	84.2	77.3	58.2	79.5
Repeat Patents	31.9	68.0	107.0	64.6	113.0
Total Patents	68.2	152.2	184.3	122.8	192.5
First Patents per Million Population	1.05	2.20	1.84	1.26	1.58
Nodal Firm Sales	69.7	139.7	365.0	368.1	n.a.
Total Agencies	259	330	621	631	709

Sources: See Tables 8.1, 8.2, 8.5.
Notes: Sales and agency figures assume a two-year lag, so that 1860–65 data are used for the 1862–67 patenting period. Nodal sales are in thousands of machines. Population is estimated by interpolation between decadal census years.

Massachusetts and other nodal states varied from a high of 64 percent from 1862 through 1867 to a low of 48 percent in the 1875–82 period, far above their population share (see Table 10.3). The closer match of patenting with the agency share in each period and the similar declining trend of both suggest that the learning coming from sales—and not the size of the potential national market—fostered invention in nodal states. The small but growing share of both patents and agencies in tertiary states was the other side of the same coin.

Patents remained disproportionately concentrated in nodal states, as measured by the higher-than-average first patent-agency ratios in each period (see Table 10.4). Nodal states also differed significantly among themselves. Massachusetts and Connecticut regularly had the most first patents per agency, and after 1867 only they had a patent-agency ratio significantly above average.[23] These two states were centers of the sewing machine industry, of machinists, and of using industries, and each of these factors may have added to their inventiveness.

Because of their higher ratios of interstate to intrastate agencies, Massachusetts (at least until the decline of Grover and Baker in the mid-1870s) and Connecticut benefited most from interstate learning. They were also centers of mechanical skills, and their considerably greater numbers of machinists per capita than New York might have increased their responsiveness to technological opportunities. But the independent significance of this factor is reduced by the case of Rhode Island, far and away the highest in machinists per capita but the lowest of the nodal states in first patents per agency.

Finally, Massachusetts may have faced more technical opportunities. Per capita, it had far more employees in industries using the sewing machine than any other state, as Table 10.4's User Industries Index indicates. Such industries utilized sewing machines more intensively and faced more specialized

Table 10.3
Geographic Concentration of Sewing Machine Agencies and
First Patents, 1862–1882
(annual averages, population in millions)

	1862-1867		1868-1874		1875-1882	
	N	(%)	N	(%)	N	(%)
Massachusetts						
Patents	8.3	23	13.6	17	13.0	19
Agencies	34	13	53	11	53	8
Population	1.3	4	1.5	4	1.7	4
Other Nodal States						
Patents	15.0	41	26.3	32	20.0	29
Agencies	75	29	152	32	194	29
Population	4.8	14	5.2	13	5.9	12
Secondary States						
Patents	8.5	23	23.6	29	19.0	28
Agencies	83	32	130	27	198	30
Population	8.9	26	10.2	26	11.7	24
Tertiary States						
Patents	4.5	12	17.9	22	16.9	25
Agencies	67	26	140	29	225	34
Population	19.7	57	22.8	58	29.1	60

Sources: See Tables 8.1, 8.5, 10.2.
Notes: Other Nodal States = Connecticut, New York, and Rhode Island; Secondary States = Ohio, Pennsylvania, Illinois, New Jersey, and New Hampshire; Tertiary States = all other states, territories, and the District of Columbia. Population is interpolated between census years.

needs than families, so that the resulting learning may have stimulated more invention. The shoe industry may thus have contributed to Massachusetts' distinctiveness as a center of sewing machine invention.

Repeat Inventors

Continuing mechanization occurred in part through the continued inventing of sewing machine patentees. Repeat patents formed 53 percent of the 2,832 sewing machine patents issued to American residents from 1862 through 1882. Some were taken out by pre–Civil War inventors; their 255 repeat patents after 1861 were more than their repeats through 1861. Very few of these were issued to inventors who had formed nodal companies; Grover took out 8, Singer 3, and Howe 1. Only three inventors who had assigned their pre-1862 patents to nodal firms at the time of patenting had repeat patents after 1861 (though, of course, nodal companies bought or licensed other patents). The vast majority remained independent. James Gibbs, the inventor of the most successful single-thread chain-stitch machine, is a notable example; after

Table 10.4
Influences on Sewing Machine Invention, 1862–1882

	1862 - 1867	1868 - 1874	1875 - 1882
Massachusetts			
F/A Index	1.75	1.50	2.39
Interstate Agencies	29%	40%	31%
S/P Index	4.28	3.78	3.07
M/P Index	2.81	2.88	3.20
User Industries Index	7.35	6.82	6.69
Other Nodal States			
F/A Index	1.43	1.01	1.00
Interstate Agencies	58%	43%	36%
S/P Index	5.01	5.42	3.16
M/P Index	1.66	1.69	2.26
User Industries Index	1.69	1.82	2.47
Secondary States			
F/A Index	0.73	1.06	0.93
Interstate Agencies	13%	17%	31%
S/P Index	0.51	0.57	2.03
M/P Index	1.53	1.65	1.54
User Industries Index	1.17	1.13	1.11
Tertiary States			
F/A Index	0.48	0.75	0.73
Interstate Agencies	0%	0%	3%
S/P Index	0.02	0.01	0.03
M/P Index	0.48	0.43	0.40
User Industries Index	0.32	0.38	0.32

Sources: See Tables 8.1, 8.5, 10.1; U.S. Census Office, Eighth Census, *Manufactures of the United States in 1860,* Ninth Census, *Statistics of the Wealth and Industry of the United States,* and Tenth Census, *Report on the Manufactures of the United States.*

Notes: As in Table 8.7, the F/A Index, the S/P Index, and the M/P Index—the First Patent-Agency Index, the Per Capita Sewing Machine Employment Index, and the Per Capita Machinists Index, respectively—are the ratios within each region of the first patents to agencies, sewing machine employment to population, and machinists to population, respectively, relative to the ratios for the nation as a whole. Thus, for all indices, the United States as a whole equals 1. The User Industries Index is analogous. User industries here include men's and women's clothing and shoes. For region i, the index, UI, is:

$$UI = \text{User Industries Employment per Capita}_i/\text{User Industries Employment per Capita}_{US}$$

For nodal, secondary, and tertiary state classifications, see Table 10.3. Population and employment are estimated by linear interpolation between census years.

his original patent in 1856, he took out 12 additional patents, including 5 after 1861, and his associate, Charles Willcox, was issued his first sewing machine patent in 1860 and took out 25 later.

The pattern of those beginning to invent after 1861 was similar. Nodal companies were more important for technological communication than for invention. Only 2 percent of the 1,541 new sewing machine inventors after 1861 patented for nodal firms. Virtually none of the second generation of nodal company owners or major officers were inventors. Assignments helped make up the loss. The 28 inventors who assigned patents to nodal firms at the time of patenting had a combined total of 142 patents (not all assigned to these firms). Eighteen were multiple inventors. A few of these were a new breed, professional inventors employed by or regularly selling to nodal companies, including the two House brothers, who developed Wheeler and Wilson's buttonhole attachment and were issued 24 and 16 sewing machine patents, and Phillip Diehl, who assigned several shuttle patents to Singer by 1882 and later developed an electric motor for this company.

Learning from nodal machines may have been instrumental in first patents, but repeat patenting depended more on inventors' experience with their inventions, especially through usage. Of those first involved in sewing machine invention after 1861, almost a quarter gained commodity usage for at least one patent. No doubt there was also usage in the inventor's own plant, but, because self-usage is hard to trace and use as a commodity had become the norm, we will focus only on commodity usage. Success led to more inventing; over half of those with used patents took out further patents, and these multiple inventors averaged about four patents each (see Table 10.5). By contrast, inventors who failed to gain commodity usage repeated less often and less persistently. Under a quarter took out additional patents, and they averaged but two. As a result, the number of repeats per inventor was five times as high when commodity usage was secured.[24]

Repeat patenting also varied with the kind of user. Among inventors with commodity usage, those securing use by nodal firms had a higher frequency of repeat invention and, more importantly, took out more repeats for each multiple inventor. Just 2 percent of all patentees, nodal company inventors took out 14 percent of used repeat patents.

Different in scale, postbellum invention was in other ways similar to that before the war. First patentees remained located near sewing machine agencies and companies. Both before and after 1861, about 30 percent of new inventors took out repeat patents. The 2.4 repeat patents averaged by multiple inventors in the earlier period were somewhat less than the 2.9 of later multiple inventors. For both periods the extent of repeat patenting was twice as high when patents were used as capital goods, was highest when used by nodal companies, and decreased in steps when utilized by multiple-agency and single-agency firms.

Table 10.5
Repeat Sewing Machine Invention and Patent Usage, 1862-1882

Patent Type	Used	Not Used	Total	Used by Nodal Firms
Single (S)	163	916	1,079	10
Multiple (M)	204	258	462	18
Total Patentees (S+M)	367	1,174	1,541	28
Repeat Patents (R)	821	515	1,336	114
Frequency [M/(S+M)]	0.56	0.22	0.30	0.64
Extent (R/M)	4.02	2.00	2.89	6.33
Rate [R/(S+M)]	2.24	0.44	0.87	4.07

Sources: See Table 8.1; city and business directories for 48 U.S. cities; Grace Cooper, *The Sewing Machine.*

Note: Only inventors first patenting after 1861 are included; 255 other sewing machine patents were issued from 1862 through 1882 to U.S. residents whose first patents came before 1862.

The inventive experience of multiple patentees was similar over much of the product cycle. The repeat patenting of multiple inventors beginning their inventive careers in different time periods is compared in Table 10.6. For those without commodity use, the number of repeat patents was nearly identical in each period. Inventors with used patents averaged nearly five repeats in all but the last period, when sales stagnated, patent use was harder to secure and maintain, and repeats fell. (The shorter period in which repeats could occur— from the time of patenting until 1882—was also a factor.) The difficulties of later phases of the product cycle also decreased the share gaining usage from over half from 1858 through 1867 to just over 40 percent for the remainder of the period. The fall of the share of multiple inventions used and the number of repeats by inventors who gained use both contributed to the decline in the number of repeat patents per multiple inventor from about four for those issued first patents from 1862 through 1867 to three for those of the next period and just over two for inventors beginning after 1874.

The pattern of repeat patenting was also similar in spatial distribution. Repeat patenting continued to depend on use of earlier patents and not on location independent of use. The variation among types of states in the rate of repeat patenting was due to differences in the share of inventors gaining use, which was twice as high in nodal than in tertiary states. (See Table 10.7.)

Because first patents were locationally concentrated, repeats were also. Inventors who were issued their first patents in nodal states took out over 60 percent of repeat patents, and, through patent assignments and inventor movement, nodal states controlled about 70 percent of all used repeat patents. The concentration of sewing machine firms and invention in nodal states, established in the early 1850s, was well entrenched in the 1860s and 1870s.[25]

Table 10.6
Repeat Sewing Machine Patenting by Date of First Patent

| | Patents Used | | Patents Not Used | | Share of |
	Multiple Inventors	Extent (R/M)	Multiple Inventors	Extent (R/M)	Used First Patents
1842–57	43	4.72	15	1.53	74%
1858–61	39	4.85	35	1.91	53
1862–67	50	5.62	43	2.28	54
1868–74	89	4.38	126	2.10	41
1875–80	48	2.60	61	1.79	44

Sources: See Tables 8.1, 10.5.

Refining the Standard Machine

Sewing machine invention after 1861 proceeded on a broad front. Inventive efforts refined and extended the operations of standard dry-thread machines and, more dramatically, developed specialized machines to stitch bags, gloves, books, carpets, hats, embroidery, and buttonholes. The breadth of invention is indicated in Table 10.8. Stitch-forming patents comprise stitching and feeding mechanisms. Elements include needles, hooks and shuttles, take-ups, presser foots, thread cutters, and starting and stopping mechanisms. Work-manipulating patents encompass trimmers, binders, rufflers, and other attachments, as well as mechanisms to fold, tuck, and turn the material. Products form a small category, which includes alterations in machine-sewed objects. The vast majority of patents in these four categories were designed for standard sewing machines or applied to all sewing machines. In this they were distinct from the last category, special machines.[26]

Each major category of invention was consistently well represented. The four major patent categories each had at least 15 percent of patents in each of the periods after 1861. Within categories, patenting was also widely dispersed. In each period, feeding and lockstitch shuttle mechanisms each made up at least 20 percent of stitch-forming patents. Shuttles, needles, presser foots, and take-ups each regularly formed a tenth of element patents. Attachments varied more, but rufflers and gatherers consistently made up a fifth of work-manipulating patents.

Invention overcame many bottlenecks. A bottleneck entails some objective that cannot be achieved because of a constraining operation, part, mechanism, or machine; for Mantoux, it was an increase of output that the supply of labor constrained. To overcome limits of speed, shuttle design was altered and—as part of an economy-wide change in engineering practice—cranks and eccentrics replaced slower springs and cams in drive mechanisms. Two- and three-needle parallel seam machines were introduced. To reduce downtime, bobbin winding was quickened and tension adjustments were automated. Altered

Table 10.7
Rate of Repeat Sewing Machine Patenting by
Type of State, 1842–1882

	Nodal States	Secondary States	Tertiary States
All	1.04	0.98	0.74
Used	2.36	2.68	2.37
Not Used	0.45	0.41	0.43
Share Used	31%	25%	16%

Sources: See Tables 8.1, 10.5.

take-up, shuttle, and tension mechanisms reduced thread breakage. To accurately tighten stitches, take-ups were improved. To extend applicability, the cylinder-shaped table for trouser legs and shoe uppers was developed. Attachments proliferated, both for family use and for specialized manufacturing operations. Some inventors developed a series of related attachments. The most prolific sewing machine inventor, Harry Goodrich, manufactured attachments; among his 32 patents were 13 creasers and markers, 3 rufflers, 3 braiders, 3 hemmers, and 4 other attachments.[27]

Even when widely recognized, bottlenecks need not be overcome. By 1880, inventors had taken out about 75 patents for motors to drive machines in homes and small plants. Motors were invented that wound springs like a watch, used air or water to store power, and ran off Bunsen batteries. But to no avail; none proved superior to the standard foot treadle. Sewing machine firms had to await the electric motor of the 1890s; the practical sewing machine motor thus rested upon the birth of a technology quite distinct from all of mechanical engineering. But sewing machine firms were relevant for the generation of the technology. One of the first practical electrical motors was developed in the 1880s by Phillip Diehl, a Singer inventor who also headed Singer's gauge department at Elizabethport, New Jersey. When Diehl's firm succeeded in building a motor for sewing machines, he sold out to Singer.[28]

The continuously wide range of invention does not deny that bottlenecks directed invention, but it does suggest that no single bottleneck dominated. The importance of bottlenecks is clear from patent specifications, which frequently identify limitations that the invention was designed to overcome. But invention had many objectives, there often were several solutions to the same problem, and which was adopted in turn posed different problems for later invention. Just as reciprocating shuttles and hooks both occasioned further inventions, so did the vibrating and oscillating shuttles introduced in the 1870s and 1880s. Sewing machine invention was composed of hundreds of bottleneck-invention-new bottleneck sequences, and as a result technical change was wide ranging.[29]

Table 10.8
Types of Sewing Machine Patents, 1842-1882

	Stitch Forming	Elements	Work Handling	Products	Special Machines
1842-61	58%	23%	9%	3%	8%
1862-67	39	16	24	6	15
1868-71	29	21	33	1	16
1872-74	21	21	38	1	19
1875-78	25	28	18	2	27
1879-82	23	23	21	2	30

Sources: See Table 8.1.
Note: See note 24 for a discussion of the method of classification.

Specialized Machines

Over time, the content of patenting changed. Among standard machines, stitch-forming patents fell and attachment inventions rose. But the most significant trend was the expansion of special-purpose machines. Their share of patents increased steadily from 8 percent before 1861 to 30 percent in the 1879–82 period (see Table 10.8). This increase is notable because it occurred at a time when general-purpose family machines were expanding relative to manufacturing machines.

The development of special machines brings us back to shoemaking. For the period as a whole, leather-sewing machines formed over one-third of special machine patents. Leather-sewing machines were unique among special machines. Practical before 1860, they declined as a share of all sewing machine patents and fell greatly in relation to other special machines. (See Table 10.9.) Moreover, unlike most other special machines, leather stitchers developed separately from the process of general sewing machine invention. Although by 1890 Singer sold more machines to shoe producers than any other company, dry-thread firms had little influence on waxed-thread invention, which made up the vast majority of leather-sewing patents.

New products accounted for the ascendancy of special machine patents— machines to make buttonholes, books, quilts, hats, embroidery, carpets, bags, gloves, brooms, belts, and a host of other products. An observer at an international exhibition in 1862 wrote, "it has been the aim of inventors and improvers in the sewing machine [*sic*] to do all that human fingers can accomplish with the common needle and thread."[30] This aim had been achieved when, two decades later, the *Sewing Machine Journal* wrote: "There are few conquests left for the sewing machine of the future to make in the line of variety. So various have been the uses to which our present machines have been adapted that little is left the hand needle to do."[31]

Sewing machines evolved in a number of distinct processes, as manifested

Table 10.9
Types of Special Sewing Machine Patents, 1862–1882

	1862-1867		1868-1874		1875-1882	
	N	(%)	N	(%)	N	(%)
Buttonhole	10	(16)	25	(12)	66	(18)
Button Attaching	0	(0)	1	(0)	16	(4)
Book Sewing	0	(0)	8	(4)	21	(6)
Embroidery	5	(8)	31	(15)	44	(12)
Hat	0	(0)	5	(2)	24	(7)
Leather	38	(60)	94	(46)	93	(25)
Quilt	0	(0)	16	(8)	24	(7)
Straw	0	(0)	7	(3)	25	(7)
Other	10	(16)	16	(8)	52	(14)

Sources: See Table 8.1.

in the location of patenting. Regional shares of various types of standard patents varied closely; Massachusetts had 13 or 14 percent of each major type (see Table 10.10). But Massachusetts had 29 percent of special machine patents. Moreover, special machines had varying locations. Massachusetts had leather and button-attaching concentrations, but New York and Connecticut were more important for book-, embroidery-, hat-, and straw-sewing machines.

Buttonhole machines were the most important and perhaps the most technologically innovative of the types of special machines developed after 1861. Kasmir Vogel and D. W. G. Humphrey invented the first major buttonhole machine and around 1864 organized the Union Buttonhole Company to produce it. In 1859 Vogel, a Chelsea, Massachusetts, machinery producer, designed an attachment that could stitch over the edge. Humphrey, working as Vogel's bookkeeper, recognized that a specialized buttonhole machine was needed and that to gain speed and accuracy its feed would have to be completely automatic. He patented such a machine in 1862. It formed an over-edge stitch by using a vibrating needle that alternated between penetrating the cloth and going over the edge. A looper on the underside of the machine enchained the loops left by the needle. An automatic feed was constructed by securing the cloth to a rotating worktable which moved the cloth straight for the length of the buttonhole, rotated the cloth around the point of the buttonhole, and then progressed down the other side. This machine achieved significant success, but not as the product of Union Buttonhole. Unable to develop its own machine, Singer arranged to manufacture and sell the Union machine, improved it, and finally bought Union Buttonhole in 1867.[32]

A second buttonhole machine was patented in 1862 by James and Henry House of Brooklyn and was soon purchased by Wheeler and Wilson, along with the services of the House brothers. Its principal innovation was its feed,

Table 10.10
Regional Shares of Sewing Machine Patents
by Type, 1862-1882

	Massachusetts	Other Nodal States	Nonnodal States
Stitch Forming	13%	41%	46%
Elements	14	33	53
Work Manipulating	13	32	55
Special Machines	29	44	26
Buttonhole	21	41	39
Button Attaching	47	35	18
Book	28	59	14
Embroidery	18	48	35
Hat	10	76	14
Leather	48	36	15

Sources: See Table 8.1.

which used a screw and wheel mechanism to move the entire stitching apparatus around the stationary cloth, thereby eliminating the problem of rotating bulky cloths. With this machine, an operative with two assistants to finish the ends could sew 1,000 buttonholes in a day, far above the 40 that could be made by hand. The Houses also designed an attachment for making buttonholes on family machines that Wheeler and Wilson considered to be its most important attachment. The connection to the Houses had an added benefit for Wheeler and Wilson; after taking out 9 buttonhole patents, James House was issued another 15 in the process of designing a new generation of Wheeler and Wilson machines.[33]

Buttonhole machines were developed in a process largely internal to the relation of buttonhole machine producers and users. After the sale of their machine, both Vogel and Humphrey continued to invent buttonhole machines. Humphrey designed two others, one of which came to be produced by John Lufkin. Both Union and Lufkin machines came to be used widely in shoe factories. A shoe factory buttonhole machine operative, J. J. Sullivan, contrived an attachment to automatically stop the machine when the buttonhole was completed, which allowed one operative to tend two machines. Singer and other companies bought this attachment. Finally, John Reece, an agent of a buttonhole machine firm, invented a machine in the early 1880s that formed a lockstitch; it rotated around the stationary material, finished the hole, and stopped itself automatically. Organized to sell this machine, the Reece Buttonhole Machine Company brought large numbers into use in the 1880s and 1890s.[34]

The principles of buttonhole machines were applied to other special sewing machines. The eyeletting machine sewed in much the same way. The oscillating needle mechanism was adopted in overseaming machines made by Singer and by Willcox and Gibbs to finish the edges of hosiery, knit goods, cloth, and leather. The carpet-sewing machine also used the over-edge stitch to allow stitched carpets to lie flat without straining the stitch. Singer was the key innovator; beginning with the principles of its Union machine, it developed a mechanism to feed the sewing machine across the tops of two suspended carpet pieces.[35]

Other dry-thread machines emerged. Singer made machines for the lightest gloves and the heaviest belting. Willcox and Gibbs developed a straw-hat-sewing machine. Independent inventors were also active; making use of 23 patents, including 12 book-sewing machine and 8 complementary material-feeding patents, David Smyth became an important book-sewing machine producer. Other machines used wire to stitch brooms and brushes; still others stitched around the dashes in carriages.[36]

The role of major standard dry-thread firms differentiated the evolution of special machines from the earlier development of waxed-thread machines. In both cases, the first major inventions were undertaken by inventors independent of the major firms. But for the new dry-thread machines of the 1860s and 1870s, nodal firms relatively quickly bought up patents or took out substitutes, applied their financial resources and technological skills to develop practical machines, and sold special machines through their marketing systems. Established dry-thread firms thus accelerated the development of new kinds of sewing machines.

This diversification was analogous to marketing changes; in both cases firms faced barriers to the expansion of sales that their profits, accumulated knowledge, and innovations overcame. New product development was soon institutionalized in research and development facilities. Singer organized a research department in 1868. Even smaller companies formed research staffs; an 1878 issue of the *Scientific American* stated that the relatively small Wilson Sewing Machine Company had "a corps of ingenious and competent workmen constantly employed in improving the machine and devising new means and methods of manufacture."[37]

The stagnation of domestic sales in the 1870s gave added impetus to diversification. Singer, the only major firm to increase output each year through the 1870s, had substantial profits invested in part in government bonds and railroad stocks. Its principal strategy to overcome domestic stagnation was to invest in marketing at home and especially abroad. But it also intensified its development of new sewing machines. Through this channel, the maturity of the product cycle for one kind of sewing machine fostered the birth of the product cycle for others.[38]

Still, diversification by dry-thread firms faced limits. It was confined not simply to sewing machines, but to dry-thread sewing machines. Dry-thread firms remained outside waxed-thread markets, but more strikingly they never entered the market for button-attaching machines. Like leather stitchers, button-sewing machines were used in shoe fitting rooms and had patents concen-

trated in Massachusetts; they can be understood only in relation to the quite
distinct process developing waxed thread machines.

The Novelty of Continuing Mechanization

Initial and continuing mechanization were stages in a sequence, a cumulative process of development largely internal to the industry. The commodity path followed by initial mechanization structured continuing mechanization. The learning-by-selling process would continue to tie sales to invention. Nodal firms, already integrated into marketing, would reap the fruits of the market penetration process already begun. Other firms would continue to copy their lead. Sales growth would account for one principal difference from initial mechanization: the greater scale of invention. The technological principles and limitations of the sewing machine would help grasp another: the origin of special machines. Continuing mechanization was a process of maturation of the new commodity.

Institutional evolution continued, directed in part by imperatives of the maturing product. Profits grew, market barriers were faced at a time when sales were still surging, and new markets for established commodities and new commodities were pursued. Led by Singer, firms integrated further into marketing. To develop the appeal of the commodity to the family market, they integrated backward to make stylish cabinets. Wheeler and Wilson built its own cabinets from the 1850s, but Singer did not establish its own factory until 1868.[39] The growth of the market for sewing machines led to some vertical disintegration in machine tools (though most continued to be made in-house), but for the most part Stigler's thesis that growing markets are associated with vertical disintegration was not supported. Not only did integration into marketing, credit provision, and cabinets increase, but also growing markets provided the revenues that accomplished this integration.

Neither did firms specialize by type of machine. Accumulation out of the profits from one new product sustained the development of others. Firms purchased patents, bought whole firms, and hired inventors. Even though their agency share fell somewhat and their patenting share noticeably, nodal firms still led the development of new sewing machines.

The inventive process also evolved. For some, invention became a way of life, a profession. Inventors regularly worked for or assigned their patents to particular companies. Organized channels communicated the needs of the firms with which they worked. Through assignment or licensing to many companies and through the competition of these firms, they learned about the needs of the whole industry. Inventors also related to each other. Copatenting was one form where knowledge was shared among inventors. More generally, a community of inventors was formed, tied together by employment and off-the-job contacts. How machinists invented when not employed in the sewing machine industry is in considerable part understandable in terms of sharing of information in families, neighborhoods, churches, clubs, and bars, as well as in machine shops. The success of the commodity path of mechanization depended on the institutional structuring of both sharing and self-interest.

Finally, the inventive process fractured by type of machine. Each took its own dynamic; standard machines developed separately from buttonhole machines, and even more from waxed-thread machines. Diversification integrated some into the accumulation of dry-thread firms. But not all; an account of shoe mechanization must go outside the dynamic of dry-thread firms.

11

Leather-Sewing Machines

Continuing mechanization was a varied process. At times it occurred prior to the formation of well-developed capital goods firms, such as in American firearms production in 1840 or British cotton textile manufacturing in 1800. Differences existed even within the commodity path, as the divergent paths of dry- and waxed-thread sewing machines exemplified. Like their dry-thread counterparts, waxed-thread machines grew in sales, gained in refinement, and found new applications. But unlike dry-thread machines, where new products were dominated by nodal firms and formed a small share of the revenue of these firms, new waxed-thread machines were more independent and important. The two principal new waxed-thread machines stitched bottoms, not uppers. Established waxed-thread and dry-thread firms had little role in their formation, and the companies that developed and sold them came to lead the shoe machinery industry. In contrast to the continuity of dry-thread sewing, shoe sewing broke with the dominant machines and firms of initial mechanization.

Because of their novelty and importance, this chapter focuses principally on bottom-sewing machines. Their independence makes this task easier: both major bottom-sewing machines emerged out of the dynamic of sewing machine development in the 1850s, and thereafter they exerted at least as much influence on upper waxed-thread machines as upper machines did on them. Their independence also raises a problem: was development hampered by separation from the knowledge and financing generated by the ongoing dynamic of the shoe machinery industry?

The McKay Machine

Invention

A machine is constrained by the product it is to fabricate, and in some cases invention is considerably simplified by transforming the product. One such case was the most important shoe-bottoming machine of the nineteenth century, the McKay sole-sewing machine. Its inventor, Lyman Blake, conceived a new kind of shoe bottomed by a single waxed-thread seam penetrating the

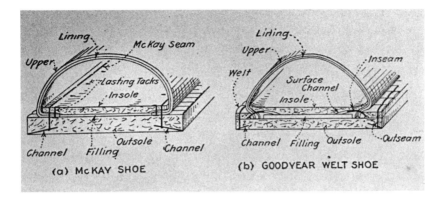

Figure 11.1 The McKay and Goodyear Welt Shoes. (Roe, *The Mechanized Equipment*, p. 463)

upper and both soles. (See Figure 11.1.) This shoe differed from pegged shoes by its mode of sole attachment, from hand-sewed welt shoes by its single seam construction, and from the lighter turn shoes and slippers because it was not sewed inside out.

The novelty of Blake's shoe lay in its distinctively technological conception, a conception that would not have arisen within a craft principle of production. The operations required to produce the Blake shoe could not readily be performed by hand. The single stitch uniting soles and upper penetrated the entire thickness of the inner sole and thus required sewing inside the shoe. This sewing was extremely difficult to complete by hand, especially around the toe; hand-sewed shoes were stitched from the outside. Blake's shoe was machine-made in principle.

Blake's shoe design determined characteristics of his machine. A machine stitch formed by a waxed thread and a barbed needle was required. The sewing apparatus had to be both inside and outside the shoe; the shoe therefore could not be sewed on the last. Rather it had to be stitched on a horn that was part of the machine. Finally, the bulkiness of the needle mechanism entailed that the looping apparatus be inside the horn.

These requirements were satisfied in Blake's 1858 patent. It stated: "The nature of my invention consists in arranging the shoe-rest on the end of an arm or projection to extend from the table or supporting-frame of the machine and enter the shoe; also, in arranging the looper as well as a thread-passage within such horn."[1] (See Figure 11.2.) The working of the machine is depicted in Figure 11.3. The shoe was mounted upside down on the horn. The barbed needle, functioning as an awl, penetrated the leather of the outer sole, inner sole, and upper. A device in the horn deposited the thread in the barb, and the needle then rose to form a chain stitch in a manner similar to that of the Wickersham machine.[2]

Figure 11.2 Blake's Patent Model. This machine had a stationary horn containing a mechanism to complete a chain stitch. (Smithsonian Photo 50361)

Blake's invention was an outcome of his experience in initial shoe mechanization. Employed by his brother in a South Abington central shop, Blake was sent to a Singer agency in East Abington to learn how to use a sewing machine. His brother then set up a shop under Blake's direction using Singer and Grover and Baker machines; Elmer Townsend's New England waxed-thread machines were soon added. An expert operator of both dry- and waxed-thread machines, Blake trained operatives and superintended the workings of the shop. Knowledge of sewing machines, particularly waxed-thread machines, helped in deriving the principles and mechanisms of his machine. His barbed needle and chain stitch were features of the Townsend machine, as Gordon McKay, who purchased the Blake patent, learned when he had to pay Townsend royalties of $25 per machine to use the Wickersham patent.[3]

Experience as a shoemaker stimulated and directed Blake's inventive efforts. At the time of his invention, Blake was a contractor and then a partner in the South Abington firm of Gurney & Mears. This employment provided a rationale for his invention which Blake identified in a patent renewal application: "We had frequent orders for sewed boots and shoes, but we could not fill

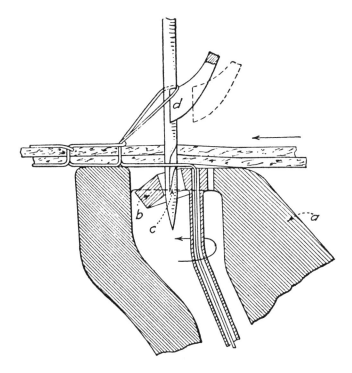

Figure 11.3 The McKay Stitching Mechanism. The looper or whorl (b) in the horn (a) placed the thread in the needle's barb (c); when the needle ascended, the hook or guard (d) held the new thread loop and enchained it within the previous loop. (Roe, *The Mechanical Equipment*, p. 477)

them because we could not get workmen skilled enough to make them, it being possible only to get a case made once in a great while by sending the work to a distance, and I saw that we might increase our trade very much if a means could be attained to make such work in sufficient quantities; and having acquired great familiarity with the use of sewing machines in uniting uppers, I was led to consider the possibility of uniting soles and uppers by sewing machines."[4] Like Mantoux's account of textiles in Britain, invention was stimulated by a bottleneck in labor supply.

Shoemaking practice also supplied the principle of uniting soles and upper with a single seam. Hand-sewed shoes were not the source; Blake said that he had never observed the hand-sewing process when he invented his machine. Here is a case where knowledge would have hindered invention; Blake later wrote that, had he known the hand-sewing process, "I now believe that my early efforts would have been directed to producing my mechanism in imitation of hand sewing, which the experience of fourteen years leads me to believe would have been futile."[5] Rather, his machine bore the same construction as the pegged shoe made in his and other South Shore shops. Pegging thus supplied a model by means of which the pegged shoe would be supplanted.[6]

As the creation of a shoemaker during the birth of the shoe machinery industry, Blake's invention took a craftlike form which limited its success. His machine was perfected by a local wheelwright and, like a craft tool, it was produced by a local foundryman. Blake intended his invention for use in his own shop. His first machine was completed in 1857 and was used for three years by Gurney & Mears and its successor. By 1859, Blake had the idea of producing and selling his machines, but was unable to do so. As he said, "I was not a machinist, had little business experience, and had no knowledge of the necessary steps to introduce my inventions into public use." Moreover, he had little enough money to support his family, much less finance the development and sale of his machine.[7] Like Elias Howe before him, Blake found that a sound invention was not enough; it would take others to realize the potential importance of his machine.

Practicality

Whereas Howe's machine had been developed by the infringing efforts of others, Blake's invention had a different fate. In 1859 he sold his patent, together with related future patents, to Gordon McKay for $70,000, of which $8,000 was paid in cash and the rest out of revenues from machine use; in the United States, both the machine and the distinctive shoe it made would be named after McKay. That this invention could be sold for such a sum attested to the importance that the sewing machine had acquired over the decade. Earlier in the 1850s, Howe had offered monopoly usage of his invention to Singer for $2,000, only to be turned down for lack of funds. Later Howe had sold a half interest in his patent for the cost of carrying on litigation against his infringers. Even in the mid-1850s, when the machine was a commercial success, the Bachelder patent was sold for only $4,000. A half decade later, McKay was willing to pay far more for a patent of much more limited applicability.[8]

The sale of Blake's patent also attested to the birth of a machinery sector. McKay was not the only one interested in the Blake invention. Boston formed a supportive environment; McKay was preceded by two earlier agreements to sell the patent for $50,000, but each foundered for financial reasons. One of these would-be purchasers was Edgar Stevens, the initial producer of the Wickersham sewing machine and a pegging machine assignee, patentee, and producer. As much as anyone of the time, Stevens understood the value of Blake's invention.[9]

Blake described McKay as "having considerable means and an extensive business acquaintance, and being a skilled machinist and engineer."[10] McKay had produced machinery for 16 years before meeting Blake. In 1858 he was the superintendent of the Lawrence Machine Works. He took out two printing press patents and, according to the Boston directory, sold printing presses from 1859 to 1862. McKay already had an interest in shoe bottoming; at almost exactly the same time Blake was issued his patent, McKay was a witness for Edgar Stevens's pegging machine patent. Through contact with J. B. Crosby, a patent solicitor who also witnessed Stevens's patent, McKay knew of Stevens's attempt to purchase the Blake patent. McKay's experience convinced him of the potential of Blake's invention and provided contacts who supplied finance and skill, including Isaac Bates, the president of the Boston Inland Mutual Insurance Company until he joined McKay.[11]

To develop the patent, McKay pooled his own talents with those of Blake and hired inventors. In 1860, Blake patented the form of sewed shoe construction inherent but unclaimed in his earlier patent. In 1862 McKay patented a minor improvement to sew around the heel. The major improvements came in a patent issued to McKay and Robert Mathies in 1862; these replaced Blake's stationary horn by a rotating horn to better sew around heel and toe, and modified the thread-drawing mechanism to let the operative sew varying thicknesses of leather without readjustment. (See Figure 11.4.) The machine was also made heavier and a feed mechanism was introduced that worked in the channel rather than on the surface of the sole. By 1862 an adequate machine was placed on the market; unlike the sewing machine, it was the result of invention within a single firm.[12]

But development did involve interaction with others through machine usage. Blake used the machine in his own firm for three years. Communication with other shoe manufacturers improved the machine. Blake developed his invention in the machine shop of the Gilmore shoe factory in Raynham. In the presence of Lynn manufacturers, including Samuel Bubier, Lyman Frazier, and William Porter, Blake tested the applicability of the machine to making women's shoes; this contact proved useful in making Lynn an early center of McKay shoes. The most important usage McKay and Blake undertook themselves; they made about 150,000 pairs of shoes for the Northern army and had another 125,000 pairs made by others. These large, homogeneous orders provided much-needed revenue, but had a further purpose that Blake well understood: "This army work was very heavy, and was undertaken with a view to test the machine, that it might be rendered as perfect as possible before it was sold to the public." Just as large army orders for firearms had helped develop mass-production machine tools, so Civil War orders aided shoe machinery.[13]

By improving machine design, self-usage prepared the way for commodity usage. It could have had this effect for several reasons. First, self-usage was undertaken by a firm organized to produce a capital good. If it were only to be self-used, McKay would not have expended the sums or hired the mechanics needed to develop the machine to practicality. Without the mechanical skill McKay assembled, use would not have translated so readily into machine

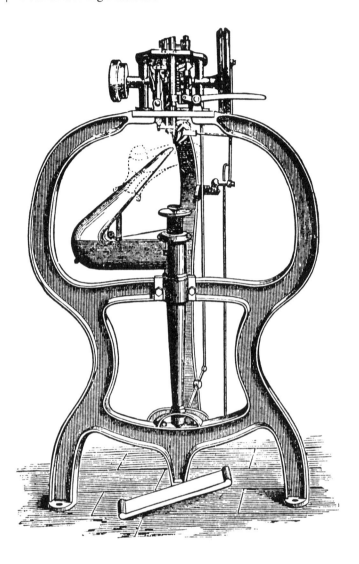

Figure 11.4 The McKay Rotating Horn Machine. (*Ure's Dictionary of Arts, Manufactures and Mines*, 4:128)

improvement—indeed, without prior improvement, army contracts might never have been secured. Second, ties to shoe producers were welcomed; there was no effort to monopolize the machine in order to maintain competitive advantages. Third, large markets provided the scale of usage needed to identify flaws of design and durability. The revenue from army sales allowed a new firm to make investments more typical of much larger firms that could call on revenues from the sale of other commodities.

Sales and Ongoing Technical Change

A gap lies between technical adequacy and commercial success even when a product addresses a significant potential market, as McKay soon observed. The problem was how to make the machine available to dispersed shoe producers, usable by companies without trained operatives and repair skills, and affordable to small firms.

Sewing machine producers had confronted the problem a decade earlier, and McKay followed their example. He defined the market to be national and international. He advertised in specialized journals, including the major trade journal, the *Shoe and Leather Reporter*, which began publishing in 1857. With some pride the *Reporter* noted that McKay took out the second full-page advertisement in the weekly's history. McKay also established a series of branch sales and servicing offices. Along with Boston and the Massachusetts shoe towns, New York and Philadelphia received early agencies. Export markets to England and the Continent were pursued from the start. The problem of usability was addressed by employing machinists to maintain and repair machinery, and experts, including Blake, to train operatives. There can be no doubt that adoption of the most advanced machine marketing system in the world fostered the diffusion of McKay's machine and the growth of his firm.[14]

Where needed, McKay modified this system. To reduce the cost and risk of fixed capital investment, McKay defined his commodity to be not the machine per se, but rather use of the machine. To a moderate set-up charge of $400 for the stitcher and auxiliary machines, he added royalty payments of three cents per pair for men's shoes, two cents for women's and boys', one cent for slippers and girls' and youths' shoes, and one-half cent for younger children's. Recognizing the complementarity of bottom sewing with other operations, McKay provided auxiliary machines such as bobbin winders and channelers at nominal cost and without additional royalty payments.[15]

Based on these innovations, the McKay machine diffused quickly. Machines were first leased where McKay and Blake had personal contacts. South Shore shoe firms (including McKay's own) used the machine to produce more than one-half of the shoes purchased by the Northern army during the Civil War. Lynn became a major center. It used 17 machines in 1862 and 62 a year later; its 150 machines in 1867 produced one-third of the McKay shoes made in the United States (see Table 11.1). The growth of machines in Lynn slowed, but many of the largest McKay producers continued to center in Lynn, some with as many as 9 machines in operation in 1877.[16]

Other shoe centers followed. Royalties of almost $100,000 in 1864 financed the extension of the agency system, which in turn fostered the rapid spread of

Table 11.1
Number of McKay Machines Used in the United States

	1862	1863	1867	1870	1871	1873	1875
Lynn	17	62	150	—	180	179	162
Haverhill	—	—	—	—	—	48	40
Massachusetts	—	—	300	—	—	526	—
New York	—	—	—	—	—	96	85
Philadelphia	—	—	—	65	—	88	102
United States	—	—	>700	—	—	—	1,154

Sources: Shoe and Leather Reporter 10 (November 21, 1867): 4; 14 (November 24, 1870): 1; 15 (May 2, 1872): 4; 17 (May 28, 1874): 1; 21 (1876): 210.

McKay stitching after the war. Haverhill became a leading center. Towns farther west adopted the machine; the eight machines used by the Bay State Shoe and Leather Company of Worcester in 1874 were the most of any firm of the time. New York and Philadelphia joined Lynn and Haverhill as premier McKay centers. Edwin Burt of New York was one of the first to apply the McKay machine to the highest quality shoes; his output of McKay shoes was eclipsed by that of two other firms which each made over one-half million pairs in 1873. Use spread to New Hampshire, Maine, and Rochester, New York. By 1871 states outside Massachusetts used most McKay machines and made 15 million of the nation's 32 million pairs of McKay shoes—about the same as their share of total shoe output.[17]

Moreover, the McKay machine spread among many sizes of shoe firms. The Lynn manuscripts of the 1870 manufacturing census list 100 firms producing shoes valued at over $5,000 in 1870. Thirty-six firms indicated that they made McKay shoes. These firms were disproportionately large; they included 9 of the 12 firms making 200,000 or more pairs of shoes annually, and 12 of the 27 firms selling from 100,000 to 200,000 pairs. McKay producers were also represented among smaller firms, forming 29 percent of firms with output between 40,000 and 100,000 and 19 percent of smaller firms. By transforming fixed capital into circulating capital costs, McKay made the machine accessible to firms that could not expect to fully utilize it.[18]

As sales expanded, the machine was further developed. McKay and Blake adapted it to sew turn shoes. Blake modified the presser foot to overcome a tendency of the shoe to rip during stitching. Steam devices were introduced to keep the wax at the proper consistency. Design changes increased the durability of parts. Altogether, from 1862 through 1901, 25 inventors took out 36 patents aimed at modifying the McKay machine, at least 5 of whom were associated with McKay. All but 2 were residents of Massachusetts. The capacity output of the McKay machine increased from 300 pairs per day in 1865 to 600 pairs in 1880 and 1,260 pairs in 1900.[19] But productivity increases in the 1880s and 1890s were not enough; the McKay machine and its characteristic product were losing ground to another machine and machine-made shoe.

The Goodyear Machine

With the Goodyear shoe, shoemaking had come full circle. The transformation of the shoe began with the birth of the pegged shoe around 1810 and continued with its ascendance through mid-century. The McKay machine brought sewing back into the bottoming shop, albeit sewing that adopted the principle of the pegged shoe. The Goodyear sewing machine returned the hand conception of bottom sewing to dominance; it challenged the McKay late in the century and exceeded McKay output by 1909.

Goodyear shoes were not identical to handmade shoes; their chain stitches and lockstitches were unknown to craft shoemakers, as were the fineness and regularity of stitches. But they had the same welt and turn shoe designs that shoemakers had made for centuries. These designs imposed difficult technical problems to mechanization, including the necessity of using a curved needle and a stitching apparatus small enough to operate inside the semicircle formed by the upturned channel lip. While in retrospect it is clear that Blake was incorrect to maintain that efforts to solve these problems were futile, it took 30 years of technical development to prove him wrong.

Goodyear machinery evolved out of a turn and welt shoe-sewing machine invented by August Destouy around 1860 and patented in 1862. This machine formed a chain stitch by means of a rotary hook and an oscillating circular needle and awl, which allowed the shoe to be sewed without penetrating to the inside. A New York mechanic, Destouy was certainly familiar with the operation of sewing machines. He assigned his patent to a New York shoe producer, James Hanan, but so many mechanical difficulties existed that Hanan attempted to sell the patent.[20]

Hanan found a purchaser in Charles Goodyear, Jr., who managed his father's vulcanization patents, produced rubber goods, and was president of the American Shoe Tip Company. His patent purchase initiated the Goodyears' second connection between shoemaking and major technological changes. Stimulated by Massachusetts wholesale shoe production, Charles Goodyear, Sr., had taken out a minor patent for gum elastic shoes in 1837. The inadequacy of these shoes fostered the experimentation that led to the discovery of vulcanization in 1839 and the production of the first pair of vulcanized rubber shoes in the same year.[21]

After buying the Destouy patent, the younger Goodyear employed Destouy and an English mechanic, Daniel Mills, to develop practical machines. Destouy took out two patents for stitching, feeding, and work support mechanisms. Mills's contributions were more important. He added a needle guard to prevent breakage of the circular needle, made the needle and awl operate independently of one another, included devices to ensure that the thread loop would be deposited in and taken out of the barb of the needle at the right time, and improved the gauges that positioned the leather for stitching. He also developed a second machine to stitch the outsole to the inner sole and welt.[22]

By 1870 Goodyear thought that success had come. He felt that his six patents formed the basis of a practical machine. He built six machines based on Mills's improvements and employed a shoemaker to use them. Aware of "the danger of introducing a new thing before being fairly tested," he and his associates "devoted themselves unremittingly to making all the improvements suggested by more than eight months [sic] practical working of the machines, since the first complete shoes were sewed in a satisfactory manner." In 1870 Goodyear issued a prospectus for the Goodyear Boot and Shoe Sewing Machine Company, a publicly held corporation to be capitalized at $1,000,000. The company was formed and numbered among its directors shoe manufacturers including Edwin Burt, an early New York McKay machine user.[23]

But success did not come so easily. Another decade was needed before the turn-sewing machine was practical and two before adequate welt and outsole machines were available. To perfect these machines Goodyear himself took out four patents, was assigned patents by six other inventors through 1887, and employed inventors and such consultants as Frederick Howe, who, as superintendent at Providence Tool and at Brown and Sharpe, was a sewing machine producer and a mass-production machinery inventor. On turn- and welt-sewing machines, the awl was eliminated but later reintroduced. For lighter leathers, the seam of entwined loops in the channel of the inner sole showed through the sole, which required that the direction of the stitching be changed so that the loops were next to the upper. To avoid ripping light or spongy soles, Christian Dancel developed a mechanism to displace the strain of the thread during tightening.[24]

The outsole stitcher was modified most importantly by introducing the lockstitch. The thickness of the chain stitch was a source of problems, as noted by Daniel Mills in an 1872 lockstitch patent: "In the channel wherein the thread is laid there is only a limited space, and the bulk of the thread is so great that, when the lip of the channel is closed down upon it, a protuberance is formed on both sides of the sole, which is inconvenient and unsightly, and causes considerable difficulty in finishing the shoe."[25] On the welt machine, the chain stitch was taken out of the channel, but for outsole machines this left the ridge of thread appearing on the top of the welt. The lockstitch, which had no ridge of thread, was the solution.

This stitch had recently been applied to upper sewing by Wardwell and Campbell around 1880 and to outsole stitching soon after. Goodyear responded to this threat by developing its own lockstitch machine which had the advantage that its curved needle could sew closer to the upper than could the straight needle of competing machines. Dancel again was the inventor.[26] By 1890, the Goodyear machines were at last adequate to make welted shoes.

These technical problems implied that revenues were low and development costs high. Goodyear had spent about $30,000 to develop the Destouy patent by 1870. By 1884 his firm had spent about $250,000. Some funds were generated from turn shoe-sewing machine revenues. Turn shoe machines sewed about 3 million pairs of shoes in 1880 and 5 million in 1883, after which output slowly increased. Funds also came from elsewhere in the industry; in 1875 Goodyear reorganized to form the Goodyear and McKay Sewing Machine Company and in so doing made use of McKay's profits and patents.[27]

Goodyear followed the McKay marketing model. The Goodyear shoe was a new product with no place in the shoe market. To counteract manufacturers' doubts about its salability, Goodyear advertised widely in newspapers and trade journals that its shoe was superior to those made by hand. To sell and service machines, Goodyear adopted the McKay agency system. By the end of the century, Goodyear had agencies in Boston, Haverhill, Brockton, and Worcester; Auburn, Maine; New York City and Rochester; Philadelphia; Burlington, New Jersey; Chicago; Cincinnati; San Francisco; St. Louis; and foreign countries.

Goodyear also introduced a McKay-type leasing system. Initially somewhat higher, fees in 1890 were four cents per pair for men's welted shoes; three cents for women's and boys'; two for stitchdowns, brogans, and girls' and youths' welted shoes; and one or one and one-half cents for turn shoes. But Goodyear did not define the fee to be a royalty on active patents, as McKay had done. Instead, fees were charged for the use of its machinery, so that, unlike McKay, Goodyear continued to lease out machines on the same terms after its basic patents had expired. Finally, it followed McKay's practice of including auxiliary machines in its leases, but sold a far wider system of bottoming machines.[28]

Belatedly, its innovations brought the success Goodyear had expected 20 years earlier. The number of leased turn- and welt-sewing machines increased from 250 in 1880 to 800 in 1888, 1,500 in 1890, 2,500 in 1895, and 3,000 in 1897. Usage grew apace, principally among welt shoe producers. From about 3 million pairs in 1880, 12 million were bottomed in 1890, 25 million in 1895, and 50 million in 1899.[29] In another 10 years, the Goodyear would become the most widely sold shoe.

The McKay and Goodyear machines transformed the inventive environment. Over the half century from 1860 they grew to bottom 90 percent of American shoes. Learning from the use of these machines led to further bottom-sewing invention, and also influenced waxed-thread sewing invention more broadly. Bottom-sewing machines thus joined upper leather-sewing machines in sustaining ongoing waxed-thread invention.

Table 11.2
Leather-Sewing Machine Patenting, 1862–1901
(annual averages)

Patenting Period	Patents			Bottom-Sewing Machines[a]	Shoe Workers	Shoe Output
	First	Repeat	Total			
1862–66	3.8	2.6	6.4	47%	128.2	32
1867–71	5.4	5.0	10.4	62	134.6	59
1872–76	6.2	6.8	13.0	40	135.1	82
1877–81	6.0	6.2	12.2	44	134.0	98
1882–86	6.0	6.0	12.0	33	140.4	137
1887–91	7.4	11.0	18.4	56	148.7	162
1892–96	9.8	17.6	27.4	58	151.2	179
1897–1901	7.6	15.0	22.6	59	152.2	200

Sources: See Table 8.1; U.S. Census Office, Eighth Census, *Manufactures of the United States in 1860;* Ninth Census, *Statistics of the Wealth and Industry of the United States;* Tenth Census, *Report on the Manufactures of the United States;* Eleventh Census, *Report of the Manufacturing Industries in the United States at the Eleventh Census,* pt. I; and *Twelfth Census: Manufactures.* Shoe output measures are taken from the appendix to this chapter.

Notes: Shoe employment, measured in thousands of workers, includes factories and custom and repair, and excludes proprietors in all periods. Employment is interpolated between census years. Shoe output, measured in millions of pairs, leads the patenting period by two years; thus, for the 1862–66 patenting period, output from 1860 through 1864 is considered.

[a]As a share of total leather-sewing machine patents.

Waxed-Thread Invention as a Whole

Ongoing invention was by its nature more anonymous than initial mechanization. It refined what others created. To the few major leather-sewing inventions of Blake, McKay, Destouy, Mills, and Dancel were added hundreds of improvements. From 1862 through 1901, 612 leather-sewing machine patents were issued to American residents (see Table 11.2). The 6 patents per year from 1862 through 1866 were about four times as many as in the years of the birth of the waxed-thread machine but were exceeded by the inventions of the 1890s in the same proportion.[30]

Like the sewing machine more generally, leather-sewing machines evolved through learning processes centered around commercially successful machines. Learning and invention grew with the expansion of leather-sewing machine sales. The correlation of patenting with use is harder to document than for dry-thread machines because leather-sewing machine firms were rarely listed in commercial directories and reliable company sales data are only irregularly available. Indications come from shoe employment and output, which set upper limits to shoe-sewing machine usage. First patenting grew along with both, more rapidly than employment, more slowly than pairs of shoes. The 1890s indicate the autonomy of patenting from output levels; shoe sales grew slowly, but patenting was brisk, reflecting the great expansion of the Goodyear shoe.

Moreover, differences in the timing of upper- and bottom-sewing machine diffusion were tied to their varying paces of patenting. Upper machines were invented and diffused first, and formed four-fifths of leather-sewing machine patents through 1861. The share of bottom-sewing machine inventions was highest during the two periods in which the expansion of bottoming machines was concentrated: from 1864 through 1870, when McKay shoes expanded from 5 to 25 million, and the 1890s, when the Goodyear shoes grew in number from 12 to over 50 million.[31]

Inventors were those best situated to learn. The learning nexus that had formed around leather-sewing machines connected occupations of machinist and shoemaker, and, as a survey of city directories reveals, these were the principal occupations of first patentees. Of the 85 inventors from 1862 through 1901 for whom occupations could be identified prior to their first patents, 50 were professional machinists, engineers, or inventors, including 19 who made sewing machines. An additional 24 were shoemakers, at least 9 of whom were manufacturers or foremen. Others included leather producers, ironworkers, carpenters, and merchants.[32]

Invention also centered near mechanized shoe production. Massachusetts led the way. Over the period as a whole, it had 56 percent of all first leather-sewing machine patents, whereas other New England states had 9 percent, Middle Atlantic states 22 percent, and western and southern states 13 percent (see Table 11.3). Shoe production (as measured by shoe employees or by output in value or pairs) was similarly distributed among regions. As evidenced by the wide geographic diffusion of the McKay machine by 1870, leather-sewing machine usage paralleled shoe output; leather-sewing machine patenting and usage were hence closely correlated by region. When seen on a per capita basis, the geographic concentration of patenting is striking. Massachusetts had an annual average of 1.53 first patents per million population in 1867–71, its least productive period, and 2.52 in its most productive period, 1892–96. By contrast, western and southern states varied from 0.01 annually per million in 1862–66 to a high of 0.03 in 1897–1901.

Although regions varied in the scale of invention, they were remarkably similar in the occupational composition of first inventors. Among Massachusetts' 43 first shoe patentees with known occupations, 58 percent were machinists and professional inventors, almost exactly equal to the national average. Another 33 percent were shoe producers, only 5 percent above the nation as a whole. The same is not true within regions. Among shoe patentees with known occupations, Massachusetts shoe towns (Lynn, Haverhill, Worcester, and Brockton) had 7 machinists and inventors and 12 shoe producers, whereas other towns (Boston, Lawrence, and Fitchburg) had 18 machinists and inven-

Table 11.3
Shares of First Leather-Sewing Machine Patents and Shoe Employment,
1862-1901

	Massachusetts		Other New England States		Middle Atlantic		West and South	
	Pat-ents	Employ-ment	Pat-ents	Employ-ment	Pat-ents	Employ-ment-	Pat-ents	Employ-ment
1862-66	63%	46%	0%	9%	32%	28%	5%	17%
1867-71	41	41	11	7	33	29	15	22
1872-76	39	43	13	7	38	28	10	21
1877-81	50	46	20	8	17	27	13	19
1882-86	57	46	3	9	23	26	17	19
1887-91	68	46	16	10	5	25	11	19
1892-96	63	43	8	12	16	24	12	22
1897-1901	53	40	3	13	21	23	24	25

Sources: See Tables 8.1, 11.2.

Notes: On shoe employment, see Table 11.2. Other New England states = Connecticut, Rhode Island, New Hampshire, Vermont, and Maine; Middle Atlantic = New York, New Jersey, Pennsylvania, Delaware, Maryland, and the District of Columbia; the West and South = the remaining states and territories.

tors and only 2 shoe producers. But the structure of capital goods sale integrated towns using shoe machines, towns producing machines (Lawrence), and towns where machinery firms located (Boston). The contact between machinists and shoemakers fostered invention by both, and this contact occurred most readily within regions.

Similar to dry-thread invention, first patenting was more concentrated in the machine-producing states than was usage. Interstate learning by national leather-sewing machine firms may account for this concentration. McKay and the biggest waxed-thread producers had offices, research staffs, and usually factories in Massachusetts. Goodyear began as a New York firm, but, on forming Goodyear and McKay, transferred some operations to Massachusetts in the 1870s. That Middle Atlantic states changed from having a larger patent share than output share to the reverse may be explained by Goodyear's move.[33]

Learning by selling fostered repeat patenting. From 1853 through 1901, 321 American residents took out leather-sewing machine patents, and 112 took out more than one (see Table 11.4). Even when patents are not known to have been used as capital goods, learning spurred further invention; 17 percent of such inventors were issued repeats. The communication coming with commodity usage led to more frequent repeat invention—by 57 percent of those with used first patents—and more inventions for each repeater—four repeats compared to less than two for multiple inventors without used first patents.[34]

Table 11.4
Repeat Leather-Sewing Machine Patenting and Use, 1853-1901

Type of Patent	Used	Not Used	All
Single (S)	61	148	209
Multiple (M)	82	30	112
Total Patentees (S+M)	143	178	321
Repeats (R)	329	53	382
Frequency [M/(S+M)]	0.57	0.17	0.35
Extent (R/M)	4.01	1.77	3.41
Rate [R/(S+M)]	2.30	0.30	1.19

Sources: See Tables 8.1, 10.5.

An apparent anomaly arises when sequenced patenting is considered. Like dry-thread patentees, inventors gaining commodity usage within one year were more likely to take out sequenced repeat patents than those without usage, but, unlike the earlier case, the number of repeats issued to multiple inventors varied little with use. (See Table 11.5.) The similar extent of repeat inventing resulted from the fact that many commercially successful inventors did not secure usage at the beginning of their careers. When usage is considered within five years of the first patent, multiple inventors with usage within this period had 3.7 sequenced repeats, compared to 2.6 for other inventors.

As was true of dry-thread machines, repeat patenting varied little by region. Except for the West and the South, the rate of repeat inventing was similar among regions for inventors with used patents, for those without, and for all inventors, as Table 11.6 indicates. In each region, use of some inventions and the pursuit of others were connected activities.

Path or Paths?

To understand the process of waxed-thread inventing, a by now familiar question must be confronted: did the various waxed-thread machines develop in autonomous paths, separated from one another and from machinery more widely? The development of waxed-thread machines took autonomy from their diverse technical requirements and from the specialization of firms developing them. But development was integrated by shared technological principles, the actions of inventors and machinery firms, and connected markets for products and labor. Machines were more closely connected in their evolution when and where these shared factors were stronger.

The Relation to Dry-Thread Machines

Waxed- and dry-thread sewing machines maintained the relative autonomy that their development had taken in the 1850s. Their sales and ongoing inven-

Table 11.5
Sequenced Repeat Leather-Sewing Machine Patenting, 1853–1896

	Within One Year		Within Five Years	
	Used	Not Used	Used	Not Used
No Sequenced Repeats (N)	70	138	86	144
With Sequenced Repeats (Y)	35	38	35	16
Total Patentees (N+Y)	105	176	121	160
Sequenced Repeat Patents (R)	134	134	128	42
Frequency [Y/(N+Y)]	0.33	0.22	0.29	0.10
Extent (R/Y)	3.83	3.53	3.66	2.62
Rate [R/(N+Y)]	1.28	0.76	1.06	0.26

Sources: See Tables 8.1, 10.5.

Note: When considering patent use within one (five) year(s) after the first patent, sequenced repeat patents are those repeats issued two (six) or more years after the first patent. On the measures of sequenced repeat patenting, see the notes to Table 8.10.

tion were organized around different nodes of communication associated with the organization of separate dominant firms. Because the location of markets and firms varied, learning and invention did also. As Table 11.7 shows, from 1862 through 1881, Massachusetts had a far larger share of waxed-thread than dry-thread patents. Other New England states had distinct concentrations of dry-thread and waxed-thread firms, the former in Connecticut and the latter in Rhode Island, and types of sewing machine patents varied accordingly. The remainder of the country had relatively larger shares of dry-thread usage, production, and invention.

Still, there were important ties between dry- and waxed-thread development. Crossover inventors—those with both kinds of patents—were common; through 1882, 46 American residents, about one-third of waxed-thread patentees, fell into this category.[35] Four-fifths lived in nodal dry-thread states. Massachusetts led with 18, but these were only 25 percent of its waxed-thread inventors. By contrast, crossover inventors formed 39 percent of the waxed-thread patentees in New York and 73 percent in Rhode Island and Connecticut. The connection of dry-thread and waxed-thread inventors was strongest where shoe production was weakest; in Massachusetts, the direct tie of waxed-thread firms to shoemaking provided a different avenue for invention.

Crossover inventors formed an unusually successful and innovative group. Two-thirds gained usage as capital goods, roughly double the share of other waxed-thread patentees. Almost one-half of all crossover inventors took out more than one waxed-thread patent (in addition to their other patents), well above the one-third for other waxed-thread patentees, and crossover multiple inventors took out more repeat patents over the rest of the century, about 4.1 compared to 3.2 for other inventors.

Their inventions were pivotal. Crossover patentees included such central upper-sewing machine inventors as William Wickersham, Edwin Bean, whose

Table 11.6
Repeat Leather-Sewing Machine Patenting by Region

	Massachusetts	Other New England States	Middle Atlantic	West and South
Used Patents				
Single (S)	37	8	11	5
Multiple (M)	51	11	16	4
Total Patentees (S+M)	88	19	27	9
Repeats (R)	211	44	65	9
Frequency [M/(S+M)]	0.58	0.58	0.59	0.44
Extent (R/M)	4.14	4.00	4.06	2.25
Rate [R/(S+M)]	2.40	2.32	2.41	1.00
Unused Patents				
Single (S)	73	13	34	28
Multiple (M)	18	1	9	2
Total Patentees (S+M)	91	14	43	30
Repeats (R)	26	3	22	2
Frequency [M/(S+M)]	0.20	0.07	0.21	0.07
Extent (R/M)	1.44	3.00	2.44	1.00
Rate [R/(S+M)]	0.29	0.21	0.51	0.07
Share Used	0.49	0.58	0.39	0.23

Sources: See Tables 8.1, 10.5.

Notes: Inventors are categorized by the location of their first patents. For definition of measures, see Table 11.4; for regional classifications, see Table 11.3.

Consolidated Wax Thread Sewing Machine Company was the Townsend interest's biggest competitor in the 1870s, and Simon Wardwell, the first to design a practical waxed-thread lockstitch machine. Their significance for bottom sewing was also clear; their numbers included Lyman Blake, Everett Richardson, who helped perfect the McKay machine, and Daniel Mills.

The prior experience of crossover inventors helped develop both dry-thread and waxed-thread sewing machines. Knowledge of dry-thread machines surely aided many, including Wickersham and Blake. But the influence also ran the other way. Twenty-five of the 46 crossover inventors first patented waxed-thread machines. Surprisingly, this was especially true of early waxed-thread inventing. Five of the 6 crossover inventors through 1861 first invented waxed-thread machines, as did 13 of the 20 in the next decade. Thirteen of Massachusetts' 18 crossover inventors began in this manner, suggesting that the tie of waxed-thread invention to shoemaking was more important in that state.[36]

Among crossover inventors of major importance for waxed-thread machine design, all but one took out waxed-thread patents before moving to dry-thread invention. They were, of course, aware of dry-thread machines, but all except

Table 11.7

Regional Distribution of Sewing Machine Patents by Type, 1862–1881

	Total Number	Regional Shares within Types			
		Massachusetts	Other New England States	Middle Atlantic	West and South
Dry Thread	2,321	15%	12%	44%	29%
Waxed Thread	210	49	12	30	8
Bottoming	100	48	6	41	5
Other	110	50	18	21	11

Sources: See Table 8.1.

Note: For regional classifications, see Table 11.3.

Wickersham were familiar with waxed-thread machines and probably found waxed-thread design more immediately relevant for leather-sewing invention. The only major crossover inventor to begin with dry-thread inventions, Simon Wardwell, surely found his long experience with lockstitch mechanisms helpful in adapting this stitch to waxed-thread use. But even in this innovation the waxed-thread machine played a key role. Wardwell was hired to perfect an inadequate lockstitch waxed-thread machine, and his machine only applied to a narrow range of shoes. Duncan Campbell, who had been in charge of machinery construction for Townsend, overcame this limit in the early 1880s, and Christian Dancel, already employed by Goodyear for a decade, applied the stitch to outsole sewing.[37]

Ties between leather-sewing and other sewing invention were closer for machines with related technology or markets. Dry-thread invention was more important for upper leather machines than for sole stitching. Only 30 percent of the crossover inventors concentrated on sole sewing, and all but 5 of these 14 first invented leather-sewing machines. Sole-sewing inventors took out different kinds of crossover patents. They concentrated not on stitch forming and parts, but on attachments, altered products, and special machines. Three of them patented attachments to ruffle, braid, and guide strips. Two took out designs for shoes and leather products, including Blake; Blake also patented a boot-making pattern. Five others were issued patents for machines to sew buttonholes, straw braid, hats, and embroidery.

Integration through the operation of dry-thread firms was less direct. They no doubt spread knowledge relevant for waxed-thread invention. Some tried to develop their own waxed-thread machines, but without success; Singer is reported to have invested thousands to make a lockstitch waxed-thread machine.[38] Employees of dry-thread companies were more successful. To take an important example, James Morley, the principal inventor of the button-sewing machine, was the Holyoke, Massachusetts, agent for the Florence Sewing Machine Company around 1880, when he took out his button-sewing patents. He adapted some dry-thread mechanisms; the adjusting screw that regulated the length of stitches solved the problem of feeding the upper between buttons.

He also relied on techniques formed in the waxed-thread sector. To feed buttons to the stitcher, he adapted the automatic eyelet-feeding mechanism that had been developed in the early 1860s by a series of inventors including Joseph Sargent, a Townsend inventor who had designed sewing and pegging machines. Morley's machine was developed by others connected to shoemaking. Joseph Mathison, the foreman of a stitching room where the Morley machine had been tested, developed a machine that could sew on buttons after the upper had been closed.[39]

The influence of the dry-thread machine on waxed-thread invention dwindled over time. As waxed-thread inventors focused on specialized technical problems, the share of crossover inventors among new waxed-thread patentees fell steadily from 46 percent through 1861 to 21 percent from 1877 through 1881. The new machine tools used by dry-thread companies were quickly adopted by waxed-thread firms but had little to do with waxed-thread design. Waxed-thread invention depended increasingly on a dynamic within the leather-sewing machine sector.

Among Waxed-Thread Machines

Waxed-thread upper machines, McKay machines, and Goodyear machines shared many technological principles, influenced each others' development, and yet evolved along separate paths. Differences in technology and markets surely mattered, but how they mattered depended on the social organization and sequencing of waxed-thread evolution.

The division between types of machines is exhibited by the categorization of patents. Invention spanned the mechanisms of waxed-thread sewing. Stitch-forming patents were most numerous and were regularly complemented by inventions to wax and handle thread, to support the work, and to feed and guide the material (see Table 11.8). The persistent breadth of invention expresses the complementarity of sewing machine mechanisms.

But there were clear trends in the direction of patenting, the most important of which manifested the sequencing of new machine types. The introduction of lockstitch upper machines was associated with a marked rise in the share of lockstitch patents in the 1870s and 1880s. More fundamental were sole-sewing machines. From 18 percent prior to 1862, sole-sewing patents surged to 44 percent in the next decade when the McKay machine was introduced, stabilized at about 30 percent in the next two decades, and again rose to 44 percent when the Goodyear machines were spreading in the 1890s. The growth of bottom-sewing machines was also associated with a doubling of the share of channeling and welt-handling mechanisms and guides.

The inventive processes of waxed-thread machines were more integrated with one another than they were with dry-thread development. In location, bottom-sewing machines were far more similar to other leather-sewing machines than either were to dry-thread machines, as Table 11.7 indicates for the

Table 11.8

Leather-Sewing Machine Patents by Type, 1853–1901

	Share within Periods						Number
	1853- 1861	1862- 1871	1872- 1881	1882- 1891	1892- 1901	1853- 1901	1853- 1901
Chain Stitch	38%	11%	10%	5%	1%	6%	37
Lockstitch	12	4	13	15	2	8	50
Sole Sewing:							
Chain Stitch	12	36	25	12	17	20	125
Lockstitch	0	1	5	6	12	7	46
Other	6	7	2	12	15	10	65
Heat and Wax	6	7	6	10	10	8	53
Thread Handling	6	4	6	10	15	10	65
Channeling and							
Welt Guides	6	8	9	11	15	12	73
Work Support	6	7	9	10	3	7	41
Other	6	15	17	8	10	12	73

Sources: See Table 8.1.

1862–81 period. Massachusetts was striking in this regard; it had 48 percent of bottoming patents, 50 percent of other sewing machine patents, but only 15 percent of dry-thread patents.[40]

The locational similarity of bottom- and other leather-sewing patents was not accidental; the same individuals often invented both. Fifty-two of the 112 waxed-thread multiple inventors throughout the 1853–1901 period took out both types of patents, so that 30 percent of inventors with bottom-sewing patents also had other leather-sewing patents, and 26 percent with nonbottoming patents held bottom-sewing patents.

Convergent technologies were recognized and utilized. Use of a waxed thread entailed common technological principles and problems involved in stitch forming, thread handling, and wax heating and applying. Solutions for one type of machine were applied, perhaps with modification, to others. Newer machines were at first the beneficiaries, but they then contributed to the evolution of earlier machines. The locational congruence among waxed-thread machines facilitated this spread.

The introduction of the lockstitch nicely illustrates this diffusion. The lockstitch was long recognized as superior because it left no thread ridge, but, due to the difficulty of tightening stitches without ripping the material or breaking the thread or needle, it had not been used. In the late 1870s many inventors designed upper machines that addressed this difficulty, and the number of upper lockstitch patents rose from 4 in the 1872–76 period to 12 over the next five years and continued at this level for another decade.

Wardwell's solution and Campbell's improvements not only brought success to their companies, they also led to attempts to introduce the lockstitch into bottom sewing. Lockstitch sole-sewing patents rose from 1 in 1882–86 to 8, 17, and 13 in the next three periods. Although only 3 of these patents were issued to inventors with earlier upper lockstitch patents, inventors were aware of upper lockstitch machines, and half of them had taken out previous leather-sewing machine patents. Goodyear had a special incentive to invent. In the early 1880s, shoe firms began to introduce the Campbell machine for outsole stitching, and, seeing the opportunity, Campbell began to develop a welt-sewing machine. To offset this threat, Goodyear set Dancel to work to adapt the lockstitch upper machine to outsole stitching; the successful curved needle machine was the result.[41]

Still, the activities developing each kind of machine were more integrated among themselves than they were with activities improving other machines. Major waxed-thread machines were brought to practicality by different firms. These firms acquired or took out the basic patents, and further technical development was largely a cumulative process using the firm's own resources and knowledge. Once established, their domination was maintained by continued product refinement; for this reason, Goodyear was assigned patents by 14 inventors from 1892 through 1901. Around each firm grew a group of inventors who assigned or licensed patents to it. Competitors also appeared, at times forcing mergers, such as the merger, when Consolidated Wax Thread gained control of the Haskell post patent, of Consolidated with Townsend's successor to form the National Sewing Machine Company. But major firms and their surrounding inventors and competitors formed nexuses that seldom overlapped.

That separate firms developed the major machines partitioned the inventive process. Diversification did not overcome this separateness because of technological and patent barriers to entry and the pull of other investment opportunities. Just as Singer needed revenues for its dry-thread growth and made no effort to enter waxed-thread production, so also Townsend was drawn toward pegging and other shoe machines at a time when McKay was designing its machine. Likewise, Gordon McKay did not merge McKay Sewing Machine with Goodyear and McKay and sold his Goodyear interests when other shoe machines appeared more lucrative.

The separation of firms by type of machine persisted even after basic patents expired. New firms arose; Andrew Eppler challenged Goodyear, and with greater success Campbell and Frank Merrick took on National Sewing Machine. But these new firms each came out of earlier firms making the same kind of machine. Eppler had copatented Goodyear improvements along with Dancel, had superintended Goodyear's mechanical department, and had also made shoe machinery in two other concerns. Merrick had headed production for National and had also worked for Goodyear. Training within the major firms made entry easier by providing detailed technical knowledge and opening communication channels with inventors, with machinery producers, and with shoe manufacturers who might buy machines or shares in the company.

Only Campbell made a sustained attempt to make both upper and sole machines.[42]

The autonomy of the inventive processes of different machines was manifested in the kinds of patents issued to repeat patentees. About four-fifths of inventors with used patents were associated with a single company, mostly by patent assignment. Because firms typically specialized in a single kind of machine, so did inventors connected to them. Of the other fifth, only a quarter had patents used by firms that together made more than one kind of machine. Inventors often specialized even more narrowly. For example, after 1886 two-thirds of the sole lockstitch patents were taken out by inventors who already had patents of this type. Ties to Goodyear structured this inventive process; 6 of the 10 inventors to take out more than one sole lockstitch patent had assigned patents to Goodyear prior to 1890, and 2 others were well-established welt shoe inventors.

The location of invention expressed the separateness of inventive processes. From 1862 through 1881 New England states other than Massachusetts had only 6 percent of bottoming patents but 18 percent of other sewing machine patents. By contrast, the Middle Atlantic region's 41 percent share of bottom-sewing machines was twice its share of other leather-sewing patents (see Table 11.7). These concentrations were associated with the location of Wardwell and Campbell in Rhode Island and Goodyear in New York. Wardwell and Campbell together took out 8 of the 20 nonbottoming patents in the New England region, and Goodyear used 14 of the 41 bottom-sewing patents in the Middle Atlantic region.

Regional shares changed over the next 20 years. When Goodyear moved out of New York, the Middle Atlantic region's concentration of bottom-sewing machines dissipated. Whereas all of the patents Goodyear used through 1881 were taken out within the Middle Atlantic region, Massachusetts inventors took out two-thirds after 1881. New England outside Massachusetts continued to center on upper machines, led by Campbell and Wardwell. But the movement of the Campbell Machine Company and the Lincoln Sewing Machine Company into welt machines narrowed the gap between bottom and upper patents. Finally, Massachusetts maintained its share of upper machines but surged from half of bottom-sewing patents before 1881 to 70 percent after.

The growing concentration of patenting in Massachusetts—notable because its share of shoe output was decreasing—derived from the growth of welt-sewing machines. The rise of the Goodyear system engendered a growth of patents for welt or turn machines and outsole stitchers from 14 percent of all leather-sewing machine patents in the 1862–71 period to 23 percent in 1892–1901 (see Table 11.9).[43] From 43 percent of welt and turn patents from 1862 through 1881, Massachusetts' share rose to 72 percent for the next 20 years. Goodyear accounted for little of this expansion directly; it was assigned only 7 welt- and turn-sewing patents from Massachusetts inventors. But its success

Table 11.9
Welt- and Turn-Sewing Patents, 1862–1901

	1862- 1871	1872- 1881	1882- 1891	1892- 1901
Number of Patents	12	23	29	57
Share Assigned to Goodyear	50%	22%	21%	5%
Share in Massachusetts	33%	48%	83%	67%
Share in Middle Atlantic Region	67%	43%	10%	23%
Share of Leather-Sewing Patents	14%	18%	19%	23%

Sources: See Table 8.1.

Notes: The first three shares compare the numbers assigned to Goodyear, in Massachusetts, and in the Middle Atlantic region to the total number of welt- and turn-sewing machine patents (line one). The last share compares the number in line one to the total number of leather-sewing machine patents.

induced other firms to develop and produce welt-sewing machines. Eppler took out 4 welt and turn patents, and Massachusetts inventors assigned 4 to Campbell. Six other Boston-based firms took out 10 welt- and turn-sewing patents. Eastern Massachusetts had become a center of welt-sewing machine firms and invention at a time when machine-made welt and turn shoes were rapidly diffusing; the resulting learning and invention consolidated Massachusetts' position as the premier center of bottom-sewing machine firms and invention.

The separate paths taken by major waxed-thread machines also led in different directions. Just as dry-thread firms did not penetrate the waxed-thread market and instead diversified into other dry-thread machines, so standard waxed-thread firms, separated from bottoming, spread into other leather-sewing operations. By 1891, the National Sewing Machine Company sold machines not only to fit shoes but also to stitch harnesses, horse collars and horse brushes, trunks, bags, and pamphlets.[44] It had become a generic leather-sewing machine company. Bottom-sewing firms also diversified but remained tied to shoemaking. From sewing machine companies, they became shoe machinery firms, the core of the developing shoe machinery industry.

Appendix: Estimates of Annual Shoe Output, 1859–1899

From an annual series of cases of shoes shipped from Boston, an estimate of annual national shoe output can be derived if (1) the number of pairs in a case can be determined, (2) the proportion of New England output that was shipped can be estimated, and (3) the share of New England output in the nation's total can be ascertained.

Case size can be estimated from U.S. census data. Boston shipments measured the number of cases shipped by land transportation from Boston to

Table 11.10
The Size of Shoe Cases

	New England Output (millions of pairs)	Boston Shipments (millions of cases)	Pairs per Case
1870	62.4	1.31	35.7
1880	93.0	2.15	32.4
1890	124.7	3.52	26.6
1900	136.7	4.82	21.3

Sources: See Table 11.2. Boston shipments are taken from *Shoe and Leather Reporter* 10 (January 9, 1868): 1; 12 (January 14, 1869): 1; 14 (December 22, 1870): 5; 16 (December 26, 1872): 5; 17 (January 15, 1873): 8; 20 (1875): 593; 33 (1882): 13; 45 (1888): 30; 48 (1889): 206; 57 (1894): 82; 61 (1896): 130; 63 (1897): 167; 65 (1898): 858; 67 (1899): 250; 69 (1900): 35; 87 (1907): 205.

Note: Shipments are for June 1 through May 31.

places outside New England. The *Shoe and Leather Reporter* estimated that shipments regularly comprised 75 percent of total New England output. The average number of shoes per case, C, is therefore given by equation 1:

$$SC = (0.75)O_{NE'} \tag{1}$$

where S is the number of cases shipped from Boston and O_{NE} is the total wholesale New England output reported in the U.S. censuses. The average case size for census years is estimated in Table 11.10.

From these estimates of case size in census years, total annual U.S. output can be approximated. Total U.S. output, O_{US}, is given in equation 2:

$$O_{US} = [SC/(0.75)](O_{US}/O_{NE}). \tag{2}$$

An estimate of U.S. wholesale output for noncensus years can be derived by linear interpolation of the case sizes and New England output share in surrounding census years. Because the 1860 census did not include the number of cases, estimates from 1859 through 1869 are derived by assuming that the size of shoe cases was constant through 1870 and that the average price of New England's shoes relative to the national average was the same in 1860 and 1870. The results are presented in Table 11.11.

Table 11.11
Boston Shoe Shipments and Estimated U.S. Shoe Output,
1859–1899
(millions)

Year	Boston Shipments (cases)	U.S. Output (pairs)	Year	Boston Shipments (cases)	U.S. Output (pairs)
1859	0.68	39	1880	2.26	131
1860	0.68	39	1881	2.31	132
1861	0.46	27	1882	2.41	136
1862	0.51	30	1883	2.57	143
1863	0.57	34	1884	2.58	142
1864	0.52	31	1885	2.72	148
1865	0.72	43	1886	2.87	154
1866	0.82	50	1887	3.07	162
1867	0.92	56	1888	3.28	171
1868	1.01	62	1889	3.40	175
1869	1.34	82	1890	3.53	179
1870	1.25	77	1891	3.47	175
1871	1.31	80	1892	3.71	185
1872	1.45	88	1893	3.43	169
1873	1.34	81	1894	3.81	186
1874	1.39	84	1895	4.05	195
1875	1.45	87	1896	3.94	188
1876	1.52	90	1897	4.18	197
1877	1.76	104	1898	4.32	201
1878	1.65	96	1899	4.73	217
1879	1.96	114			

Sources: See Tables 11.2, 11.10.

12

Ongoing Shoe Invention

Continuing shoe mechanization consisted in part of the evolution of shoe machines that existed in 1860, but more of the birth and development of new machines. From a few machines to prepare, sew, and peg leather in 1860, shoe machinery was transformed into a system of dozens of machines in 1900. A few operations were performed by new types of sewing machines, but many more were carried out with new machines to mold, last, channel, level, trim, heel, and finish. A broad front of technical change spread machinery to every department of the shoe factory except upper cutting.

That so many shoe machines originated after 1860 raises a problem about the sense in which the period was one of continuing mechanization. Here again is the question of the relation of existing machines to the origin of others. Each new machine formed a dynamic that built upon itself. Each also originated and developed in relation to other machinery: machines in the economy as a whole, machines developed in initial shoe mechanization, and machines invented within ongoing shoe invention itself. The problem is to understand how the independent dynamics of individual shoe machines combined with broader processes of growth and mechanization to account for the ongoing evolution of shoe machinery.

Continuing shoe mechanization was distinguished by the fact that shoe machines evolved through a dynamic already shaped by the process originating shoe machinery. Initial mechanization had formed capital goods firms, marketing structures, and a group of inventors that together structured a process of technical change. This process had already connected the evolution of shoe machines and would continue to do so. To understand ongoing mechanization, it is on this process and its evolution over time—rather than on mechanization elsewhere in the economy or the growth of potential demand—that we must focus. We will begin by treating shoe manufacturing invention (other than sewing machines) as a whole, and consider the connections between the evolution of different machines in later chapters.

Table 12.1
Shoe Patents, Employment, and Output, 1862-1901
(annual averages)

| | Patents | | | Workers | Output (million | Boston Machine |
	First	Repeat	Total	(000s)	pairs)	Firms
1862–66	20.2	7.2	27.4	128.2	32	8.0
1867–71	38.2	19.0	57.2	134.6	59	16.4
1872–76	54.6	47.6	102.2	135.1	82	20.0
1877–81	45.2	53.6	98.8	134.0	98	23.8
1882–86	63.4	72.4	135.8	140.4	137	43.4
1887–91	56.8	85.0	141.8	148.7	162	72.4
1892–96	48.0	69.6	117.6	151.2	179	88.2
1897–1901	39.4	74.2	113.6	152.2	200	85.0

Sources: See Tables 11.2, 11.11. Patents were identified from class 12, U.S. Department of Commerce, *U.S. Patent Classification–Subclass Listing,* and were then individually consulted. Boston shoe machinery firms are listed in Boston business directories, 1860–99.

Notes: On shoe employment, see Table 11.2. Boston machine firms are shoe machinery companies or agencies listed in the Boston business directory. Output and Boston firms are for the period two years earlier than patenting periods–for example, for 1860–64 for the 1862–66 patenting period.

Learning by Selling and New Inventors

Shoe machines continued to develop through market-mediated learning. Propelled by early machine usage, secondary invention proliferated, firms formed, sales expanded, and invention proceeded anew. Ongoing mechanization was shaped by the now familiar relation of use to first and repeat invention.

Shoe patenting grew rapidly after 1860. The Civil War interrupted the expansion of inventing, but did not reduce its level. From the plateau of 28 annually in the decade from the mid-1850s, shoe patents—excluding those for shoe-sewing machines, leather-cutting and leather-rolling machines, and most metallic fastening machines—doubled after the war, redoubled to 100 per year in the 1872–76 period, peaked at about 140 annually around 1890, and fell somewhat in the next decade.[1] (See Table 12.1.)

First patents grew rapidly, then slackened off. From the steady 20 per year from 1857 through 1866, they crested above 60 in the early 1880s and then gradually fell to 40 at the end of the century. First patenting varied with shoe employment but was more volatile; in both the 1870s and 1890s, the stagnancy of employment was accompanied by a fall in first patents during the decade.

First patents declined greatly relative to machinery use. Patenting declined in relation to shoe output; the ratio of annual first patents per million pairs of shoes fell from about 0.65 from 1862 through 1877 to 0.46 in the next decade,

Table 12.2
Regional Shares of First Shoe Patents and Shoe Employment,
1862-1901

	Massachusetts		Other New England States		Middle Atlantic		West and South	
	Pat-ents	Employ-ment	Pat-ents	Employ-ment	Pat-ents	Employ-ment-	Pat-ents	Employ-ment
1862-66	49%	46%	13%	9%	26%	28%	13%	17%
1867-71	39	41	5	7	26	29	30	22
1872-76	45	43	10	7	25	28	21	21
1877-81	48	46	11	8	24	27	17	19
1882-86	54	46	6	9	21	26	19	19
1887-91	55	46	11	10	20	25	14	19
1892-96	51	43	12	12	22	24	15	22
1897-1901	50	40	9	13	22	23	20	25

Sources: See Tables 11.2, 12.1.
Notes: On shoe employment, see Table 11.2. On the classification of states by region, see Table 11.3.

and then fell in regular steps to 0.20 in the 1897–1901 period. Because the spread of machinery after 1860 greatly increased the ratio of machinery sales to shoe sales, first patenting declined even faster in relation to machinery usage. An aggregate measure of all shoe machinery usage cannot be formed, but the number of shoe machinery firms advertising in the Boston business directory provides some indication.[2] These agencies grew tenfold from the early 1860s to the 1890s, and annual first patenting per agency fell steadily from 2.52 from 1862 through 1866 to 0.46 in the 1897–1901 period. Patenting was disproportionately concentrated in the early stages of the product cycle, and fell off relatively when the product had taken adequate form.

Unlike the extent of patenting, the location was highly stable. Massachusetts regularly took out half of the first patents, the Middle Atlantic region a fifth to a quarter, and the remainder of New England a tenth (see Table 12.2). The close relationship of the regional distribution of shoe patents to shares of shoe output would be expected if learning through the interaction of shoe machinery producers and users structured the inventive process. Moreover, the stability of Massachusetts' patenting share in light of its falling share of all shoe output, shoe factory output, and employment of machinists may be accounted for by a dynamic taken on within shoe machinery production, largely concentrated in Massachusetts and a surrounding ring including Rhode Island; Hartford, Connecticut; and southern New Hampshire and Maine.

By similar reasoning, the learning-by-selling thesis implies that invention would be concentrated among occupations best placed to learn from the use, sale, production, and servicing of shoe machines, and not simply those with the highest level of mechanical skills. From a study of city directories, occupa-

Table 12.3
Occupations of Shoe Inventors, 1837–1901

	1837–1901 (N)	1837–1861	1862–1871	1872–1881	1882–1891	1892–1901	1837–1901
Shoemakers	368	36%	60%	52%	55%	49%	52%
Machinists	189	24%	23%	29%	26%	27%	27%
Inventors	37	5%	3%	7%	5%	5%	5%
Leather	15	5%	0%	2%	2%	3%	2%
Trade	32	9%	7%	2%	3%	6%	5%
Other	69	20%	7%	8%	10%	10%	10%
Total Number	710	55	73	207	219	156	710

Sources: City and business directories for 76 U.S. cities.
Notes: Occupations are taken from one to three years prior to the first shoe patent. In addition to the 710 inventors listed here, another 42 could not be classified by industry. Shoemakers include those making shoe lasts, patterns, tools, and shoe parts. Machinists include those listed as engineers. Inventors are those listing their occupation as inventor, patent solicitor, patent draftsman, or model builder. Trade includes all those specializing in retail and wholesale sales.

tions prior to first shoe manufacturing patents were located for 752 inventors, almost one-third of all American shoe patentees. For 710 inventors, the industries in which they worked could be identified; the remainder were classified simply as foremen, managers, clerks, and agents.[3]

Most inventors were from the two occupations closest to shoe mechanization: shoemaking and machinery. The shoemaking sector remained a fertile source of inventors. Defined to include shoe lasts, patterns, and such parts as soles, heels, tips, linings, and laces, it supplied 368 inventors, over half those classifiable by industry. (See Table 12.3.) Remarkably, given the growing complexity of patents, its share of classifiable first patentees was constant after 1861.

Inventors from this sector were of two types. One made shoe inputs. Thirty-seven were employed making nonmachine instruments of production, principally lasts but also patterns and tools. Another 27 made shoe parts. Shoe input makers increased their share of classifiable new inventors from 7 percent from 1862 through 1881 to 11 percent over the next two decades. As manufacturers of capital goods sold only to shoemakers, they took out far more shoe patents in proportion to their numbers than did shoemakers or machinists. They thus continued the innovative practices of input manufacturers of the craft period.

Shoe producers were the second and, with 300 inventors, the more numerous type. Their continuous inventiveness points to the importance of learning at the point of production. Learning was unevenly distributed; those in positions of authority were disproportionately represented among inventors, including 57 manufacturers; 38 foremen, superintendents, and contractors; and many classified as shoemakers who ran their own shops. Their share of inventors decreased slowly from a high of 51 percent in the 1862–71 period to 39 percent from 1892 through 1901.

As in initial mechanization, about a quarter of all classifiable shoe inventors had been machinists and engineers, a share that remained constant throughout the period. Some produced machinery used in shoemaking; 20 were categorized as such, another 12 made sewing machines, and no doubt some listed simply as machinists should be added. Others learned of shoemaking problems less directly, from repairing, from proximity with shoe machinery shops, and from communication with other machinists. Breaking-in problems were overcome most readily where shoe machinery firms were located; Massachusetts had 65 percent of the nation's machinist-shoe inventors.

Groups other than machinists and shoemakers took out about a fifth of classifiable first patents. One group was intrinsically tied to invention. Five percent of shoe patents were issued to professional inventors, including not only inventors proper but also draftsmen, designers, patternmakers, model makers, and patent solicitors. Of course, drafting, patterns, and models were also used for purposes other than invention, but advertisements indicate that patenting formed an important and sought-after part of the business. Especially in shoemaking areas, the very nature of this business brought contact with shoe invention. Through professional inventors, the institutionalization of technological change elsewhere in the economy supported shoe mechanization.

Shoe patents were also issued to other producers. Fifteen made leather, 12 fabricated iron, 9 worked wood, and others worked stone, sewed, printed, photographed, hung paper, and made watches, paper, and beer. A few were attorneys, teachers, physicians, bartenders, and bookkeepers. Finally, only 32 could, even in the broadest sense, be classified as merchants; as Marx emphasized, it was producers who transformed techniques of production. But these were not simply producers—rather, they were producers in those times, locations, and occupations for which the sale of shoe machines provided a medium of technological communication.

Kinds of Use and Repeat Invention

Repeat patenting followed a pattern similar to dry-thread and waxed-thread sewing invention. From 1837 through 1901, 4,266 shoe patents were issued to 2,416 American residents. Twenty-nine percent of these inventors were issued more than one shoe patent. Nine percent of multiple inventors took out first patents through 1861; this group took out 115 repeat patents after 1861—almost twice as many as they had been issued previously. The remaining 91 percent of inventors took out all but 5 percent of the repeat patents after 1861.

The tie of repeat inventing to use is clear, as Table 12.4 demonstrates. Over three-fifths of those whose inventions spread as commodities were multiple

Table 12.4
Repeat Shoe Patenting, 1837-1901

	Commodity Usage	Without Commodity Usage	All	Self-Usage	Unused
Single (S)	176	1,550	1,726	87	1,463
Multiple (M)	303	387	690	41	346
Total Patentees (S+M)	479	1,937	2,416	128	1,809
Repeats (R)	1,633	750	2,383	76	674
Frequency [M/(S+M)]	0.63	0.20	0.29	0.32	0.19
Extent (R/M)	5.39	1.94	3.45	1.85	1.95
Rate [R/(S+M)]	3.41	0.39	0.99	0.59	0.37

Sources: See Table 12.1; city and business directories for 76 U.S. cities; McDermott, *A History of the Shoe and Leather Industries.*

Notes: "Commodity Usage" refers to inventors whose patents are embodied in commodities sold as capital goods; "Self-Usage" pertains to inventors who used inventions in their own or their assignees' shoe factories. Self-usage and unused (the fourth and fifth columns) sum to patents without commodity usage (the second column).

inventors, in marked contrast to the one-fifth of those without such use.[4] Moreover, multiple inventors with used patents took out close to three times as many repeats as those who did not. Because of their greater frequency and extent of repeat inventing, inventors securing commodity usage took out about nine times as many repeats as those without such usage.

The examination of sequenced repeat patenting leads to the same conclusion. Inventors whose patents were embodied in new capital goods within one year of the initial patent had four times as many sequenced repeat patents as had inventors without such usage (see Table 12.5). The contrast is stronger when longer lag periods are considered. Inventors gaining use within three years had five times as many repeats four and more years after the first patent, and those with use within five years had over six times as many repeats six and more years after beginning to patent.

Among those attaining use through the sale of capital goods, repeat patenting varied widely. As the distribution in Table 12.6 suggests, single inventors formed 37 percent of the group but took out only 8 percent of the 2,112 patents so used (remember that patents issued to more than one person are counted separately for each inventor). Single patentees and those with one repeat, together a majority of inventors, were issued just 17 percent of patents. The one-tenth of inventors with 10 or more patents took out 45 percent of all used shoe patents. They typically had regularized relations with successful companies, whether as members, employees, or independent assignors. Of the five most prolific inventors, Erastus Winkley was engaged in developing leveling machines for Goodyear, Matthias Brock and George Copeland worked on the Copeland lasting machine, and the two with the most patents—Charles

Table 12.5
Sequenced Repeat Shoe Invention, 1837–1896

	Within One Year		Within Three Years		Within Five Years	
	Used	Not Used	Used	Not Used	Used	Not Used
No Sequenced Repeats (N)	167	1,529	200	1,616	231	1,653
With Sequenced Repeats (Y)	132	362	129	245	119	187
Total Patentees (N+Y)	299	1,891	329	1,861	350	1,840
Sequenced Repeat Patents (R)	692	1,143	662	820	667	561
Frequency [Y/(N+Y)]	0.44	0.19	0.39	0.13	0.34	0.10
Extent (R/Y)	5.24	3.16	5.13	3.35	5.61	3.00
Rate [R/(N+Y)]	2.31	0.60	2.01	0.44	1.91	0.30

Sources: See Tables 12.1, 12.4.

Notes: On the definition and measures of sequenced repeat invention, see Table 8.10. Usage here refers only to patents used as capital goods.

Table 12.6
Distribution of Used Shoe Patents
by Inventor, 1837-1901

Repeats per Inventor	Inventors with Used Patents		Used Patents	
	Number	Cumulative Share	Number	Cumulative Share
0	176	37%	176	8%
1	91	56	358	17
2	55	67	523	25
3	35	75	663	31
4	23	79	778	37
5	15	82	868	41
6	18	86	994	47
7-8	19	90	1,158	55
9-10	5	91	1,209	57
11-12	10	93	1,332	63
13-15	9	95	1,468	70
16-20	10	97	1,651	78
21-25	5	98	1,771	84
26-30	3	99	1,853	88
Over 30	5	100	2,112	100

Sources: See Tables 12.1, 12.4.
Note: Used patents are restricted to those used as capital goods.

Glidden with 69 and Freeborn Raymond with 79—both invented heeling machines for McKay.

The tie of use and repeat invention is more complex than the preceding analysis suggests. The learning-by-selling mechanism refers to use mediated by the purchase of capital goods. Self-usage was also a source of learning to the inventor, to workers trained in the new technique, and to acquaintances outside the shop. Besides improving the use of new equipment, learning led to modifications of the equipment and as such constituted a kind of embodied learning by using.

In an industry with many machine users, self-usage was inferior to learning by selling as a social form for ongoing mechanization. It limited learning and first patenting to those few who came in contact with the invention. It also limited repeat invention because the inventor learned only from the feedback of those in the shop and often had little technological knowledge to solve observed problems. The wide diffusion coming from commodity usage overcame limits to both the number who learned and the breadth of feedback that inventors received.

Measuring both self-usage and the invention it fostered is difficult, the former because usage was not manifested in the growth of specialized firms and the latter because such invention had less reason to be patented. Nevertheless, there was some reason to patent in order to get remuneration for—or to inhibit –use by others, and insights into the role of self-usage in ongoing invention can be gathered by a study of patenting.

The tie of self-usage and repeat inventing can be explored by assuming that a shoe manufacturing patent was self-used when the inventor or assignee was a shoe manufacturer, foreman, or superintendent at or after the time of patenting. This assumption is analogous to that made for commodity usage. Thus a shoe manufacturing patent made by or sold to a shoe machinery firm will be considered used as a capital good, but the same patent when made by or sold to a shoe manufacturer and not sold to a shoe machinery producer will be considered self-used.[5]

Based on the survey of occupations of patentees and assignees, 128 inventors had patents that can be classified as self-used; a few others had both self-usage and commodity usage and were counted with the latter. As expected, repeat patenting by inventor-users was intermediate between inventors with commodity usage and those without known usage. About a third took out repeat patents, well above the 19 percent of those not gaining use, but well below 63 percent of those securing commodity usage. (See Table 12.4.) For multiple patentees, the number of repeats was a third of that of inventors with commodity usage and no more than that of inventors who failed to gain use. The most striking conclusion is the contrast between self-usage and capital goods use, as expressed in the far higher rate of repeat patenting of inventors finding use as commodities.[6] Continuing mechanization thus depended on the social form taken by technical change.

Repeat inventing followed its own logic, and as such depended little on the factors that determined first inventing. It varied by location, primarily because use also varied by region. The rate of repeat patenting was over twice as high in Massachusetts as in other New England states or in the Middle Atlantic states, and these regions were twice as high as the West and the South combined (see Table 12.7). This difference was primarily due to the larger share utilized in Massachusetts.

Yet its significantly higher rate of repeat patenting for both those with and without use suggests that Massachusetts had other advantages, in particular the concentration of the shoe machinery industry in that state and the connected establishment of shoe invention as a profession. Massachusetts was not much different in the frequency of repeat inventing among inventors with used patents, but had a much higher extent of repeat patenting due to the residence of the most prolific inventors within its borders. The 28 inventors with 15 or more repeats took out 43 percent of used repeat patents (and 34 percent of all used patents). Twenty-five of these inventors were located in Massachusetts. They all worked for well-known, relatively long-lived companies. Half worked for McKay, Goodyear, or Townsend firms, and others worked in smaller, more specialized companies often of their own forming. If these 28 inventors are excluded, the number of repeat patents for each of the remaining

Table 12.7
Repeat Shoe Patenting by Region

	Massachusetts	Other New England States	Middle Atlantic	West and South
Inventors with Commodity Usage				
Single (S)	117	16	32	11
Multiple (M)	223	25	44	11
Total Patentees (S+M)	340	41	76	22
Repeats (R)	1,313	85	186	49
Frequency [M/(S+M)]	0.66	0.60	0.58	0.50
Extent (R/M)	5.89	3.40	4.23	4.45
Rate [R/(S+M)]	3.86	2.07	2.45	2.23
Inventors without Commodity Usage				
Single (S)	634	153	407	356
Multiple (M)	211	34	92	50
Total Patentees (S+M)	845	187	499	406
Repeats (R)	442	64	169	75
Frequency [M/(S+M)]	0.25	0.18	0.19	0.12
Extent (R/M)	2.09	1.88	1.84	1.50
Rate [R/(S+M)]	0.52	0.34	0.34	0.18
Share Used	0.29	0.18	0.13	0.05

Sources: See Tables 12.1, 12.4.
Note: For definition of regions, see Table 11.3.

inventors who gained use lies between 3.2 in the Middle Atlantic region and 3.4 in Massachusetts and other New England states.[7] Repeat inventing was strongest where the shoe machinery industry had institutionalized technical change among specialized inventors.

Repeat inventing was also largely independent of the occupations before patenting. At first sight this does not seem so; machinists and professional inventors averaged two repeats, and shoemakers and others only one. But this result is due to the fact that over twice as many machinists and inventors gained use. (See Table 12.8.) (Use here is confined to commodity usage; self-usage and nonusage are grouped together.) The frequency, extent, and rate of repeat inventing varied greatly between used and nonused for each occupation type but, within each use category, were remarkably constant among occupations.

The higher share used among machinists and professional inventors resulted from their occupational knowledge of design, production, and marketing, especially when they patented machines. This surely helped those who made

Table 12.8
Repeat Patenting by Occupation and Commodity Usage

	Mechanical	Shoemaking	Other
Inventors with			
Commodity Usage			
Single (S)	38	31	7
Multiple (M)	71	52	16
Total Patentees (S+M)	109	83	23
Repeats (R)	383	264	97
Frequency [M/(S+M)]	0.65	0.63	0.70
Extent (R/M)	5.39	5.08	6.06
Rate [R/(S+M)]	3.51	3.18	4.22
Share of Inventors[a]	0.48	0.23	0.20
Inventors without			
Commodity Usage			
Single (S)	83	218	78
Multiple (M)	34	67	15
Total Patentees (S+M)	117	285	93
Repeats (R)	78	119	29
Frequency [M/(S+M)]	0.29	0.24	0.16
Extent (R/M)	2.29	1.78	1.93
Rate ([R+(S+M)]	0.67	0.42	0.31
Share of Inventors[a]	0.52	0.77	0.80

Sources: See Tables 12.1, 12.3, 12.4.

Notes: Mechanical occupations refer to machinists and professional inventors. Other occupations include leather, trade, and others. For categorization of occupations, see Table 12.3.

[a] Refers to the share of inventors within each occupation who have or have not gained use as a capital good.

shoe and sewing machinery, four-fifths of whom gained use. It also assisted the 43 percent of other machinists and professional inventors who secured use. The advantage of machinists and professional inventors is manifested in the time taken to bring inventions into use. Among multiple inventors securing commodity usage, 75 percent of machinists and professional inventors gained use within one year and 86 percent within five years. By contrast, 53 percent of shoemakers, shoe manufacturers, and foremen found usage within one year and 69 percent within five.

Prior occupation did influence repeat inventing through the content of the first patent. Technologically skilled occupations were more likely than others to patent machines. A rough measure of the share of machine patents can be derived by grouping together tools, forms, work support devices, and processes as nonmachine patents; other patents were for burnishing, heeling, lasting, pegging, sole-manipulating, and upper machines. Machines comprised 55 percent of first patents for inventors with classifiable occupations (and 53 percent of all first patents), but formed 75 percent for machinists and professional inventors, compared to 45 percent for shoemakers and 46 percent for others. In the occupational composition of inventors, patents for shoe machines were more like those for leather-sewing machines than like nonmachine shoe patents; machinists and professional inventors took out 44 percent of first shoe machine patents, 59 percent of leather-sewing machine patents, and only 17 percent of other shoe manufacturing patents.[8]

Further, those who began with machines—whatever their earlier occupations—were more successful repeat inventors. Within each category of usage, inventors with machines as first patents were more likely to take out repeats and, when they did, took out more repeats. (See Table 12.9.) The rate of repeat patenting hence was much higher. The differential was especially pronounced for those with commodity usage. Moreover, with 27 percent gaining commodity usage, inventors who began with machines were over twice as likely to attain such use as were other inventors.[9] Among machine inventors with known occupations, machinists and professional inventors did especially well; 53 percent secured commodity usage, well above the 28 percent for shoemakers and 30 percent for others.

Why inventive paths that began with machines were so distinctive is not clear. One factor was the concentration of professional shoe inventors on machinery. First patents often directed the inventor toward similar or complementary invention. The 28 inventors with 15 or more repeats all primarily invented machines, and all but 3 had machines for first patents. Without these inventors, machine inventors had only marginally higher extents of repeat patenting among those with commodity usage—3.46 patents per inventor to 3.25 for nonmachine inventors.[10]

Learning by selling reproduced the locational advantages of Massachusetts as a shoe machinery center. Learning was greatest where the inventor could secure regular interactions with shoe machinery producers and users; the higher share of Massachusetts inventors gaining use and the higher rate of repeat patenting among those with use followed from the concentration of machinery firms in that state. The concentration fostered communication about shoe machinery which induced disproportionate numbers of machinists and professional inventors to join the ranks of shoe inventors—38 percent versus 24 percent for other states—and also occasioned an exceptionally large share of machines among first patents—64 percent. The greater likelihood of usage for both machinists and machines reinforced the concentration of shoe machinery firms and the dynamic of ongoing mechanization in that state, closing the circle of cumulative causation.

Table 12.9
Repeat Patenting by Type of First Patent and Usage

	Commodity Usage		Self-Usage		Unused	
	Machine	Nonmachine	Machine	Nonmachine	Machine	Nonmachine
Single (S)	115	61	38	49	689	774
Multiple (M)	231	72	23	18	189	157
Total Patentees (S+M)	346	133	61	67	878	931
Repeats (R)	1,360	273	44	32	385	289
Frequency [M/(S+M)]	0.67	0.54	0.38	0.27	0.22	0.17
Extent (R/M)	5.89	3.79	1.91	1.78	2.04	1.84
Rate [R/(S+M)]	3.93	2.05	0.72	0.48	0.44	0.31
Share of Inventors[a]	0.27	0.12	0.05	0.06	0.68	0.32

Sources: See Tables 12.1, 12.4.

Notes: Nonmachine patents include tools, forms, processes, and work support devices; all others are machines. For categorization of usage, see Table 12.4.

[a]Shares by kind of use of inventors with the same kind of first patent (machines or nonmachines).

Internal versus External Determinants

Embedded in a broader economy, shoe invention was affected by factors quite outside the learning-by-selling process. The economy's mechanical skills and the potential demand for shoes and hence shoe machinery conditioned ongoing mechanization as they had initial mechanization. But these economy-wide factors cannot by themselves account for the growth of shoe invention.

To see this, a distinction must be made. Clearly outside forces conditioned mechanization. Shoemakers took the potential demand for shoes and the supply of inputs as givens. Machinists and professional inventors were needed to produce machines and took out one-third of shoe manufacturing patents. But the critical question is whether *changes* in demand and skills independent of shoe mechanization induced later shoe invention.

Shoe output expansion was one such change. The rising income from rapid capital accumulation and the growing per capita income from technical change contributed to the doubling of U.S. per capita shoe consumption and the fivefold growth of shoe output from 1860 to 1900. Growing output may have induced invention, and increased incentives may have been the mechanism. Yet, as has been seen, incentive-based accounts fail to explain the concentration of patenting in Massachusetts, the occupations of inventors, or the pattern of repeat inventing. As an alternative, learning by selling expects that patenting and shoe machine usage would move together, and that machine usage would grow in proportion to shoe output only when market penetration was well advanced.

However, the learning-by-selling thesis ties invention to the process developing and diffusing new machines, and as such denies that invention was determined by an independently given shoe output. First, shoe output was not independent; it was influenced by the cost-cutting and product-altering results of technical change. Second, both the reality and the perception of potential machinery demand depended on the course of mechanization. Once firms built factories and formed managerial systems to use upper-sewing machines, leather-preparing machines, and particularly bottom-sewing and pegging machines, they found it easier to introduce other machines. The rise of new, national and international machinery markets and appropriate marketing methods improved expectations quite outside any increase in the demand for shoes. Third, actual machine usage varied with the progress of the product cycle. During the penetration phase, usage grew whatever happened to output levels. Even when the market for any machine had been saturated, other new machines could arise and expand machine usage for any level of shoe output. Indeed, the maturation of some machines may have called forth the development of others. Until the potential markets for all machines had been penetrated, the dynamics of new product development were the major determinants of shoe machine usage.

Consider next the machinery sector. Machinists and shoe patenting both

Table 12.10

Shoe Patenting, Output, and Machinists, 1857–1901

Patenting Period	Shoe Patents Index (1857-66=1)	Shoe Output Index (1859-64=1)	Per Capita Machinists Index (1857-66=1)	Total U.S. Patent Index (1857-66=1)
1867–76	2.84	2.11	1.95	2.82
1877–86	4.17	3.53	3.38	3.82
1887–96	4.62	5.12	5.54	4.94
1897–1901	4.04	5.99	7.16	5.23

Sources: See Tables 11.2, 12.1; U.S. Bureau of the Census, *Historical Statistics of the United States,* ser. W-99.

Notes: All indices are ratios of the annual level in any period to the annual level in the base period. Machinists are interpolated between census years, and output periods are two years earlier than patent periods.

grew after 1860, but neither the timing nor the location of growth suggests that the increase of machinists brought about the expansion of shoe invention. The disparity was pronounced in the 1890s; from the 1887–96 period to the 1897–1901 period, machinists increased by 29 percent but shoe patenting fell by 12 percent (see Table 12.10). As might be expected, machinists were more closely related to patenting in the whole economy. Moreover, the location of machinists differed significantly from that of shoe invention. Massachusetts regularly had one-tenth of the country's machinists but three-fifths of total shoe patents, and its decline from 11 percent of U.S. machinists in 1860 to 9 percent in 1900 coincided with its rise from 54 percent of shoe patents in the 1857–66 decade to 68 percent from 1892 through 1901.

The growing technological sophistication of machinists no doubt influenced shoe machinery, especially in motor and transmission mechanisms. Mechanical knowledge expanded among the increasing numbers of college-trained mechanical engineers and also among practicing machinists. But the technology of shoe machinery was distinctive, and there is no evidence that any of the major innovations rested on recent advances in general mechanical knowledge.

Moreover, if the growing numbers or knowledge of machinists accounted for the expansion of shoe invention, then one would expect the share of machinists and professional inventors among all shoe inventors to rise over time. The rising share of machinery in shoe manufacturing patents and the greater share of machines used give added weight to this expectation. But this was not so; the share remained constant. Learning by using among shoemakers retained its importance throughout the period.

The location of inventors also suggests that machinist-inventors were tied to the internal dynamic of mechanization. If shoe invention were independent of the dynamic of shoe machinery, then one might expect invention by members of an occupation in any region to be in proportion to their numbers. This was roughly so for shoemakers; Massachusetts had 52 percent of the country's shoemaker-inventors and a slightly lower share of employment throughout the period. But it was not so for machinists; Massachusetts' 65 percent of the nation's machinist-inventors (and 70 percent of the professional inventors who took out shoe patents) far exceeded its 10 percent of machinists. To put the point differently, although it had the highest share of shoe producers in its labor force, Massachusetts had the largest share of patents issued to machinists and professional inventors—38 percent—of any region. It thus appears that the proclivity of Massachusetts machinists and inventors to develop shoe machines can be attributed to the presence of the shoe machinery sector.[11]

Factors outside the shoe machinery industry clearly supported ongoing shoe mechanization, but principally as they conditioned the industry's own learning-by-selling process. Or, rather, processes; there were many machines each with its own development process. The questions that remain are whether and how the organization of the shoe machinery industry connected the evolution of the various shoe machines.

13

Integration by Inventors

Within the shoe machinery sector, the development of separate machines was connected by both inventors, responding to technical problems and opportunities, and firms, pursuing strategies of growth. The two kinds of integration were related; shoe machinery firms hired inventors and communicated technical problems within the broader inventive community, and the resulting inventions fostered the growth of these firms. But as will be seen, inventors and firms integrated the process of continuing mechanization in different ways and with different outcomes; we will thus consider them separately.

Machines developed in a sequence. The commodity path of technical change structured the way that earlier machines could lead later ones. Two technological links pertained to any path: convergences and bottlenecks. As mechanisms used in a production process, machines embodied technical principles applicable to other machines. Because they could function adequately only if other steps in the production process were adequate, machines focused attention on limiting operations. But technological links would have meant little if not communicated; as commodities, machines were embedded in social relations that governed the spread of knowledge about convergences and bottlenecks to potential inventors. Those who took out patents for earlier machines made up one important group of potential inventors, particularly when their earlier inventions had gained use. For firms, the profits and knowledge gained from developing and selling earlier machines could provide the means and in part the direction for diversification. Through inventors and firms, the sequencing of new commodity development processes integrated the evolution of machinery.

To argue for the integrating role of inventors and firms is in effect to argue against the notion that machines evolved as similar but unconnected responses to similar extraindustry circumstances. Schmookler, for example, used the incentive effect of output growth to account for the evenness of patenting among types of inventions.[1] But as the preceding chapter argued, learning by selling offers a superior account of the location and occupations of inventors and of the dynamics of repeat invention. Similar intraindustry factors tied together the development of different shoe machines.

Table 13.1
Share of Shoe Patents by Type, 1837–1901

	1837–1861	1862–1871	1872–1881	1882–1891	1892–1901	All
Sole Machines	17%	18%	23%	21%	33%	24%
Trimmers & Stiffeners	10	10	16	19	17	16
Heel Machines	1	4	5	8	7	6
Burnishers	1	5	12	10	4	8
Upper Machines	14	8	10	8	8	9
Tools	18	21	9	4	4	8
Work Support	9	11	7	9	6	8
Lasts & Trees	12	19	11	11	17	14
Processes	20	5	7	10	3	8

Sources: See Table 12.1.

The Break between Initial and Ongoing Mechanization

Virtually every shoemaking operation was the object of inventive effort, almost all with some success by 1900. Table 13.1 divides shoe patents by type. Sole patents include machines to last, peg, channel, level, mold, and handle welts. Trimmers and stiffeners are used for both sole and heel formation. Heeling machines assemble, compress, and nail heels. Burnishing machines finish soles and heels, and upper machines crimp, fold, assemble, and trim uppers. Forms include lasts and trees. Tools, work support devices, and new processes complete the types of patents. Machines to sew, to cut and prepare leather, and, for the most part, to bottom with metallic fastenings are excluded.

It is striking to note how continuously widespread shoe invention was. Each kind of patent was well represented in each period, particularly after 1861. The question is whether connections among inventions led to the evenness of inventing across operations.

Earlier shoe mechanization met conditions for the spread of shoe machinery after 1860, but generated neither the critical machines of ongoing mechanization nor the inventors and firms that would develop these machines. The shoe machines of the 1850s continued to develop later in the century. Machines to roll and split leather and to cut it into strips and sole blanks were refined, as were devices to crimp upper leather. A practical pegging machine came into use. But their evolution had little significance for the birth of the major new shoe machines.

All but one of these initial machines performed operations with little technological linkage to later machines. Since the craft period, shoemaking had been divided into five kinds of operations. Leather preparing and some finishing had been the domain of the central shop, upper fitting of women home-workers, and bottoming, heeling, and some finishing of the ten-footer.

Whereas the major new machines after 1860 bottomed, heeled, and finished, most machines of the 1850s performed other operations. Leather preparing had few technical links to other operations and in the factory system was conducted in separate departments or even in specialized firms. Upper sewing and crimping had some bearing on machinery for other upper operations; Elmer Townsend, for example, developed eyeletting machines in the 1860s and 1870s. And, of course, the sewing machine was relevant for bottom stitching, but upper machines had little direct influence on other bottoming and heeling machines.[2]

Nor was the pegging machine significant for the evolution of other machinery, but for a different reason: as machine-sewed shoes expanded, the pegged shoe declined, and with it the pegging machine. Although the pegged shoe linked pegging to complementary bottoming operations, its decline reduced the need and occasion to mechanize these operations.

Limitations to the prospects of the pegging machine were hardly evident in 1860. The machine was well on the way to practicality and widespread use. Townsend employed inventors to perfect Benjamin Sturtevant's invention. David Whittemore, a North Bridgewater shoe-dressing manufacturer, developed a work support device that pivoted from side to side to more readily peg shoes at the shanks. Both Townsend and Whittemore developed well-functioning machines in the mid-1860s. Use spread quickly, aided by the fact that pegged shoe firms could sell in accustomed markets. In 1870, 901 pegging machines were reported in use, seven-tenths of them in Massachusetts. Large producers often used many machines; in 1871, the Batchellers of North Brookfield used 30 in their factory yet still put out most of their bottoming. By 1873, pegging machines bottomed about 30 million pairs of shoes.[3]

But 1873 was the zenith; machine-pegged shoes fell off to 22.5 million pairs in 1876 and but 4 million in 1899. The pegging machine succumbed to the superior quality and higher price of McKay shoes. Pegging invention declined with the pegged shoe. The 33 pegging machine patents issued before 1861 were followed by 42 from 1862 through 1881 and only 10 in the next 20 years.[4]

The pegging machine had one important legacy. During its development, Townsend had become interested in metallic pegging. Spurred by a bottom-nailing machine that was coming into use, he directed his mechanics to develop a screw-wire-bottoming machine. Around 1870 they introduced a machine that achieved some success in making heavy shoes.[5]

The development of metallic-fastened shoes also depended on another process within continuing mechanization, the birth of sole-sewing machinery, as Townsend discovered in the mid-1870s when enjoined from using his machine due to infringement of Gordon McKay's channeling patents. Lyman Blake had become interested in nailing a decade earlier. In 1865 he took out his first patent for nailed shoes, and in 1868 he adapted the rotating horn of the McKay machine to nail soles. In the early 1870s, Blake took out two more nailing patents, and McKay patented a machine with strong resemblance to his sole-

Table 13.2
Share of Sole Machine Patents by Type, 1837–1901

	1837-1861	1862-1871	1872-1881	1882-1891	1892-1901	All
Lasting	8%	10%	30%	42%	36%	33%
Pegging	67	13	14	3	0	8
Channeling	0	33	16	12	10	13
Leveling	12	11	11	19	20	17
Molding	0	9	8	5	2	6
Other	12	23	21	19	32	24

Sources: See Table 12.1.

stitching machine. To avoid litigation, Townsend joined McKay in the McKay Metallic Fastening Association in 1877, as later several other firms did as well. McKay placed 800 or 900 machines in 1889, but metallic-fastened shoes never formed more than 15 percent of industry output.[6]

The inconsequence of the machines of the 1850s for later mechanization was one instance of a broader break between initial and ongoing mechanization. The content of invention changed. Heeling, burnishing, and sole machines expanded, and tools, upper machines (especially crimpers), and process patents declined (see Table 13.1). A remarkable transformation occurred among bottoming machines other than trimmers (which cannot be easily distinguished from heel trimmers). Pegging machines, two-thirds of sole machines through 1861, fell to 14 percent from 1862 to 1881 and to 2 percent thereafter (see Table 13.2). Its place was taken by machines to mold, channel, level, and last.

Just as the type of invention changed, so did firms and inventors. Beyond waxed-thread and pegging machines, Townsend's role was limited to efforts to develop an eyeletting machine and a sole trimmer. Only ten inventors beginning before 1861 later took out patents that were used. Two of these, William Landfear and Alpheus Gallahue, remained confined to pegging machines. Only one, Seth Tripp, had major importance in developing new machines, and he was well connected with the emergence of the McKay machine. (Another, David Knox, had invented sole leather machines, which are not included in the patent survey.) The machines, inventors, and firms that continued mechanization were only exceptionally those that had begun it.

Thus, continuing mechanization, although conditioned by initial mechanization, developed through its own, distinctive processes. It is to these processes that we must turn to account for the integration of shoe machine development.

Table 13.3
Regional Distribution of Shoe and Sewing Machine Patents

	Total Number	Regional Shares within Types			
		Massa-chusetts	Other New England States	Middle Atlantic	West and South
1862–1881					
Shoemaking	1,428	57%	7%	22%	14%
Leather Sewing	210	49	12	30	8
Other Sewing	2,321	15	12	44	29
1882–1901					
Shoemaking	2,544	66	7	17	10
Leather Sewing	402	63	11	17	8

Sources: See Tables 8.1, 12.1.
Note: For definition of regions, see Table 11.3.

Leather-Sewing Machine Leadership

Although the inventors and firms of the 1850s did little to invent later shoe machines, they did foster the development of a machine that would lead ongoing mechanization, the bottom-sewing machine. Its technological principles converged with those of other machines, its dependence on complementary bottoming operations directed technological change, and its success spread knowledge of convergent principles and needed complements.

The plausibility of leadership by bottom-sewing machines is indicated by the locational similarity of shoe patenting and shoe-sewing machine invention. Massachusetts led in both, with from one-half to two-thirds of each type of patent (see Table 13.3). In the 1862–81 period, its shares of shoe- and leather-sewing machines were much closer to each other than either were to the share of dry-thread sewing machines. The same was true of other regions except other New England states, with their concentration of dry-thread and upper waxed-thread firms. Moreover, shares of shoe- and leather-sewing machine patents changed together; for Massachusetts, both rose in the 1882–1901 period.

Crossover Inventors

Machines could have developed in the same regions without connection; stronger evidence for integration is provided by the involvement of inventors in developing many kinds of machines. From 1837 through 1901, 101 inventors took out patents for both leather-sewing machines and shoe manufacturing improvements, 4 percent of shoe inventors and 32 percent of leather-sewing patentees. Unlike the tie of dry-thread and waxed-thread machines, crossover inventors between leather-sewing and shoe patents formed a steady share of shoe inventors throughout the second half of the nineteenth century. Crossover

Table 13.4
Crossover Leather-Sewing Machine and Shoe Invention,
1837–1901

	Crossover Inventors		Other Inventors	
	Used	Not Used	Used	Not Used
Shoe Patents				
Single (S)	11	20	165	1,530
Multiple (M)	51	19	252	368
Total Patentees (S+M)	62	39	417	1,898
Repeats (R)	395	58	1,238	692
Frequency [M/(S+M)]	0.82	0.49	0.60	0.19
Extent (R/M)	7.75	3.05	4.91	1.88
Rate [R/(S+M)]	6.37	1.49	2.97	0.36
Leather-Sewing Patents				
Single (S)	16	34	44	113
Multiple (M)	42	9	40	22
Total Patentees (S+M)	58	43	84	135
Repeats (R)	200	24	129	30
Frequency [M/(S+M)]	0.72	0.21	0.48	0.16
Extent (R/M)	4.76	2.67	3.22	1.36
Rate [R/(S+M)]	3.45	0.56	1.54	0.22

Sources: See Tables 8.1, 10.5, 12.1, 12.4.

Notes: Crossover inventors were those who patented both leather-sewing machines and shoe manufacturing improvements. Used patents are restricted to those used as capital goods.

inventing also extended beyond shoe machinery; of the 51 crossover inventors through 1881, 15 also took out dry-thread machine patents.

These inventors came predominantly from mechanical trades. Of 40 with known occupations before their first shoe patents, 25 had been machinists or professional inventors, including 10 who made sewing machines and 2 who made shoe machinery. Another 11 had been shoemakers.

Crossover inventors had a far greater importance for shoe mechanization than their share of shoe patentees would suggest. First of all, more secured usage. The 61 percent of them with patents used as capital goods far exceeded the 18 percent of other shoe inventors, as Table 13.4 indicates. Second, crossover inventors were more active in repeat patenting. When compared to other shoe inventors, they took out additional shoe patents more frequently and in greater numbers, so that their rate of repeat patenting was twice as high for those who secured use and over four times as high for those without use. Only 4 percent of patentees, they took out a quarter of used repeat patents.

The inventive proclivity of crossover patentees is even more notable because it extended to leather-sewing machines. Virtually all of the major leather-sewing machine inventors also patented shoe manufacturing improvements, including such upper-sewing innovators as William Wickersham, William Butterfield, and Elmer Townsend; such McKay shoe inventors as Lyman Blake, Gordon McKay, Everett Richardson, and Hadley Fairfield; and, among welt-sewing patentees, Charles Goodyear, Jr., Christian Dancel, Zachary French, and Andrew Eppler. Crossover inventors more successfully brought their sewing machines into use; the 57 percent gaining use exceeded the 38 percent of other leather-sewing inventors. Higher shares of crossover patentees took out repeat leather-sewing patents, and those who did were issued more repeats. Therefore, both crossover inventors gaining use and those who did not had rates of repeat leather-sewing invention over twice as high as their counterparts with only leather-sewing inventions.

Among crossover inventors, the 63 who patented bottom-sewing machines were the most successful. Sixty-seven percent gained commodity usage for shoe patents, compared to 58 percent for inventors with only upper-sewing machine inventions. Among those who secured use, a higher share took out other shoe patents—86 to 68 percent—and these inventors averaged a remarkable 9.1 repeats, compared to 4.5 for upper-sewing machine inventors.

The Direction of Crossover Inventing

Invention and the attendant social experience provide skills that foster repeat invention of any type, but may also direct attention to complementary or technically convergent operations. Crossover inventors concentrated their efforts on the former. The quality of sole stitching depended on the accuracy of complementary operations. Bottoming comprised a sequence of steps. The upper had to be accurately lasted to the inner sole. Soles had to be shaped to the last. Channeling in the outsole for the McKay shoe and both soles for the Goodyear required sufficient precision that the stitching inside the channel would be properly positioned. To improve shoe quality, the soles had to be reshaped after sewing in an operation called "beating out" or "leveling." Inadequate performance of complementary operations formed bottlenecks that gave direction to bottoming invention.

Channeling was the most critical complementary operation. On the McKay shoe, the outer sole was channeled on its outer surface; after sewing, the channel was cemented shut to protect the completed seam. Channeling required great accuracy; the channel had to be deep enough to cover the stitches yet not so deep that the stitch could pull through the sole. It also had to be cut a specific distance from the edge of the sole; if too far the upper would not be sewed, and if too close the stitch might not penetrate the insole. The Goodyear shoe channeled both the insole and the outsole, and imposed different technical requirements on each. The welt had to be properly positioned, and the channels had to be located so that the seams did not cross.[7]

From the initial penetration of the McKay machine in the early 1860s, channeling received much attention. Absent before 1862, channeling machine patents rose to 7 from 1862 through 1866 and then to 18 in the next five years, a level that continued throughout the century. Crossover inventors were active. They comprised 19 of the 24 who began shoe patenting with channelers. Thirty-two took out 40 percent of the channeling inventions, including almost all of the most important. Blake was issued 5 channeling patents, and McKay copatented 1 with Blake and took out another by himself. Goodyear and Dancel took out the first of several Goodyear channeling patents in 1874. Wickersham was issued 2 channeling patents.

Because channeling was located by reference to the sole, its adequacy was contingent on the accuracy of sole rounding, which roughly cut the sole blank to the size of the finished sole. Crossover inventors played little role in developing an adequate rounder for the McKay shoe. The key patent was issued in 1880 to Jason Smith, a Rockland, Massachusetts, shoe machinery producer, for a machine that both rounded and channeled the sole against an iron sole pattern. Goodyear crossover inventors were decisive for the Goodyear shoe. The most important innovation, the outsole rough rounder and channeler, was patented by Henry Briggs in 1891 and improved by Briggs and Christian Dancel two years later. Prior to this machine, the outsole seam sometimes crossed and cut the inseam, causing the shoe to rip. The problem was that the channeled outsole often shifted when it was temporarily attached to the welt and upper in preparation for stitching. The solution was to round and channel the outsole after it had been cemented to the welted upper by using as gauges the inseam and the last on which the shoe was mounted.[8]

Crossover inventors also developed other bottoming machines. Three-quarters began shoe inventing with machines, and many who did not were issued manufacturing process patents to better use sewing machines. Issued 12 percent of all shoe manufacturing patents, they took out 82 percent of the patents for stitch separating, 20 percent for sole leveling, 16 percent for molding machines, 18 percent for lasting machines, 12 percent for sole- and heel-trimming machines, and about 25 percent for other sole machines. In total, crossover inventors took out 20 percent of sole machine patents.

Some complementary inventions were of major significance. Eppler developed the most successful sole-laying machine, and John Hadaway came out with a useful stitch-separating machine. Paths also led in other directions. Landfear was one of the last to follow the earlier pattern of moving from sewing to pegging machines. Some moved toward technically convergent machines. Blake, Louis Goddu, and Eppler developed metallic fastening machines. Many tried to mechanize lasting, including a few who tried to adapt the sewing machine to this task.

Leather-sewing machine inventors were major agents in the birth of some but not all bottoming machines. They mattered most in operations closely bound with sewing, especially channeling, rounding, and stitch separating. They were active but not central in developing machines to level, mold, and last, and did little to develop heeling or finishing machines, tools, and forms.

The activity of crossover inventors cannot account for the evenness of patenting among types of operations.

The Mutuality of Leadership

An earlier machine can lead the evolution of a later one when its dissemination and development contribute both to its own progress and to the birth and evolution of the later machine. Leadership differentiates the roles of machines, but does not deny that the later machine can support the improvement and sales of the earlier. The leader and the led can bolster one another.

Leather-sewing machines led shoe machines in this way. The role of their inventors in developing shoe machines is complemented by the activities of sewing machine firms considered in the next chapter. The great expansion of patents for sole machines after 1861, especially new machines for channeling and molding, was one result. But the influence was not one way. Shoe inventors improved the sewing machine. Indeed, the path of crossover invention led from shoe to shoe-sewing machines more often than the converse. Fifty-eight first took out shoe patents, compared to the 43 who were first issued leather-sewing patents. Through 1871 most started with sewing machine inventions, including Wickersham, Butterfield, Blake, and Richardson. But over the next 20 years, 70 percent began with shoe inventions.

Goodyear inventors often began with shoe patents. Dancel's first patent was a channeling machine in 1874; three years later he began his series of basic welt-sewing patents. He then interspersed 6 shoe machine patents with 8 leather-stitching inventions over the two decades before his death. Zachary French began with a lasting jack in 1883, and continued with 12 sole-sewing patents and 19 shoe manufacturing patents, almost all of the latter for trimming, channeling, welt-handling, and other bottoming machines. Henry Briggs is another case in point. He began with his important rough-rounding patents before turning to a series of take-up and chain-stitch patents. Of the 12 crossover inventors with patents used by Goodyear, only 3 began with leather-sewing machines, and these 3 together were issued only 14 percent of the shoe patents taken out by Goodyear crossover inventors and 11 percent of the leather-sewing machine patents.

Without question the sewing machine aided the invention and use of shoe machines, but the converse is true as well. Complementary machines added to the usefulness and sales of sewing machines, as McKay recognized when he added a channeler to improve the accuracy of his sewing and a spooler to reduce the time needed to wind the bobbin in the horn of his machine.[9] Leveling machines improved the shape of the sole after stitching. Molding machines eliminated the bagginess that had limited the sale of McKay shoes to lower-quality markets. The importance of the molding machine is emphasized by Charles McDermott, the longtime editor of the *Boot and Shoe Recorder*: "To this method of sole moulding more, perhaps, than any other single feature was due the great increase in the popularity of McKay sewed shoes. . . . With the moulded soles the fit and style of the last were retained and there was nothing in the general appearance to distinguish the McKay sewed from the hand sewed work."[10] Likewise, a series of complementary machines, led by the rough rounder and channeler, sped the introduction of the Goodyear sewing machines.

A mutual reinforcement of sole-sewing and other bottoming machines had originated. The shoe machines that the sewing machine had fostered took on their own dynamics and in cases contributed to sewing machine design and sales. Growing sewing machine sales added to the use of other machines, to usage and repeat patenting for inventors of other machines, and to the expansion of new inventors. Sole-sewing and other shoe machines had come to evolve as a system.

Ties among Shoe Machines

The processes developing shoe machines were connected among themselves, particularly when machines performed similar or complementary operations. This was manifested in the location of patenting. The broadest contrast was between machines and other patents. Massachusetts inventors took out 70 percent of shoe machine patents but only 46 percent of others. The state had over three-fifths of every major kind of machine patent except crimpers, peggers, and molders. This concentration on machinery reflects Massachusetts' domination of shoe machinery firms and its associated 65 percent share of known machinist-inventors.

Machine development was also interrelated when inventors patented more than one kind of machine. To ascertain the extent of this phenomenon, patents have been broken down into 20 types: 9 kinds of bottoming machines, 3 types of upper machines, heeling machines, finishing machines, stiffeners, tools, 2 types of forms, work support devices, and new processes. Of these types, only work support mechanisms and new processes need not refer to functionally specific devices (although some inventions combined more than one type of device).

Over 400 inventors took out more than one type of patent, 60 percent of multiple inventors and 17 percent of all inventors. A finer division of machine types—there were many kinds of heeling machines and more types of tools yet they formed but two categories—would increase the share issued more than one type of patent. Multiple inventors with a single type of invention were concentrated among those with one or two repeat patents.

Much patenting improved the devices for which first patents had been issued. Forty percent of repeats were in the same category as inventors' first patents, and another few percent were for altered processes or work support mechanisms for the same devices. Those changing patent types often specialized in lines to which they moved; the two most prolific inventors, Freeborn

Table 13.5
Single- and Multiple-Category Shoe Inventors, 1837–1901

| | With Commodity Usage | | Without Commodity Usage | |
	Single Category	Multiple Category	Single Category	Multiple Category
Number (M)	132	171	215	172
Share	44%	56%	56%	44%
Repeats (R)	397	1,236	367	383
Repeat Share	24%	76%	49%	51%
Extent (R/M)	3.01	7.23	1.71	2.23

Sources: See Tables 12.1, 12.4.
Note: A multiple-category inventor is a multiple inventor with patents in more than one category; the remainder are multiple inventors with patents in one category.

Raymond and Charles Glidden, began respectively with lasting and burnishing machines, but then together took out 76 heel machine patents, 19 related work support and process patents, and 24 heel-trimming patents.

Most repeat patenting took the inventor away from the operation originally addressed. Multiple-category patenting was most common among prolific inventors. Table 13.5 characterizes multiple inventors by use as a capital good and concentration of patents in a single category. The same categories are used, except that heel and sole trimmers are separated. To focus on the distinction between operations, categories are widened to include complementary patents; for example, an inventor with patents for lasting machines, lasting pincers, lasting jacks, and lasting processes would be classified as a single-category inventor. Even with this expanded notion of a category, half of the multiple inventors took out patents in more than one category. Many developed three types of machines, though few invented more. The share inventing in more than one category was higher among those with commodity usage than those without—56 to 44 percent. Moreover, multi-category inventors took out more repeat patents among those with commodity usage and also among those without; the difference was especially marked for the former. As a result, multiple-category inventors took out 76 percent of used repeat patents and 68 percent of all repeat patents. A virtuous circle connected machines; use led to learning which facilitated invention of other kinds of machines, which in turn added to use, learning, and further invention.

The Path and Importance of Redirection

Multiple-category inventors related the development of all shoe machines, but the degree of integration varied widely. Insights into the direction of inventive diversification can be gained by classifying inventors by the primary and secondary categories of their inventions—defined to be the categories with the highest and next-to-highest number of patents—and then examining

Table 13.6
Inventive Redirection for Shoe Inventors with Used Patents, 1837-1901

Secondary Category	Primary Patent Category						
	Burnish- ing	Heel	Last- ing	Other Sole	Sole Trimming	Upper	All
Processes	0%	8%	24%	9%	4%	0%	8%
Forms	0	0	0	5	0	23	6
Tools	0	4	6	7	4	15	5
Work Support	0	0	6	7	0	0	5
Stiffeners	7	8	0	0	7	0	3
Burnishers	–	25	12	2	26	8	11
Heel	14	21	0	16	15	15	14
Lasting	14	12	–	7	7	0	6
Other Sole	14	17	24	27	30	15	21
Sole Trimmers	43	4	0	14	–	0	8
Upper	7	0	29	7	7	23	13

Sources: See Table 12.1.

Notes: The primary category is the category in which the inventor had the most patents; the secondary category is the category with the next highest number of patents. Columns list the share of secondary patents for each primary category. The last column indicates the share of secondary categories among all 171 multiple patentees with used patents—including both the primary categories listed in this table and those not listed. Note that the columns for burnishing, lasting, and sole trimming have no entries in their own rows; because they are single categories, they cannot be both primary and secondary categories. Other columns group more than one category and can have entries in rows of the same type.

the distribution of secondary categories for each type of primary invention. The categories are the 20 used earlier. Table 13.6 presents this distribution for inventors with used patents. Only the most common primary categories are listed; inventors whose largest number of patents were machines for burnishing, heeling and heel trimming, lasting, sole trimming, other sole operations, and uppers formed 81 percent of the 171 multiple-category patentees who secured usage.[11] Columns list the secondary categories associated with each primary category, and the last column indicates the shares of secondary categories for all 171 inventors. In any row, shares significantly above that in the last column indicate an inventive affinity between the primary and secondary categories.

Each type of machine had inventive affinities with some kinds of devices and not others. Burnishing machine inventors developed sole trimmers far more often than did other inventors.[12] Sole-trimming inventors were connected to burnishers and to other sole machines. Heeling patentees were tied to burnishing and other heeling machines. Lasting machines were especially closely related to lasting tools and to machines that assembled upper pieces in preparation for lasting. More broadly, sole machines and upper machines were each most closely related to other machines of their own type.

A second conclusion may also be drawn. Inventors of each type of machine were distributed widely enough among secondary categories that no single dominant mechanism directed attention from one operation to another. Many directing influences coexisted. McKay's movement from sewing and channeling to heeling and then to lasting did not follow lines of technological convergence or close complementarity of operations. Because of the technological wholeness of the shoe factory and the range of communication with shoe producers, inventors could and did follow many paths of machine development.

The very multiplicity of their paths united all shoe machinery into one system. Virtually all pairs of major machines were connected by successful inventors, although to different degrees. Through this mechanism, the internal development of each machine, even by the efforts of inventors who concentrated solely on that machine, was informed by the relationship of machines to one another.

Leveling and molding machines illustrate the importance of diversification among types of shoe machines. To improve fit and appearance, shoes had long been leveled (or beaten out) after bottoming, a process in which soles were hammered to ensure their evenness. The need for leveling was especially felt on McKay shoes; sewed when the lasts were removed, early McKay shoes lost the shape of the last and were distinctively baggy at the sides. Leveling and molding machines solved this problem. The inventive effort grew dramatically after 1860. The 6 patents prior to 1862 grew to 15 in the 1862–71 period, tripled in the next decade, then expanded to 68 in the 1882–91 period and to 82 over the next 10 years.

This effort generated several practical leveling machines. In 1867 Joseph Johnson patented a machine to shape the bottomed soles by pressure on iron lasts. He developed this machine while working in a Lynn shoe factory, and, to make and sell the machine, he joined the owners of that factory to form Swain, Fuller & Company. As in the case of Lyman Blake, self-use gave way to the commodity path of mechanization. Within a year Johnson added a second last "to enable an attendant to prepare for being pressed a sole, while another may be in the act of being pressed by the machine."[13]

In 1868 Seth Tripp modified the Johnson process and, after a series of patents including one that used six simultaneously working lasts, came out with the successful Little Giant leveler. In 1884 Maurice Bresnahan, who had worked with Johnson, patented a leveler and produced it in the shoe machinery firm that he and his brothers ran. A quite different solution was arrived at by Othniel Gilmore in 1880. The son of the owner of the Raynham shoe factory where Blake had perfected his sewing machine, Gilmore used rollers to copy the hand-leveling process. Goodyear developed an improved version of the Gilmore leveler, which it added to its system of bottoming machinery.[14]

All but Bresnahan had previously taken out other kinds of patents. Johnson had been issued channeling machine and last patents, and, at the time of his first leveling patent, Tripp was a Lynn inventor who already had to his credit one shank-cutting, two pegging, and four burnishing patents. Gilmore's leveler was patented 16 years after he had used a roller to provide even pressure in a patented polishing machine and 1 year after receiving burnishing and stiffening patents. After their first leveling patents, Johnson and Bresnahan concentrated on levelers and took out five and three more leveling patents respectively. Tripp and Gilmore each took out two more leveling patents, but Tripp also took out a number of burnishing and other patents and Gilmore went into channeling invention.

The sole-molding machine was new to shoemaking. Invented around 1860 by David Knox, it applied pressure to form both soles to the shape of the last prior to sewing. By means of this machine, the soles retained much of their shape through sewing; together with the leveler, the molder largely overcame the bagginess of early McKay shoes.[15]

The molder was one of the few bottoming machines that depended on earlier leather-preparing innovations. From his experience designing and selling strippers, rolling machines, and sole blank machines, Knox had acquired knowledge of the properties of sole leather that he put to use in his molding machine. The importance of this machine extended beyond sole molding; Knox's fellow Lynn resident Joseph Johnson adapted the molder to form his beating-out machine, which was in turn the basis for the later Lynn improvements of Tripp and Bresnahan. On the same day Tripp took out his leveler patent, he was issued a patent for a molding machine. Knox later applied the molding principle to shape counters and heel stiffeners.

As molding and leveling machines exemplify, the birth of new machines often benefited from earlier patents of the central inventors. This was also true of other machines, such as Glidden's heeling machines, preceded by a heel burnisher. The machines of such inventors, developed and marketed by their own or other firms, were then improved by many, including some who specialized on a single machine, as was the case with Bresnahan and the principal inventor of the Goodyear leveler, Erastus Winkley. One result of successful integration was the initiation of independent processes of ongoing machine development.

Inventive Leadership and Integration

Established and potential inventors were integrated in a communications network that tied the diffusion and improvement of some machines to the birth and introduction of others. As the leading machine penetrated its market, it provided inducements and knowledge not only to improve the machine, but also to develop complementary and technologically convergent machines. The deepening of the product cycle for some machines was thus connected to the beginning of cycles for others. New machines came to sustain their own learning processes, pulled inventors in to improve them, but at the same time generated inventors oriented to other new operations.

The sequencing of product cycles influenced the distribution of patents by type and the level of shoe manufacturing patenting as a whole. The marked decline of pegging patents and the equally rapid growth of channeling and molding patents in the 1860s were both due to the rise of the McKay shoe. As the McKay shoe matured and McKay stitching patents declined relatively, so did patents to channel and mold (offset only partially by the rise of the Goodyear shoe). Sole machine invention was then led by patents for the most complex bottoming operation, lasting.

The sewing machine played three different roles in the birth of shoe machines. Upper-sewing machines had been critical to the origin of pegging machines and eyeletters. The McKay machine supplied inventors who took out important patents and redirected the efforts of established inventors toward complementary machines. By the time Goodyear developed its system of machines, it could call on well-established solutions and professional inventors. Most of its crossover inventors adapted machines to the requirements of manufacturing the Goodyear shoe.

One other factor structured ongoing invention. Shoemaking was tied to invention through shoe machinery firms. The activities of these firms influenced the use of inventions and the learning that arose from use. The medium informs the message; the pace and direction of technical change depended on the accumulation processes of machinery firms.

14

Integration by Firms

Shoe machinery firms connected the development of shoe machines inadvertently by spreading technological and marketing knowledge and intentionally through policies of diversification. Here is another kind of machine leadership; as either a result or a condition of the sale of leading machines, firms undertook to develop other machines.

Successful new product development generated financial and technological reasons for diversification. Over the course of the product cycle, revenues available for investment rarely equaled funds needed to penetrate potential markets. In the early stages of the cycle, the financing required to develop, produce, and sell the new machine far exceeded revenues, and, although credit made up part of the gap, finance constrained firm growth. As penetration proceeded, the dramatic growth of sales eased this constraint; a golden age began. Accumulation led to rapid sales growth which generated the funds to continue or accelerate the pace of accumulation. But the successful invasion of the potential market undercut the golden age. As market saturation approached, the growth of revenues slackened, reducing the sustainable rate of accumulation.

Revenue deceleration was not necessarily the binding limit to expansion; even before this limit came about, the financial requirements for reinvestment in the same line diminished. The plant and sales network had already been established, and falling unit production costs—and, as designs improved, perhaps also servicing costs—increased the profit margin. The coincidence of large profits with limited investment opportunities in the same line of business provided an impetus to enter new markets, in part through developing new products.[1]

Diversification had a second source. Machines formed a system in which the adequate functioning of each depended on the adequacy of others. A firm could more readily sell one machine if others were also available. If others did not exist or were not adapted for use with the firm's machine, an incentive existed for diversification. Expanding the system of machinery thus fostered movement through the product cycle, and could furthermore provide competitive advantages over other firms making the primary but not the auxiliary machines.

Firms began to diversify in the process of initial mechanization when Elmer Townsend spread from waxed-thread sewing into pegging machines. He continued his outward expansion by moving from pegging into technically convergent metallic fastening machines. He bought promising eyeletting inventions and set his own inventors to work to bring out an adequate machine; by 1871, he owned 37 eyeletting patents. He also bought and developed patents for edge-setting machines. Foreshadowing the formation of United Shoe Machinery a quarter century later, in the early 1870s the Townsend interests combined with those of David Whittemore to form the Shoe Machinery Manufacturing Company, valued at $1.2 million and employing 250. But upper-sewing and pegging machines were not to lead the consolidation of the shoe industry; the Townsend-Whittemore concern dissolved in 1875.[2]

McKay

Just as—in part because—the McKay machine surpassed the pegging machine, so also McKay and not Townsend led the diversification process. The success of the McKay machine provided technological and marketing knowledge used to develop and sell other machines, and leasing revenues supplied needed financing. Revenues from leasing fees grew from $39,000 in 1863 to $210,000 in 1867, $356,000 in 1869, $400,000 in 1870, $565,000 in 1872, and about $750,000 annually in the late 1870s.[3]

Revenue growth both depended on and fostered diversification. Complementary machines introduced in the 1860s bolstered sewing machine sales. This was the rationale for the invention of a channeling machine. In 1864 Gordon McKay began his own shoe patenting with a channeler; he and Lyman Blake copatented another in the same year and Blake was issued four more through 1871. McKay also developed a spooling machine adapted to the horn construction of his stitcher. Recognizing the complementarity of channeling and spooling machines with the sole sewer, McKay made them available with the sewing machine at no change in royalty and a nominal increase in set-up payments. McKay spread little further into complementary machines, partly because others developed machines to mold, trim, and level McKay shoes.

Diversification after 1870 was more a result than a cause of the expanded use of the McKay machine. Until 1867 or 1868, growing revenue was needed to overcome a financial constraint; McKay did not pay a dividend until 1866. But from about 1869 or 1870, it is unlikely that the increasing revenues were required to expand production and marketing networks. The number of machines in use grew by only 450 between 1867 and 1875, a considerably lower absolute annual increase than before 1867, and remained roughly constant from 1873 until 1883. Old machines were replaced, but the Sewing Machine Combination licensed over 200 McKay machines in only one of five years for which records are available. Likewise, the marketing system had been established in the major shoemaking centers by the late 1860s. The problem of the absorption of profits continued until 1881, when the basic patents expired, the royalty system was abandoned, and with it the main revenue basis of the firm was eliminated.[4]

McKay addressed the problem in several ways. He established an international marketing system to export machinery, principally to England and to a lesser extent to the Continent and Canada. Exports began in 1862 and by 1876 some 846 machines were used in foreign countries.[5] He improved his machine, doubling its daily capacity from 1865 to 1880. The resulting fall of labor costs encouraged adoption by the unmechanized and by pegged shoe producers. Already controlling the market, McKay had little to gain by the price competition to which shoe firms resorted in the 1870s; per pair royalties remained constant until 1881.

But neither entry into foreign markets nor investment in further product improvement absorbed all the retained profits of the firm. Diversification was the key solution. Beginning around 1870, McKay entered four new markets within a decade. He developed turn-sewing patents and in 1875 joined with Goodyear in the only consolidation that McKay would not see through to success. He bought heeling machine patents, formed the McKay Heeling Association in 1870, and in 1875 consolidated with his chief competitor to form the McKay and Bigelow Heeling Machine Association. Lasting was his next target. Again he bought patents, formed the McKay Lasting Association in 1872, and, propelled by patent overlaps, joined with Henry Thompson and then with George Copeland. Finally, after two years of infringement suits, McKay merged with a Townsend company to form the McKay Metallic Fastening Association in 1877.[6]

In control of basic patents, McKay undertook to develop practical machines. Goodyear and McKay should be considered a Goodyear company, but the other McKay associations took out (or were assigned at the time of patenting) 160 shoe patents and others for shoe-sewing machines. Two-thirds of these patents were for heel and heel-trimming machines, and another one-fifth for lasting.

These inventions, combined with the marketing experience and retained earnings of the McKay Sewing Machine Association, brought success to the newer McKay companies. McKay and Bigelow machines heeled 10 million pairs of shoes in 1871, 27 million in 1876, 45 million in 1881, and 72 million in 1890. Annual revenues rose to about a quarter-million dollars. Some 500 metallic fastening machines were sold through 1886 and another 300 in the following two years. In 1888, McKay sold peg wire to fasten about 20 million pairs of shoes. Lasting machines diffused more slowly, but in 1895, McKay and Copeland machines lasted about 20 million pairs.[7]

Table 14.1
Shoe Inventors by Type of User, 1837-1901

	McKay Inventors	Goodyear Inventors	Others
Single (S)	11	6	127
Multiple (M)	39	18	224
Total Patentees (S+M)	50	24	351
Repeats (R)	436	175	967
Frequency [M/(S+M)]	0.78	0.75	0.64
Extent (R/M)	11.18	9.72	4.32
Rate [R/(S+M)]	8.72	7.29	2.75

Sources: Tables 12.1, 12.4.

Note: McKay inventors are shoe patentees who had at least one patent used by McKay, and analogously for Goodyear inventors. Other inventors had patents used by neither company.

McKay Inventors

For each type of machine, invention had begun before McKay's involvement and continued outside his firm. But his diversification surely added to invention in areas he entered. His sales brought about learning and invention by those outside his firms. More to the point here, McKay organized ongoing invention within his associations. Fifty inventors assigned shoe machinery patents to McKay at the time of patenting. Most were technologically skilled. Of the 24 for whom occupations are known prior to their first shoe patents, 18 had been machinists, draftsmen, or model makers. The other 6 came from the shoemaking sector, including 2 factory foremen and 2 last makers.

Through employment and regular patent purchase, McKay professionalized invention. As a result, McKay inventors were more productive than other inventors with commodity usage. Ten were among the 28 with 15 or more repeat patents. When compared to inventors with patents used by firms other than Goodyear, a larger share of McKay inventors were multiple patentees and these averaged far more repeats. (See Table 14.1.) Both factors combined to give all McKay inventors three times as many repeat patents. Eleven also patented leather-sewing machines.

The association with McKay was not the only reason for the success of these inventors. Some had already been successful. Louis Goddu patented his bottom-screwing machine prior to the formation of McKay Metallic Fastening, George Copeland was an important inventor before his merger with McKay, and Freeborn Raymond had a decade's experience with the National Heeling Machine Company before joining McKay and Bigelow. Some achieved success after leaving McKay, including Goddu and Copeland.

But for many the ties to McKay were paramount. For Blake and McKay this is clear. It was also so for the second most prolific shoe inventor, Charles

Glidden. Originally a Lynn heel contractor, Glidden began his long association with McKay in the late 1860s and over the next three decades assigned 40 patents to McKay companies, mostly for heeling and heel-trimming machines. Often teamed with McKay, Hadley Fairfield assigned 14 shoe patents to McKay firms, as well as 1 sewing machine patent. Matthias Brock began with Copeland but most of his 33 patents were assigned to McKay and Copeland or its successors.

Moreover, inventors often changed direction as McKay diversified. Glidden moved from heel machine invention to lasting machines from 1873 through 1881, and then returned to heeling and heel-trimming machines. Fairfield developed burnishing and heeling machines from 1873 through 1875, sewing machines in 1876, lasting machines in the early 1880s, and heel-trimming machines in the late 1880s and early 1890s. From the McKay sole stitcher in the 1870s, Everett Richardson moved to lasting machines in the mid-1880s and then back to sewing machines.

As Glidden, Fairfield, and Richardson exemplified, among multiple inventors with used patents, McKay inventors were more likely to take out a variety of kinds of shoe patents than were other, non-Goodyear inventors. Over 70 percent of McKay inventors took out more than one type of patent, well above the 53 percent of inventors for non-Goodyear firms. Furthermore, McKay multiple-category inventors took out 95 percent of the repeat patents of all McKay inventors; among those gaining use outside McKay and Goodyear, only two-thirds of the repeat patents were issued to multiple-category inventors. The scope of McKay inventors was broadened by the 11 with sewing machine patents.

The diversification undertaken by McKay thus integrated the development of at least some shoe machines. His machines spanned most of the operations of the ten-footer; they lasted, bottomed, and heeled. Whereas use of these machines was locationally widespread, invention was not; 90 percent of McKay inventors were from Massachusetts. As such, McKay's activities help account for the concentration of first inventions in Massachusetts and the greater rate of repeat inventing and easier shifts of inventive focus by residents of that state.

Integration was furthered by indirect effects. The sales of the McKay firms directed others to improve heeling, lasting, and metallic fastening machines. Some had invented machines of other types, but many specialized in single types of machinery. Yet even this specialization by inventors and firms attests to the leadership of McKay and of its sole-sewing machine.

Goodyear

Besides McKay, the most significant diversification effort was undertaken by another sewing machine company, Goodyear. Goodyear had a different rationale. The slow diffusion of the Goodyear machine implied that retained earnings were hardly abundant. When rapid diffusion came in the 1890s, Goodyear readily invested its earnings in such undertakings as a plant large enough to employ 20 men as toolmakers and to devote a floor each for milling machines, screw-making machines, planers, and drillers.[8] Goodyear diversified not as a result but as a condition of market penetration.

The difference in rationale entailed distinct directions of diversification. After its early move into channeling, McKay invested in machines that were either substitutes for or largely independent of its other machines. Its welt and turn machines and screw machines in part substituted for McKay stitchers. Heeling machines performed operations after bottoming was completed. Lasting machines were most closely connected to sewing machines, but there is no evidence that McKay developed lasting machines because of any complementarity with sewing.

By contrast, Goodyear focused on machines to complement its sewing machines. Of the 36 patents taken out by Goodyear and its assignors, 4 were for channeling, 14 for sole leveling, 3 for sole rounding and trimming (including Briggs's rough rounder and channeler), 2 for sole assembling, 1 for stitch separating, 6 for lasting, and 6 for other sole operations. By 1897, Goodyear had diversified into 25 different bottoming machines, including machines to cut channels, open channels, turn the channel lip down, split and beat welts, and temporarily lay soles before outsole stitching. To complete its bottoming system, Goodyear tried to develop a lasting machine. By improving the accuracy and decreasing the cost of complementary operations, this diversification succeeded in increasing sewing machine sales.[9]

Goodyear's diversification redefined the commodity sold. Unlike McKay, whose new commodities generated a series of machines sold separately, Goodyear's new product development yielded a new commodity: a system of welt-sewing machines. The system was a unit defined by the sole-sewing machines. Other machines were auxiliary. They were added with only a minor set-up charge; the channel-lip-turning machine, placed for $60 without a leasing fee, formed the precedent. Auxiliary machines had no market independent of the sewing machines. Initial leases of the rough-rounding and channeling machine restricted its use to shoe producers employing Goodyear stitchers. Later machines were added on the same principle. The purpose of introducing new auxiliary machines was, in the words of Goodyear's general manager, S. V. A. Hunter, "to strengthen the welt system."[10]

Goodyear's new product development acquired a competitive rationale in the 1890s. Andrew Eppler and Duncan Campbell each developed turn- and welt-sewing machines, Eppler with the backing of several of the largest Goodyear users, seven of whom were directors of Eppler's firm. Goodyear effectively countered by extending its welt system. It added a number of new machines in the mid-1890s, the most important of which was the Copeland Rapid Laster. This was the first time that the lasting machine had been integrated into the bottoming system. Goodyear also tried to protect its superiority in auxiliary machines by announcing that infringers of its rough-rounding and channeling and its stitch-separating and indenting machines would be prosecuted.[11]

The development of the Goodyear system utilized a core of inventors attracted, as were McKay inventors, from mechanically adept occupations. Ten of the 13 with known occupations had been machinists or professional inventors, and the other 3 had been shoemakers. Goodyear inventors were almost as prolific as McKay inventors. As Table 14.1 indicates, the 7.3 patents of Goodyear inventors, a bit under the 8.7 of McKay patentees, were far above the 2.8 of other inventors with used patents. Goodyear inventors spread out their inventive efforts even more than McKay inventors. Sixteen of the 18 Goodyear multiple inventors were issued shoe patents of more than one type; these 16 took out all but 3 of the 175 repeat patents issued to Goodyear inventors.

A few inventors began their shoe patenting with Goodyear, including Christian Dancel and also Zachary French, whose 20 shoe patents and 12 sewing machine patents put him among the most prolific of crossover inventors. But because most of its patents came later in the period, Goodyear benefited from the prior inventive experience of its patentees. Joseph Crisp had taken out 22 patents for Copeland lasting and treeing firms before working on Goodyear lasting machines, and William Gordon had as many for several companies before patenting a sole-assembling machine for Goodyear. In 10 years of inventing before joining Goodyear, Peter Coupal had patented 3 leather-sewing machines and 3 sole-laying machines.

The centrality of the leather-sewing machine in the Goodyear system is also expressed in the role of sewing machine inventors in developing the Goodyear system: one-half of the Goodyear shoe machine inventors were crossover inventors who held a total of 59 leather-sewing machine patents. Clearly their inventions depended on Goodyear's experience with sewing machines. On the other hand, three-quarters of Goodyear crossover inventors started with shoe patents, and the shoe machines they formed helped account for the diffusion of the sole-stitching machine. The sewing machine was not just a leader, it was also led.

The Extent of Integration by Firms

Diversification was not confined to Townsend, McKay, and Goodyear. Other firms developed and marketed a variety of machines. Eppler had the most active minor sewing machine firm. Firms organized or managed by Eppler were issued or assigned 5 channeling patents and about 25 other patents for such bottoming operations as metallic fastening and sole laying. At least eight other bottom-sewing machine firms took out channeling patents.

Burnishing and trimming firms were often integrated, as in the cases of Dodge Trimmer, Flagg Manufacturing, and James Busell. Companies that integrated lasting with other operations included those of Busell; Copeland, who entered treeing; Albert Preston, who combined lasting and crimping; and Sidney Winslow, who spread from buffing machines.[12]

A sense of the relation of diversification to invention can be gained by examining shoe machinery companies listed in Boston business directories. From 1860 through 1901, 101 of these firms were issued shoe patents. Twenty-two took out patents for more than one type of shoe machine. Eighteen patented trimming or channeling machines, 10 in combination with burnishing machines, 5 with sole levelers, and 4 each with heel and lasting machines. If sewing machine patents are added, 18 firms were issued patents for both sewing and shoe machines, led of course by McKay and Goodyear. Ten of these took out trimming and channeling patents, and 8 combined lasting and sewing patents in an effort to use the sewing machine to last.

Important limits to diversification existed. Many firms specialized in a single type of machinery, including the most important heel-burnishing firm, the Tapley Machine Company. If firms did diversify, one line of machinery often remained dominant, as was true for Copeland, the Tripp Giant Leveler Company, and even Goodyear. Diversification took firms into only a few lines of machinery. The most successful, McKay, focused on a few bottoming and heeling operations. Until the formation of United Shoe Machinery, companies were significantly less diversified than Elmer Townsend, who sold machines to sew uppers, to eyelet, to peg and screw bottoms, and to trim soles.

Even within bottoming, new machines often took practical form outside the diversification of bottoming machine firms. This had been true of molding, leveling, and rounding in the 1860s and 1870s. It remained true of machines developed well after McKay and Goodyear began to diversify. The most important example was the lasting machine.

Lasting was the hardest bottoming operation to mechanize. It involved assembling the insole, upper, and some minor parts on the last; pulling the toe of the upper over the last and tacking it to the insole and last; and, finally, lasting proper, which drew the upper over the last and tacked its sides, toe, and heel to the insole. The accuracy of construction and the appearance of the shoe rested on the quality of lasting. The upper had to be evenly stretched to avoid bagginess and folded around the toe and heel in a way that did not show on the finished shoe.

The complexity of the operation and the variability of the material accounted for the difficulty of mechanization. The pull-and-twist motion of the hand laster proved hard to duplicate. Just as the hand motions of cotton picking were more difficult to mechanize than the arm motions of reaping, so also the grasping, pulling, and twisting made hand lasting harder to mechanize than trimming, pegging, or sewing. The problem was complicated by the heterogeneity of the material. Some leather could be stretched only a little, but other leather had to be stretched a lot to avoid looseness in the finished shoe. Care had to be taken to ensure that pincers stretching the leather did not rip the thin uppers. Moreover, welt shoes had to be tacked in a certain way to be sewed without ripping. It was no surprise that lasting was still largely a hand operation in the 1890s.[13]

The need for a lasting machine was felt early. Inaccuracies in lasting were a significant cause of ripped leather and poor shoe quality. Like other bottoming machines, lasting patents grew with the expansion of the factory in the 1860s. The early 1870s saw invention take off. The 8 patents from 1862 through 1871 grew to 68, 120, and 135 in the next decades.

Both of the major sole-sewing companies took up the problem. In 1872 McKay bought up the patents of an earlier lasting company and to develop them hired such inventors as Charles Glidden, who already had a McKay heeling machine to his credit. After combining with Henry Thompson and George Copeland, the McKay & Copeland Lasting Association controlled over 100 patents in 1881 and made a machine having limited use for heavy shoes. Much effort was expended on this machine in the 1880s, and in 1895 it lasted about 20 million pairs of shoes. But it would not dominate the field. Neither would the Copeland rapid laster, which Goodyear took into its system in 1893. Goodyear claimed that this machine saved from two to five cents per pair compared to hand lasting, but it was never widely used.[14]

It was the product of a new company that would mechanize lasting. The Hand Method lasting machine, so named because it copied the movements of hand lasters, was invented by Jan Matzeliger, a machinist from Dutch Guiana. Matzeliger was hired to operate a McKay stitcher in a Lynn factory in 1875 and began trying to develop a lasting machine soon after. His work gave him an advantage over other inventors: he regularly observed hand lasters and was able to incorporate their movements into the machine he patented in 1883. His was the only machine to apply equally well to shoes of all lightnesses, shapes, and modes of construction. Like the Goodyear machine and the Gilmore leveler, it illustrates that successful shoe machinery often closely copied hand principles of production; all machinery did not have to depart from hand-type operations as radically as had the sewing machine. It is a tribute to Matzeliger's accomplishment that his machine took practical form for some shoes in a decade, whereas the Goodyear welt system required a quarter century.[15]

But development, production, and marketing proved too much for Matzeliger, as for Lyman Blake and August Destouy before him. The Hand Method Lasting Machine Company was formed in the mid-1880s and joined another firm to form the Consolidated Hand Method Lasting Machine Company, controlled by Sidney Winslow, a promoter of a shoe-buffing machine, and George Brown, agent and then New England general manager for Wheeler and Wilson. Through the efforts of company inventors, who were issued a dozen patents, Consolidated introduced a practical lasting machine for McKay shoes by 1890 and adapted this machine to Goodyear shoes in 1897. To disseminate its machines, Consolidated spread agencies throughout the principal shoe towns and in 1897 established a training school in Lynn large enough to use 50 practice machines. Well-marketed, excellent products brought rapid growth; the 2,900 machines used in 1899 lasted 80 million pairs of shoes. Just applied to Goodyear shoes, Consolidated machines would continue to spread in the decade to come.[16]

One final machine completed the mechanization of lasting. Shortly after 1900 a machine was introduced to accurately pull the upper over the last. This machine was not produced by any of the major bottoming companies— McKay, Consolidated, or Goodyear—but rather by all three; their merger in the late 1890s formed the United Shoe Machinery Company which developed a machine based on the principles of an earlier pulling-over machine.[17]

Planned and Independent Product Development

In some ways the social organization that initiated major inventions late in the century would have been familiar to Elias Howe. New machines were still often developed by small inventors acting on their own behalf. Matzeliger's inventive process, taking place on his own time with his own funds in a small rented room, was much like Howe's. That Matzeliger would sell the patent to a relatively small firm was similar to the experience of Howe in England, and of William Wickersham, Lyman Blake, and August Destouy in America. Sale continued to bring learning by selling; success greatly increased the share of patents outside nodal firms for welt sewing in the 1890s, as it had for dry-thread sewing in the late 1850s.

But the differences were striking. Bound up with shoe machine sales, a dynamic of ongoing mechanization had originated. Technical knowledge disseminated, marketing practices spread, shoe firms readily purchased machinery, and professional inventors appeared. A McKay stitcher in a Lynn factory, Matzeliger was just as affected by this dynamic as were McKay and Goodyear inventors. Established shoe machinery firms typically developed and sold new machines; unlike in the case of Wickersham, Blake, or Destouy, it was a shoe machinery company that bought Matzeliger's patent.

Between dry-thread and Goodyear machines, invention had changed in a way that gave planned development a much greater role. The dry-thread machine had taken practical form quickly through an interaction of firms spreading knowledge by means of sales efforts. Already a change had occurred when waxed-thread and McKay machines each achieved practicality within a single firm. The firm had come to plan and organize technical change.

A further step was taken when companies diversified into new products. When Singer entered buttonhole and carpet-sewing markets, when Townsend undertook pegging and eyeletting, and when McKay went into heeling, they benefited from their firms' own histories. Earlier innovation supported all inventors, including those whose patents were purchased by diversifying firms. But for these firms, their own past innovations influenced their present profits, organization, and personnel in a way that facilitated ongoing technical change. Within a decade, their product development brought out practical buttonholing, pegging, eyeletting, and heeling machines.

A last step came when the time needed to develop machines was protracted. Practicality arrived a quarter century after Goodyear took up welt-sewing machines or McKay addressed lasting. At about the same time Matzeliger was issued his patent, Matthias Brock was taking out his fifteenth lasting patent, which he assigned to the McKay and Copeland Lasting Machine Association. A decade and a half later, when the lasting machine finally was successful, he would have taken out as many again, assigned now to Consolidated and McKay, a merger of his old firm and that formed to develop Matzeliger's machine. In the absence of significant sales, learning by selling was relatively less important and company research and development more so.

In such cases, the process of commodity definition was prolonged, and invention occurred ahead of demand, front-loading the product cycle. Sales came quickly for dry-thread, upper waxed-thread, McKay, and heeling machines, after which patenting leaped to a much higher level. The matter was quite different with lasting and welt-sewing machines, as a comparison of heeling and lasting machines indicates. Heeling machines penetrated the market in earnest from around 1871, when McKay and Bigelow machines heeled about 12 percent of American shoes, on their way to 30 percent in 1876. From less than 2 per year in the previous decade, heel machine patents rose to 5 annually from 1872 through 1881 and about 10 for the rest of the century. Lasting machines did not mechanize a tenth of output until the 1890s, and patenting, which had averaged 11 annually from 1877 through 1891, only grew to 13 per year in the next decade. The point is not that learning by selling declined, only that it was supplemented by much more intensive presale invention by machinery firms.

Companies developing all major machines took out a large share of patents before their commodities were practical. Because welt-sewing and lasting machines took so long to become practical, major companies took out many more patents. In the quarter century through 1891, Goodyear took out or was assigned at the time of patenting 18 shoe-sewing machine patents and 7 complementary shoe patents. Major lasting machine companies, including McKay, Copeland, Thompson, and Consolidated, took out 61 patents from 1876 through 1891. In both cases, firms began with very large patent shares and their shares then fell. Goodyear's 8 turn- and welt-sewing patents from 1869 through 1871 were virtually all for this type of machine, but it only had 10 more in the next 20 years. The 45 issued to major lasting firms from 1877 through 1886 were over half of all lasting patents, a share that fell to 13 percent in the next decade.

Falling shares were often associated with entry, and welt-sewing and lasting machines were no exception. Sales of turn machines and inadequate welt machines spread knowledge of Goodyear machines. Goodyear employees entered, especially Andrew Eppler, who after patenting for Goodyear in 1881 formed his own company and took out four welt-sewing patents through 1892. Lasting machine companies proliferated from 1885. Frank Chase took out seven patents through 1891 and eight more in the next five years. Four other firms entered with at least two lasting patents through 1891, including one by Christian Dancel assigned to Scott Lasting in New York. Six more firms new to lasting were issued two or more patents from 1892 through 1896, Goodyear among them.

With practicality came learning, invention, and entry; but major companies retained center stage. Having declined to 12 percent of patents in the 1892–96 period, major lasting companies rose to 26 percent in the next 5 years. From 5 per decade in the previous 20 years, Goodyear's sewing machine patents grew to 19 from 1892 through 1901, to which it added 30 shoe patents. Its earlier shoe patents had been for channelers and rounders, but in the 1890s machines to level soles, separate stitches, assemble soles, and last were paramount. Just when its welt- and outsole-sewing machines became practical, Goodyear redefined its commodity to be a system of bottoming machines.

From the time of the sewing machine, nodal firms had formed early and retained their lead as the market was penetrated. But now major firms organized product development for far longer periods in anticipation of growth, found other well-funded firms willing to do the same, and readily diversified. Technical change in the shoe industry and new institutions in the capital goods sector had emerged together, and in their evolution had altered the process generating new techniques. The practices of the upcoming century were coming into being.

15

Two Results

Results of technical change cannot be separated from the process generating this change. It is at best one-sided to argue, as economic theory frequently does, that the economic effects of new machines are outcomes of the technical properties of these machines. For the economic institutions governing the diffusion of new machines have effects of their own. The same process that increased the productivity of shoemaking labor also concentrated the shoe machinery industry. The commodity path that structured the generation of technical change also shaped its results.

Mechanized Shoe Production

Though hardly unique, the mechanization of shoemaking still stood out, as recognized by the 1898 report of the Commissioner of Labor, entitled *Hand and Machine Labor*: "There is probably none of the older industries of the country in which the introduction of machinery has been more rapid, or has played a more important part in saving time and reducing labor cost, than in that pertaining to the manufacture of boots and shoes."[1] This report documented the transformation of shoemaking for seven factories it carefully surveyed in 1895 and 1896. Machinery had come to every branch of shoemaking except for upper cutting, which remained the domain of pattern, knife, and board. The sewing and skiving machine populated the upper fitting room along with eyeletting, buttonholing, and upper-folding machines. Sole-cutting, rolling, rounding, molding, and channeling machines filled the stock fitting room, and heel-cutting, compressing, nailing, and trimming machines made and attached heels. The lasting machine was only coming into use, and its complement, the pulling-over machine, was still awaited. But the system of bottoming machines to channel, sew or peg, lay, level, and trim was generally used. Machines to burnish and buff soles and heels were fixtures in finishing rooms. Steam engines ran almost all machines, as they had for a quarter century.[2]

Mechanization continued the transformation of labor begun before the Civil War. The worker became an operative whose actions were determined by the requirements of the machine. The McKay stitcher removed the last, mounted the shoe upside down on the machine horn, activated the machine, and guided the shoe as the machine rotated it. The worker made a difference; if he or she tipped the shoe, the needle would be mispositioned in the channel of the shoe, and the stitching would be misplaced and perhaps cut during trimming. But it was the machine that stitched; the worker had become a condition of the machine's activity.[3]

Mechanized production was by no means complete. Machines were utilized in only one-half of the operations into which *Hand and Machine Labor* divided shoemaking. Some were not prospects for mechanization, including sorting, marking, and supervising. But over one-third were unmechanized yet employed such tools as brushes, sponges, sprinklers, knives, hammers, pincers, and tack pullers. Still, the most time-consuming hand operations except upper cutting and in part lasting had been mechanized. About three-quarters of the labor time of craft shoemakers had been expended on operations mechanized by 1898. Upper sewing itself formed 25 percent of hand labor time, and in welt shoes, welt and outsole stitching comprised another 12 to 16 percent.[4]

Even hand activities were affected by mechanization. The extent of the division of labor was increasingly structured by the system of machines. David Johnson, a Lynn shoemaker, listed 33 positions in the shoe factory of 1875, whereas a description of the Goodyear shoe factory of the turn of the century listed 95. The 13 positions in the bottoming department had expanded to 32, and nonmechanized operations were defined in relation to the machines that surrounded them.[5]

The use of machinery markedly improved labor productivity. For the industry as a whole, annual output per laborer among firms producing for the wholesale market stood at 880 pairs in 1870 and grew to 1,530 pairs in 1900.[6] In 1870 some of the most labor-saving shoe machines had already been introduced, including the upper-sewing machine, the McKay stitcher, the pegger, and leather-rolling, stripping, blank-cutting, and skiving machines. Measures of the pairs manufactured appear in the federal census for the first time in 1870 (except for partial figures in 1810), but the Massachusetts state census measured output earlier. Within Massachusetts, output per worker rose from 580 pairs in 1855 to 1,090 in 1870 and 1,750 in 1900; the transition from craft to factory production tripled productivity.[7] In at least this state, the first decade and a half of mechanization increased productivity as rapidly as did the next three.

The connection between mechanization and productivity growth is documented in *Hand and Machine Labor*. When compared to hand producers who worked from 1855 to 1875, factory laborers at the end of the century produced almost 9 times as many pairs of shoes per labor hour. Not all of this productivity increase can be attributed to mechanization. The productivity of upper cutters tripled, and other hand operations were similar. But productivity growth was much higher for mechanized operations. Labor productivity in mechanized upper sewing and in welt sewing was 23 times as high as hand methods, and outsole stitching was 40 times as high. Other operations were only by comparison less revolutionary. Sole rounding was 12 times as high; leveling, 8; sole trimming, 13; sole burnishing, 7; and heel attaching, 9. Other operations had little or no advantage over hand methods, including sole laying, outsole channeling, and insole channeling. Lasting offers a useful contrast of measured productivity growth coming with mechanization. In units retaining hand techniques, productivity was 3 times as high as earlier hand techniques, just as for upper cutting. But it was 6 times as high for units using the lasting machine.[8]

In accounting for productivity growth, the generation and the introduction of new techniques were inseparable. The very fact that the shoe manufacturer was confronted with a choice of techniques manifested the commodity form of technical change. Because the capital goods producer marketed finished machinery along with training in its usage, the shoe manufacturer did not have to undertake the technical development associated with self-usage or with the spread of knowledge through the movement of workers. The marketing of shoe machinery firms also determined the locations and sizes of shoe producers confronted with the choice of technique.

Moreover, the availability of techniques did not account for productivity growth by itself. Use of the machines was associated with short-run learning by doing, as well as perhaps with the intensification of labor. No doubt short-run learning took place largely through the agency of shoe firm management and contractors. Yet both it and the disembodied learning by using associated with the development of machine maintenance and repair procedures depended on the training and servicing undertaken by machinery firms.[9]

In addition, introduction and generation were tied together more dynamically. Learning from communication with users, machine firms improved the design and durability of machines and developed other new products. As inventors they were joined by shoe manufacturers, foremen, and workers; over 40 percent of shoe manufacturing patentees got their start in shoe factories and shops. Efforts to market products led to collaboration and investment by shoe manufacturers in the development of new capital goods, as Goodyear was pleased to experience in the 1870s but not so pleased when his competitors did the same in the 1890s.

Mechanization could not but alter the structure of the shoe industry. Just as, in Mantoux's interpretation, textile machinery helped shape the factory, the industrial firm, and class relations in factory regions, so too did shoe machines; technical and institutional changes were once again connected. As McKay and pegging machines were introduced, bottoming teams were brought into the factory, managed often at first by contractors but later by company foremen. The relationships among shoe firms were altered by competitive advantages coming from falling unit costs and from higher prices for the McKay and then the Goodyear shoe. These advantages in turn made mechanization compulsory.

To examine these effects is beyond our scope; it is enough to note that they depended not simply on the existence of machinery but also on its social form.[10] Machines only spread as rapidly and widely as they did because companies formed marketing systems to make machinery available in many locations, usable by operatives without prior training, and affordable by firms of all sizes. The broad diffusion evened unit costs and thus limited the advantages of larger firms. United Shoe Machinery defended its agency system on these grounds; that one of the great U.S. monopolies at the turn of the century could justify itself as the protector of the small firm is among the more ironic implications of the commodity form taken by technical change.

The Concentration of the Shoe Machinery Industry

The mechanization process that so broadly spread machinery among 1,600 factory shoe producers in 1900 also concentrated the bulk of the production of that machinery in a few firms and then a single firm. The two results were connected; new products and marketing methods gave powerful advantages to the growth and consolidation of innovating machinery firms. The growth of the market did lead to specialization, but specialization within firms, not among them.

The tendency toward the consolidation of firms had three aspects. The novelty of the machine and its markets led to vertical integration. Growth, Gordon McKay discovered as had Isaac Singer before him, was greatly aided by integration into marketing. The regular contacts with shoe producers required by the complexity of the product and the practice of leasing machinery could not be met by existing marketing methods; firms had to organize this function themselves. Firms also integrated into research and development.

Second, consolidation was common among producers of individual machines in the period when practical products were originating. Often motivated by the risk and disruption of patent litigation, such consolidation had been a common practice of McKay in heeling, metallic fastening, and lasting in the 1870s and 1880s. It continued in the 1890s with the acquisition of Campbell by Goodyear and the merger of Consolidated, McKay and Copeland, and two smaller firms to form the Consolidated and McKay Lasting Machine Company in 1897.[11] Once firms made and sold practical machines, entry by others was limited by barriers of capital cost, marketing organization, accumulated knowledge, breadth of product line, and, for a period, patent control.

Third, diversification spread the influence of successful firms among commodities, as McKay's expansion illustrated. To better coordinate its diversified, yet independent operations, McKay consolidated its heeling and metallic fastening companies to form the McKay Shoe Machinery Company in the mid-1890s. Goodyear integrated shoe machinery evolution more closely by leasing a system of machines as a single commodity.

Each of these tendencies of consolidation persisted as shoe machinery expanded. Indeed, each was partly responsible for the growth of sales. Integration into marketing clearly had this effect. The organization of technical development within the firm was especially important when practicality was a long time coming. Mergers made possible the appropriation of technical advance without litigation (although other means, such as the sewing machine industry's patent pool, could have accomplished the same end). Diversification made use of finance and knowledge to develop new machines more rapidly and was, as Goodyear learned, a condition for selling the principal machine.

The pinnacle of consolidation was reached with the formation of the single firm that dominated the industry. In February 1899, the United Shoe Machinery Company was incorporated out of the merger of five firms: Goodyear and its international marketing subsidiary, McKay Shoe Machinery, the Consolidated and McKay Lasting Machine Company, the Eppler Welt Machine Company and its marketing subsidiary, and the Davey Pegging Machine Company. There were many reasons for this merger. In testimony before the Industrial Commission, Elmer Howe, a member of United's executive committee, focused on the marketing savings gained from reducing the duplication of servicing networks.[12]

The merger also resulted from the same factors that had supported earlier consolidation in the industry, especially as they came together around the lasting machine. United Shoe Machinery was not the result of competition of major firms producing the same machines; except for the minor instance of McKay and Davey in pegging, firms had little overlap of product lines. More important was the development of a new product; both Goodyear and Consolidated and McKay attempted to develop a turn- and welt-lasting machine but each was blocked by patents held by the other. A rationale for consolidation existed much like the one that had brought McKay together with Thompson, then Copeland, and then Consolidated.[13]

But this overlap did not directly lead to merger. The more immediate factor was the diversification of Consolidated and McKay into bottom-sewing machinery. Consolidated and McKay had faced a limit to its growth in the booming welt market coming from Goodyear's integration into lasting. The threat came not from Goodyear's lasting machine itself—it was inferior to the Hand Method machine—but because Goodyear could tie use of its welt inseamers to use of its lasting machine. Consolidated and McKay took the offensive; it bought a controlling interest in the Eppler Welt Machine Company. It then had a system of machines superior to the Goodyear system in one critical regard: its lasting machine. Consolidated and McKay then took the lead in further consolidation. Aware that sales would fall if shoe firms could use adequate welt machinery along with the Hand Method laster, the Goodyear officers soon agreed to merge. Somewhat more reluctantly, McKay agreed to combine, responding in part to the competitive threat posed by the prospects of a system combining the Davey pegging machine with Consolidated lasters.[14]

The formation of United Shoe Machinery integrated the industry in several ways. Its product line included virtually all sole fastening, lasting, and heeling machines and as such was far wider than the lines of its predecessors Its continuation of Goodyear's practice of leasing a line of machinery integrated the sale of machinery because of its wider product line. Initially United aimed at selling a single commodity: the use of all machinery appropriate for a shoe firm's factory. Thus, a firm using its lasting machines would also have to use its heeling and bottoming machinery. After negotiation with the New England Association of Boot and Shoe Manufacturers, United relaxed this requirement a bit, offering to lease machinery in only one department of the factory at a higher fee. It integrated servicing by merging the agencies and teams of its component firms. Soon after the turn of the century it also concentrated production in its Beverly, Massachusetts, factory, called "The home of the United Shoe Machinery Company—the largest and most modern machinery manufacturing plant in the country."[15]

Furthermore, United integrated product development far more than had its predecessors. It established an experimental division that employed the inventors of the constituent firms, hired a few more, and expended about one-half million dollars annually in the 15 years after consolidation. The division brought together inventors with wide experience in product development. Twenty-two American inventors assigned 22 shoe patents and 11 leather-sewing machine patents to United in 1900 and 1901. Eighteen of these inventors took out more than 1 shoe or sewing machine patent through 1901 and averaged about 15 patents per inventor. United inventors included three of the five most prolific shoe patentees: Freeborn Raymond, Matthias Brock, and Erastus Winkley.

United developed or refined 150 machines through 1914. The most important for bottoming was the pulling-over machine introduced in 1904. Having cost $900,000 to develop, it completed the mechanization of lasting. To sell a complete line of shoe machinery, United diversified into stock-fitting machines, finishing machines, and a few upper-fitting operations, along with tools, gauges, dies, and supplies. Acquisition was a principal means to diversify. Soon after the consolidation, United bought out 2 companies making eyeletting machines, 1 manufacturing eyelets, 1 making edge setters, the Gem Flexible Insole Company, and Gordon, Coupal and Co., the manufacturer of the Rockingham line of finishing machinery. Altogether United made 43 acquisitions from 1899 through 1904 and another 16 through 1911. It then used its own inventors to develop the acquired machinery.[16]

The shoe machinery industry was taking its twentieth-century form. From an industry of firms concentrating in single machines or lines of machinery, it had come to be dominated by one generic shoe machinery firm. Based on the inherited expansion in welt-sewing and lasting machine use, United increased its assets almost 10 percent per year through 1910. Its retained earnings were used to enter foreign markets; its foreign sales helped foreign firms resist the strong penetration efforts that American shoe firms began in the 1890s. Its profits also extended its product line through most shoe machinery, with exceptions such as the products of another giant, Singer.[17]

United also used its profits to diversify out of the shoe machinery industry. It developed generic leather-working machinery such as eyeletters and cutting and finishing machinery, and then went into heavy machine tools and capital equipment, industrial fastenings, and industrial chemicals—products it makes today. But all this belongs to the history of the twentieth-century capital goods sector; with the formation of United's shoe machinery line, the origin of mechanized shoe production had been completed.

Part IV

Conclusion

16

Continuity and Change

The mechanization of American shoemaking revolutionized techniques and institutions, and as such exemplifies the problem with which the book began: how to account for industrialization when techniques and institutions were both qualitatively changed in the process. It is appropriate to conclude by considering the solution that has been advanced.

Starting the Commodity Path

The first step to a solution is often to clarify the problem. We have advanced the thesis that shoe machinery developed according to the logic of the commodity path of technical change. According to this thesis, industrialization results from structured social processes that generate and diffuse technical change. These processes take different social forms, but in any form technical change establishes a cumulative process tying together invention, diffusion, and use. In the commodity form, machine sale is a medium for diffusion, learning, and the growth of machinery firms; these together lead to ongoing technical improvement.

This thesis implies that industrialization can only be understood as the outcome of two sequential processes: a process originating techniques and institutions, and a later process in which these institutions sustain technical change. Moreover, it follows that starting the process faces greater barriers, especially structural barriers to communication. Before a commodity exists, the need it is to satisfy is unsettled, and knowledge of technical problems, skills to solve these problems, awareness of machine marketing, and access to finance are isolated from each other. Even in modern capitalism, the birth of new commodities involves innovation in both techniques and institutions.

The discontinuity was much greater in the origins of mechanized capitalist production. When production was conceived in craft terms, there was no expressed need for machines. Substantial expenditure and reorganization were needed to introduce the factory system. The separation of shoemaking and engineering knowledge, embedded in distinction between crafts of shoemakers and machinists, made invention difficult. Mechanization required not merely technical innovation, but also novel marketing mechanisms and new machinery firms. Nor was there the stimulus of competition to force innovation; until there were commodities, there could be no competition over market shares, and there was no meaningful competition with shoe tool producers or indirectly from rubber shoes. Leadership was required.

The very terms used—discontinuity, innovation, leadership—invite comparison with Schumpeter. His notion of innovation takes full cognizance of the discontinuity of technical change from the state of the economy. Innovation is for him "a feat not of intellect, but of will." It requires "supernormal energy and courage" possessed by "a distinct type which is rare." It requires, in short, the entrepreneur. Entrepreneurship itself is understood in terms of the psychology of the type: the will to conquer, the dream of forming a private kingdom, the joy of creating. The theory of capitalist change examines not the sources but the consequences of innovation, the effects—on interest rates, profits, growth, and instability—of the entrepreneurial function "which will, *by its mere working and from within*—in the absence of all outside impulses or disturbances and even of 'growth'—destroy any equilibrium." [1] With regard to the economy, the entrepreneur is the unmoved mover.

Our approach has been quite distinct. Schumpeter rightly argues that a theory of capitalist change cannot be subordinated to a doctrine of equilibrium; innovation is distinguished from an adjustment to conditions in the economy at large.[2] But in one way he resembles many theorists of equilibrium: technical change does not emerge from prior economic processes. For us the problem is more how the institutional structure of premechanized production could create conditions and agents of mechanization; how, in other words, continuity could underlie change.

It is in addressing this problem that the manufacturing dynamic takes on importance. The prospects for a new capital good depend on the organization of the sectors to use and make it. The evolution of shoemaking integrated the market, concentrated production locationally, and increased the size of the firm; each of these changes supported the introduction of new techniques. Agents and social forms of innovation emerged; merchants and especially producers transformed production through a path of self-usage, and specialized input producers introduced a commodity path of technical change. Mechanization elsewhere also fostered the birth of shoe machines. From outside the shoe industry, potential demand grew and skill expanded, both tied in part to mechanization. New innovative institutions, especially machinery firms and the machinists' trade, applied technical knowledge to develop machines and formed marketing practices to sell them. Relative to the Industrial Revolution, the problem of inventing, developing, and producing machines was much lessened.

That such changes facilitated the birth of shoe machinery does not, of course, deny the reality of innovation. Individuals who altered established practice made a difference, led both by inventors such as Elias Howe, Allen Wilson, Isaac Singer, Lyman Blake, August Destouy, Christian Dancel, and

Jan Matzeliger and by the marketing innovators and company builders, Singer and his partner Edward Clark, Gordon McKay, Charles Goodyear, Jr., and Sidney Winslow.

But their innovations were conditioned by economic processes. The very institutions that limited communication of technological skills, market expectations, and shoemaking problems made innovation necessary if techniques were to arise and spread. Capital goods firms and independent inventors had generated ongoing mechanization processes in already mechanized sectors, but they had no organized means to discover and solve problems in other sectors. Mechanization could only occur along many distinct paths; shoe machinery innovators might call on other sectors for help, but had to develop to the point when they could do the calling.

Moreover, innovators were hardly unconditioned. They were embedded in institutions that structured potential demand, skills, and learning. In its timing, location, personnel, and operations, innovation took place where barriers were least. One need not doubt Schumpeter's claim that factors of will mattered; after all, not everyone who might have innovated did so. But factors of intellect—the learning and insight critical for invention and diffusion—also mattered, and the intellectual advances of the innovator depended on institutions of firm, craft, and market to communicate knowledge of technical problems, solutions, and modes of diffusion.

The importance of the institutional framework to innovation was exhibited by the interactions that brought Howe's machine to practicality. Although the earliest inventors failed commercially, together they succeeded in forming a communications network enmeshing, often by accident, those who would develop and sell Howe's machine. The network was structured around sale, and prior institutional changes on the sides of supply and demand—among those who produced and sold machines, and among those who bought them—together fostered the dynamic that brought success to innovations where earlier stitching inventions had failed. That innovators were not investing ahead of demand, manifested by the ready reception of machines, was both a result of institutional evolution and a source of further machine evolution. The outcome of the process was not simply a new technique, but also complementary innovations in marketing, new capital goods firms, and a commodity path of ongoing mechanization.

New commodities were collective efforts, embodying the contributions of many. Cooperation was often an inadvertent result of the inability to appropriate the results of one's own efforts. But at times it was intentional, the sharing of knowledge and interests that regularly occurred in shop and community. It was the everyday interactions among the multitude of manufacturers, craftsmen, and merchants that occasioned even the most original innovators. And as the result of the institutionally grounded activity of many, new machines gained commodity usage and new firms formed that would carry forth the mechanization process. Shoe machinery had created its own dynamic.

On the Commodity Path

The significance of an invention lies not simply in itself but also in the dynamic it starts. The commodity path accounts for mechanization through a process structured by the commodity and the institutions making and selling it. The path is cumulative; it proceeds through virtuous circles overcoming limits to growth and sales. As a means of profit making and a medium of communication, the commodity is at the intersection of twin circles of learning and accumulation. (See Figure 16.1.) Firms attempt to sell; interactions around sales communicate knowledge of technology and marketing; new and established inventors undertake secondary invention; with new techniques, sales grow again. The usual cycle of accumulation is fused with another of learning because the firm has to define the product and the needs it is to fulfill, and to embody that definition in machines and marketing institutions. Only through such institutionalization do sales grow and spread, which expands the extent and alters the location of invention. Sales are both a result and a condition of development, an end and a means.

Once started, the twin processes of growth and learning solve the problems of industrial revolution. Techniques and institutions evolve together, each limiting the other, each transformed by means of the other, until such new institutions as capital goods firms that internalize product development, well-formed marketing networks, and a corps of professional inventors can sustain a process of ongoing technical change. As some users mechanize, others are forced to follow. Competition follows innovation; as Schumpeter would agree, innovations are more a condition than a result of competition. The learning coming from the spread of machinery is concentrated in firms and inventors in the center. The advantages gained by some firms and regions sustain their leadership in the evolution of the commodity and in the birth of others.

It is worth reflecting on the character of this process. Economic theory frequently conceives technical change as an adjustment—for example, in the attempt to tie technical change to relative factor proportions. The coherence of this attempt has been faulted,[3] but the strategy of conceiving technical change as a response to the state of the economy persists—for example, in Schmookler's notion of demand-induced technical change.

That the dynamic of the commodity path was largely internal to the emerging sewing and shoe machinery industries implies that it cannot be understood as the approach to an equilibrium, even one shifting over time. It was, of course, conditioned by potential demand and called on inputs from the broader economy, but it had its own agents, created its own conditions, and formed its own momentum. Rapidly changing internal contexts were a far more important determinant of change than the slowly evolving economy-wide structure of demand and skills. The autonomy of machine development was tied to its social status as a new commodity. Its potential demand was indeed influenced by the economy, and, when it had penetrated its market, this limit became

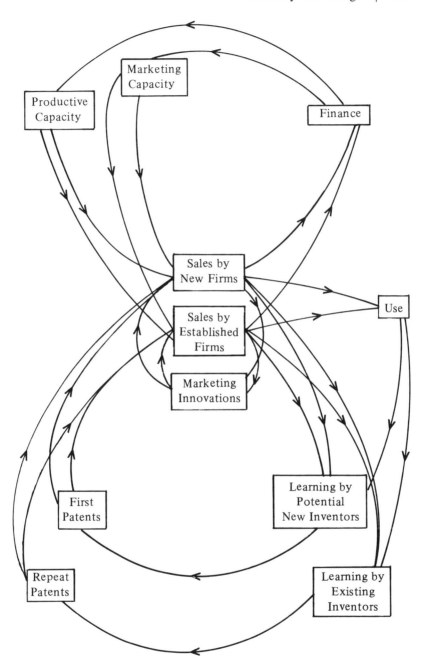

Figure 16.1 Learning by Selling and Ongoing Invention.

pertinent. But the protracted period when the commodity was defined and its market penetrated cannot be grasped by any notion of adjustment to equilibrium.

The notion of a commodity form of technical change gives a fuller account of the role of sales than does Schmookler's formulation. His is a variant of the equilibrium notion: exogenously given changes in demand, taken as a proxy for future demand, increase incentives and spur invention. Because invention responds to an exogenous force, there is no need to examine the institutional structure of the innovating industry. This idea only makes sense, however, once the potential market has been fulfilled. Potential sales can obviously exceed actual sales when the market is being defined and penetrated; no one would ever begin to invent otherwise. But by implicitly limiting his notion to mature commodities, Schmookler can say little about how these commodities emerged.

Learning by selling is not so limited. It connects sales and invention throughout the product cycle, because interactions around sales lead to learning and invention. Due to its explicit grounding in the structure of the innovative process, learning by selling can account for the dissemination of the knowledge conducive to invention. It can therefore identify who invents—those in occupations and locations exposed to learning—and how much they invent, which varies with the use of earlier patents. To complete an account of mechanization, the circle of sales and invention must be closed; to do so, the effect of technological and marketing innovations on sales, neglected by Schmookler, must be grasped.

The importance of the commodity path can also be seen by contrasting it to other plausible paths, particularly that of self-usage. Sales overcome barriers to diffusion, learning, and hence ongoing invention. Institutional effects also differ: with commodity usage, capital goods firms spread technology and marketing innovations elsewhere and can encourage a transformation of machine tools and their social form of diffusion.

Old Paths and New

The processes developing shoe machines differed in part because they formed a sequence in which earlier machines influenced the development of later ones. Singer, Blake, Goodyear, and Matzeliger all benefited from earlier sewing and shoe mechanization. A series of product cycles developed, linked principally by sewing machines, as Figure 16.2 depicts. The complex lasting machine was heir to the simple dry-thread sewing machine by way of the upper waxed-thread machine, the bottom-sewing machine, and complementary bottoming machines.

These machines were integrated with each other in a way that none of them was tied to textile or transportation machinery. Channels of communication through firms, common markets among shoe producers, and the networks of

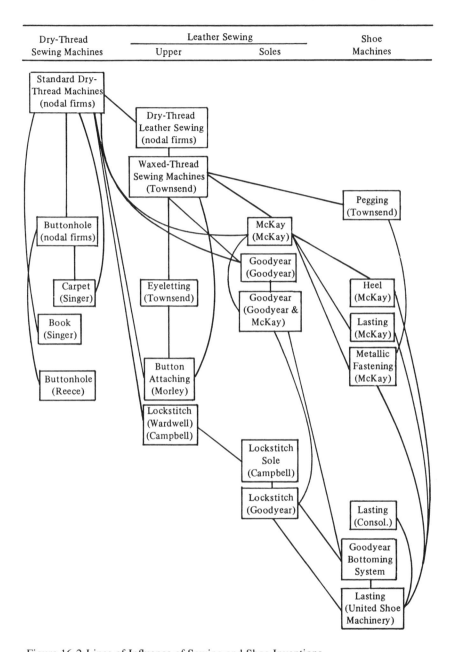

Figure 16.2 Lines of Influence of Sewing and Shoe Inventions.

machinists and inventors all facilitated the recognition of technological convergence and complementarity and marketing similarity. For latecoming machines, barriers of capacity and isolation were lessened.

The result was a widening of the focus of invention, the formation of firms to develop and sell new commodities, and the ensuing dynamics of the product cycle. This repeats the experience that formed the path. As sales grew, vertical disintegration occurred; mass-production machine tools became commodities, as did cut soles and in cases even uppers.

The multiplication of firms came up against the logic of accumulation by existing companies. The commodity form imposed limits to firm growth. Requirements of sale were only met by integrating into marketing. The need to overcome machine bottlenecks brought organized product development within the firm; diversification into other machines was often the result. The very success of market penetration led in time to limitations of market growth and investment opportunities, and solutions entailed further integration. Agencies became both closer and farther away; sewing machine and even shoe firms formed outlets near the home, and machinery companies spread agencies around the world.

Another solution was to diversify into other machines. Diversification influenced the product cycle. On the one hand, existing firms foreshortened the cycle by providing funds, knowledge, and organization to market and develop machines. On the other hand, firms undertook product development for prolonged periods prior to sale. Here was the internality that Schumpeter associated with entrepreneurship—building ahead of demand, the concentration of invention prior to sale—but it came with the institutionalization of technical change, the routinization of change that for Schumpeter spelled the end of the entrepreneurial function.[4]

But the transition was between sets of innovational institutions, not from the individual entrepreneur to the organized research of the large firm. This is not at all to deny the reality of the large firm; to the contrary, as the market for shoe machinery grew, machinery companies became more—not less—consolidated. Compared to United Shoe Machinery, the largest shoe toolmaker in 1860 had a far smaller share of a far smaller market. Rather, it is to emphasize that institutions of innovation existed before the research divisions of machinery firms, and that these institutions help account for both mechanization and the machinery firm.

Generality

This account of the evolution of shoemaking has implications beyond one industry. It suggests that all studies of technical change must grasp the social structure of the generation and diffusion of technology. Diffusion not only spreads machines, it spreads knowledge, which fosters later technical change; the pace and direction of invention can vary with the social structure of learning. Moreover, institutional change may well attend technical progress; techniques, marketing organization, and the structure of firms evolve together. Finally, technical change is path-dependent; it builds contexts that condition later technical change.

This conception of technical change, as has been argued, overcomes the principal deficiency in the accounts of industrialization forwarded by Marx and Mantoux. It also can clarify issues in the conception of history. A tension in the Marxian account of history arises from the fact that Marx posits historical evolution to be both socially created and yet determined by the autonomous evolution of the forces of production, which mediate between man and nature. The tension can be resolved by reference to the social structures of technical change. New techniques are socially generated; they emerge from the social relations of economy and community. But technical change takes autonomy from its cumulative process; as such, it does not respond directly to demands for it. At the same time, because the process depends on the use of new techniques, it can hardly be independent of users and the knowledge they provide. Finally, technical change—seen as a socially structured process of the generation and diffusion of techniques—surely affects the evolution of relations of production, marketing, and competition, as seen in the origin and growth of industrial capital.

Three features of the evolution of technical change follow. Because there are many social forms of technical change, there can be no single answer to the question of why, within capitalism, mechanization occurred. The determinants of technical change vary not only with the social path followed but also with the diversity of scales of use, numbers of users, technologies employed, and the relation to the paths of other techniques.[5] Second, many paths coexist at any time, each with its own autonomy. Third, the cumulative nature of technical change can alter its own social form. The shoe industry began with self-usage, added commodity usage, and finally combined both with planned development within firms.

The conceptualization of shoe mechanization pertains also to a wide range of industries. Many processes of technical change took the form of new product development, commonly initiated by new firms. Ties to the machinery sector conditioned virtually all industrialization processes except the first. Communications barriers were critical for many. More narrowly, sewing and shoe machines resembled other machinery with wide markets and small users, including agricultural machinery, cash registers, office machinery, elevators, automobiles, much electrical machinery, and small-scale computers.

The case of shoemaking carries implications for technical change in the whole economy. Techniques evolve in separate paths. They are connected to the broader economy in their origins and are influenced by changes elsewhere without losing their internal dynamics. Path specificity implies that the pace of technical change varies widely among sectors. Furthermore, the pace of technical change for the whole economy is the outcome of the separate paths developing new products, the stream of secondary inventions of established paths, and the learning by doing and using associated with each path.

The degree of integration among paths increases when machines become capital goods, when regular markets for machinists arise, and when capital goods industries are concentrated in the same regions. As exemplified by Massachusetts, Rhode Island, and Connecticut in the second half of the nineteenth century, concentration can stimulate new product development which reinforces concentration. For the economy as a whole, as well as for the shoe industry, the geographic spread of mechanization need not imply a commensurate spread of machine production.

Shoemaking also contributed to the cumulative development for the whole economy. Shoemaking was surely less important for mechanization elsewhere than were textiles after the Industrial Revolution in Britain because the United States had many mechanized sectors; the same factors that eased the mechanization of shoemaking reduced the importance of that mechanization for others. But the process that generated sewing and shoe machinery shaped inventors who developed major machines of other types, added to the economy's pool of mechanical skills, created widely applicable mechanisms, fashioned marketing techniques that were extensively copied, helped generate mass-production machine tools and diffuse them as machines, and, at the century's end, formed companies such as United Shoe Machinery and Singer. These contributions were the result not simply of shoe mechanization, but of the commodity form it had taken.

Notes

Chapter 1

1. Marx, *Capital*, 1:501, 508. Marx's notions of craft and mechanized production are developed in *Capital*, 1, chaps. 13–15, and in *Grundrisse*, esp. pp. 585–88, 690–711, 767–76. Along with dispersed sections of *Capital*, precapitalist economic formations are analyzed in *Grundrisse*, pp. 459–514, and in Marx and Engels, "The German Ideology." For definitions of machinery that also focus on constrained motion, see Reuleaux, *Kinematics of Machinery*. While seeking to avoid the use of gender-specific language in this book, I have retained the words "craftsman," "journeyman," "tradesman," and "foreman" because most of these people were men during the period described.

2. *Capital*, 1:616.

3. Mantoux is in essential agreement with Marx in the formulation of the question. He adopts Marx's notions of machinery, the contrast of mechanized and craft production, and manufacturing as a stage. See *The Industrial Revolution*, pp. 25–44. On Marx's idea of the manufacturing stage, see Thomson, "Primitive Capitalist Accumulation."

4. Marx, *Capital*, 1:873–913; Mantoux, *The Industrial Revolution*, pp. 136–85.

5. *Capital*, 1:918. More generally, see ibid., 1, chap. 31, and 3, chap. 20. Eric Hobsbawm builds fruitfully on Marx's notions in "The General Crisis."

6. Mantoux, *The Industrial Revolution*, pp. 91, 41. See also the notion of a Smithian dynamic in Parker, "Opportunity Sequences in European History," *Europe, America, and the Wider World*, 1:191–213.

7. *The Industrial Revolution*, p. 206. One ambiguity should be pointed out. The opposition of tradesmen to those with "theoretic" knowledge is overdrawn; Mantoux elsewhere argues that millwrights had mathematical and mechanical knowledge. The real issue is whether the trades supplied sufficient knowledge to solve the technological problems of initial industrialization. Mantoux grants a role to autonomous scientific developments, especially in considering the steam engine, but maintains that the "empirical" phase of initial industrialization was necessary for the emergence of science as a determinant of industrial technology (pp. 205–6).

8. Ibid., pt. II. Marx emphasizes the role of the corn mill in developing principles of friction. *Capital*, 1:468, 498. On the role in developing industrial techniques of agents formed within the manufacturing stage, see ibid., 1, chaps. 14, 15, and 3, chap. 20.

9. *The Industrial Revolution*, p. 206.

10. *Capital*, 1:490–91. Marx's notion of constant capital implies that in capitalism machines are purchased commodities. We may infer that their genesis would therefore be influenced by this commodity form, but Marx never drew this inference.

11. *The Industrial Revolution*, p. 206. The point is not to deny that personality

matters, but merely that how it matters cannot be established without a fuller characterization of economic institutions.

12. The term "shoes" in this book refers to all footwear, including boots, slippers, and shoes in the narrow sense.

Chapter 2

1. Commons, "American Shoemakers"; Hazard, "The Organization of the Boot and Shoe Industry" and *The Organization of the Boot and Shoe Industry*.

2. Commons, "American Shoemakers," p. 78. Note that the merchant function could be performed by a manufacturer. Both Commons and Hazard ground their periodizations in the work of Bucher, *Industrial Evolution*, esp. pp. 150–84.

3. Commons, "American Shoemakers," p. 76. Hazard's more descriptive, less causal account does not explicitly address the issues separating Commons and Marx.

4. Marx, *Capital*, 3:449–50.

5. Ibid., pp. 452–54. The distinction between paths to capitalism has been ably brought out in Dobb, *Studies in the Development of Capitalism*, pp. 123–76.

6. *Shoe and Leather Reporter* 54 (1892): lxviii; Bragg, *The Origin and Growth of the Boot and Shoe Industry*, pp. 4–6; Depew, *One Hundred Years of American Commerce*, 2:567; U.S. Census Office, Eighth Census, *Manufactures of the United States in 1860*, p. lxix; Hazard, *The Organization of the Boot and Shoe Industry*, pp. 37–39; Wooster, "Manufacturer and Artisan," pp. 62–64.

7. Commons, "American Shoemakers," p. 59.

8. Depew, *One Hundred Years of American Commerce*, 2:567; Bryant, *Shoe and Leather Trade*, p. 38; Hazard, *The Organization of the Boot and Shoe Industry*, pp. 28, 35.

9. Depew, *One Hundred Years of American Commerce*, 2:567; George, *London Life in the Eighteenth Century*, pp. 195–202; Thompson, *The Making of the English Working Class*, pp. 258–60; Clapham, *An Economic History of Modern Britain*, 1:167, 169, 181; Unwin, *Industrial Organization in the Sixteenth and Seventeenth Centuries*.

10. On Britain, see Hobsbawm, "Artisans and Labour Aristocrats?" *Worlds of Labor*, pp. 252–72. On European shoemakers, see Hobsbawm and Scott, "Political Shoemakers," pp. 103–30. On the urban American craft tradition, see Wilentz, *Chants Democratic*, pp. 23–60. For a fascinating study of a Boston shoemaker, see Alfred Young, "George Robert Twelves Hewes," pp. 561–623. On a path in which craftsmen gained tight control over their training and employment, see Jackson, *The Formation of Craft Labor Markets*.

11. Hazard, *The Organization of the Boot and Shoe Industry*, p. 22.

12. Hall, "The Gentle Craft," p. 62.

13. Hazard, *The Organization of the Boot and Shoe Industry*, pp. 32–33, 135.

14. Exports and imports were insignificant in 1810 and remained so in 1832. U.S. Census Office, Eighth Census, *Manufactures of the United States in 1860*, p. lxix; U.S. Treasury Department, *Documents Relative to the Manufactures in the United States*, passim.

The estimates of Table 2.1 can only roughly approximate sales for two reasons. In forming the 1810 estimates, the assumption that nonreporting states equaled regional averages may overestimate output. If, for example, New Hampshire and Connecticut are assumed to have output equal to New England states other than Massachusetts (which would underestimate their importance), then total U.S. output would fall by $1.1 million. If we assume that the ratio of per capita shoe output of reporting states to that of nonreporting states is the same as in 1850, 1810 output would be about $10.5 million. On the other hand, Tench Coxe put 1812 shoe output at over $15 million in nominal terms, far in excess of the estimates here. U.S. Census Office, *Eighth Census, Manufactures of the United States in 1860*, p. lxx.

The second source of imprecision concerns the price index used. I have relied on the Warren-Pearson index for hides and leather products, because if accurate this gives a better estimate of the number of pairs of boots and shoes made. If the index for all producers' goods had been used, then, in 1860 dollars, the outputs for 1810, 1840, and 1850 would have been $7.5, $27.4, and $59.7 million respectively. The most important difference is the more rapid growth between 1810 and 1840 (and between 1850 and 1860). The general producers' price index may be superior since it provides better estimates of Massachusetts shoe prices in 1845 and 1855.

15. The *McLane Report* asked manufacturers to list their markets, but the respondents overestimated Massachusetts markets by listing the locations of wholesalers rather than the ultimate market. Awareness of this distinction was conveyed in the Weymouth returns, which stated, "1/2 disposed of first in Boston; principal part finally sold in the southern states," and in the Brookfield returns, which said that its shoes were sold in "N.Y., Philadelphia and other middle and southern cities, for Southern, Western, West Indies, and South American markets." U.S. Treasury Department, *Documents Relative to the Manufactures in the United States*, 1:88–89, 480–81. Unfortunately, similar data on the location of markets are not available for other years.

16. On the location of shoe markets, see ibid, passim; various issues of *Shoe and Leather Reporter*; Bryant, *Shoe and Leather Trade*; Hazard, *The Organization of the Boot and Shoe Industry*, passim. On the earliness of competition in wholesale markets, see Hazard, ibid., p. 33, 144n; Mulligan, "Mechanization and Work in the American Shoe Industry," p. 61.

On western and southern markets in general, see Taylor, *The Transportation Revolution*; Sherry, "Petty Bourgeois Agriculture"; North, *The Economic Growth of the United States*; Chandler, *The Visible Hand*; Garrett, "The Marxian Theory of Primitive Accumulation." On the limits of these markets, see Fishlow, "Antebellum Interregional Trade Reconsidered." On the primacy of intraregional trade, see Lindstrom, *Economic Development in the Philadelphia Region* and "American Economic Growth before 1840," pp. 289–301. On the markets for another Massachusetts manufacture, see Zevin, "The Growth of Cotton Textile Production after 1815," pp. 122–47.

17. The ratio of regional per capita incomes to the national average—1.32 for New England and 1.36 for the Middle Atlantic region—is taken from Easterlin estimates for 1840. U.S. Bureau of the Census, *Historical Statistics of the United States*, F287–296. The proportions of per capita income among regions varied over time, but the basic conclusions would persist with any plausible changes.

18. This measure of interregional shipments understates wholesale markets by neglecting intraregional wholesale production and, because only net shipments are considered, by disregarding shipments among exporting regions.

19. Polanyi, *The Great Transformation*, chap. 5.

20. Commons, "American Shoemakers," p. 72.

21. On the United States, see Gallman, "Gross National Product in the United States," pp. 8–26; Poulson, *Value-added in Manufacturing, Mining, and Agriculture*; David, "The Growth of Real Product," pp. 151–97; Williamson, "Inequality, Accumulation, and Technological Imbalance," pp. 231–53; Lindstrom, "Macroeconomic Growth," pp. 679–705. For a study of a region, see Lindstrom, *Economic Development in the Philadelphia Region*. Useful discussions of the eighteenth-century English home

market include John, "Agricultural Productivity and Economic Growth," pp. 19–34; Eversley, "The Home Market and Economic Growth," pp. 206–59.

22. On transport development for the whole country, see Taylor, *The Transportation Revolution*; Fishlow, *American Railroads*. On intraregional transportation, see Lindstrom, *Economic Development in the Philadelphia Region*.

23. *Shoe and Leather Reporter* 10 (October 31, 1867): 1, 23 (1877): 49; Bryant, *Shoe and Leather Trade*, pp. 26, 38–43; Hazard, *The Organization of the Boot and Shoe Industry*, pp. 13–14, 45–47. Tanners and merchants also changed marketing forms.

24. Bryant, *Shoe and Leather Trade*, pp. 26–27; *Shoe and Leather Reporter* 45 (1888): 323; Depew, *One Hundred Years of American Commerce*, 2:571; U.S. Census Office, Eighth Census, *Manufactures of the United States in 1860*, p. lxxii. The jobber system is summarized in Chandler, *The Visible Hand*, pp. 19–28.

25. *Shoe and Leather Reporter* 10 (October 3, 1867): 1, 20 (1875): 331, 45 (1888): 323, 54 (1892): lxxvi; Bryant, *Shoe and Leather Trade*, pp. 25–26; Hazard, *The Organization of the Boot and Shoe Industry*, pp. 81–82, 99–101, 108n; Hoover, *Location Theory*, p. 173; U.S. Census Office, Eighth Census, *Manufactures of the United States in 1860*, p. lxxii.

Chapter 3

1. *Shoe and Leather Reporter* 54 (1892): lxix–lxxv; Dawley, *Class and Community*, p. 29.

2. Quoted from Hazard, *The Organization of the Boot and Shoe Industry*, p. 14; U.S. Treasury Department, *Documents Relative to the Manufactures in the United States*, 1:216, 220, 410, 490; Bryant, *Shoe and Leather Trade*, pp. 45–47; Bragg, *The Origin and Growth of the Boot and Shoe Industry*, pp. 4–6; Hall, "The Gentle Craft," pp. 129–45.

3. U.S. Census Office, Seventh Census, *Abstract of the Statistics of Manufactures*, p. 15.

4. Johnson, *Sketches of Lynn*, p. 44. Massachusetts was preceded by England in developing the division of shoemaking labor, but may have been the American initiator.

5. Hazard, *The Organization of the Boot and Shoe Industry*, pp. 44–45. Lynn shoe workers recognized this distinction when they addressed "Shoe Binders, Journeymen Cordwainers, and Apprentices" in their magazine, *The Awl* 1 (December 4, 1844): 1.

6. U.S. Census Office, Seventh Census, *Abstract of the Statistics of Manufactures*, p. 15. The increased share of women may also have resulted from the expansion of finishing operations performed by women and the substitution of pegging for bottom sewing among men.

7. Hazard, *The Organization of the Boot and Shoe Industry*, pp. 43, 92n; *Shoe and Leather Reporter* 45 (1888): 479.

8. Depew, *One Hundred Years of American Commerce*, 2:567; Hazard, *The Organization of the Boot and Shoe Industry*, p. 86. The bottoming gang was born in Philadelphia at about the same time as in Massachusetts. How extensively the bottoming gang had spread by 1850 is unclear; in Lynn, it was common in the 1840s to train workers in the whole bottoming process. Mulligan, "Mechanization and Work in the American Shoe Industry," p. 62.

9. P. 476.

10. *Capital*, 3, chap. 20.

11. *Class and Community*, pp. 20–32. Dawley goes further: "The master did not simply wither away; he was done in. The agents of the master's demise were the shopkeepers" (p. 25). This statement is particularly notable because Dawley criticizes Commons's emphasis on the merchant function. Commons gives a greater role to shoemakers, whom he groups among those reorganizing production. In this regard, I believe Commons is right; even in Lynn, as attested by the data Dawley presents on the restricted but regular mobility of cutters into the ranks of employers, capitalist production and the division of labor were not simply the impingement of an outside elite on resisting producers but were in part the result of producers' own innovations. Wilentz's characterization of craft entrepreneurs is superior in grasping innovation by American craftsmen. *Chants Democratic*, pp. 35–42, 107–42.

12. Hazard, *The Organization of the Boot and Shoe Industry*, pp. 95, 68–71; *Shoe and Leather Reporter* 45 (1888): 479; "Henry Wilson," *Dictionary of American Biography*.

13. Quoted respectively from Hazard, *The Organization of the Boot and Shoe Industry*, p. 14, and Torrey, *The Shoe Industry of Weymouth*, p. 15. Not only merchants but also tanners participated in the reorganization of Massachusetts shoe production. Bryant, *Shoe and Leather Trade*, p. 136; Hazard, *The Organization of the Boot and Shoe Industry*, pp. 200–202.

14. *Shoe and Leather Reporter* 54 (1892): lxxi; U.S. Treasury Department, *Documents Relative to the Manufactures in the United States*, 1:231; Ballou, *History of the Town of Milford*, pp. 359–60.

15. U.S. Treasury Department, *Documents Relative to the Manufactures in the United States*, 1:224–35. William Mulligan suggests that in Lynn the family was the typical medium of skill transmission in the craft period. "Mechanization and Work in the American Shoe Industry," pp. 59–63, and "The Transmission of Skill in the Shoe Industry," pp. 234–46.

16. *Shoe and Leather Reporter* 54 (1892): lxix–lxxv; Hazard, *The Organization of the Boot and Shoe Industry*, pp. 57–58, 113; Dawley, *Class and Community*, p. 55; Faler, "Workingmen, Mechanics, and Social Change," p. 309.

17. *Shoe and Leather Reporter* 54 (1892): lxxi.

18. Prentiss, *Recollections of an Old Boot and Shoe Maker*.

19. Ballou, *History of the Town of Milford*, pp. 359–60; *Shoe and Leather Reporter* 10 (October 31, 1867): 1, 11 (July 30, 1868): 1, 14 (April 6, 1871): 1, 14 (May 25, 1871): 1, 23 (1877): 49, 54 (1892): lxxiii; Hazard, *The Organization of the Boot and Shoe Industry*, pp. 21n, 52, 58, 200–202; Bryant, *Shoe and Leather Trade*, p. 55. Massachusetts shoemakers also spread large-scale production to cities outside the state, including Baltimore, Philadelphia, and Chicago. *Shoe and Leather Reporter* 10 (December 26, 1867): 1, 21 (1876): 179, 54 (1892): lxviii.

20. *Shoe and Leather Reporter* 14 (April 6, 1871): 1; Hazard, *The Organization of the Boot and Shoe Industry*, p. 69.

21. Depew, *One Hundred Years of American Commerce*, 2:567; Hazard, *The Organization of the Boot and Shoe Industry*, p. 86.

22. Sokoloff, "Transition from the Artisanal Shop to the Nonmechanized Factory," pp. 351–82; Dawley, *Class and Community*, pp. 55–56.

23. U.S. Census Office, Seventh Census, *Abstract of the Statistics of Manufactures*, p. 15.

24. U.S. Treasury Department, *Documents Relative to the Manufactures in the United States*, passim. Cost reductions from putting out work to women are difficult to assess because, prior to the capitalist division of labor, fitting by women may have

influenced the piece rates paid their husbands. One indication that the division of labor decreased costs was that the daily wage for men was as high when the share of women was less.

25. U.S. Census Office, Seventh Census, *Abstract of the Statistics of Manufactures*, p. 15; Hazard, *The Organization of the Boot and Shoe Industry*, p. 144n. Already in 1810, Massachusetts shoes, at $1.00 per pair, far undersold those of the Middle Atlantic region, which averaged $1.44, and this difference persisted. Massachusetts shoes were also lower in quality and sold in somewhat different markets than shoes of other states. Still, markets overlapped and price competition existed. U.S. Treasury Department, Third Census, *Arts and Manufactures of the United States*.

26. Hazard, "The Organization of the Boot and Shoe Industry," pp. 248–49.

27. On the predominance of circulating over fixed capital in 1832, see Sokoloff, "Investment in Fixed and Working Capital," pp. 545–56. Elsewhere Sokoloff shows that in many antebellum industries, economies of scale in nonmechanized production were exhausted at relatively low output levels. "Transition from the Artisanal Shop to the Nonmechanized Factory."

28. *Capital*, 1, chaps. 26–33. See also Thomson, "Primitive Capitalist Accumulation." The tie of the ease of getting land to the difficulty of securing labor power is central to the frontier thesis of Turner (*The Frontier in American History*), and forms the starting point for Habakkuk's influential account of the greater mechanization of American production (*American and British Technology in the Nineteenth Century*).

29. On the protoindustrialization thesis, see Mendels, "Proto-industrialization," pp. 241–61; Kriedte, Medick, and Schlumbohm, *Industrialization before Industrialization*. See also Jones, "The Agricultural Origins of Industry," pp. 58–71.

30. Dawley, *Class and Community*, p. 29.

31. "Sectoral Shift in Antebellum Massachusetts," pp. 146–71. On the decline of New England agriculture, see the classic study of Bidwell and Falconer, *History of Agriculture*.

32. The growing distance shoes were put out did not equally increase transport costs due to improvements in carriage and wagon making in such towns as Concord, New Hampshire, and Amesbury, Massachusetts; to better road building; and to the introduction of the railroad. Innovations by shoemakers also helped; in 1821 Nathan Chase introduced the covered wagon to put out and market Lynn shoes. Dawley, *Class and Community*, pp. 75–76; Hazard, *The Organization of the Boot and Shoe Industry*, passim; *Shoe and Leather Reporter* 54 (1892): lxxiii.

Transportation costs in the putting-out system can be only roughly estimated. Hoover puts the commercial charges for transporting merchandise by wagon on good roads at about 20 cents per ton-mile in the 1870s and 1880s. Shoes averaged 1 to 2 pounds in weight (boots somewhat more), so that round-trip costs for transporting shoes to be made at a distance of 20 miles would be 0.4 to 0.8 cents. Because back roads were often poor, time was spent packing and unpacking, and goods might not be ready, costs were correspondingly greater. The cost of transporting uppers for fitting must be added. The total cost of transporting shoes by road to outworkers 20 miles away was a few percent of labor costs. See Hoover, *Location Theory*, p. 169.

33. U.S. Treasury Department, *Documents Relative to the Manufactures in the United States*, 1:224–35, 238–39; *Shoe and Leather Reporter* 14 (April 6, 1871): 1.

34. Sokoloff, "The Puzzling Record of Real Wage Growth."

35. U.S. Census Office, Sixth Census, *Statistics of the United States*, p. 408.

36. Wooster, "Manufacturer and Artisan," pp. 61–77; Sokoloff, "Transition from the Artisanal Shop to the Nonmechanized Factory."

37. *The Industrial Revolution*, p. 89.

Chapter 4

1. *Capital*, 1:492.
2. *Scientific American* 21 (December 4, 1869): 362.
3. Bryant, *Shoe and Leather Trade*, pp. 42, 48. The Spanish trade referred to Cuba. Bryant was something of an authority; he said that he had known all the shoe dealers since 1820. On the introduction of the pegged shoe, see *Shoe and Leather Reporter* 10 (December 26, 1867): 1, 11 (July 16, 1868): 1, 21 (1876): 36, 23 (1877): 49. Shoe pegs were used in the eighteenth century, but as far as is known only to attach heels. Hazard, *The Organization of the Boot and Shoe Industry*, p. 174.
4. U.S. Census Office, Eighth Census, *Manufactures of the United States in 1860*, p. lxxi; Hazard, *The Organization of the Boot and Shoe Industry*, pp. 80n, 221; U.S. Treasury Department, *Documents Relative to the Manufactures in the United States*, 1:410–11. J. Leander Bishop estimated the share of pegged shoes to be seven-eighths of all shoes in 1860. *A History of American Manufactures*, 2:125.
5. The distinction between style and construction is reflected in the U.S. Patent Office classification of patents, which differentiates "footwear" from "shoe manufacturing" patents.
6. U.S. Bureau of Labor, *Thirteenth Annual Report*, 2:526–77. The dates of the cases considered varied from 1855 to 1868, but lower labor time of pegging was true even when pegged shoes were made earlier than sewed shoes.
7. Hazard, *The Organization of the Boot and Shoe Industry*, p. 221. Nailed shoes, similar in construction to pegged shoes, never gained much use in the craft period. If American shoes were anything like their British counterparts, the nails could penetrate the foot of the wearer; this was one reason for the failure of the system of machines designed by the celebrated engineer Isambard Brunel of Portsmouth block-making fame. Roe, *English and American Tool Builders*, pp. 26–32; Church, "Labour Supply and Innovation," p. 30; Brooke, *Footwear*, p. 89.
8. Frederick Allen, *The Shoe Industry*, pp. 72–73.
9. *Lynn Business Magazine* 2 (1902): 125; *Shoe and Leather Reporter* 18 (1874): 300; Hazard, *The Organization of the Boot and Shoe Industry*, pp. 67n, 202. On the spread of standard lasts, see Carolyn Cooper, "The Roles of Thomas Blanchard's Woodworking Inventions."
10. U.S. Census Office, Eighth Census, *Manufactures of the United States in 1860*, p. lxxi.
11. The shank was a part of the shoe extending from the heel about halfway to the toe. Johnson, *Sketches of Lynn*, p. 17. The importance of this change was emphasized by another shoemaker, William Stone. *Lynn Item*, March 2, 1901.
12. *Capital*, 1:460–61. The instruments of labor include those objects mediating between the laborer and the material: tools, forms, work support devices, and the workshop itself.
13. Hazard, *The Organization of the Boot and Shoe Industry*, pp. 28, 30, 67n, 91, 189.
14. Quotation from U.S. Census Office, Eighth Census, *Manufactures of the United States in 1860*, p. lxxi. See also Bishop, *A History of American Manufactures*, 2:381; U.S. patents 9,340, 10,316, 13,901, 14,060, 27,514.
15. A survey of all American shoe manufacturing patents forms the basis for patent references. McDermott, *A History of the Shoe and Leather Industries*, pp. 109–13; Johnson, *Sketches of Lynn*, p. 332.
16. Lewis and Newhall, *History of Lynn*, p. 91, as quoted from Hazard, *The Organization of the Boot and Shoe Industry*, p. 29. Apparently Dagyr was not enough

by himself; Americans continued to attempt to recruit British shoemakers to Lynn. "Ebenezer Breed," *Dictionary of American Biography.*

17. Roe, *English and American Tool Builders*; Rosenberg, *Perspectives on Technology*, pp. 9–31; Gibb, *The Saco-Lowell Shops*; Merritt Smith, *Harpers Ferry Armory.*

18. *Shoe and Leather Reporter* 10 (December 26, 1867): 1, 23 (1877): 49.

19. Marx, *Capital*, 1:503.

20. Quimby, *The Story of Lasts*; *Shoe and Leather Reporter* 18 (1874): 300; *Lynn Business Magazine* 2 (1902): 125; Hazard, *The Organization of the Boot and Shoe Industry*, pp. 67n, 80n, 202; U.S. Census Office, Eighth Census, *Manufactures of the United States in 1860*, p. lxxi.

21. Smith, *The Wealth of Nations*, pp. 3–21. Smith recognizes that learning, improved dexterity, and invention are all consequences and sources of the growth of the division of labor. See also George Stigler's discussion of vertical disintegration in "The Division of Labor Is Limited by the Extent of the Market." On the difference between the technical and social divisions of labor, see Marx, *Capital*, 1, chap. 14.

22. *Lynn Business Magazine* 2 (1902): 125; Quimby, *Pacemakers of Progress*, pp. 140, 142, 281; U.S. Census Office, Eighth Census, *Manufactures of the United States in 1860*, p. lxxi; 1860 city directories of Boston and Lynn.

23. The distinction between machines and nonmachines largely follows the classification in U.S. Department of Commerce, *U.S. Patent Classification—Subclass Listing*. Machines are not always clearly distinct from nonmachines; many work support and crimping devices have mechanisms to hold and manipulate the material that are similar to those used on machines. Ten rubber shoe patents have also been excluded from the table.

24. The decline of New England from 1826–45 to 1846–55 is due to Massachusetts' fall from 35 to 18 percent between these two periods. The reason is not clear; Massachusetts' share of nonmachine patents rose to 48 percent from 1856 through 1860.

25. *Shoe and Leather Reporter* 11 (July 16, 1868): 1.

26. Ibid. How Pillsbury came to reconceive the problem of heeling into one of bottoming is not documented.

27. *Journal of the Franklin Institute* 47 (1849): 259–62; Greeley, *The Great Industries of the United States*, p. 701; McDermott, *A History of the Shoe and Leather Industries*, p. 131; Rosenberg, *The American System of Manufactures*, p. 171; Carolyn Cooper, "The Roles of Thomas Blanchard's Woodworking Inventions."

28. Rosenberg, *Perspectives on Technology*, pp. 9–31, and *The American System of Manufactures*, introduction and passim; Roe, *English and American Tool Builders*; Carolyn Cooper, "The Roles of Thomas Blanchard's Woodworking Inventions."

29. Rosenberg, *The American System of Manufactures*, p. 387; U.S. Census Office, Eighth Census, *Manufactures of the United States in 1860*, pp. lxxi, lxxii; Hazard, *The Organization of the Boot and Shoe Industry*, pp. 217–18; Carolyn Cooper, "The Roles of Thomas Blanchard's Woodworking Inventions."

30. Rosenberg, "America's Rise to Woodworking Leadership," *Perspectives on Technology*, pp. 297–98.

31. Ibid., pp. 32–49; Rosenberg, *The American System of Manufactures*, p. 171; *Scientific American* 21 (December 4, 1869): 362; U.S. Census Office, Eighth Census, *Manufactures of the United States in 1860*, p. lxxi; Hazard, *The Organization of the Boot and Shoe Industry*, p. 80n.

32. Quimby, *Pacemakers of Progress*, pp. 27, 140, 142, 281; Johnson, *Sketches of Lynn*, p. 20.

33. Quoted from Hazard, "The Organization of the Boot and Shoe Industry," p. 259; Depew, *One Hundred Years of American Commerce*, 2:567.

34. U.S. Bureau of Labor, *Thirteenth Annual Report*. The data in this report lead to similar conclusions; the savings in labor time from substituting pegged for sewed shoes ranged from 8 to 14 percent for different types of shoes.

35. Quoted from *Lynn Item*, April 10, 1908. Hazard suggests that such uniformity was a competitive requirement. *The Organization of the Boot and Shoe Industry*, p. 94.

36. Commons, "American Shoemakers," p. 76. For a similar criticism and a positive theory of new product development, see Levine, *Economic Theory*, 2, chaps. 4, 5.

Chapter 5

1. Bryant, *Shoe and Leather Trade*, p. 47. See also *Shoe and Leather Reporter* 28 (1879): 780.

2. McDermott, *A History of the Shoe and Leather Industries*, pp. 109–10.

3. *Shoe and Leather Reporter* 10 (December 12, 1867): 4, 54 (1892): lxxiii; Dawley, *Class and Community*, pp. 76–78.

4. Bolles, *Industrial History of the United States*, p. 456.

5. Business directories of Boston, Lynn, Worcester, Lowell, and Haverhill for 1860; manuscripts of 1860 census of manufacturing.

6. *Shoe and Leather Reporter* 54 (1892): lxxiii.

7. *The Organization of the Boot and Shoe Industry*, p. 98. Hazard follows Carl Bucher in this definition. *Industrial Evolution*, pp. 173–76. On awareness of the utilization of time in centralized workshops, see Thompson, "Time, Work Discipline, and Industrial Capitalism," pp. 56–97.

8. Marx, *Capital*, 1, chaps. 14, 15. Marx's usage was closer to that of the time; Hazard notes that central shops of the 1840s and 1850s were called manufactories. *The Organization of the Boot and Shoe Industry*, p. 94n.

9. The contrast of Marx and Hazard took an ironic twist in recent times when, in a broadly Marxist interpretation, Stephen Marglin argued that the factory was instituted to control workers and had no technological superiority over other forms of work organization. This argument was aimed at notions that changes in technique were introduced because they increased productivity and more specifically at the tradition of interpretations of the Industrial Revolution extending from Mantoux to Landes, and, in at least one reading, to Marx himself. See "What Do Bosses Do?" and "Knowledge and Power." In response to Marglin, Landes contends that textile machinery did reduce costs and that the factory would not have come about without machinery. "What Do Bosses Really Do?"

10. Note that this idea of standardization does not require interchangeable parts. U.S. Census Office, *Twelfth Census: Manufactures*, 1:xxxvi.

11. Ibid., p. 765.

12. Johnson, *Sketches of Lynn*, p. 345. The splitting machine also saved material; both the flesh and hair sides of the leather could be used, whereas formerly the flesh side was cut away and discarded. Bryant, *Shoe and Leather Trade*, p. 47.

13. *Eighty Years' Progress*, p. 428.

14. Johnson, *Sketches of Lynn*, p. 336.

15. Bolles, *Industrial History of the United States*, p. 456; McDermott, *A History of the Shoe and Leather Industries*, p. 67; Bishop, *A History of American Manufactures*, 2:509.

16. Marglin recognizes that technological change since the Industrial Revolution has

increased productivity, but holds that the direction of later technological change was determined by the earlier factory system because factory owners formed the demand for new techniques and patents were more enforceable than in putting-out systems. "What Do Bosses Do?" pp. 89–90.

It is not clear whether Marglin is referring to later technical change in the cotton textile industry alone or to change in all industries. It is difficult to see how the latter could be true. Machines were demanded outside the factory, as the reaper and sewing machine exemplify. Moreover, the enforceability of patent rights may depend less on the kind of users than on the social form of diffusion: machines spreading through sale can be policed more readily than machines diffusing through the movement of workers. By confining his attention to machine users, Marglin ignores the social organization of the diffusion and generation of new techniques, and as such only partially grasps the "economic and social institutions" on which, he argues, innovation depends. Ibid., p. 64.

17. February 28, 1863, as quoted from Dawley, "The Artisan Response to the Factory System." Employment from Dawley, *Class and Community*, p. 346.

18. U.S. Census Office, Seventh Census, *Abstract of the Statistics of Manufactures*, and Eighth Census, *Manufactures of the United States in 1860*. Some but not all of this shift reflected the employment of men as sewing machine operatives in some towns.

19. Dawley, *Class and Community*, pp. 134–39.

20. Johnson, *Sketches of Lynn*, pp. 151–52; Hazard, *The Organization of the Boot and Shoe Industry*, pp. 89–101.

21. Dawley, *Class and Community*, p. 75. The limitations of development of the manufactory in the absence of heat or power requirements are emphasized by Mantoux and the protoindustrialization literature.

22. Other shoe operations became separate commodities, including shoe blanks. *Shoe and Leather Reporter* 10 (June 6, 1867): 1, 14 (May 11, 1871): 4; Hazard, *The Organization of the Boot and Shoe Industry*, p. 77.

23. Marglin too quickly assumes that mechanization concentrated authority in the capitalist. Subcontracting, inside contracting, and workers' control over the use of machinery were widespread in the nineteenth-century American economy. See Buttrick, "The Inside Contracting System"; Clawson, *Bureaucracy and the Labor Process*; Montgomery, *Workers' Control in America*. On the autonomous evolution of management, see Braverman, *Labor and Monopoly Capital*. Marglin acknowledges the dispersion of authority in "Knowledge and Power."

24. U.S. Census Office, Eighth Census, *Manufactures of the United States in 1860*, p. lxxi.

25. One of the themes of modern investigations of the social organization and determinants of mechanization is that in market economies machinery need not lead to the capitalist factory system. One form this takes is the emphasis on divergent paths of industrialization in Berg, *The Age of Manufactures*, and Sabel and Zeitlin, "Historical Alternatives to Mass Production."

26. Hazard, *The Organization of the Boot and Shoe Industry*, pp. 95–96; Dawley, *Class and Community*, p. 77. Cf. *Eighty Years' Progress*, p. 428, which argues that in Essex County in 1864 machine ownership by operatives was the general case.

27. Quoted from Bishop, *A History of American Manufactures*, 2:509; *Lynn Item*, November 10, 1903, March 2, 1901; *Lynn Business Magazine* 1 (June 1901): 24–26.

28. *Scientific American* 7 (July 4, 1863): 102. Putting-out continued in nonmechanized bottoming and upper-finishing operations.

29. Bishop, *A History of American Manufactures*, 2:509. Though it seemed almost

complete compared to hand work, the degree of mechanization would have seemed modest by later standards.

30. *Scientific American* 7 (July 4, 1863): 102. See also *Rice & Hutchins: A Retrospect*, p. 30.

31. *Shoe and Leather Reporter* 14 (October 13, 1870): 1, 18 (1874): 4, 36 (1883): 136, 54 (1892): lxxxiv; Hazard, *The Organization of the Boot and Shoe Industry*, p. 78.

32. Quoted from Johnson, *Sketches of Lynn*, p. 18; *Shoe and Leather Reporter* 14 (October 13, 1870): 1.

33. *Eighty Years' Progress*, p. 325.

34. Commons, "American Shoemakers," p. 72.

35. Of course, the factory may not have been welcomed by workers, but their reservations did not materialize into effective opposition to, or even widespread struggles around, the introduction of machinery. Continued usage of craft training and subcontracting systems undoubtedly facilitated acceptance of the factory, as did the weakness of the craft tradition in the United States. On workers' organization in the Lynn shoe industry, see Dawley, *Class and Community*.

36. Hazard, *The Organization of the Boot and Shoe Industry*, p. 219. It must be presumed that the value of machinery would have been higher in 1860.

37. Atack, "Firm Size and Industrial Structure," pp. 470, 472. See also Atack, "Economies of Scale and Efficiency Gains."

Chapter 6

1. This classification differs from the more common "supply" and "demand" division, which would group together market narrowness, lack of marketing knowledge, and marketing isolation under demand factors, as distinct from supply factors such as skills, finance, and inputs to production. The classification used here better identifies the critical communication processes. I have formulated the classification of barriers and used it to examine why only one of the first 18 stitching mechanisms achieved practicality in "Between Invention and Practicality."

2. Variants on these forms also modify the measures of threshold usage. Self-usage can be accompanied by licensing, which would combine elements of both measures. In a distinct form, inventions may be shared within a community, spread by informal contact or publications; community-wide usage is the appropriate measure. On this mode, see Robert C. Allen, "Collective Invention"; Sabel and Zeitlin, "Historical Alternatives to Mass Production." On threshold models of diffusion, see David, "The Mechanization of Reaping in the Ante-bellum Midwest," *Technical Choice*, pp. 195–232.

3. U.S. Census Office, Eighth Census, *Manufactures of the United States in 1860*. The nominal value of clothing output has been deflated by the Warren-Pearson index for textile products. U.S. Bureau of the Census, *Historical Statistics of the United States*, E 56.

4. U.S. Census Office, Eighth Census, *Manufactures of the United States in 1860*; U.S. Bureau of the Census, *Historical Statistics of the United States*, E 55, 56.

5. Feldman, *Fit for Men*, p. 96; *Eighty Years' Progress*, pp. 310–11; Wilentz, *Chants Democratic*, pp. 119–24.

6. For inventors, another source of uncertainty was the share of the potential usage that they could expect to control. Capital requirements to produce machines were low enough that many could do so. Patent rights, while never totally enforceable, surely

offered some protection to patent owners, but here was another source of uncertainty: if basic rights were controlled by others, the inventor could be excluded from the usage. For a careful discussion of the role of uncertainty in nineteenth-century American technical change, see Strassmann, *Risk and Technological Innovation*. Barriers to appropriating the results could dissuade individuals from investing in socially beneficial invention. On this, see Arrow, "Economic Welfare."

7. Labor time figures are for years ranging from 1855 through 1875; relative labor times of sewing and pegging are roughly constant over the period. In machine production, upper sewing falls to about one-tenth of total labor time. U.S. Bureau of Labor, *Thirteenth Annual Report*, 1:28, 2:526–72.

8. Family sales were also uncertain; it was unclear whether sewing machines were more like spinning wheels and hand looms, which left the house, or the coal stove, the washing machine, and the standing clock, which entered the home. Nor was it evident that the family could afford the sewing machine, though the $12 to $50 stove and the $10 to $45 standing clock suggested that purchase was not out of the question. Brady, "Consumption and the Style of Life," pp. 86–87.

9. On real wages, see Sokoloff, "The Puzzling Record of Real Wage Growth"; Margo and Villaflor, "The Growth of Wages." Published annual wages are consistent with their findings. Annual money labor income in the shoe industry increased from $205 to $250 from 1850 to 1860, but rising prices and the fall in the share of women employed in shoemaking from 31 to 23 percent largely eliminate any real wage increase associated with this money wage growth.

10. For a good description of the operations of hand sewing, see Burlingame, *March of the Iron Men*, pp. 360–61,

11. Rosenberg, "Technological Change in the Machine Tool Industry, 1840–1910," *Perspectives on Technology*, pp. 9–31.

12. "Technology, Resources, and Economic Change in the West," p. 63. On the applicability to the sewing machine of Parker's conception of technical change as an "eco-technic process," see Thomson, "The Eco-Technic Process and the Development of the Sewing Machine," pp. 243–69.

13. Machinists are here measured by employment of the machinery industry as listed in manufacturing censuses. Such machinists had considerable technological skill; most machine shops had small machine runs. The average machinery establishment employed 26 in 1850 and 30 in 1860. Wages provide one indicator of the persistence of skills in large shops. In 1850, Massachusetts and Rhode Island paid the same annual wages as other New England states but their 33 workers per shop were far higher than the 19 in the rest of the region. Of course, skill levels differed; particularly in large shops, not all workers designed machines. But the deskilling that would accompany later large-scale machinery production—notably the sewing machine—had not made much headway in the first half of the nineteenth century.

Measuring the economy's technical skills by employment in the machinery sector has deficiencies. First, employers also had skills. Second, many machinists are not included in this sector; the number working in railroad repair shops exceeded those making locomotives in 1860 (Fishlow, *American Railroads*, pp. 154–56). Third, nonmachinists had mechanical skills, including firearms manufacturers, clockmakers, patent agents, and professional inventors. Because these others generally varied in the same direction as employees in the machinery sector, using numbers of machinists to measure mechanical skills is not unrealistic.

14. Patterns of the organization, technical development, marketing, and innovativeness of the machinery sector are discussed in Roe, *English and American Tool Builders*;

Clark, *History of Manufactures*, 1; Rosenberg, *Perspectives on Technology*; Woodbury, *Studies in the History of Machine Tools*; Ware, *The Early New England Cotton Manufacture*; Gibb, *The Saco-Lowell Shops*; Cole, *The American Woolen Manufacture*; Pursell, *Early Stationary Steam Engines*; Temin, "Steam and Water Power in the Early Nineteenth Century"; Hunter, *A History of Industrial Power*; White, *American Locomotives*; Fitch, "Report on the Manufactures of Interchangeable Mechanism"; Deyrup, *Arms Makers of the Connecticut Valley*; Merritt Smith, *Harpers Ferry Armory*; Carolyn Cooper, "The Roles of Thomas Blanchard's Woodworking Inventions"; Hoopes, "Early Clockmaking in Connecticut," pp. 1–26; Landes, *Revolution in Time*; Hoke, "Ingenious Yankees"; Rogin, *The Introduction of Farm Machinery*; McCormick, *The Century of the Reaper*.

15. Alternate estimating procedures would increase Massachusetts' 1810 share, but, because its share must have been less than its 33 percent of reported 1810 output, its share of national output must have risen over time.

16. On the limited spread of mechanization in nineteenth- century Britain, see Berg, *The Age of Manufactures*; Musson, *The Growth of British Industry*.

17. Roe, *English and American Tool Builders*, p. 256; Freedley, *Philadelphia and Its Manufactures*, p. 306.

18. In accounting for the growth of nineteenth-century American cities, Allan Pred made localized learning the central link connecting manufacturing and invention. *The Spatial Dynamics of U.S. Urban-Industrial Growth*, pp. 127–31.

19. Producers in each industry were less concentrated than Table 6.2 indicates. The table lists employees but not employers and the self-employed; because major producing states had larger shops, their share of employees is somewhat higher than their share of all producers. The discrepancy for machinists is greater; the substantial numbers of machinists employed in repair and maintenance, especially in the railroad, were much more dispersed than those listed as employees of the machinery industry.

20. Pred, *The Spatial Dynamics of U.S. Urban-Industrial Growth*, p. 106.

Chapter 7

1. Parton, "History of the Sewing Machine," pp. 528–29.

2. Ibid., p. 527.

3. U.S. patent 4,750. On Howe's inventive process, see Burlingame, *March of the Iron Men*, pp. 361–62; Iles, *Inventors at Work*, pp. 318–20; Kaempffert, *A Popular History of American Invention*, 2:384–86; Parton, "History of the Sewing Machine." On Howe's stitching mechanism, see *Appleton's Dictionary of Machines*, 2:620–21; *Eighty Years' Progress*, p. 414; Gregory, "Machines, Etc. Used in Sewing," 7:8–9.

4. *Illustrated Description and Price List of the Willcox and Gibbs Silent Sewing Machine*, p. 18. See also Burlingame, *March of the Iron Men*, p. 363.

5. Parton, "History of the Sewing Machine," p. 531; Salamon, *The History of the Sewing Machine*, pp. 14–15; Gifford, *Application of Elias Howe*, pp. 29–34.

6. Parton, "History of the Sewing Machine," p. 530.

7. These early sewing machines are discussed in detail in Thomson, "Between Invention and Practicality."

8. U.S. patent 5,942. On the inadequacy of Howe's invention, see *Appleton's Dictionary of Machines*, 2:621; Bolles, *Industrial History of the United States*, pp. 244–45; Jack, "The Channels of Distribution for an Innovation," pp. 114–15; *Journal of the Society of Arts*, April 17, 1863, pp. 386–87. Salamon maintained that the baster plate could be bent to any required form, but the time involved in bending and rebending the

piece and the inaccuracy of the operation limit the usefulness of this possibility. *The History of the Sewing Machine*, p. 56.

9. Parton, "History of the Sewing Machine," p. 531.

10. I have developed the idea of learning by selling in "Learning by Selling and Invention." This notion is one component of a broader idea of technical change put forth in Thomson, "Technological Change as New Product Development."

11. On learning processes in economic history, see David, "The 'Horndal Effect' in Lowell, 1834–56: A Short-run Learning Curve for Integrated Cotton Textile Mills" and "Learning by Doing and Tariff Protection: A Reconsideration of the Case of the Antebellum United States Cotton Textile Industry," *Technical Choice*, pp. 174–91 and 95–173 respectively; Rosenberg, "Learning by Using," *Inside the Black Box*, pp. 120–40. The classical notions of bottlenecks and of challenge and response used to discuss the Industrial Revolution are kinds of learning arguments.

12. Thomson, "Technological Change as New Product Development." Related ideas are contained in Levine, *Economic Theory*, 2, chaps. 4, 5; Shapiro, "Innovation, New Industries, and New Firms," pp. 27–43. On the relation of the product cycle, firm development, and location, see Vernon, "International Investment and International Trade in the Product Cycle"; Markusen, *Profit Cycles, Oligopoly, and Regional Development*.

13. For an analysis of the failure of early machines, see Thomson, "Between Invention and Practicality."

14. *Scientific American* 4 (January 27, 1849): 145, 7 (July 17, 1852): 349; Ewers and Baylor, *Sincere's History of the Sewing Machine*.

15. U.S. patent 6,437.

16. See, for example, *Scientific American* 3 (April 22, 1848): 243, 3 (June 3, 1848): 292, 4 (January 27, 1849): 145, 4 (September 22, 1849): 1.

17. On the connections among these machines, see Grace Cooper, *The Sewing Machine*, pp. 21–31; *Sewing Machine Advance*, August 1906, p. 57. Cooper offers the best summary of the development of the sewing machine from Howe to the existence of a practical machine.

18. Grace Cooper, *The Sewing Machine*, pp. 29–30, 142–43; Lewton, "The Servant in the House," pp. 570–71; Brandon, *A Capitalist Romance*, pp. 40–43.

19. U.S. patent 6,439; Gregory, "Machines, Etc. Used in Sewing," 7:10–11; Depew, *One Hundred Years of American Commerce*, 2:526; Grace Cooper, *The Sewing Machine*, pp. 22–23.

20. U.S. patent 8,294; *Scientific American* 7 (November 1, 1851): 49; *Transactions of the American Institute*, 1856, p. 542; Depew, *One Hundred Years of American Commerce*, 2:527; Bishop, *A History of American Manufactures*, 2:606.

21. *Scientific American* 4 (January 27, 1849): 145, 1 (July 7, 1859): 32; *Eighty Years' Progress*, pp. 424–25; *Appleton's Dictionary of Machines*, 2:620–21; *Appleton's Cyclopedia of Applied Mechanics*, 1880, 2:744; Grace Cooper, *The Sewing Machine*, pp. 22–23, 35–38; Alexander, "On the Sewing Machine," p. 364; *Journal of the Franklin Institute*, 1851, p. 144; Freedley, *Leading Pursuits and Leading Men*, p. 128.

22. *Scientific American* 3 (June 3, 1848): 292, 36 (May 26, 1877): 320.

23. U.S. patent 7,776; *Scientific American* 5 (November 24, 1849): 73; Central Labor Union, *Centennial Illustrated History of Bridgeport*, p. 108; Orcutt, *A History of the City of Bridgeport*, pp. 261–63.

24. For the analysis of invention as a process of insight, see Usher, *A History of Mechanical Inventions*, pp. 56–83.

25. *Scientific American* 14 (October 30, 1858): 61; Lewton, "The Servant in the House," p. 573; *Sewing Machine Advance* 1 (1879): 66.

26. Boston city directory, 1851; Gregory, "Machines, Etc. Used in Sewing," 7:14. Some ambiguity exists about Johnson's occupation; the Boston city directory of 1847–48 identifies a J. B. Johnson as a "philosophical instrument-maker."

27. Grace Cooper, *The Sewing Machine*, pp. 19–31; Bishop, *A History of American Manufactures*, 2:606. Singer soon bought out Zieber's interest. Brandon, *A Capitalist Romance*, pp. 78–86.

28. Quoted from Gregory, "Machines, Etc. Used in Sewing," 7:14. On the mechanical inadequacy of this machine, see Grace Cooper, *The Sewing Machine*, pp. 25–26.

Chapter 8

1. Grace Cooper, *The Sewing Machine*, passim.

2. Patents are used here to measure inventive activity, not the effect of such activity on productivity change. For a careful argument in favor of this measure, see Schmookler, *Invention and Economic Growth*. Patent applications are in principle a better measure of inventive effort, but sufficiently detailed data on applications denied are not readily available. However, use of patent applications rather than patents granted would probably make little difference to the conclusions of this book, because, at least for the whole economy, the share of patents granted in all applications regularly varied between about one-half and two-thirds from 1856 through 1900.

3. Learning also occurred through other media such as the detailed accounts of sewing machines in the *Scientific American*, numerous industrial exhibitions, patents, and patent litigation. But as in the earlier period, there is little evidence that these media played much of a role in fostering invention through 1855.

4. Where there is more than one patentee, an invention is classified as a first patent if none of the patentees had earlier sewing machine patents and as a repeat patent if one or more had previous sewing machine patents.

5. For the classic formulation of the thesis of demand-induced technical change, see Schmookler, "Economic Sources of Inventive Activity" and *Invention and Economic Growth*.

6. U.S. patents 10,354, 12,233; Grace Cooper, *The Sewing Machine*, pp. 65, 72.

7. U.S. patent 12,116; *Scientific American* 8 (June 4, 1853): 297–98, 14 (January 22, 1859): 161, 3 (September 8, 1860): 166–67; Central Labor Union, *Centennial Illustrated History of Bridgeport*, p. 110; *Eighty Years' Progress*, p. 420.

8. Grace Cooper, *The Sewing Machine*, p. 33. To his chagrin, Singer was told by a competitor that he could have patented the treadle had it not been in public use for over two years.

9. These patents had the competitive purpose of avoiding infringement of earlier patents, including Wilson's own, which had come under the control of his former partners. U.S. patents 8,296, 9,041; *Scientific American* 5 (November 24, 1849): 73, 8 (June 4, 1853): 297–98; *Eighty Years' Progress*, pp. 415–19; Gregory, "Machines, Etc. Used in Sewing," 7:12–13; Grace Cooper, *The Sewing Machine*, pp. 26–28; Alexander, "On the Sewing Machine," p. 362; Orcutt, *A History of the City of Bridgeport*, pp. 263–66.

10. U.S. patents 8,876, 10,842, 10,974, 12,364, 12,969, 13,065, 13,362, 13,687, 13,966.

11. U.S. patents 10,975, 13,661, 13,662, 13,768; *Lynn Item*, November 10, 1908; Depew, *One Hundred Years of American Commerce*, 2:526.

12. The formation of sewing machine firms is ascertained from Grace Cooper, *The Sewing Machine*, passim, from city directories, and from patent assignments.

13. Jack, "The Channels for Distribution of an Innovation," pp. 113–41, presents the best statement of the evolution of marketing organization. Although his article draws almost exclusively from the Singer files, its conclusions are generally applicable to Grover and Baker and to Wheeler and Wilson.

14. Ibid., pp. 115–34; Freedley, *Leading Pursuits and Leading Men*, p. 537; Brandon, *A Capitalist Romance*, pp. 131, 136.

15. Orcutt, *A History of the City of Bridgeport*, pp. 263–67; Salamon, *The History of the Sewing Machine*, pp. 64–65; Grace Cooper, *The Sewing Machine*, p. 141.

16. The best secondary accounts of these cases are presented in Burlingame, *March of the Iron Men*, pp. 369–70, and Salamon, *The History of the Sewing Machine*, pp. 61–65. See also Gifford, *Application of Elias Howe*, pp. 39–58. These and other patent litigation cases provide an important source on the invention and development of the sewing machine.

17. Quoted from Burlingame, *March of the Iron Men*, p. 370.

18. Grace Cooper, *The Sewing Machine*, pp. 24, 33–34. By the time Singer had lost the suit, other firms had already taken out licenses and advertised this fact. The protection licensing afforded buyers was often noted. The *Scientific American* wrote of the Wheeler and Wilson machines: "As there has been much dispute about the originality and identity of sewing machines as related to Mr. Howe's original patent, no person who buys one of these machines is clogged with an impending lawsuit, as there is an arrangement between Mr. Howe and Messrs. Wheeler, Wilson & Co.; so every customer will be perfectly protected" (8 [June 4, 1853: 298]).

19. *Sewing Machine Advance*, August 1906, p. 57; Bishop, *A History of American Manufactures*, 2:607; Depew, *One Hundred Years of American Commerce*, 2:530; Lewton, "The Servant in the House," pp. 577–79; Grace Cooper, *The Sewing Machine*, p. 34.

20. The terms of the Sewing Machine Combination are summarized in Grace Cooper, *The Sewing Machine*, pp. 41–42, and Howe, *Application of Elias Howe Jr. for an Extension of His Sewing Machine Patent*.

21. The number of nodal company agencies in surveyed cities is understated because many cities either did not have business directories or did not list agents by the company they represented. Jack, "The Channels of Distribution for an Innovation," pp. 124–34; Depew, *One Hundred Years of American Commerce*, 2:530; U.S. Census Office, Eighth Census, *Manufactures of the United States in 1860*, pp. lix–lxvi.

22. Central Labor Union, *Centennial Illustrated History of Bridgeport*, pp. 112, 114.

23. *Journal of the Society of Arts* 63 (1863): 365–67; *Practical Mechanic's Journal*, cited in Brandon, *A Capitalist Romance*, p. 135.

24. Brandon, *A Capitalist Romance*, pp. 116, 120–28; Davies, *Peacefully Working to Conquer the World*, pp. 18, 38. Because growth was predominantly self-financed, manufacturing profits were especially important for penetrating the family market.

25. Freedley, *Leading Pursuits and Leading Men*, p. 147; *Eighty Years' Progress*, p. 427.

26. Brandon, *A Capitalist Romance*, pp. 116–17; Davies, *Peacefully Working to Conquer the World*, p. 20; Depew, *One Hundred Years of American Commerce*, 2:529.

27. Data on agencies come from listings in commercial directories, which understate the number of agencies for several reasons. Many towns with agencies did not issue directories. Especially early in the period, many city directories did not include busi-

ness directories or did not have a category for sewing machines. Given that exports were not yet large, the understatement of agencies would overestimate sales per agency.

28. Nonnodal output is the difference between the 111,300 machines in the census and nodal firm output. I estimate that nodal firm output was intermediate between that of the 1859 and 1860 calendar years on the grounds that, as indicated by the census manuscripts, this was so for Grover and Baker. U.S. Census Office, Eighth Census, *Manufactures of the United States in 1860*, p. cxc.

29. Table 8.3 considers only those sewing machine agencies in each city that were listed in the directory of that city; it thus excludes agencies in cities alluded to in the directories of other cities. Seven 1860 agencies were excluded for this reason, but were included in Table 8.2. The 18 cities that had directories listing no sewing machine agencies, besides the 5 listed in Table 8.3, were Haverhill, Gloucester, Springfield, and Newburyport, Massachusetts; Portsmouth, New Hampshire; Newport, Rhode Island; Oswego, New York; Lancaster, Pennsylvania; Akron, Ohio; Fort Wayne, Indiana; Quincy, Illinois; Davenport, Iowa; Petersburg, Virginia.

30. Quoted from Lewton, "The Servant in the House," pp. 575–76. See also *Sewing Machine Advance* 1 (1879): 114; Grace Cooper, *The Sewing Machine*, pp. 45–47.

31. Use of a three-year lag or a distributed lag would give much the same results. That the substantial growth of sales and agencies between 1854–56 and 1857–59 was associated with a much smaller growth of first patents is anomalous in its extent, but not in its direction. Over the period from 1851 through 1882, the ratio of first patents to agencies declined regularly, probably due to the growing technological knowledge required to invent and to the fact that learning may be more related to cumulative sales, net of abandoned machines, and through 1872 cumulated sales grew more slowly than current sales. See Thomson, "Learning by Selling and Invention."

32. It could be argued that the distribution of sewing machine patenting was an outcome of urbanization. Allan Pred has used a concept of cumulative causation similar to that used in this book to argue that urban location and invention were mutually reinforcing. The 16 cities he surveyed had 30 percent of American patents in 1860, some three times their share of population. *The Spatial Dynamics of U.S. Urban-Industrial Growth*, p. 106. The same cities had 50 percent of sewing machine patents from 1855 through 1861.

But the disproportionate degree of urbanization in nodal states does not account for their higher sewing machine patent shares. Nodal sewing machine cities were far more inventive than other cities. Cities where nodal companies were located—New York and Boston among the cities Pred surveyed—had 40 percent of sewing machine patents, over twice their 18 percent share of patents of all types. By contrast, the 14 other cities had 10 percent of sewing machine patents, somewhat beneath their 12 percent share of all patents. Moreover, among U.S. residents outside major cities, those in nodal states were far more prolific sewing machine inventors than those in nonnodal states. As Pred would agree, invention varied in kind with industrial composition.

33. Learning by selling can also account for variations of patenting within state groups. Among both nodal and secondary states, the correlation of patenting per capita with machinists per capita can be accounted for by interstate learning and the concentration of sewing machine production. Among tertiary states the correlation is largely explained by the correlation of centers of machinists and concentrations of agencies; within groups of states with similar concentrations of agencies, there is little or no correlation of patenting and machinists.

34. This definition can only approximate use, even restricting the term to use through machine purchase. It overstates use by considering that all patents of an

inventor were used if any were. This clearly was not so; even for inventors who owned firms, some of their patents must have proved impractical. Still, insofar as they learned through relating to others around the sale or potential sale of inadequate patents, these failures may have aided later invention.

On the other hand, usage is undermeasured because data are sparse on licensing and assignment after the patent grant, but both were common. (For the methods and importance of utilizing assignments over the entire course of the patent, see Carolyn Cooper's "The Roles of Thomas Blanchard's Woodworking Inventions" and "Thomas Blanchard's Woodworking Machines.") Usage is relatively understated for patents outside surveyed cities and for attachments and special-purpose machines, which were not commonly listed in business directories.

35. Grace Cooper, *The Sewing Machine*, passim.

36. That a higher proportion of first patents was used earlier in the period implies that the higher average number of repeats among inventors of used patents in part reflects the longer period they had to invent. That use mattered is seen when the extent of repeat inventing is compared for similar years of first invention. For 1854 through 1856, multiple inventors who gained use took out 4.1 repeat patents whereas those who did not took out 1.6 repeats. For multiple inventors beginning in 1857 and 1858, the average number of repeats was 2.1 if machines were used and 1.4 if unused. Therefore, repeats may have increased with time, but those with used patents better utilized this time.

37. The distribution of patents by type is taken from U.S. Department of Commerce, *U.S. Patent Classification—Subclass Listing*, class 112, and is amended by an examination of the individual patents. This distribution overstates the domination of the standard dry-thread machine, since many patents classified as stitch forming, feeding, tensioning, and so forth were designed for special-purpose machines. If leather-sewing machine patents are any indication, the number of patents classified as special-purpose machines is about half the number designed for use on these machines. This would still be under 20 percent of all sewing machine patents.

38. On the transformation of sewing effected by the progress of sewing machines, besides patents, see Alexander, "On the Sewing Machine," pp. 361–63; *American Artisan* 5 (October 23, 1867): 244; Grace Cooper, *The Sewing Machine*, pp. 46–47, 57–63; *Eighty Years' Progress*, pp. 423–24; Gregory, "Machines, Etc. Used in Sewing," 7:18–37; *Mechanic's Magazine* 8 (August 8, 1862): 76; *Scientific American* 14 (January 29, 1859): 165, 6 (January 4, 1862): 1, 8 (November 28, 1863): 1, 14 (March 10, 1866): 1; Tomlinson, *Cyclopedia of Useful Arts and Manufactures*, 3:626.

39. Chandler, *The Visible Hand*, pp. 287–314.

Chapter 9

1. *Lynn Item*, November 10, 1908; Gannon, *Shoemaking*, p. 27; Quimby, *Pacemakers of Progress*, p. 31.

2. *Scientific American* 7 (July 17, 1852): 349; *Lynn Item*, November 10, 1908.

3. Worcester city directory, 1855; *Lynn Item*, November 10, 1908; Grace Cooper, *The Sewing Machine*, p. 100.

4. From Wickersham's patent specification, it is not clear that he realized the particular appropriateness of his machine to waxed-thread sewing. The patent made no mention of waxed thread and was written as though the machine could apply to either leather or cloth. U.S. patent 9,679; McDermott, *A History of the Shoe and Leather Industries*, p. 95.

5. U.S. patents 11,571, 11,581, 11,631; Boston city directory, 1851; McDermott, *A History of the Shoe and Leather Industries*, p. 95.

6. There were surely more than 24 patents designed for sewing leather. A study of patent specifications prior to 1856 indicates that about half of the patents for leather sewing were not categorized as leather-sewing machines, but were instead classified by the character of the improvement (shuttles, tension mechanisms, attachments).

7. Assignments include only those listed on the patent grants. Occupations are taken from the survey of city directories, supplemented in a few cases by McDermott, *A History of the Shoe and Leather Industries*, passim.

8. City directories are available only for medium- and large-sized cities, typically with populations exceeding 10,000. Occupations from these directories may understate the proportion of shoemakers relative to machinists, but the availability of directories for such shoe towns as Lynn, Haverhill, and Worcester in part compensates.

9. Shoe inventions were more difficult to identify than sewing machines. Most were listed in class 12, "boot and shoe making," U.S. Department of Commerce, *U.S. Patent Classification—Subclass Listing*. In addition, leather-cutting machines were listed in class 69, "leather manufactures," and in class 83, "cutting." A few more patents were located from U.S. Patent Office, *Subject-Matter Index*, and from annual Patent Office reports. Patents were then individually consulted.

10. *Shoe and Leather Reporter* 54 (1892): lxxiii, 55 (1893): xliii.

11. McDermott, *A History of the Shoe and Leather Industries*, pp. 109–10. Knox was described as a mechanic, which, if so, may have aided his solution.

12. Quoted from McDermott, *A History of the Shoe and Leather Industries*, pp. 62–63; *Shoe and Leather Reporter* 21 (1876): 36. The lack of finance, the costs and reorganization needed to introduce the machine, the opposition of bottomers, and perhaps technical deficiencies contributed to Whittemore's failure.

13. U.S. patents 17,544, 17,998, 19,282, 21,593; Stone, *History of Massachusetts Industries*, 2:1145–46; McDermott, *A History of the Shoe and Leather Industries*, pp. 64–67.

14. U.S. patent 25,149; McDermott, *A History of the Shoe and Leather Industries*, pp. 67–68.

15. *Shoe and Leather Reporter* 14 (June 1, 1867): 1, 10 (December 12, 1867): 4; Stone, *History of Massachusetts Industries*, 2:1155; McDermott, *A History of the Shoe and Leather Industries*, pp. 95–96.

16. U.S. patent 14,269.

17. Note that Sturtevant's key peg-strip patent was the only one he did not assign to Townsend at the time of patenting.

18. Similar to sewing machines, pegging machines are said to have been used when the inventor or an assignee attempted to sell machines. The stagnancy in the number of pegging patents after 1856 reflects the slowness of machine introduction. In this regard, the pegging machine in the late 1850s was like the sewing machine a decade earlier.

19. Manuscripts of the 1860 census of manufacturing, U.S. Census Office, Eighth Census, *Manufactures of the United States in 1860*; commercial directories of Lynn and Boston, 1859 and 1860.

20. *Bulletin of the Business History Society*; Ewers and Baylor, *Sincere's History of the Sewing Machine*, pp. 19–20; Hunter, *A History of Industrial Power*, 2:263–64.

21. *Asher and Adams' Pictorial Album*, p. 114.

Chapter 10

1. Marx, *Capital*; Mantoux, *The Industrial Revolution*; Landes, *The Unbound Prometheus*; Rostow, *The Stages of Economic Growth*.

2. Mantoux, *The Industrial Revolution*, p. 91. See also Marx, *Capital*, 1:918. The effect of market growth on productivity growth is developed in Young, "Increasing Returns and Economic Progress," and elaborated in the cumulative causation explanations of Kaldor, *Causes of the Slow Rate of Economic Growth*. Kaldor takes this argument in a macroeconomic direction to conclude that technological change should have been especially rapid immediately after the Industrial Revolution. Manufacturing growth was most rapid then because (1) the income elasticity of demand for manufactured goods was high, (2) capital goods sectors grew rapidly, and (3) exports of manufactured goods expanded greatly. If, whether through learning or incentive effects, technical change increased with manufacturing output, the conclusion follows. On the character of this line of argument, see Ricoy, "Cumulative Causation."

3. Mantoux, *The Industrial Revolution*, p. 42 and passim; Marx, *Capital*, 1:15.

4. Marx, *Capital*, 1:505n.

5. Mantoux, *The Industrial Revolution*, pp. 475, 216, 338.

6. Marx does allude to the birth of machine tools as commodities in the mid-nineteenth century, but says nothing about the importance of this transition for the process of technical change. In developing Marx's interpretation of the origins of capitalism, Dobb notes the importance of institutional change. He argues that technological dynamics are ongoing in capitalism and hence cannot differentiate the Industrial Revolution from later periods. The distinctiveness of the technological dynamic of the Industrial Revolution lay more in its institutional innovations, including the birth of a textile machinery industry. *Studies in the Development of Capitalism*, pp. 255–81.

On the generation of the first textile machinists, see Musson and Robinson, "The Origins of Engineering." On the contribution of science, see Musson and Robinson, *Science and Technology*.

7. Allyn Young interprets Adam Smith's notion that the division of labor is limited by the extent of the market to mean that market growth may lead to the formation of new capital goods, but does not indicate how those goods will be generated and developed. "Increasing Returns and Economic Progress." Learning theories often associate demand growth with learning (Kaldor) or consider learning embodied in capital goods (Arrow, "The Economic Implications of Learning by Doing") without identifying the social organization of the learning process.

8. Stigler, "The Division of Labor," p. 189. In a footnote Stigler agrees that vertical disintegration and the narrowing of product lines are both implied by his interpretation of Smith. Allyn Young suggests a similar process of new industry formation. "Increasing Returns and Economic Progress."

9. Data on nodal machines are from Grace Cooper, *The Sewing Machine*, pp. 89, 112, 119. Nonnodal machine sales are the difference between census data on total sewing machine production and estimates of nodal sales for census years. Nonnodal sales are overstated to the extent that at least one important nonnodal machine, the Domestic, was controlled by a nodal firm, Singer. Hounshell, *From the American System to Mass Production*, p. 97.

10. Depew, *One Hundred Years of American Commerce*, 2:530, 534–35; U.S. Census Office, *Twelfth Census: Manufactures*, 2:411–12.

11. U.S. Bureau of the Census, *Historical Statistics of the United States*, p. 139. Given the durability of the sewing machine, population and per capita income expan-

sion after the mid-1870s may have prevented sales from falling during the period when 1870 vintage machines were still in use. After the market penetration phase, one would expect sales growth to have been regulated by those extraindustry factors determining the potential market.

12. Davies, *Peacefully Working to Conquer the World*, pp. 9–60, 74; *Scientific American* 54 (March 13, 1886): 165; Chandler, *The Visible Hand*, pp. 304–5, 403–5.

13. Surveyed city directories centered on large cities, including all cities with a population over 40,000 in 1860 and all but three over 20,000. Fifty-one surveyed cities had directories listing sewing machine agencies in 1880 (see Table 8.3). Forty-one of these already had agencies in 1860. Three of the 51 cities in 1880—Los Angeles, Fall River, and Jersey City—had partial listings over the previous 20 years; for this reason, they were excluded from calculations concerning agencies in Table 10.1 and elsewhere in this chapter. The number of multiple-agency firms is cumulative; it overstates the actual number in any year if some firms had gone out of business. In addition, a few other multiple-agency firms in the 1850s had gone out of business by 1862.

14. Cost changes are harder to assess. Singer testified in 1870 that sewing machines cost $11.83 to produce; in 1877 it was estimated that machines selling for $65 cost about $6.25 to make and an $85 machine cost under $10. Presumably these figures excluded sewing machine cabinets. On productivity and costs, see U.S. Census Office, Eighth Census, *Manufactures of the United States in 1860* (p. cxc), and Ninth Census, *Statistics of the Wealth and Industry of the United States*; Fitch, "Manufactures of Interchangeable Mechanism," p. 35; *Scientific American* 26 (May 4, 1872): 295, 36 (May 5, 1877): 277.

15. For the classic statement of the importance of technological convergence for the birth of the sewing machine, see Rosenberg, *Perspectives on Technology*, pp. 9–31. For a fine recent study of the birth of mass production, see Hounshell, *From the American System to Mass Production*, esp. pp. 15–123. Mass-production machinery produced not only firearms, but also axes, hardware, locks, and clocks. The precision sector also developed in Rhode Island. On the development of firearms, in addition to Rosenberg and Hounshell, see Fitch, "Manufactures of Interchangeable Mechanism," pp. 1–27; Roe, *English and American Tool Builders*, pp. 164–215, 231–38; Merritt Smith, *Harpers Ferry Armory*; Woodbury, "History of the Gear Cutting Machine," *Studies in the History of Machine Tools*, p. 80.

16. Merritt Smith, *Harpers Ferry Armory*; Fitch, "Manufactures of Interchangeable Mechanism," p. 20; Roe, *English and American Tool Builders*, pp. 143, 168–69, 195.

17. Hounshell emphasizes the difficulties of introducing interchangeable parts manufacturing. *From the American System to Mass Production*, pp. 67–123. See also Roe, *English and American Tool Builders*, pp. 6, 17–20, 24, 192, 197, 202–7; Durfee, "Interchangeable Construction," p. 1251; Fitch, "Manufactures of Interchangeable Mechanism," pp. 20, 26–27, 36–37; Central Labor Union, *Centennial Illustrated History of Bridgeport*, p. 112; Bishop, *A History of American Manufactures*, 2:435; Rosenberg, *The American System of Manufactures*, pp. 9–15, 71; Woodbury, "History of the Grinding Machine," *Studies in the History of Machine Tools*, pp. 59–61; "A. C. Hobbs" and "Frederick Howe," *Dictionary of American Biography*.

18. *Scientific American* 7 (December 27, 1862): 401; *American Artisan* 14 (January 27, 1872): 61; Woodbury, "History of the Milling Machine," *Studies in the History of Machine Tools*, pp. 44–51, and "History of the Grinding Machine," pp. 9, 58–66; Roe, *English and American Tool Builders*, pp. 175–76, 195, 208–14, and *The Mechanical Equipment*, pp. 221–35, 324; Fitch, "Manufactures of Interchangeable Mechanism," p. 37; *Reports of the United States Commissioners to the Vienna Exhibition of 1873*,

3:32; *Asher & Adams' Pictorial Album*, p. 48; *Scientific American* 42 (March 20, 1880): 181; Durfee, "Interchangeable Construction," p. 1251; Hounshell, *From the American System to Mass Production*, pp. 79–82.

19. Roe, *English and American Tool Builders*, pp. 137, 143, 165–66, 177, 191, 203, 207–13; Fitch, "Manufactures of Interchangeable Mechanism," pp. 26, 28, 40; Woodbury, "History of the Milling Machine," *Studies in the History of Machine Tools*, pp. 51–54; Durfee, "Interchangeable Construction," pp. 1250, 1252; Saul, "Mechanical Engineering Industries in Britain," pp. 111–30; Hounshell, *From the American System to Mass Production*, pp. 79–82.

20. Until more is known about the employees of sewing machine producers (especially foremen, superintendents, and contractors), the extent of involvement of producers in sewing machine development cannot be determined. But involvement could not have been great, because there were relatively few sewing machine inventors in the major center of Bridgeport who are not known to have had other employment.

21. Invention became less responsive to sales during the sewing machine's product cycle, as evidenced by the declining ratio of first patents to agencies (or to nodal company sales). Annual first patents per agency declined from 0.59 in the 1853–57 patenting period to 0.26 in 1868–71 and 0.11 in 1879–82. The relative concentration of patenting early in the product cycle supports the Schumpeterian expectation that patenting is bunched near the inception of the product. The decline may have resulted from different intensities of learning over time. First, models were standardized by about 1870 and obvious bottlenecks were overcome. Second, family machines rose relatively until in 1900 they formed 94 percent of the total number and 82 percent of the value of sewing machines made in the United States. Family machines were used less intensively and for a narrower range of applications than manufacturing machines, and thus posed fewer problems to be overcome. In addition, learning may be more related to cumulative sales, net of abandoned machines, and through 1872 cumulative sales grew more slowly than current sales.

22. The classification and many conclusions of this section are the same as those of my "Learning by Selling." As that article shows, if this altered state classification were applied to the pre-1860 period, the conclusions of Chapter 8 would be substantially unchanged.

23. The differential patent-agency ratios may have resulted from undercounting agencies, due in part to the availability of commercial directories. Undercounting occurred in all areas; the only factor making it particularly true of Massachusetts is the location of agencies in shoe towns without available directories.

24. Much the same is concluded by considering sequenced repeat patenting. Inventors with patents used within one year had rates of repeat patenting two and one-half times those who did not; and those gaining use within three years, compared to others, had four times as many patents four or more years later.

25. The concentration is even greater when foreign countries are taken into account. Foreign inventors took out only a few percent of American sewing machine patents, far less than the share of American inventors in foreign countries. Moreover, some foreign residents assigned patents to American firms, including a few who were agents of American companies.

26. This classification follows that of the Patent Office. A degree of arbitrariness necessarily exists. Should a shuttle mechanism for a leather-sewing machine be classified as a stitch-forming mechanism, a shuttle, or a leather-sewing machine? The U.S. Department of Commerce's *U.S. Patent Classification—Subclass Listing* divides sewing machine patents into 350 different categories. It often lists a patent in several

categories but typically identifies a principal category. I have usually classified patents according to these principal categories. Table 10.8 underestimates the share of patents made for special machines, because some are classified as elements, stitch-forming mechanisms, or attachments.

27. *Sewing Machine Advance* 1 (1879): 32; Byrn, *The Progress of Invention in the 19th Century*, pp. 192–93; *Appleton's Cyclopedia of Applied Mechanics*, 1880, 2:738–44, 750–52; *Appleton's Cyclopedia of Applied Mechanics*, 1893, 3:795; Gregory, "Machines, Etc. Used in Sewing," 7:18, 37; Urquhart, *Sewing Machinery*, pp. 86–89; Grace Cooper, *The Sewing Machine*, pp. 62–63.

28. *Scientific American* 20 (April 17, 1869): 247; *Engineering* 3 (1867): 513, 10 (1870): 6; *Mechanics of the Sewing Machine*, pp. 76–77; Depew, *One Hundred Years of American Commerce*, 2:534; Davies, *Peacefully Working to Conquer the World*, p. 107.

29. *Scientific American* 38 (November 2, 1878): 278–79; *Appleton's Cyclopedia of Applied Mechanics*, 1880, 2:738–40; *Mechanics of the Sewing Machine*, pp. 50–52, 56–61. The choice of mechanisms also influenced later development. The use of the lockstitch by most major companies and the elimination of Grover and Baker with its double-thread chain stitch altered learning and later invention; chain-stitch patents—40 percent of stitch-forming patents prior to 1861—fell to 5 percent from 1875 through 1882.

30. *Mechanic's Magazine* 8 (August 8, 1862): 76.

31. Quoted from *Scientific American* 48 (February 10, 1883): 88.

32. Strictly speaking, the buttonhole machine did not sew at all, since it did not unite separate layers of material, but was more like the embroidery machine. Yet its general mechanisms were much the same as those of the sewing machine. McDermott, *A History of the Shoe and Leather Industries*, pp. 135–36; *Engineering* 3 (1867): 513; Tomlinson, *Cyclopedia*, 3:627; Depew, *One Hundred Years of American Commerce*, 2:532, 539; *Reports of the United States Commissioners to the Paris Universal Exposition*, 2:295; Grace Cooper, *The Sewing Machine*, p. 62.

33. *Engineering* 3 (1867): 513; *Transactions of the American Institute*, 1863, pp. 470–73; *Reports of the United States Commissioners to the Paris Universal Exposition*, 2:295–96; Gregory, "Machines, Etc. Used in Sewing," 7:21; Wheeler and Wilson, *The Golden Calendar*.

34. McDermott, *A History of the Shoe and Leather Industries*, pp. 137–38.

35. *Appleton's Cyclopedia of Applied Mechanics*, 1880, 2:796; Gregory, "Machines, Etc. Used in Sewing," 7:31; Depew, *One Hundred Years of American Commerce*, 2:533, 539.

36. *Appleton's Cyclopedia of Applied Mechanics*, 1880, 2:747–50; *Appleton's Cyclopedia of Applied Mechanics*, 1893, 3:795–96; *Scientific American* 35 (October 7, 1876): 223, 43 (September 11, 1880): 163.

37. Davies, *Peacefully Working to Conquer the World*, pp. 50, 80; *Scientific American* 38 (November 2, 1878): 278; Depew, *One Hundred Years of American Commerce*, 2:533.

38. Davies, *Peacefully Working to Conquer the World*, pp. 58–76; Chandler, *The Visible Hand*, pp. 303–5, 402–5; Carstensen, *American Enterprise in Foreign Markets*.

39. On the integration into cabinets, see Hounshell, *From the American System to Mass Production*, pp. 129–46.

Chapter 11

1. U.S. patent 20,775.

2. A clear discussion of this process is given in Plunkett, *Theory and Practice of Boot and Shoe Manufacture*, p. 258.

3. See Blake's affidavit, *Application of Lyman Blake for Extension of Letters Patent*, p. 4. Patent renewal applications are a useful source because they make clear the economic significance of the machine. See also McDermott, *A History of the Shoe and Leather Industries*, p. 96.

4. *Application of Lyman Blake for Extension of Letters Patent*, p. 4.

5. Quoted from McDermott, *A History of the Shoe and Leather Industries*, p. 70.

6. That these contexts fostered his invention in no way denies Blake's originality. After all, many confronted the same contexts yet Blake alone adapted the design of the pegged shoe to sewing and introduced the horn and looper mechanism to form the new shoe. That Blake did this, rather than the trained mechanics who were designing waxed-thread and pegging machines for Townsend, suggests the extent of Blake's accomplishment. The originality of inventors can be assessed only in relation to the social contexts in which they exist.

7. Quoted from *Application of Lyman Blake for Extension of Letters Patent*, p. 5; see also McDermott, *A History of the Shoe and Leather Industries*, p. 70.

8. McDermott, *A History of the Shoe and Leather Industries*, p. 71; Grace Cooper, *The Sewing Machine*, p. 140.

9. McDermott, *A History of the Shoe and Leather Industries*, p. 71.

10. *Application of Lyman Blake for Extension of Letters Patent*, p. 5.

11. Ibid., pp. 5–6, 22–25; U.S. patent 21,091; *Shoe and Leather Reporter* 55 (1893): xliv; McDermott, *A History of the Shoe and Leather Industries*, p. 71.

12. U.S. patents 29,562, 35,165, 36,163; *Application of Lyman Blake for Extension of Letters Patent*, p. 24; *Shoe and Leather Reporter* 62 (1896): 457; testimony of Charles Buffam in *G. McKay v. Jonathan Brown*, pp. 11–12.

13. Quoted from *Application of Lyman Blake for Extension of Letters Patent*, pp. 7, 9, 25; see also Hazard, *The Organization of the Boot and Shoe Industry*, pp. 110–11; *Shoe and Leather Reporter* 54 (1892): lxxii. Another Lynn manufacturer, Abner Moore, reportedly provided the material for the first trial of the McKay machine in 1858 and 1859; Moore had previously joined other Lynn shoemakers to buy the Essex County rights to the Singer machine and manufacture a sewing machine in 1853 and 1854. *Shoe and Leather Reporter* 54 (1892): lxxxiv.

14. *Shoe and Leather Reporter* 54 (1892): xliv, 57 (1894): 1114, 64 (1897): 537, 87 (1907): 117; *Application of Lyman Blake for Extension of Letters Patent*, p. 7; *Report of the Industrial Commission*, 14:483.

15. The set-up charge was later discontinued. *Shoe and Leather Reporter* 10 (April 18, 1867): 2, 17 (July 30, 1874): 1, 32 (1881): 307.

16. *Shoe and Leather Reporter* 17 (July 30, 1874): 1, 23 (1877): 208, 32 (1881): 307, 64 (1897): 603; Hazard, *The Organization of the Boot and Shoe Industry*, p. 117; Bryant, *Shoe and Leather Trade*, pp. 77–78. Cf. *Report of the Industrial Commission*, 14:498, which puts the number of McKay machines in 1890 at 4,000.

17. *Shoe and Leather Reporter* 17 (July 20, 1874): 1, 23 (1877): 208; *Shoe and Leather Record* 4 (1873–74): 463.

18. The same conclusion follows for Essex County as a whole, though the identified McKay producers were only 14 percent of all manufacturers.

19. U.S. patents 42,622, 42,916, 45,422, 107,155, 207,340, 273,531, 415,064,

440,327; Keir, *Industries of America*, p. 457. See also *Lynn Item*, November 18, 1903 (in "Lynn Scrapbooks"); Stone, *History of Massachusetts Industries*, 2:1151.

20. *Shoe and Leather Reporter* 50 (1890): 694; Goodyear Boot and Shoe Sewing Machine Company, *Prospectus*, p. 3; United Shoe Machinery Corporation, *How American Shoes Are Made*, pp. 42–45, 59.

21. On the connection of the older Goodyear to shoe production, see *Shoe and Leather Reporter* 64 (1897): 565, 87 (1907): 217.

22. U.S. patents 34,413, 56,729, 93,731, 95,571, 96,944, 97,951.

23. Quoted from Goodyear Boot and Shoe Sewing Machine Company, *Prospectus*, pp. 3–8; see also McDermott, *A History of the Shoe and Leather Industries*, p. 87.

24. U.S. patents 112,802, 116,947, 170,547, 190,709. See also Roe, *English and American Tool Builders*, pp. 195–96, and *The Mechanical Equipment*, p. 477; *Appleton's Cyclopedia of Applied Mechanics*, 1880, 2:744; B. P. Cooper, "Shoe Machinery," pp. 30–35; Kaempffert, *A Popular History of American Invention*, 2:423; McDermott, *A History of the Shoe and Leather Industries*, pp. 86–91.

25. U.S. patent 127,423.

26. U.S. patents 240,307, 366,935; McDermott, *A History of the Shoe and Leather Industries*, pp. 86–92. Later patents substituted an eye-point for the barbed needle—for example, U.S. patent 369,563.

27. Goodyear Boot and Shoe Sewing Machine Company, *Prospectus*, p. 8; McDermott, *A History of the Shoe and Leather Industries*, 88–89.

28. *Report of the Industrial Commission*, 14:482–83; *Shoe and Leather Reporter* 50 (1890): 694, 28 (1879): 375; Kaempffert, *A Popular History of American Invention*, 2:423–24; *Goodyear Shoe Machinery Company Catalog*; McDermott, *A History of the Shoe and Leather Industries*, pp. 90–91.

29. *Shoe and Leather Reporter* 46 (1888): 1102, 50 (1890): 694, 55 (1893): 156a, 64 (1897): 1273, 67 (1899): 29, 69 (1900): 83; Depew, *One Hundred Years of American Commerce*, 2:568.

30. To identify and classify leather-sewing machine patents, the U.S. Department of Commerce's *U.S. Patent Classification—Subclass Listing* has been used. A few of these sewing machines used dry thread, but the vast majority were waxed-thread machines. Leather-sewing machine patents include more than shoe-sewing machines, because they also sewed harnesses, saddlery, hats, and books. Still, the large majority sewed shoes. The number of leather-sewing machines was underestimated because some were included among attachments, elements, and stitch-forming mechanisms. For example, 16 patents were listed as leather-sewing machines through 1861, but Chapter 9 identified 24. For consistency with 1862–1901 data, this chapter will consider only the 16 listed leather-sewing machine patents through 1861.

31. Bottom-sewing machine patents include those that could apply only to bottom sewing, such as sole-stitching, channeling, and welt guides, and those patent grants that specify their bottoming function. The remainder include upper-sewing machines and those bottom-sewing machines with generic applicability.

32. Leather-sewing machine patentees from 23 cities had known occupations, led by Boston's 19 and Lynn's 15. The directories consulted were the same as those used to determine sewing machine agencies in 1880, with the addition, in some years, of directories for Lynn, Brockton, Haverhill, Fitchburg, and Lawrence, Massachusetts, and Bridgeport, Connecticut.

33. Other factors may have worked to Massachusetts' benefit. It consistently had three times as many machinists per capita as the national average and had disproportionately more employment in sewing machine factories. However, these factors can-

not account for the state's increasing share of first patenting after 1880, because its share of machinists fell somewhat and its share of sewing machine employment fell from 22 percent in 1860 to 5 percent in 1900. We have measured total shoe output, including custom and repair. Massachusetts' share of wholesale production was higher in each period, but its 50 percent share in 1890 and its 41 percent share in 1900 are still less than its share of first patenting.

34. Data on usage are taken more from assignments at the time of patenting because fewer firms were listed in business directories than among dry-thread machines. Patent assignments mask the concentration of use, because many companies specified Portland, Maine, as their location on patent grants yet were not listed in Portland city directories. Whether this fictive location was a response to Maine's incorporation laws is unclear.

35. Inventors are said to have had waxed-thread patents when at least one patent is classified as a leather-sewing machine, and to have had dry-thread patents when at least one sewing machine was not classified as a leather-sewing machine. This overstates the linkage between dry- and waxed-thread inventors because some patents for attachments and elements were used only on leather-sewing machines but were classified as dry-thread patents.

36. That for other states dry-thread invention may have led to waxed-thread invention is seen in two states with great sewing machine concentration but little shoe-making. In Rhode Island and Connecticut, six of the eight crossover inventors first patented dry-thread machines, and the other two copatented a moistening invention that may have been intended for their book-sewing machine patented in the same year.

37. McDermott, *A History of the Shoe and Leather Industries*, pp. 95–99; Stone, *History of Massachusetts Industries*, 2:1155–56; *Appleton's Cyclopedia of Applied Mechanics*, 1880, 2:744–45; Depew, *One Hundred Years of American Commerce*, 2:478; Clark, *History of Manufactures*, 2:478; U.S. Census Office, *Twelfth Census: Manufactures*, 2:410.

38. McDermott, *A History of the Shoe and Leather Industries*, p. 98.

39. *Sewing Machine Advance* 11 (1889): 17, 12 (1890): 29; McDermott, *A History of the Shoe and Leather Industries*, pp. 126–27, 133–34.

40. This categorization understates the share of bottom-sewing machine patents because many thread-handling, work support, and presser-foot inventions were used on bottom-sewing machines but, because they were also used on other machines, were classified as upper machines.

The anomaly of the Middle Atlantic region, where the share of bottom-sewing machines was much closer to the share of dry-thread patents than to the upper patent share, can probably be attributed to the location of Goodyear in New York through most of the period; from 1882 through 1901, the share of bottom-sewing patents in this region fell to 17 percent, the same as its share of other leather-sewing machines.

41. McDermott, *A History of the Shoe and Leather Industries*, pp. 90, 97–99; Stone, *History of Massachusetts Industries*, 2:1155–56; *Appleton's Cyclopedia of Applied Mechanics*, 1880, 2:744–45.

42. McDermott, *A History of the Shoe and Leather Industries*, pp. 92, 99, 114–15, 117.

43. The actual share of welt- and turn-sewing patents was probably at least twice as high; Goodyear is known to have been assigned 40 patents but only 20 appear as welt- or turn-sewing patents in our classification.

44. Boston business directory, 1891.

Chapter 12

1. Once again, patents were taken from U.S. Department of Commerce, *U.S. Patent Classification—Subclass Listing*. It was necessary to narrow the range of patents because the source used to identify leather-cutting and leather-preparing patents went only to 1873. The excluded patents comprised 12 percent of shoe patents from 1837 through 1861, and were disproportionately concentrated in Massachusetts.

2. Only the Boston city directory was included because no others had shoe machinery listings throughout the period.

3. In the large majority of cases, occupations were identified by examining city directories from one to three years prior to the first patent. In a few cases where occupational listings were unclear, additional information was obtained from business directories. For example, when entries listed occupations as foremen with a business address, business directories at times could be used to determine the industry. In addition to the directories used to locate sewing machine agencies (listed in Table 8.3 and Chapter 8, note 29), directories for Brockton and Lawrence, Massachusetts, have been consulted for selected years. Thirty-eight cities had at least one shoe manufacturing inventor whose occupation could be determined, led by 143 inventors from Lynn and 140 from Boston.

4. Use as a capital good is underestimated because of the absence of listings for shoe machinery companies in almost all city directories. This may exaggerate the contrast in frequency of repeat patenting. But the difference is still pronounced, as attested to by the case of Boston, which had extensive shoe machinery listings but had a marked contrast of repeat inventing between its inventors who gained use and those who did not.

5. Shoe manufacturers and foremen are chosen to indicate self-usage because they had authority to introduce new techniques into factory production, whereas cutters, operatives, and shoemakers did not. What is measured is the potential to use an invention in shoe factories; little can be said about the actuality. In this, the measure for self-usage is inferior to that of commodity usage, because for the latter it is at least known that the inventor or assignee made and sold capital goods, though not whether particular patents were used in these products.

Of course, the two forms were not simply alternatives; they were at times symbiotically related. Some shoe manufacturers, including Lyman Blake, used and perfected inventions in their own factories and then sold them as capital goods. On the other hand, manufacturers also improved upon purchased machines.

6. Many other inventors for which occupational data were unavailable also used their own patents. If these inventors had characteristics of the surveyed self-users, their inclusion would heighten the contrast between self-used and unused inventions.

After two or three patents, self-using inventors may have realized that patenting was not worth the cost and therefore stopped patenting their inventions. This would account for the similar extents of repeat patenting between inventors with self-used and unused patents.

7. The choice of 15 repeats as a manifestation of regularized inventing is arbitrary. If 8 were chosen, the extent of repeat patenting for other inventors would range from 2.1 in the West and South to 2.7 in Massachusetts; if 20 were chosen, extents would range from the 3.2 of the Middle Atlantic region to 4.3 for Massachusetts and 4.5 for the West and South. In each case, exclusion of the most prolific inventors lessens or eliminates the advantage of Massachusetts over other states.

8. The border between machines and nonmachines is fuzzy in cases; some crimping machines were more like devices without self-moving parts, and some processes were strictly mechanized. For example, 36 inventors took out process patents for mecha-

nized sewing. But the ambiguous cases are too few to affect the general results.

9. A more nuanced classification of nonmachine patents would only reinforce the point. The 36 inventors who first took out mechanized sewing process patents were more like machine patentees, with rates of repeat patenting of 4.50 when they gained use as capital goods and 0.52 when they did not. In addition, these inventors took out many leather-sewing machine patents.

10. The concentration of prolific inventors on machines is greater still; two of the three starting with nonmachine patents, Lyman Blake and Frank Chase, had previously invented sewing machines and began shoe inventing with sewing process patents.

Why machine inventors were more likely to repeat is not accounted for by excluding prolific inventors. Perhaps machines were used in ways that brought more information back to inventors. Their greater complexity, the larger numbers involved in producing and marketing them, and involvement of the inventor in machinery firms may all have had this effect. Alternatively, machines may have been more remunerative.

11. The regional shares of first patents closely paralleled the shares of patentees classifiable by occupation. For example, Massachusetts had 55 percent of all those inventors classifiable by occupations and 49 percent of all inventors.

Chapter 13

1. Among other examples, Schmookler uses the similar trends of various types of shoe patenting to argue for the preeminence of demand. *Invention and Economic Growth*, pp. 95–96.

2. McDermott, *A History of the Shoe and Leather Industries*, pp. 110–12, 126–28; U.S. Census Office, *Twelfth Census: Manufactures*, 2:747.

3. *Shoe and Leather Reporter* 15 (August 10, 1871): 1, 23 (1877): 208, 64 (1897): 603; McDermott, *A History of the Shoe and Leather Industries*, pp. 63–68; U.S. Census Office, Ninth Census, *Statistics of the Wealth and Industry of the United States*, p. 591.

4. In addition, 71 work support devices for pegged work were patented in the 40 years after 1861, two-thirds through 1881. *Shoe and Leather Reporter* 23 (1877): 208, 69 (1900): 83. As early as 1868, a preference existed for McKay shoes in the Boston market. Prices for men's, women's, and boys' McKay shoes in early 1878 were 10 to 50 percent higher than for comparable pegged shoes. Similar differentials had existed throughout the 1870s. *Shoe and Leather Reporter* 11 (July 30, 1868): 4, 25 (1878): 95.

5. McDermott, *A History of the Shoe and Leather Industries*, pp. 78–80.

6. U.S. patents 49,219, 76,150, 122,985, 169,463. Metallic fastening patents are often not listed among shoe manufacturing patents and are therefore difficult to trace. Of 12 important metallic fastening inventors listed by McDermott, only 8 had shoe manufacturing patents and only 2 had metallic fastening patents. McDermott, *A History of the Shoe and Leather Industries*, pp. 75, 80–84; *Shoe and Leather Reporter* 21 (1876): 36, 37 (1884): 184, 47 (1889): 552–54, 48 (1889): 948, 54 (1892): lxxxiv, 62 (1896): 1643, 64 (1897): 605; Frederick Allen, *The Shoe Industry*, p. 132. In 1909, 8 percent of shoes were metallically fastened.

7. On the requirements of machine channeling, see *Ure's Dictionary of Arts, Manufactures and Mines*, 4:121, 129.

8. *Shoe and Leather Reporter* 10 (April 18, 1867): 2, 17 (July 30, 1874): 1, 32 (1881): 307, 52 (1891): 253, 55 (1893): 1364, xliv, 62 (1896): 97; United Shoe Machinery Company, *Goodyear Welt Shoes*, pp. 18–19; McDermott, *A History of the Shoe and Leather Industries*, pp. 112–13.

9. *Shoe and Leather Reporter* 10 (April 18, 1867): 2, 17 (July 30, 1874): 1, 32 (1881): 307.

10. *A History of the Shoe and Leather Industries*, p. 111.

11. The highest number of patents consisted of burnishing machines for 14 inventors; heel and heel-trimming machines for 24; lasting machines for 17; sole-trimming machines for 27; upper machines for 13; and channeling, leveling, pegging, molding, and other sole machines for 44. Note that categorizing inventors by the number of patents of a type implies nothing about the direction in time of changes of inventive focus.

12. Sole trimming is an ambiguous category, because it includes both rough rounding—an operation in bottoming—and the finishing trimming that occurs after bottoming.

13. Quoted from U.S. patent 75,428. See also U.S. patent 71,495; McDermott, *A History of the Shoe and Leather Industries*, pp. 116–17.

14. U.S. patents 96,638, 164,235, 231,707, 266,283, 300,039; McDermott, *A History of the Shoe and Leather Industries*, pp. 116–17; *Shoe and Leather Reporter* 47 (1889): 552–54.

15. McDermott, *A History of the Shoe and Leather Industries*, pp. 110–12. Knox's molding machine was perhaps the only major invention that was not patented. McDermott attributes this to Knox's disgust with earlier patent litigation and discouragement over the slowness of introduction of his machine.

Chapter 14

1. On the logic of diversification, see Levine, *Economic Theory*, 2, chaps. 4, 5; on the product cycle and its relation to location, see Vernon, "International Investment and International Trade in the Product Cycle"; Markusen, *Profit Cycles, Oligopoly, and Regional Development*.

2. *Shoe and Leather Reporter* 14 (June 1, 1871): 1; McDermott, *A History of the Shoe and Leather Industries*, pp. 124–27; Stone, *History of Massachusetts Industries*, 2:1145–46.

3. *Shoe and Leather Reporter* 17 (July 30, 1874): 1, 55 (1893): 156a, 64 (1897): 603, 71 (January 10, 1901): 17; Depew, *One Hundred Years of American Commerce*, 2:530.

4. Depew, *One Hundred Years of American Commerce*, 2:530; testimony of J. B. Crosby in *Application of Lyman Blake for Extension of Letters Patent*, p. 53.

5. *Shoe and Leather Reporter* 21 (1876): 210, 57 (1894): 1114.

6. McDermott, *A History of the Shoe and Leather Industries*, pp. 80–82, 100–105; Stone, *History of Massachusetts Industries*, 2:1153, 1156; *Gordon McKay et al. v. Henry Dunham*.

7. *Shoe and Leather Reporter* 50 (1890): 694, 44 (1887): 660, 45 (1888): 127, 47 (1889): 554, 60 (1895): 116; McDermott, *A History of the Shoe and Leather Industries*, pp. 80–81, 100–105; *Report of the Industrial Commission*, 14:483; Depew, *One Hundred Years of American Commerce*, 2:568.

8. *Shoe and Leather Reporter* 50 (1890): 694, 60 (1895): 709, 63 (1897): 1301; McDermott, *A History of the Shoe and Leather Industries*, p. 91.

9. *Shoe and Leather Reporter* 50 (1890): 276, 53 (1892): 1150, 55 (1893): xliv, 57 (1894): 813, 60 (1895): 811, 61 (1896): 460; United Shoe Machinery Company, *Goodyear Welt Shoes*, pp. 18–19; *Catalog of Parts of Goodyear Shoe Machinery Company's Machines*.

10. *Shoe and Leather Reporter* 59 (1895): 850. On the formation of the Goodyear system, see *Shoe and Leather Reporter* 60 (1890): 276, 52 (1891): 253, 59 (1895): 850, 61 (1896): 460.

11. *Shoe and Leather Reporter* 50 (1890): 746, 53 (1892): 92, 61 (1896): 1350, 58

(1894): 805, 59 (1895): 185, 415, 585, and 850, 62 (1896): 1428, 63 (1897): 101; *Shoe and Leather Reporter Annual*, 189?, pp. 276, 278, 286–87, 469, and 1893, p. 307; McDermott, *A History of the Shoe and Leather Industries*, p. 99. Goodyear directors who were also shoe manufacturers included George Keith, William Rice, and W. D. Brackett.

12. *Shoe and Leather Reporter* 47 (1889): 553–58, 54 (1892): lxxxiv, 59 (1895): 585, 64 (1897): 603; McDermott, *A History of the Shoe and Leather Industries*, pp. 92, 115, 119–26.

13. McDermott, *A History of the Shoe and Leather Industries*, p. 103; *Report of the Industrial Commission*, 14:307. On the difference between mechanizing hand and arm motions, see Parker, "Agriculture," p. 385.

14. McDermott, *A History of the Shoe and Leather Industries*, pp. 103–5; *Shoe and Leather Reporter* 50 (1890): 276 and 694, 55 (1893): xliv, 57 (1894): 813, 60 (1895): 116 and 811, 61 (1896): 460.

15. *Shoe and Leather Reporter* 57 (1894): 1454, 63 (1897): 35, 507; Kaplan, "Jan Earnst Matzeliger," pp. 16–22; United Shoe Machinery Company, *Illustrated Catalog of Shoe Machinery*, pp. 81, 83; McDermott, *A History of the Shoe and Leather Industries*, pp. 106–8.

16. *Shoe and Leather Reporter* 57 (1894): 1454, 61 (1896): 458 and 629, 63 (1897): 349, 419, and 523, 66 (1898): 1423, 67 (1899): 1403, 68 (1899): 169, 69 (1900): 83 and 770; Kaplan, "Jan Earnst Matzeliger."

17. United Shoe Machinery Company, *Goodyear Welt Shoes*, pp. 28–32; McDermott, *A History of the Shoe and Leather Industries*, p. 108.

Chapter 15

1. U.S. Bureau of Labor, *Thirteenth Annual Report*, 1:113.

2. Ibid., 2:524–77.

3. Workers had as much control as they did because the machine did not—and still does not—completely control the feed of the shoe. The range of activity of the McKay stitcher decreased over time. In the early McKay machine, the worker nailed the heels and toes of the shoe, but later machines took over this activity. Brodoli, *The Boot and Shoe Maker*, 3:191–92.

4. U.S. Bureau of Labor, *Thirteenth Annual Report*, 2:524–77.

5. *Hand and Machine Labor* identifies even more specializations in the factories it surveys. Johnson, *Sketches of Lynn*, p. 344; Kaven and Hadaway, "Modern Shoe Manufacture," app. 1.

6. The 1870 data are for firms with output exceeding $5,000, whereas the 1880–1900 data are for factory production, as distinct from custom and repair. By the criterion of production for the mass market, the two are largely comparable, but because some firms with output under $5,000 produced for the mass market, the 1870 data were probably more restrictive. U.S. Census Office, Ninth Census, *Statistics of the Wealth and Industry of the United States*, p. 591, and *Twelfth Census: Manufactures*, 2:760–63.

7. Massachusetts figures measure all producers and hence are not comparable with the wholesale establishments measured in federal censuses. But because custom producers were a minor part of Massachusetts output, this difference was not significant. State census measures of productivity for all producers in 1875 and 1885 fell between the federal measures for wholesale production in Massachusetts in surrounding census years.

Productivity growth from 1855 to 1870 may be overstated because part-time labor probably fell as the putting-out system declined. In Lynn, for example, the annual output per female employee, which approximated the annual productivity of fitters, fell from 843 pairs in 1832 to 716 in 1855. A rough sense of the real productivity growth from 1855 to 1870 can be gotten by assuming (1) that the fall in output per woman employee was due to the rise in part-time labor, (2) that part-time labor for men did not change, (3) that annual labor hours per worker in 1832 and 1870 were the same, and (4) that the decline in part-time labor in Massachusetts was the same as that in Lynn. The Massachusetts annual output per full-time worker in 1855 would have been 636 pairs, and productivity growth would have been 71 percent by 1870 and 175 percent by 1900. Massachusetts, *Abstract of the Census of Massachusetts for 1855*; Dawley, *Class and Community*, pp. 245–46.

8. For present purposes, the relevant point is the differential productivity growth in mechanized and nonmechanized operations. There remains the problem that the productivity growth noted in *Hand and Machine Labor* far exceeded the tripling indicated by manufacturing censuses, and the gap has no obvious explanation. Differences in systems of craft production account for part. *Hand and Machine Labor* refers to custom production undertaken by one or two workers, whereas the census refers to wholesale production undertaken by establishments with dozens of workers. Wholesale craft units dispensed with the time used by the custom shoemaker to measure feet and prepare patterns and lasts; neglecting this time would reduce hand labor time by 8 percent. Learning, specialization, improved tools, speed-up, and decreased quality could all have played a part. (On the ties of forms of industrial organization to economies of scale, see Sokoloff, "Transition from the Artisanal Shop to the Nonmechanized Factory," and Atack, "Economies of Scale and Efficiency Gains.") In addition, factories in *Hand and Machine Labor* doubled the national average in employment and were located in Massachusetts; they therefore may have captured economies of scale and organizational superiorities that increased measured productivity relative to the national average.

9. Rosenberg, "Learning by Using," *Inside the Black Box*, pp. 120–40; David, "The 'Horndal Effect' " and "Learning by Doing and Tariff Protection," *Technical Choice*, pp. 95–191. On inside contractors and managers as innovators within the factory, see Clawson, *Bureaucracy and the Labor Process*. See Lazonick and Brush, "The 'Horndal Effect' in Early U.S. Manufacturing," for an argument that the observed increase in output per hour in David's study was more a result of intensification of labor than of technological change. Because shoe machines were relatively simple and had few safety problems, disembodied learning by using was less significant than in the use of aircraft studied by Rosenberg.

10. I consider these effects in "Technological Change as New Product Development."

11. McDermott, *A History of the Shoe and Leather Industries*, pp. 102–5; *Shoe and Leather Reporter* 52 (1891): 496, 52 (1892): 1150, 57 (1894): 813, 59 (1895): 69, 60 (1895): 650, 61 (1896): 1364, 62 (1896): 213, 63 (1897): 1101.

12. *Report of the Industrial Commission*, 14:483–84; Kaysen, *United States v. United Shoe Machinery Corporation*, p. 6. This rationale may not be very strong. Though one agency could replace three if the companies combined, employment in regional agencies need not fall and, as Howe reported, did not fall with the merger. This he attributed to a business upturn, but it is not clear how employment varied over the cycle. Surprisingly, Howe did not mention reduced production costs as a rationale for consolidation.

It should be noted that Howe had an interest in portraying the purpose of the consolidation to be cost reduction rather than the overcoming of antagonistic competitive processes. As in its successful 1911 defense against the government's attempt to prosecute it under the Sherman Antitrust Act, United claimed that the amalgamation was one of firms making different machines and did not change the preexisting extent of competition. See Kaysen, *United States v. United Shoe Machinery Corporation*, pp. 6–16.

13. Elmer Howe treated the overlap of lasting patent ownership as a secondary reason for consolidation. *Report of the Industrial Commission*, 14:483.

14. *Shoe and Leather Reporter* 62 (1896): 1009, 66 (1898): 1544, 67 (1899): 319, 488; Kaysen, *United States v. United Shoe Machinery Corporation*, p. 6; McDermott, *A History of the Shoe and Leather Industries*, p. 142. Purported cost reductions from combining service centers were later taken as a rationale for requiring companies to use a complete line of United machines or pay a premium for the use of only some. *Report of the Industrial Commission*, 14:488. On the superiority of the Consolidated lasting machine, see, for example, United Shoe Machinery Company, *Illustrated Catalogue of Shoe Machinery*.

15. Quoted from *Lynn Item*, February 6, 1924, in "Lynn Scrapbooks." *Shoe and Leather Reporter* 70 (1900): 689, 71 (January 3, 1901): 13, 71 (January 24, 1901): 13; Kaysen, *United States v. United Shoe Machinery Corporation*, pp. 13–15; *Report of the Industrial Commission*, 14:488. Kaysen conservatively estimated the market share of United to have been at least 70 percent in each major type of machinery (p. 7).

16. Kaysen, *United States v. United Shoe Machinery Corporation*, pp. 8–10; United Shoe Machinery Company, *Illustrated Catalogue of Shoe Machinery*, pp. 164–65, and *Tools for the Shoemaker*; *Report of the Industrial Commission*, 14:485; *Shoe and Leather Reporter* 68 (1899): 245; McDermott, *A History of the Shoe and Leather Industries*, pp. 144–49.

17. McKenzie, *The American Invaders*, pp. 49–51; Church, "The Effect of the American Export Invasion"; *Report of the Industrial Commission*, 14:489; Kaysen, *United States v. United Shoe Machinery Corporation*, p. 7.

Chapter 16

1. Quotations from Schumpeter, "The Instability of Capitalism," pp. 379, 384, 380, 383. Schumpeter's italics. On the sources of entrepreneurship, see Schumpeter, *The Theory of Economic Development*, pp. 92–94. See also Heilbroner, *Behind the Veil of Economics*, pp. 165–84.

2. "The Instability of Capitalism," p. 383. Schumpeter believed that the two were complements. Much of Schumpeter's work concerns the conception and working out of capitalist change, including *The Theory of Economic Development*, *Business Cycles*, and *Capitalism, Socialism, and Democracy*, pt. 2. For a rejection of the complementarity of ideas of equilibrium and capitalist change and an attempt to build economic theory on other grounds, see Levine, *Economic Theory*, esp. vol. 2.

3. On the inadequacy of an inference of the direction of technical change from relative factor prices, see Salter, *Productivity and Technical Change*; Temin, "Labor Scarcity in America"; David, *Technical Choice*, pp. 20–31.

4. *Capitalism, Socialism, and Democracy*, pp. 131–34.

5. For a study of distinct paths of technical change in the modern economy, see von Hippel, *The Sources of Innovation*.

Bibliography

Alexander, Edwin. "On the Sewing Machine: Its History and Progress." *Journal of the Society of Arts* 11 (April 10, 1863): 358–70.

Allen, Frederick. *The Shoe Industry*. Boston, 1916.

Allen, Robert C. "Collective Invention." *Journal of Economic Behavior and Organization* 4 (March 1983): 1–24.

American Artisan.

Appleton's Cyclopedia of Applied Mechanics. 2 vols. New York, 1880.

Appleton's Cyclopedia of Applied Mechanics. 2d ed. 3 vols. New York, 1893.

Appleton's Dictionary of Machines, Mechanics, Engine Work and Engineering. 2d ed. 2 vols. New York, 1868.

Application of Lyman Blake for Extension of Letters Patent. Boston, 1874.

Arrow, Kenneth. "The Economic Implications of Learning by Doing." *Review of Economic Studies* 29 (June 1962): 155–73.

————. "Economic Welfare and the Allocation of Resources for Invention." In *The Rate and Direction of Inventive Activity: Economic and Social Factors*, pp. 609–25. Princeton, 1962.

Asher and Adams' Pictorial Album of American Industry, 1876. New York, 1976.

Atack, Jeremy. "Economies of Scale and Efficiency Gains in the Rise of the Factory in America, 1820–1900." In *Quantity and Quiddity: Essays in U.S. Economic History*, edited by Peter Kilby, pp. 286–335. Middletown, Conn., 1987.

————. "Firm Size and Industrial Structure in the United States during the Nineteenth Century." *Journal of Economic History* 46 (June 1986): 463–75.

The Awl.

Ballou, Adin. *History of the Town of Milford*. Boston, 1882.

Barber, John. *Historical Collections of Every Town in Massachusetts*. Worcester, 1839.

Berg, Maxine. *The Age of Manufactures: Industry, Innovation, and Work in Britain, 1700–1820*. New York, 1986.

————. "The Power of Knowledge: Comments on Marglin's 'Knowledge and Power.'" In *Firms, Organization and Labour: Approaches to the Economics of Work Organization*, edited by Frank Stephen, pp. 165–75. New York, 1984.

Bidwell, Percy, and John Falconer. *History of Agriculture in the Northern United States, 1620–1860*. Washington, D.C., 1925.

Bishop, J. Leander. *A History of American Manufactures from 1608 to 1860.* 3 vols. Philadelphia, 1868.

Bolles, Albert S. *Industrial History of the United States.* Norwich, Conn., 1878.

Bordoli, Ernest, ed. *The Boot and Shoe Maker.* 3 vols. London, 1936.

Brady, Dorothy. "Consumption and the Style of Life." In *American Economic Growth: An Economist's History of the United States*, edited by Lance Davis, Richard Easterlin, and William Parker. New York, 1972.

Bragg, Ernest A. *The Origin and Growth of the Boot and Shoe Industry in Holliston and Milford, Massachusetts, 1793–1950.* Boston, 1950.

Brandon, Ruth. *A Capitalist Romance: Singer and the Sewing Machine.* Philadelphia, 1977.

Braverman, Harry. *Labor and Monopoly Capital: The Degradation of Work in the Twentieth Century.* New York, 1974.

Brooke, Iris. *Footwear: A Short History of European and American Shoes.* New York, 1971.

Bryant, Seth. *Shoe and Leather Trade of the Last Hundred Years.* Boston, 1891.

Bucher, Carl. *Industrial Evolution.* New York, 1967.

Bulletin of the Business History Society 4 (January 1930): 4–5.

Burlingame, Roger. *March of the Iron Men.* New York, 1938.

Buttrick, John. "The Inside Contracting System." *Journal of Economic History* 12 (1952): 205–21.

Byrn, Edward. *The Progress of Invention in the 19th Century.* New York, 1900.

Carstensen, Fred. *American Enterprise in Foreign Markets: Studies of Singer and International Harvester in Imperial Russia.* Chapel Hill, 1984.

Catalog of Parts of Goodyear Shoe Machinery Company's Machines. 1897.

Central Labor Union, ed. *Centennial Illustrated History of Bridgeport, Connecticut and the Central Labor Union.* Bridgeport, 1900.

Chandler, Alfred. *The Visible Hand: The Managerial Revolution in American Business.* Cambridge, Mass., 1977.

Church, R. A. "The Effect of the American Export Invasion on the British Boot and Shoe Industry, 1885–1914." *Journal of Economic History* 28 (June 1968): 223–54.

_____. "Labour Supply and Innovation, 1800–1860: The Boot and Shoe Industry." *Business History* 12 (1970): 25–45.

Clapham, J. H. *An Economic History of Modern Britain.* 3 vols. Cambridge, England, 1926.

Clark, Victor. *History of Manufactures in the United States.* 3 vols. New York, 1929.

Clawson, Dan. *Bureaucracy and the Labor Process: The Transformation of U.S. Industry, 1860–1920.* New York, 1980.

Cole, Arthur H. *The American Woolen Manufacture.* 2 vols. Cambridge, Mass., 1956.

Commons, John R. "American Shoemakers, 1648–1895: A Sketch of Industrial Evolution." *Quarterly Journal of Economics* 24 (November 1909): 39–84.

Cooper, B. P. "Shoe Machinery." *Institute of Mechanical Engineers: Proceedings* (June 15, 1937): 30–35.

Cooper, Carolyn C. "The Roles of Thomas Blanchard's Woodworking Inventions in 19th Century American Manufacturing Technology." Ph.D. dissertation, Yale University, 1985.

_____. "Thomas Blanchard's Woodworking Machines: Tracking 19th-Century Technological Diffusion." *IA: The Journal of the Society for Industrial Archeology* 13 (1987): 41–54.

Cooper, Grace Rogers. *The Sewing Machine: Its Invention and Early Development.* Washington, D.C., 1976.

David, Paul. "The Growth of Real Product in the United States before 1840: New Evidence, Controlled Conjectures." *Journal of Economic History* 27 (1967): 151–97.

_____. *Technical Choice, Innovation, and Economic Growth.* Cambridge, England, 1975.

Davies, Robert. *Peacefully Working to Conquer the World: Singer Sewing Machines in Foreign Markets, 1854–1920.* New York, 1976.

Dawley, Alan. "The Artisan Response to the Factory System: Lynn, Massachusetts in the 19th Century." Ph.D. dissertation, Harvard University, 1971.

_____. *Class and Community: The Industrial Revolution in Lynn.* Cambridge, Mass., 1976.

Depew, Chauncey, ed. *One Hundred Years of American Commerce.* 2 vols. New York, 1895.

Deyrup, Felicia. *Arms Makers of the Connecticut Valley.* Northampton, Mass., 1948.

Dictionary of American Biography. 1946.

Dobb, Maurice. *Studies in the Development of Capitalism.* New York, 1947.

Durfee, W. F. "The History and Modern Development of the Art of Interchangeable Construction." *Transactions of the American Society of Mechanical Engineers* 14 (1893): 1225–57.

Eighty Years' Progress of the United States. New York, 1864.

Engineering.

Eversley, D. E. C. "The Home Market and Economic Growth in England, 1750–1780." In *Land, Labour and Population in the Industrial Revolution*, edited by E. L. Jones and G. E. Mingay, pp. 206–59. London, 1967.

Ewers, William, and H. W. Baylor. *Sincere's History of the Sewing Machine.* Phoenix, Ariz., 1970.

Fairfield, George A. "Report on Sewing Machines." In *Reports of the Commissioners of the United States to the International Exhibition Held at Vienna, 1873*, 3:5–34. Washington, D.C., 1876.

Faler, Paul. "Workingmen, Mechanics, and Social Change: Lynn, Massachusetts, 1800–1860." Ph.D. dissertation, University of Wisconsin, 1971.

Feldman, Egal. *Fit for Men.* Washington, D.C., 1960.

Field, Alexander James. "Sectoral Shift in Antebellum Massachusetts: A Reconsideration." *Explorations in Economic History* 15 (1978): 146–71.

Fishlow, Albert. *American Railroads and the Transformation of the Ante-Bellum Economy.* Cambridge, Mass., 1965.

_____. "Antebellum Interregional Trade Reconsidered." In *New Views on Ameri-*

can Economic Development, edited by Ralph Andreano, pp. 187–200. New York, 1965.

Fitch, Charles. "Report on the Manufactures of Interchangeable Mechanism." In U.S. Census Office, Tenth Census, 1880, *Report on the Manufactures of the United States at the Tenth Census, 1880*, pp. 1–43. Washington, D.C., 1883.

Freedley, Edwin T., ed. *Leading Pursuits and Leading Men: A Treatise on the Principal Trades and Manufactures of the United States*. Philadelphia, 1856.

———. *Philadelphia and Its Manufactures*. Philadelphia, 1858.

Gallman, Robert. "Gross National Product in the United States, 1834–1909." In *Output, Employment, and Productivity in the United States after 1800*, pp. 8–26. New York, 1966.

Gannon, Fred. *Shoemaking: Old and New*. Salem, Mass., 1911.

Garrett, Richard. "The Marxian Theory of Primitive Accumulation, with an Application to the Antebellum Cotton Plantation." Ph.D. dissertation, New School for Social Research, 1978.

George, M. Dorothy. *London Life in the Eighteenth Century*. New York, 1965.

Gibb, George. *The Saco-Lowell Shops: Textile Machinery Building in New England, 1813–1849*. Cambridge, Mass., 1950.

Gifford, George. *Application of Elias Howe, Jr. for an Extension of His Patent for Sewing Machines: Argument of George Gifford, Esq., in Favor of the Application*. New York, 1860.

G. McKay v. Jonathan Brown. Circuit Court of the United States, District of Massachusetts, 1884.

Goodyear Boot and Shoe Sewing Machine Company. *Prospectus of the Goodyear Boot and Shoe Sewing Machine Company*. New York, 1870.

Goodyear Shoe Machinery Company Catalog. Ca. 1897.

Gordon McKay et al. v. Henry Dunham. Circuit Court of the United States, District of Massachusetts, ca. 1882.

Greeley, Horace, et al. *The Great Industries of the United States*. Hartford, 1872.

Gregory, George. "Machines, Etc. Used in Sewing and Making Clothing." In *International Exhibition, 1876: U.S. Centennial Commission*, 7:1–35. Washington, D.C., 1880.

Habakkuk, H. J. *American and British Technology in the Nineteenth Century*. New York, 1962.

Hall, John Phillip. "The Gentle Craft: A Narrative of Yankee Shoemakers." Ph.D. dissertation, Columbia University, 1954.

Hazard, Blanche. "The Organization of the Boot and Shoe Industry in Massachusetts before 1875." *Quarterly Journal of Economics* 27 (1913): 236–62.

———. *The Organization of the Boot and Shoe Industry in Massachusetts before 1875*. Cambridge, Mass., 1921.

Heilbroner, Robert. *Behind the Veil of Economics*. New York, 1988.

Hobsbawm, Eric. "The General Crisis of the European Economy in the 17th Century." *Past and Present* 54 (May 1954): 33–53, 54 (November 1954): 44–65.

———. *Workers: Worlds of Labor*. New York, 1984.

Hoke, Donald. "Ingenious Yankees: The Rise of the American System of Manufactures in the Private Sector." Ph.D. dissertation, University of Wisconsin-Madison, 1985.

Hoopes, Penrose. "Early Clockmaking in Connecticut." In *Connecticut Tercentenary Commission: Committee on Historical Publications* 2 (May 1935): 1–26.

Hoover, Edgar. *Location Theory and the Shoe and Leather Industries*. Cambridge, Mass., 1939.

Hounshell, David. *From the American System to Mass Production, 1800–1932*. Baltimore, 1984.

Howe, Elias, Jr. *Before the Honorable Philip F. Thomas, Commissioner of Patents, in the Matter of the Application of Elias Howe Jr. for an Extension of His Sewing Machine Patent*. New York, 1860.

Hunter, Louis. *A History of Industrial Power in the United States, 1780–1930*. 2 vols. Charlottesville, Va., 1985.

Iles, George. *Inventors at Work*. New York, 1906.

Illustrated Description and Price List of the Willcox and Gibbs Silent Sewing Machine. New York, 1869.

Jack, Andrew. "The Channels of Distribution for an Innovation: The Sewing Machine Industry in America, 1860–1865." *Explorations in Entrepreneurial History* 9 (1956): 113–41.

Jackson, Robert. *The Formation of Craft Labor Markets*. New York, 1984.

John, A. H. "Agricultural Productivity and Economic Growth in England, 1700–1760." *Journal of Economic History* 25 (March 1965): 19–34.

Johnson, David. *Sketches of Lynn or the Changes of Fifty Years*. Lynn, Mass., 1880.

Jones, E. L. "The Agricultural Origins of Industry." *Past and Present* 40 (July 1968): 58–71.

Journal of the Franklin Institute.

Journal of the Society of Arts.

Kaempffert, Waldemar, ed. *A Popular History of American Invention*. 2 vols. New York, 1924.

Kaldor, Nicholas. *Causes of the Slow Rate of Economic Growth of the United Kingdom*. Cambridge, England, 1966.

Kaplan, Sidney. "Jan Earnst Matzeliger." *Journal of Negro History* 40 (1955): 8–33.

Kaven, M. B., and J. B. Hadaway. "Modern Shoe Manufacture." *Meeting of the American Association of Mechanical Engineers*, December 1910, pp. 1961–87.

Kaysen, Carl. *United States v. United Shoe Machinery Corporation: An Economic Analysis of an Anti-Trust Case*. Cambridge, Mass., 1956.

Keir, Malcolm. *Industries of America: Manufacturing*. New York, 1928.

Kriedte, Peter, Hans Medick, and Jurgen Schlumbohm. *Industrialization before Industrialization: Rural Industry in the Genesis of Capitalism*. Cambridge, England, 1981.

Landes, David. *Revolution in Time: Clocks and the Making of the Modern World*. Cambridge, Mass., 1983.

————. *The Unbound Prometheus: Technological Change and Industrial Devel opment in Western Europe from 1750 to the Present*. Cambridge, England, 1969.

————. "What Do Bosses Really Do?" *Journal of Economic History* 46 (September 1986): 585–623.

Lazonick, William, and Thomas Brush. "The 'Horndal Effect' in Early U.S. Manufacturing." *Explorations in Economic History* 22 (1985): 53–96.

Levine, David. *Economic Theory*. 2 vols. London, 1981.

Lewis, Alonzo, and James Newhall. *History of Lynn*. Boston, 1844.

Lewton, Frederick L. "The Servant in the House: A Brief History of the Sewing Machine." *Annual Report of the Smithsonian Institution* 84 (1929): 559–83.

Lindstrom, Diane. "American Economic Growth before 1840: New Evidence and New Directions." *Journal of Economic History* 29 (1979): 289–301.

————. *Economic Development in the Philadelphia Region, 1810–1850*. New York, 1978.

————. "Macroeconomic Growth: The United States in the Nineteenth Century." *Journal of Interdisciplinary History* 13 (1983): 679–705.

Lynn Business Magazine.

Lynn Item.

"Lynn Scrapbooks." Lynn, Mass., undated.

McCormick, Cyrus. *The Century of the Reaper*. New York, 1931.

McDermott, Charles. *A History of the Shoe and Leather Industries of the United States*. Boston, 1918.

McKenzie, F. A. *The American Invaders*. New York, 1976.

Mantoux, Paul. *The Industrial Revolution in the Eighteenth Century: An Outline of the Beginnings of the Modern Factory System in England*. New York, 1961.

Marglin, Stephen. "Knowledge and Power." In *Firms, Organization and Labour: Approaches to the Economics of Work Organization*, edited by Frank H. Stephen, pp. 146–64. London, 1984.

————. "What Do Bosses Do? The Origins and Functions of Hierarchy in Capitalist Production." *The Review of Radical Political Economics* 6 (Summer 1974): 60–112.

Margo, Robert, and Georgia Villaflor. "The Growth of Wages in Antebellum America: New Evidence." *Journal of Economic History* 47 (December 1987): 873–95.

Markusen, Ann. *Profit Cycles, Oligopoly, and Regional Development*. Cambridge, Mass., 1985.

Marx, Karl. *Capital*. 3 vols. New York, 1977.

————. *Grundrisse*. Harmondsworth, England, 1973.

————, and Engels, Frederick. "The German Ideology." In *Collected Works*, 5: 19–452. New York, 1976.

Massachusetts. *Abstract of the Census of Massachusetts for 1855*. Boston, 1857.

Mechanic's Magazine.

Mechanics of the Sewing Machine.

Mendels, Franklin. "Proto-industrialization: The First Phase of the Industrialization Process." *Journal of Economic History* 32 (March 1972): 241–61.

Montgomery, David. *Workers' Control in America: Studies in the History of Work, Technology, and Labor Struggles.* Cambridge, England, 1979.

Mulligan, William. "Mechanization and Work in the American Shoe Industry: Lynn, Massachusetts, 1852–83." *Journal of Economic History* 41 (March 1981): 59–63.

_____. "The Transmission of Skill in the Shoe Industry: Family to Factory Training in Lynn, Massachusetts." In *The Craftsman in Early America*, edited by Ian Quimby, pp. 234–46. New York, 1984.

Musson, Albert E. *The Growth of British Industry.* New York, 1978.

_____, and Eric Robinson. "The Origins of Engineering in Lancashire." *Journal of Economic History* 20 (June 1960): 209–33.

_____, and Eric Robinson. *Science and Technology in the Industrial Revolution.* Toronto, 1969.

North, Douglass. *The Economic Growth of the United States, 1790–1860.* New York, 1961.

Orcutt, Samuel. *A History of the City of Bridgeport, Connecticut.* New Haven, 1887.

Parker, William. "Agriculture." In *American Economic Growth: An Economist's History of the United States*, Lance Davis, Richard Easterlin, William Parker, et al., pp. 369–417. New York, 1972.

_____. *Europe, America, and the Wider World.* Cambridge, England, 1984.

_____. "Technology, Resources, and Economic Change in the West." In *Economic Development in the Long Run*, edited by A. J. Youngson, pp. 62–78. London, 1972.

Parton, J. "History of the Sewing Machine." *Atlantic Monthly* 19 (May 1867): 527–41.

Plunkett, Frank. *Introduction to the Theory and Practice of Boot and Shoe Manufacture.* London, 1916.

Polanyi, Karl. *The Great Transformation.* Boston, 1957.

Poulson, Barry. *Value-added in Manufacturing, Mining, and Agriculture in the American Economy from 1809 to 1839.* New York, 1975.

Pred, Allan. *The Spatial Dynamics of U.S. Urban-Industrial Growth, 1800–1914.* Cambridge, Mass., 1966.

Prentiss, Lewis. *Recollections of an Old Boot and Shoe Maker from 1815 to 1898.* Mansfield, Mass., 1898 or 1899.

Pursell, Carroll. *Early Stationary Steam Engines in America: A Study in the Migration of a Technology.* Washington, D.C., 1969.

Quimby, Harold. *Pacemakers of Progress: The Story of Shoes and the Shoe Industry.* Chicago, 1946.

_____. *The Story of Lasts.* New York, 1948.

Report of the Industrial Commission. 19 vols. Washington, D.C., 1901.

Reports of the United States Commissioners to the Paris Universal Exposition, 1867. 6 vols. Washington, D.C., 1870.

Reports of the Commissioners of the United States to the International Exhibition

Held at Vienna, 1873. 4 vols. Washington, D.C., 1876.

Research Publications, Inc. *Early Unnumbered United States Patents, 1790–1836.* Woodbury, Conn., 1980.

Reuleaux, Franz. *Kinematics of Machinery: Outlines of a Theory of Machines.* London, 1876.

Rice & Hutchins: A Retrospect, 1866–1916. Cambridge, Mass., 1916.

Ricoy, Carlos. "Cumulative Causation." In *The New Palgrave: A Dictionary of Economics*, edited by John Eatwell, Murray Milgate, and Peter Newman, 1:730–36. London, 1987.

Roe, Joseph W. *English and American Tool Builders.* New Haven, 1916.

———. *The Mechanical Equipment.* New York, 1918.

Rogin, Leo. *The Introduction of Farm Machinery and Its Relation to the Productivity of Labor in Agriculture in the United States during the Nineteenth Century.* Berkeley, 1931.

Rosenberg, Nathan. *Inside the Black Box: Technology and Economics.* Cambridge, England, 1982.

———. *Perspectives on Technology.* Cambridge, England, 1976.

———, ed. *The American System of Manufactures.* Edinburgh, 1969.

Rostow, W. W. *The Stages of Economic Growth.* Cambridge, England, 1968.

Sabel, Charles, and Jonathan Zeitlin. "Historical Alternatives to Mass Production: Politics, Markets and Technology in Nineteenth-Century Industrialization." *Past and Present* 108 (May 1985): 133–76.

Salamon, N. *The History of the Sewing Machine from the Year 1750.* London, 1863.

Salter, W. E. G. *Productivity and Technical Change.* Cambridge, England, 1966.

Saul, S. B. "The Market and the Development of Mechanical Engineering Industries in Britain, 1860–1914." *Economic History Review* 20, 2d ser. (1967): 111–30.

Schmookler, Jacob. "Economic Sources of Inventive Activity." *Journal of Economic History* 22 (March 1962): 1–20.

———. *Invention and Economic Growth.* Cambridge, Mass., 1966.

Schumpeter, Joseph. *Business Cycles.* 2 vols. New York, 1939.

———. *Capitalism, Socialism, and Democracy.* New York, 1942.

———. "The Instability of Capitalism." *Economic Journal* 38 (September 1928): 361–86.

———. *The Theory of Economic Development.* New York, 1961.

Scientific American.

Sewing Machine Advance.

Shapiro, Nina. "Innovation, New Industries, and New Firms. *Eastern Economic Journal* 12 (January–March 1986): 27–43.

Sherry, Robert. "Petty Bourgeois Agriculture in the 19th Century United States." Ph.D. dissertation, Yale University, 1979.

Shoe and Leather Record.

Shoe and Leather Reporter.

Shoe and Leather Reporter Annual.

Smith, Adam. *An Inquiry into the Nature and Causes of the Wealth of Nations*. New York, 1937.

Smith, Merritt R. *Harpers Ferry Armory and the New Technology: The Challenge of Change*. Ithaca, N.Y., 1977.

Sokoloff, Kenneth. "Investment in Fixed and Working Capital during Early Industrialization: Evidence from U.S. Manufacturing Firms." *Journal of Economic History* 44 (June 1984): 545–56.

_____. "The Puzzling Record of Real Wage Growth in Early Industrial America, 1820 to 1860." UCLA Institute of Industrial Relations Working Paper, Los Angeles, 1988.

_____. "Was the Transition from the Artisanal Shop to the Nonmechanized Factory Associated with Gains in Efficiency? Evidence from the U.S. Manufacturing Censuses of 1820 and 1850." *Explorations in Economic History* 21 (1984): 351–82.

Stigler, George. "The Division of Labor Is Limited by the Extent of the Market." *Journal of Political Economy* 59 (June 1951): 185–93.

Stone, Orra. *History of Massachusetts Industries*. 2 vols. Boston, 1930.

Strassmann, W. Paul. *Risk and Technological Innovation: American Manufacturing Methods during the Nineteenth Century*. Ithaca, N.Y., 1959.

Taylor, George R. *The Transportation Revolution, 1815–1860*. New York, 1951.

Temin, Peter. "Labor Scarcity in America." *Journal of Interdisciplinary History* 1 (Winter 1971): 251–64.

_____. "Steam and Water Power in the Early Nineteenth Century." *Journal of Economic History* 26 (June 1966): 187–205.

Thompson, E. P. *The Making of the English Working Class*. New York, 1963.

_____. "Time, Work Discipline, and Industrial Capitalism." *Past and Present* 38 (1967): 56–97.

Thomson, Ross. "Between Invention and Practicality: The Development of the Sewing Machine." Unpublished manuscript, 1986.

_____. "The Eco-Technic Process and the Development of the Sewing Machine." In *Technique, Spirit, and Form in the Making of the Modern Economies: Essays in Honor of William N. Parker*, edited by Gavin Wright and Gary Saxenhouse, pp. 243–69. Greenwich, Conn., 1984.

_____. "Learning by Selling and Invention: The Case of the Sewing Machine." *Journal of Economic History* 47 (June 1987): 433–45.

_____. "Primitive Capitalist Accumulation." In *The New Palgrave: A Dictionary of Economics*, edited by John Eatwell, Murray Milgate, and Peter Newman, 3:963–66. London, 1987.

_____. "Technological Change as New Product Development." *Social Concept* 3 (June 1986): 3–26.

Tomlinson, Charles, ed. *Cyclopedia of Useful Arts and Manufactures*. 3 vols. London, 1866.

Torrey, Bates. *The Shoe Industry of Weymouth*. Weymouth, Mass., 1933.

Transactions of the American Institute.

Turner, Frederick. *The Frontier in American History*. New York, 1962.

United Shoe Machinery Company. *Goodyear Welt Shoes: How They Are Made.* Boston, 1911.

———. *Illustrated Catalogue of Shoe Machinery Manufactured by the United Shoe Machinery Company.* Boston, ca. 1902.

———. *Tools for the Shoemaker.* Boston, ca. 1902.

United Shoe Machinery Corporation. *How American Shoes Are Made.* Boston, 1916.

Unwin, George. *Industrial Organization in the Sixteenth and Seventeenth Centuries.* Oxford, 1904.

Ure, Andrew. *A Dictionary of Arts, Manufactures and Mines.* 2 vols. New York, 1842.

Ure's Dictionary of Arts, Manufactures and Mines. 4 vols. London, 1879.

Urquhart, J. W. *Sewing Machinery.* London, 1881.

U.S. Bureau of the Census. *Historical Statistics of the United States, Colonial Times to 1957.* Washington, D.C., 1960.

U.S. Bureau of Labor. *Thirteenth Annual Report of the Commissioner of Labor: Hand and Machine Labor.* 2 vols. Washington, D.C., 1898.

U.S. Census Office. Eighth Census, 1860. *Manufactures of the United States in 1860.* Washington, D.C., 1865.

———. Eleventh Census, 1890. *Report of the Manufacturing Industries in the United States at the Eleventh Census, 1890.* Washington, D.C., 1895.

———. Ninth Census, 1870. *Statistics of the Wealth and Industry of the United States.* Washington, D.C., 1872.

———. Seventh Census, 1850. *Abstract of the Statistics of Manufactures.* Washington, D.C., 1858.

———. Sixth Census, 1840. *Statistics of the United States of America [at] the Sixth Census.* Washington, D.C., 1841.

———. Tenth Census, 1880. *Report on the Manufactures of the United States at the Tenth Census, 1880.* Washington, D.C., 1883.

———. *Twelfth Census of the United States, Taken in the Year 1900: Manufactures.* 3 vols. Washington, D.C., 1902.

U.S. Department of Commerce. Patent and Trademark Office. *U.S. Patent Classification—Subclass Listing.* 30th ed. Washington, D.C., 1985.

Usher, Abbott P. *A History of Mechanical Inventions.* rev. ed. Cambridge, Mass., 1954.

U.S. Patent Office. *Annual Report of the Commissioner of Patents.* Washington, D.C. 1850 through 1900.

———. *Subject-Matter Index of Patents for Inventions Issued by the United States Patent Office from 1790 to 1873, Inclusive.* Washington, D.C., 1874.

U.S. Treasury Department. *Documents Relative to the Manufactures in the United States, Collected and Transmitted to the House of Representatives by the Secretary of the Treasury.* 3 vols. New York, 1969.

———. Third Census, 1810. *A Statement of the Arts and Manufactures of the United States of America for the Year 1810.* Philadelphia, 1814.

Vernon, Raymond. "International Investment and International Trade in the Product Cycle." *Quarterly Journal of Economics* 80 (May 1966): 190–207.

von Hippel, Eric. *The Sources of Innovation*. New York, 1988.

Ware, Caroline. *The Early New England Cotton Manufacture*. Boston, 1931.

Wheeler and Wilson. *The Golden Calendar*. 1870.

White, John. *American Locomotives: An Engineering History, 1830–1880*. Baltimore, 1968.

Wilentz, Sean. *Chants Democratic: New York City and the Rise of the American Working Class, 1788–1850*. New York, 1984.

Williamson, Jeffrey. "Inequality, Accumulation, and Technological Imbalance: A Growth-Equality Conflict in American History?" *Economic Development and Cultural Change* 27 (1979): 231–53.

Woodbury, Robert. *Studies in the History of Machine Tools*. Cambridge, Mass., 1972.

Wooster, Harvey. "Manufacturer and Artisan, 1790–1840." *Journal of Political Economy* 34 (February 1926): 61–77.

Young, Alfred. "George Robert Twelves Hewes (1742–1840)." *William and Mary Quarterly* 38, 3d ser. (October 1981): 561–623.

Young, Allyn. "Increasing Returns and Economic Progress." *Economic Journal* 38 (December 1928): 527–42.

Zevin, Robert. "The Growth of Cotton Textile Production after 1815." In *The Reinterpretation of American Economic History*, edited by Robert Fogel and Stanley Engerman, pp. 122–47. New York, 1971.

Index

Agency system, 98, 101–2, 260–61 (n. 27), 261 (n. 29); directories for, 105 (table), 113; for McKay machine, 163–64; for Goodyear machine, 167
Agriculture, 3–4, 31
Alvord, J. D., 141, 142
American Shoe Tip Company, 165
Ames Manufacturing, 141
Apprentices, 13, 14, 25
Association of Boot and Shoe Manufacturers, 230

Bachelder, John, 83–84, 89, 100
Baker, William, 84, 86, 90
Baldwin, Matthias, 67
Bartholf, A., 93
Bates, Isaac, 161
Bay State Shoe and Leather Company, 164
Bean, Edwin, 172–73
Bean running-stitch machine, 86–87
Billings, Joseph, 141
Blake, Lyman, 156–61, 173, 200, 210, 272 (n. 10); bottom-stitching patent of, 121; channeling patents to, 205; and diversification process, 214
Blake shoe. *See* McKay shoe
Blanchard, Thomas, 42
Bliss, George, 99, 119
Blodgett, Sherburne, 90, 92, 131
Blodgett and Lerow (company): sales by, 93–94; infringement suits against, 99
Blodgett and Lerow machine, 83, 84; as contractor-built, 91
Boot and Shoe Recorder, 206–7
Boston, Mass.: shoe shipments from, 181 (table)
Bottlenecks, 258 (n. 11), 266 (n. 21); overcoming, 148–49; and invention, 198, 204
Bottoming gang, 248 (n. 8)
Bottoming machines: and crossover inventors, 205
Bottom-sewing machines. *See* Goodyear machine; Leather-sewing machines; McKay machine
Bradshaw, John, 83, 84, 99, 127
Breaking-in problems, 67, 70; for sewing machines, 76–77, 120; for shoe-sewing machines, 118, 119; for shoe machines, 122; easing of, 131
Bresnahan, Maurice, 210, 211
Briggs, Henry, 205, 206
Britain: mechanization in, 67
Brock, Matthias, 187, 217, 223
Brown, George, 221
Brown, Joseph, 141, 142
Brown and Sharpe (company), 141, 166
Bubier, Samuel, 161
Burt, Edwin, 164, 166
Butterfield and Stevens (company), 120, 121, 127
Buttonhole machines, 151–52

Campbell, Duncan, 174, 178, 218; and lockstitch, 176–77
Campbell Machine Company, 178
Canton Boot and Shoe Machine Company, 50, 128–29, 130
Capacity: for mechanization, 60; as mechanization barrier, 63–66
Capital: accumulation of, 2; and learning, 116–17
Capital goods: and shoemaking, 43; sale of, 187; purchase of, 189
Capitalism: processes of, 1–2; paths to, 12, 25; and development, 26, 236
Capitalist production: establishment of, 22–25; origins of, 25; geographic spread of, 27, 28 (figure); relation to division of labor, 29
Central shop system, 23–24; origins of, 26–27; diffusion of, 26–27, 28 (figure); labor transformation in, 49, 50; elimination of, 53; machinery in, 61
Channeling, 204–5
Chase, Frank, 224, 272 (n. 10)
Civil War, 161, 183
Clothing industry, 60–61, 66
Commission agents, 98
Commodities: and competition, 236
Commodity definition. *See* Product cycle
Commodity path, 80–82; problems with, 82; for shoe machine invention, 119; starting, 235–37; process of, 238–40; ties among,